Building successful
intelligence and
achieving your goals

Keys to Success

FOURTH CANADIAN EDITION

CAROL CARTER | JOYCE BISHOP | SARAH LYMAN KRAVITS | PETER J. MAURIN

PEARSON

Prentice
Hall

Toronto

Library and Archives Canada Cataloguing in Publication

Keys to success : building successful intelligence and achieving your goals /
Carol Carter ... [et al.]. — 4th Canadian ed.

Includes index.
ISBN 0-13-197331-2

1. College student orientation—Canada—Handbooks, manuals, etc. 2. Study
skills—Handbooks, manuals, etc. 3. College students—Canada—Life skills guides.
I. Carter, Carol

LB2343.34.C3K48 2006   378.1'98   C2005-907812-X

ISBN 0-13-197331-2

Vice President, Editorial Director: Michael J. Young
Acquisitions Editor: Dave Ward
Sponsoring Editor: Carolin Sweig
Marketing Manager: Toivo Pajo
Developmental Editor: Jennifer Murray
Production Editor: Richard di Santo
Copy Editor: Julie Fletcher
Proofreader: Nancy Carroll
Production Coordinator: Janis Raisen
Permissions Manager: Susan Wallace-Cox
Art Director: Julia Hall
Interior Design and Composition: Susan Thomas
Cover Design: Michael Stokely
Cover Image: Getty Images

1 2 3 4 5   11 10 09 08 07

Printed and bound in the United States of America.

Brief Contents

QUICK START TO COLLEGE AND UNIVERSITY   *xvii*

Chapter 1   **WELCOME TO YOUR POST-SECONDARY CAREER**   *2*

Chapter 2   **VALUES, GOALS, TIME, AND STRESS**   *30*

Chapter 3   **LEARNING STYLES, MAJORS, AND CAREERS**   *62*

Chapter 4   **CRITICAL, CREATIVE, AND PRACTICAL THINKING**   *92*

Chapter 5   **READING AND STUDYING**   *130*

Chapter 6   **LISTENING, NOTE TAKING, AND MEMORY**   *162*

Chapter 7   **RESEARCHING AND WRITING**   *194*

Chapter 8   **TEST TAKING**   *230*

Chapter 9   **RELATING TO OTHERS**   *264*

Chapter 10   **PERSONAL WELLNESS**   *296*

Chapter 11   **MANAGING CAREER AND MONEY**   *322*

Chapter 12   **CREATING YOUR LIFE**   *354*

Contents

Preface   xi

Acknowledgements   xiv

About the Authors   xv

QUICK START TO COLLEGE AND UNIVERSITY   xvii

HOW COLLEGES AND UNIVERSITIES ARE STRUCTURED   xviii

Teaching takes centre stage • Administrators provide support

HOW TO GET ACADEMIC HELP   xx

Help from instructors and teaching assistants • Help from academic advisors • Help from a mentor • Help from learning specialists

WHAT YOUR SCHOOL EXPECTS OF YOU   xxii

Understand and apply for financial aid • Understand curriculum and graduation requirements • Choose and register for classes • Follow procedures • Pursue academic excellence • Have academic integrity • Master the school's computer system • Get involved

Chapter 1
WELCOME TO YOUR POST-SECONDARY CAREER   2

WHERE ARE YOU NOW—AND WHERE CAN YOUR EDUCATION TAKE YOU?   4

What education can do for you • How education promotes life success

HOW DO YOU MAKE A SUCCESSFUL TRANSITION TO COLLEGE OR UNIVERSITY?   7

HOW CAN SUCCESSFUL INTELLIGENCE HELP YOU ACHIEVE YOUR GOALS?   7

Defining successful intelligence • Why successful intelligence is your key to success

HOW WILL KEYS TO SUCCESS HELP YOU BUILD SUCCESSFUL INTELLIGENCE?   10

The chapter material • The in-chapter activities • The end-of-chapter exercises

GET CREATIVE! *See Yourself at Your Best*   12

HOW CAN YOU GET MOTIVATED?   13

Make a commitment • Develop positive habits • Be responsible • Face your fears • Build self-esteem

GET PRACTICAL! *Face Your Fears*   17

HOW CAN WHAT YOU LEARN NOW HELP YOU SUCCEED IN SCHOOL, WORK, AND LIFE?   20

Education prepares you to learn from failure and celebrate success • Education builds a foundation for learning throughout life

GET ANALYTICAL! *Learn from a Mistake*   21

BUILDING SKILLS
For Academic, Career, and Life Success   25

SUGGESTED READINGS   28

INTERNET RESOURCES   29

Chapter 2
VALUES, GOALS, TIME, AND STRESS   30

WHY IS IT IMPORTANT TO KNOW WHAT YOU VALUE?   32

Identifying and evaluating values • How values affect your educational experience • Academic integrity: How ethical values promote success at school • Values and cultural diversity • Cultural competence

GET ANALYTICAL! *Explore Your Values*   34

HOW DO YOU SET AND ACHIEVE GOALS?   36

Set long-term goals • Set short-term goals • Prioritize goals • Work to achieve goals

GET CREATIVE! *Map Out a Personal Goal*   40

HOW CAN YOU EFFECTIVELY MANAGE YOUR TIME?   40

Identify your time-related needs and preferences • Build a schedule • Use scheduling techniques • Fight procrastination • Be flexible

GET PRACTICAL! *Make a To-Do List*   47

HOW DO YOU COPE WITH THE STRESS OF COLLEGE LIFE?   50

Successful time management and goal setting relieve stress • Stress-management strategies

BUILDING SKILLS
For Academic, Career, and Life Success   54

SUGGESTED READINGS   61

INTERNET RESOURCES   61

Chapter 3
LEARNING STYLES, MAJORS, AND CAREERS   62

WHAT IS A LEARNING STYLE?   64

The two parts of learning style ● Getting perspective on learning style

HOW CAN YOU DISCOVER HOW YOU LEARN?   66

Multiple intelligences ● Personality spectrum ● Scoring the assessments

MULTIPLE PATHWAYS TO LEARNING   69

PERSONALITY SPECTRUM   70

WHY IS IT IMPORTANT TO KNOW HOW YOU LEARN?   74

Study benefits ● Classroom benefits ● Workplace benefits

HOW CAN YOU CHOOSE A MAJOR?   77

Short-term goal #1: Use learning styles assessments to identify interests and talents ● Short-term goal #2: Explore academic options ● Short-term goal #3: Establish your academic schedule ● Be flexible as you come to a decision

GET ANALYTICAL, CREATIVE, AND PRACTICAL! *Link Your Interests to Intriguing Majors   79*

HOW CAN MULTIPLE INTELLIGENCES HELP YOU EXPLORE MAJORS AND CAREERS?   83

Career exploration strategies

HOW CAN YOU IDENTIFY AND MANAGE LEARNING DISABILITIES?   84

Identifying a learning disability ● Managing a learning disability

PERSONAL TRIUMPH *Michaëlle Jean   86*

BUILDING SKILLS
For Academic, Career, and Life Success   88

SUGGESTED READINGS   91

INTERNET RESOURCES   91

Chapter 4
CRITICAL, CREATIVE, AND PRACTICAL THINKING   92

WHAT IS SUCCESSFULLY INTELLIGENT THINKING?   94

Successfully intelligent thinking is balanced ● Successfully intelligent thinking means asking and answering questions ● Successfully intelligent thinking requires knowing your purpose ● Successfully intelligent thinking is yours to build

HOW CAN YOU IMPROVE YOUR ANALYTICAL THINKING SKILLS?   97

Gather information ● Analyze and clarify information ● Evaluate information

GET ANALYTICAL! *Assess Analytical Thinking Skills   101*

HOW CAN YOU IMPROVE YOUR CREATIVE THINKING SKILLS?   103

Brainstorm ● Shift your perspective ● Set the stage for creativity ● Take risks

GET CREATIVE! *Assess Creative Thinking Skills   108*

HOW CAN YOU IMPROVE YOUR PRACTICAL THINKING SKILLS?   108

Experience helps develop practical thinking skills ● The emotional intelligence connection ● Practical thinking means action

GET PRACTICAL! *Assess Practical Thinking Skills   111*

HOW CAN YOU PUT ANALYTICAL, CREATIVE, AND PRACTICAL THINKING TOGETHER TO SOLVE A PROBLEM OR MAKE A DECISION?   113

Solving a problem ● Making a decision ● Keeping your balance

BUILDING SKILLS
For Academic, Career, and Life Success   119

SUGGESTED READINGS   124

INTERNET RESOURCES   124

STUDY BREAK: GET READY FOR EXAMS   125

SELF STUDY QUIZ   128

Chapter 5
READING AND STUDYING   130

WHAT WILL HELP YOU UNDERSTAND WHAT YOU READ?   132

GET CREATIVE! *Be the Author of Your Life   133*

HOW CAN YOU SET THE STAGE FOR READING?   133

Take an active approach to difficult texts ● Choose

the right setting ● Define your purpose for reading ● Match strategies to different areas of study ● Build reading speed ● Expand your vocabulary

MULTIPLE INTELLIGENCE STRATEGIES FOR READING 138

HOW CAN SQ3R HELP YOU OWN WHAT YOU READ? 142

Survey ● Question ● Read ● Recite ● Review

GET ANALYTICAL! *Find the Main Idea* 148

HOW CAN YOU RESPOND CRITICALLY TO WHAT YOU READ? 150

Use knowledge of fact and opinion to evaluate arguments ● Media literacy

HOW AND WHY SHOULD YOU STUDY WITH OTHERS? 152

Leaders and Participants ● Strategies for Study Group Success ● Benefits of Working with Others

GET PRACTICAL! *Form a Study Group* 153

BUILDING SKILLS
For Academic, Career, and Life Success 157

SUGGESTED READINGS 161
INTERNET RESOURCES 161

Chapter 6
LISTENING, NOTE TAKING, AND MEMORY 162

HOW CAN YOU BECOME A BETTER LISTENER? 164

Know the stages of listening ● Manage listening challenges ● Become an active listener

HOW CAN YOU MAKE THE MOST OF NOTE TAKING? 168

Recording information in class ● Reviewing and revising your notes

GET ANALYTICAL! *Discover Yourself as a Listener* 168

GET PRACTICAL! *Face a Note-Taking Challenge* 170

MULTIPLE INTELLIGENCE STRATEGIES FOR NOTE TAKING 171

WHICH NOTE-TAKING SYSTEM SHOULD YOU USE? 174

Taking notes in outline form ● Using the Cornell note-taking system ● Creating a think link ● Using other visual note-taking strategies

HOW CAN YOU WRITE FASTER WHEN TAKING NOTES? 179

HOW DOES MEMORY WORK? 181

How your brain remembers: Short-term and long-term memory ● Retaining information in long-term memory

WHAT MEMORY STRATEGIES CAN IMPROVE RECALL? 184

Develop helpful strategies ● Use mnemonic devices

GET CREATIVE! *Craft Your Own Mnemonic* 188

PERSONAL TRIUMPH *Daniel Igali* 190

BUILDING SKILLS
For Academic, Career, and Life Success 191

SUGGESTED READINGS 193
INTERNET RESOURCES 193

Chapter 7
RESEARCHING AND WRITING 194

HOW CAN YOU MAKE THE MOST OF YOUR LIBRARY? 196

Start with a road map ● Learn how to conduct an information search ● Conducting research using a search strategy

GET PRACTICAL! *Discover Your School's Library* 197

HOW CAN YOU DO RESEARCH ON THE INTERNET? 201

The basics ● Search directories and search engines ● Use analytical thinking to evaluate every source

GET CREATIVE! *Google (Yes, it's a verb)* 203

WHAT ARE THE ELEMENTS OF EFFECTIVE WRITING? 205

Writing purpose ● Knowing your audience

WHAT IS THE WRITING PROCESS? 206

Planning ● Drafting ● Revising ● Editing

GET ANALYTICAL! *Avoid Plagiarism* 215

MULTIPLE INTELLIGENCE STRATEGIES FOR WRITING 217

HOW CAN YOU DELIVER AN EFFECTIVE ORAL PRESENTATION? 222

Prepare as for a writing assignment ● Practise your performance

BUILDING SKILLS
For Academic, Career, and Life Success 224

SUGGESTED READINGS 229
INTERNET RESOURCES 229

Chapter 8
TEST TAKING 230

HOW CAN PREPARATION IMPROVE TEST PERFORMANCE? 232

Identify test type and material covered ● Create a study plan and schedule ● Prepare through careful review ● Take a pretest ● Prepare physically ● Make the most of last-minute studying

GET CREATIVE! *Write Your Own Test* 233

MULTIPLE INTELLIGENCE STRATEGIES FOR TEST PREPARATION 237

HOW CAN YOU WORK THROUGH TEST ANXIETY? 238

Preparation ● Attitude ● Test anxiety and the returning student

WHAT GENERAL STRATEGIES CAN HELP YOU SUCCEED ON TESTS? 240

Write down key facts ● Begin with an overview of the exam ● Read test directions ● Work from easy to hard ● Watch the clock ● Master the art of intelligent guessing ● Follow directions on machine-scored tests ● Use critical thinking to avoid errors ● Maintain academic integrity

HOW CAN YOU MASTER DIFFERENT TYPES OF TEST QUESTIONS? 243

Multiple-choice questions ● True-or-false questions ● Matching questions ● Fill-in-the-blank questions ● Essay questions

GET ANALYTICAL! *Write to the Verb* 250

HOW CAN YOU LEARN FROM TEST MISTAKES? 252

GET PRACTICAL! *Learn from Your Mistakes* 253

BUILDING SKILLS
For Academic, Career, and Life Success 254

SUGGESTED READINGS 257
INTERNET RESOURCES 257

STUDY BREAK: GET READY FOR EXAMS 258

SELF STUDY QUIZ 261

Chapter 9
RELATING TO OTHERS 264

HOW DO YOU EXPERIENCE DIVERSITY? 266

The diversity within you ● Diversity on campus

HOW CAN YOU DEVELOP CULTURAL COMPETENCE? 268

Identify and evaluate personal perceptions and attitudes ● Be aware of what happens when cultures interact ● Build cultural knowledge ● Adapt to diverse cultures

GET CREATIVE! *Expand Your Perception of Diversity* 270

HOW CAN MINORITY STUDENTS MAKE THE MOST OF COLLEGE OR UNIVERSITY? 273

Define your experience

GET PRACTICAL! *Make a Difference* 274

HOW CAN YOU COMMUNICATE EFFECTIVELY? 275

Adjust to communication styles
Constructive and non-constructive criticism
Understand body language

GET ANALYTICAL! *Give Constructive Criticism* 279

MULTIPLE INTELLIGENCE STRATEGIES FOR COMMUNICATION 277

Communicate across cultures ● Manage conflict ● Manage anger

HOW DO YOU MAKE THE MOST OF PERSONAL RELATIONSHIPS? 284

Use positive relationship strategies ● Avoid destructive relationships ● Sexual harassment ● Violence in relationships ● Rape and date rape ● Choose communities that enhance your life

PERSONAL TRIUMPH *Tooka Shahriari* 289

BUILDING SKILLS
For Academic, Career, and Life Success 290

SUGGESTED READINGS 293
INTERNET RESOURCES 293

Chapter 10
PERSONAL WELLNESS 296

HOW CAN YOU MAINTAIN A HEALTHY BODY AND MIND? 298

Eat right ● Exercise ● Get enough sleep ● Stay safe ● Recognize mental health problems

GET PRACTICAL! *Improve Your Physical Health* 303

HOW ARE ALCOHOL, TOBACCO, AND DRUGS USED AND ABUSED? 306

Alcohol ● Tobacco ● Illegal drugs ● Identifying and overcoming addiction

MULTIPLE INTELLIGENCE STRATEGIES FOR STRESS MANAGEMENT 307

GET ANALYTICAL! *Evaluate your Substance Abuse* 309

GET CREATIVE! *Find More Fun* 313

HOW CAN YOU MAKE SMART DECISIONS ABOUT SEX? 313

Sex and critical thinking ● Birth control ● Sexually transmitted diseases

BUILDING SKILLS
for academic, career, and life success 317

INTERNET RESOURCES 321

SUGGESTED READINGS 321

Chapter 11
MANAGING CAREER AND MONEY 322

HOW CAN YOU PREPARE FOR WORKPLACE
SUCCESS? 324

Investigate career paths ● Know what employers
want ● Stay current ● Expect change

GET ANALYTICAL! *Connect Values to Career* 328

WHAT DOES YOUR LEARNING STYLE MEAN FOR
YOUR CAREER? 329

HOW CAN YOU FIND A CAREER THAT'S RIGHT
FOR YOU? 331

Use available resources ● Make a strategic job
search plan ● Your résumé, cover letter, and
interview

GET CREATIVE! *Make a Dream Résumé* 335

WHAT WILL HELP YOU JUGGLE WORK AND
SCHOOL? 335

Effects of working while in school ● Establishing
your needs

HOW CAN YOU CREATE A BUDGET THAT
WORKS? 336

The art of budgeting ● Savings strategies ●
Making successfully intelligent financial decisions ●
Use bank accounts wisely

*MULTIPLE INTELLIGENCE STRATEGIES FOR
BUDGETING* 340

GET PRACTICAL! *Map Out Your Budget* 343

HOW CAN YOU MANAGE YOUR CREDIT CARDS? 345

How credit cards work ● Managing debt

BUILDING SKILLS
for academic, career, and life success 349

SUGGESTED READINGS 352

INTERNET RESOURCES 352

Chapter 12
CREATING YOUR LIFE 354

HOW WILL WHAT YOU'VE LEARNED BRING
SUCCESS? 356

New attitudes and skills prepare you to succeed ●
Flexibility helps you adapt to change ● Lifelong
learning

GET CREATIVE! *Think 50 Positive Thoughts* 359

HOW CAN YOU MAKE A DIFFERENCE IN YOUR
COMMUNITY? 360

You can help others ● You can get involved locally
and nationally ● You can help to preserve your
environment

GET ANALYTICAL! *Evaluate Your Involvement in
Communities* 362

HOW CAN YOU CONTINUE TO ACTIVATE YOUR
SUCCESSFUL INTELLIGENCE? 363

HOW CAN YOU CREATE AND LIVE YOUR PERSONAL
MISSION? 365

GET PRACTICAL! *Explore Your Personal Mission* 366

PERSONAL TRIUMPH *Shania Twain* 367

BUILDING SKILLS
for academic, career, and life success 370

SUGGESTED READINGS 373

INTERNET RESOURCES 373

STUDY BREAK: GET READY FOR EXAMS 374

SELF STUDY QUIZ 377

Answer Key 379

Index 381

Photo Credits 388

Mission Statement

Our mission is to help students know and believe in themselves, take advantage of resources and opportunities, set and achieve their goals, learn throughout their lives, discover careers that fulfill and support them, build fruitful and satisfying relationships with others from all backgrounds and walks of life, and experience the challenges and rewards that make life meaningful.

A Great Way to Learn and Instruct Online

The Pearson Education Canada Companion Website is easy to navigate and is organized to correspond to the chapters in this textbook. Whether you are a student in the classroom or a distance learner you will discover helpful resources for in-depth study and research that empower you in your quest for greater knowledge and maximize your potential for success in the course.

Companion Website

[**www.pearsoned.ca/carter**]

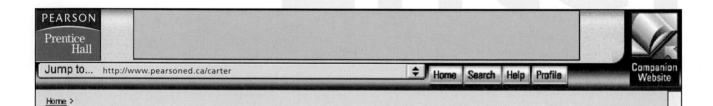

PEARSON Prentice Hall

Jump to...   http://www.pearsoned.ca/carter   Home Search Help Profile

Companion Website

Home >

Companion Website

Keys to Success, Fourth Canadian Edition, by Carol Carter, Joyce Bishop, Sarah Lyman Kravits, and Peter J. Maurin

Student Resources

The modules in this section provide students with tools for learning course material. These modules include:
- Objectives
- Multiple Choice
- Essay Questions
- Destinations
- Additional Articles

In the quiz modules students can send answers to the grader and receive instant feedback on their progress through the Results Reporter. Coaching comments and references to the textbook may be available to ensure that students take advantage of all available resources to enhance their learning experience.

Instructor Resources

A link to this book on the Pearson Education Canada online catalogue (vig.pearsoned.ca) provides instructors with additional teaching tools. Downloadable PowerPoint Presentations and an Instructor's Manual are just some of the materials that may be available. The catalogue is password protected. To get a password, simply contact your Pearson Education Canada Representative, or call Faculty Sales and Services at 1-800-850-5813.

Preface

Since the last edition of *Keys to Success*, we have focused our energies and research on the following question: How can students get the most out of college or university and use what they learn to achieve their goals in an ever-changing world? We found an important answer in the concept of successful intelligence, developed by psychologist Robert Sternberg.[1]

This book builds successful intelligence

Successful people, says Sternberg, are more than their IQ score. Focus on the two most important parts of Sternberg's message and you can change your approach to education in a way that will maximize your learning and *life success*.

One: *Successful intelligence gives you tools to achieve important goals.* Successful intelligence goes beyond doing well on tests (analytical thinking). Only by combining that analytical skill with the ability to come up with innovative ideas (creative thinking) and the ability to put ideas and plans to work (practical thinking) will you get where you want to go.

Two: *Intelligence can grow.* The intelligence you have when you are born does not stay the same for the rest of your life. You can build and develop your intelligence in the same way that you can build and develop physical strength or flexibility.

Every chapter of the fourth Canadian edition of *Keys to Success* helps you to build successful intelligence. How?

- *Chapter coverage:* The successful intelligence theme is introduced in Chapter 1 and covered in more detail in the thinking chapter (Chapter 4). Successful intelligence concepts are referenced throughout all chapters of the text.
- *In-text exercises:* Three exercises within the chapter text—"Get Analytical!", "Get Creative!", and "Get Practical!"—develop each skill in the context of the chapter material and your personal needs.
- *Synthesis exercise:* At the end of each chapter, the "Putting It All Together" exercise gives you an opportunity to combine all three skills and apply them toward a meaningful task.

This book connects you with the ideas and experiences of others

To help you excel in a world that is increasingly diverse, this fourth Canadian edition of *Keys to Success* introduces the concept of *cultural competence*, using the following features:

- *Descriptions of real Canadian students' experiences* have been woven into the text in areas where they enhance the topic being discussed.
- *A focus on cultural competence*, in Chapter 9, shows the value of going beyond tolerance to actively adapt to and learn from people different from you. References to cultural competence and diversity are also woven throughout every chapter, showing how diversity is part of many aspects of school, the workplace, and personal life.
- *Personal Triumph* stories, real-life accounts of how people have overcome difficult circumstances in the pursuit of education and fulfillment, appear near the end of every third chapter. These inspiring stories motivate you to step up your personal efforts to succeed.
- *Chapter summaries* introduce a word or phrase from a language other than English and suggest how you might apply the concept to your own life.

- *A continuing focus on multiple intelligences* highlights individual diversity and confirms that each individual has a unique way of learning, with no one way better than another. Chapter 2 introduces and explains this concept, and subsequent chapters include grids with strategies for applying various learning styles to the chapter content.

This book provides strategies and resources that help you do your work

With successful intelligence as the foundation of this edition, and cultural competence as an underlying theme, *Keys to Success* presents the following learning tools and materials that will help you succeed in college and beyond.

A post-secondary primer. Because there's so much to know right off the bat, the section "Quick Start to College and University" appears at the beginning of this text. Quick Start helps you get a feel for the structure of your school, the people who can help you with academic and life issues, the resources available to you, and expectations from instructors, administrators, and fellow students. Your instructor can use this introduction to post-secondary life and tailor it to your particular institution.

Skills that prepare you for college, career, and life. The ideas and strategies that help you succeed in college also take you where you want to go in your career and personal life. The three parts of this text help you develop a firm foundation for lifelong learning:

- *Defining yourself and your goals:* Chapter 1 provides an overview of today's post-secondary experience and an opportunity to evaluate your personal starting point. Chapter 2 gets you on track with ways to manage yourself effectively, focusing on values, goal-setting strategies, time-management skills, and handling stress. Chapter 3 helps you identify complementary aspects of your learning style (your multiple intelligences and your personality spectrum), choose strategies that make them work for you, and begin to think about your major.

- *Developing your learning skills:* Chapter 4 puts your learning into action by exploring the concept of successful intelligence in depth, helping you to build analytical, creative, and practical thinking skills and put them together in order to solve problems, make decisions, and achieve goals. The next few chapters build crucial skills for the classroom and beyond—Reading and Studying (Chapter 5), Listening, Note Taking, and Memory (Chapter 6), Researching and Writing (Chapter 7), and Test Taking (Chapter 8).

- *Creating success:* Recognizing that success includes more than academic achievement, Chapter 9 focuses on developing the interpersonal and communication skills you need in a diverse society. Chapter 10 helps you to manage the stress and wellness issues that so many college students face, and Chapter 11 covers the money-management and career-planning skills you need in college and beyond. Finally, Chapter 12 helps you think expansively: What path have you travelled during the semester? What plans do you have for your future?

Skill-building exercises. Today's graduates need to be effective thinkers, team players, writers, and strategic planners. The set of exercises at the end of each chapter—"Building Skills for Academic, Career, and Life Success"—encourages you to develop these valuable skills and to apply thinking processes to any topic or situation:

- *Developing Successful Intelligence: Putting It All Together.* These exercises encourage you to combine your successful intelligence thinking skills and apply them to chapter material.

- *Team Building: Collaborative Solutions.* This exercise gives you a chance to interact, problem solve, and learn in a group setting, building your teamwork and leadership skills in the process.

- *Writing: Discovery Through Journaling.* This journal exercise provides an opportunity to express your thoughts and develop your writing skills.

- *Career Portfolio: Plan for Success.* This exercise helps you gather evidence of your talents, skills, interests, qualifications, and experience. The "Career Portfolio" exercises build on one another to form, at the end of the semester, a portfolio of information and insights that will help you in your quest for the right career and job.

This book is just a start—only you can create the life of your dreams

As you work through this course and move forward toward your goals, keep this in mind: Studies have shown that when students feel that they have a fixed level of intelligence, they improve less, put less effort into their work, and have a harder time in the face of academic challenges. However, students who feel that they can become more intelligent over time are more likely to improve, tend to work harder, and handle academic challenges with more success.[2] *Believe that your intelligence can grow*—and use this book to develop it this semester, throughout your college experience, and afterward as you build the future of your dreams.

Notes

1. Successful intelligence concepts from Robert Sternberg, *Successful Intelligence*. New York: Plume, 1997.
2. David Glenn, "Students' Performance on Tests Is Tied to Their Views of Their Innate Intelligence, Researchers Say," *The Chronicle of Higher Education*, June 1, 2004 [on-line]. Available: http://chronicle.com/daily/2004/06/2004060103n.htm. (Web site available by subscription only.)

Acknowledgements

We would like to thank all those students across the country who helped us (and their fellow students) by providing *Stressbuster* tips: Alejandra Gonzalez, Michael Murray, Kevin Forseth, Gabriel Schroedter, Claire Douglas, Anna Griffin, Alicia Brett, Stephanie Jack, Nancy E. Shaw, Soumik Kanungo, Sonya Beel, and Jennifer Armour. We would also like to thank the many instructors from across Canada who assisted us with the preparation of the *Stressbuster* tips: Sue Ann Cairns, Kwantlen University College; Sharon Cameron, Algonquin College; William Christian, Guelph University; Les Hanson, Red River College; Selia Karsten, Seneca College; Gail McClintock, Champlain College; Trudy McCormack, St. Francis Xavier University; Joan McKibbon, St. Lawrence College; and Doug McLean, Sprott-Shaw Community College.

Thanks also to our reviewers, whose comments and suggestions have helped us in the preparation of this Fourth Canadian Edition: Elizabeth Bishop, Confederation College; Jacqueline Cottingham, Confederation College; Debbie Cox, Conestoga College; Tracy Fawcett, SAIT; Carlos Frewin, Humber College; Tom Groulx, St. Clair College; Bryan Hartman, UNBC; Kerry Johnston, Humber College; Selia Karsten, Seneca College; Kathy Mitchell, University College of the Cariboo; Lazarus Simeon, George Brown.

Thanks to the staff at Pearson Education Canada: Carolin Sweig, Sponsoring Editor; Jennifer Murray, Developmental Editor; and Richard di Santo, Production Editor.

While I am the Canadian author for this, the fourth Canadian edition of *Keys to Success*, the contents of the book are really the product of years of teaching at several institutions. Thanks to my current and former students at Mohawk College and to the many former students at Brock University and Niagara College. Whether it was Communications, Media, or Sociology, you always taught me something in the process.

Finally, to my gifted crew at home—Kim, Sonja, and Joshua: You are my "keys to success." Thanks for your love, patience, and understanding. I love you all very much.

Peter J. Maurin, M.A.

About the Authors

Carol Carter is founder of LifeBound, a career coaching company that offers individual coaching sessions and seminars for high school students, college students, and career seekers. She has written *Majoring in the Rest of Your Life: Career Secrets for College Students*, and *Majoring in High School*. She has also co-authored *Keys to Preparing for College, Keys to College Studying, The Career Tool Kit, Keys to Career Success, Keys to Study Skills, Keys to Thinking and Learning*, and *Keys to Success*. She has taught welfare-to-work classes, team taught in the La Familia Scholars Program at the Community College of Denver, and conducted numerous workshops for students and faculty around the country. Carol is a national college and career expert and is interviewed regularly for print, radio, and television news programs. In addition to working with students of all ages, Carol thrives on foreign travel and culture; she is fortunate enough to have been a guest in more than 40 foreign countries. Please visit her website and write her at www.lifebound.com.

Joyce Bishop holds a Ph.D. in psychology and has taught for more than 20 years, receiving a number of honours, including Teacher of the Year for 1995 and 2000. For five years she has been voted "favorite teacher" by the student body and Honor Society at Golden West College, Huntington Beach, California, where she has taught since 1987 and is a tenured professor. She worked with a federal grant to establish Learning Communities and Workplace Learning in her district, and she has developed workshops and trained faculty in cooperative learning, active learning, multiple intelligences, workplace relevancy, learning styles, authentic assessment, team building, and the development of learning communities. Joyce is currently teaching on-line and multimedia classes, and she trains other faculty to teach on-line in her district and region of 21 colleges. She co-authored *Keys to College Studying, Keys to Success, Keys to Thinking and Learning*, and *Keys to Study Skills*. Joyce is the lead academic of the Keys to Lifelong Learning Telecourse, distributed by Dallas Telelearning.

Sarah Lyman Kravits comes from a family of educators and has long cultivated an interest in educational development. She co-authored *Keys to College Studying, The Career Tool Kit, Keys to Success, Keys to Thinking and Learning*, and *Keys to Study Skills*, and has served as program director for LifeSkills, Inc., a non-profit organization that aims to further the career and personal development of high school students. In that capacity she helped to formulate both curricular and organizational elements of the program, working closely with instructors as well as members of the business community. She has also given faculty workshops in critical thinking. Sarah holds a B.A. in English and drama from the University of Virginia, where she was a Jefferson Scholar; and an M.F.A. from Catholic University.

Peter J. Maurin received his Master's degree in sociology from McMaster University in 1992. He currently teaches in the Media Studies Department at Mohawk College in Hamilton, Ontario. He has been a student advisor for the General Arts and Science Program at Mohawk, and has taught at Seneca College, Niagara College, and Brock University. The fourth Canadian edition of *Keys to Success* is Peter's eighth book for Pearson Education. Besides teaching, Peter is a professional communicator: He is a freelance writer and broadcaster, logging more than 20 years on the air for several radio stations in Ontario. He's also an old rock and roller. His weekly radio show "Oldies Without Borders" can be heard Sundays from 10 a.m. until noon online at http://www.mohawkcollege.ca/msa/cioi/.

Quick Start to College and University

A Guide to Knowing What to Do, How to Do It, and Where to Get Help

Welcome, or welcome back, to your post secondary education! Ahead of you are opportunities to learn more than you can imagine. Over the next years, you will explore the world of ideas, acquire information, and develop skills that will last a lifetime.

With these wonderful opportunities comes the challenge of adjusting to the realities of college. It may help you to know that nearly every college student—no matter what age or level of experience—feels overwhelmed as college begins.

Quick Start to College and University is designed to help you feel in control as you start the most important educational journey of your life. As you read, consult your school handbook and/or website to learn about its specific resources, policies, and practices. The exercises interspersed throughout *Quick Start* will also help you focus on your school.

Remember that you, along with instructors, advisors, administrators, support personnel, and fellow students, are a full participant in the educational process. Take the first steps toward a future filled with opportunity by

- taking an active role in your courses from the first day of class.
- being in charge of your learning, which involves setting goals, managing your time, completing assignments on schedule, and seeking help, if necessary.
- striving to do your best and making a commitment to quality.
- being an advocate for yourself as you relate to others.
- taking care of your mind, body, and relationships.
- getting involved in activities that interest you and that help develop your talents.
- deciding what you want to study—what you are passionate about.
- pursuing meaningful academic goals (honours or awards, involvement in academic organizations, internships, or other work experiences that support your academic path).

One of the first steps in creating your own success is learning what your college expects of you—and what you have a right to expect in return as a consumer of higher education.

How colleges and universities are *structured*

Think of your school as a large organization made up of arms that perform specific functions and that is run by hundreds and sometimes thousands of people. The two primary functional arms of your school focus on teaching and administration.

Teaching takes centre stage

The primary mission of most colleges and universities is teaching—communicating to students the knowledge and thinking skills needed to become lifelong learners. Although the term "instructor" is used in this text, teachers have official titles that show their rank within your college. Instructors with the highest status are *full professors*. Moving down from these are *associate professors, assistant professors, lecturers, instructors,* and *assistant instructors*, more commonly known as *teaching assistants* or *TAs*. (Remember that titles may vary from school to school and from college to university.) *Adjuncts* may teach several courses, but are not official staff members. Later in *Quick Start*, you will see how to communicate with and get help from your instructors.

Administrators provide support

The administrative staff enables your school—and the student body—to function. *Vice-presidents* deal with the nuts and bolts of operations; they make sure buildings are repaired, instructors are hired, students are registered, tuition is collected. *Deans,* in contrast, are in charge of operations and issues that directly involve students—for example, a Dean of Student Affairs and a Dean of Admissions. (These divisions and titles do not always apply, so learn the system at your school.)

Large institutions may be divided into *schools* that have separate administrative structures and staffs—for example, a School of Business or a School of Social Work. Each school normally has its own dean, and each department has a *chair* or *chairperson*—an instructor named to head the department.

One of the most important administrative offices for students is the *Office of the Dean of Student Affairs,* which, in many schools, is the centre for student services. Staff members try to answer your questions or direct you to others who can help. Learn how the student-help system works so you can identify specific people to turn to in case of a problem.

Administrative offices dealing with tuition issues and registration

Among the first administrators you will meet are those involved with tuition payments, financial aid, and registration.

The *bursar's office* (also called the *office of finance,* the *accounting office,* and *cashiering services*) issues bills for tuition and room and board and collects payments from students and financial aid sources. Direct your questions about tuition payments to this office.

The *financial aid office* helps students apply for financial aid and understand the eligibility requirements of different programs. The three main sources of financial aid are student loans, grants, and scholarships. You will learn more about these sources below.

The *registrar's office* (also called the *admissions office* in many community colleges) handles course registration, sends grades at the end of the semester, and compiles your official transcript, which is a comprehensive record of your courses and grades. Graduate schools require a copy of your official transcript before considering you for admission, as do many employers before considering you for a job. Transcripts are requested through the registrar's office.

Administrative services for students

A host of services is designed to help students adjust to and succeed in school and to deal with problems that arise. Here are some services you are likely to find:

Academic enhancement centres, including reading, writing, math, and study-skills centres. These centres offer consultations and tutoring to help students improve skills at all levels and become more confident. Don't be shy or embarrassed about using these services. If you find yourself struggling at the start of term, get help as soon as possible.

Academic computer centre. Most schools have sophisticated computer facilities equipped with computers, software, printers, and other equipment. At many schools, these facilities are open every day, and are staffed by technicians who can assist you with computer-related problems. Many facilities also offer training workshops.

Student housing or commuter affairs office. Most colleges and universities provide on-campus housing for undergraduate students. The housing office handles room and roommate placement, establishes behavioural standards, and deals with special situations and problems (e.g., an allergic student's need for a room air conditioner). Schools with commuting students may have programs to assist students with transportation and parking.

Health services. Your school's health centre is staffed with medical professionals who may include physicians, nurse practitioners, registered nurses, and support staff. If you are not feeling well, visit the clinic for help. Available services generally include prescriptions for common medicines, routine diagnostic tests, vaccinations, and first aid. All clinics are affiliated with nearby hospitals for emergency care. In addition, psychological counselling is sometimes offered through the health clinic, or it may have a separate facility. Remember that, although services are available, it is up to you to seek them out.

Career services. This office helps students find part-time and full-time jobs, as well as summer jobs and internships. Career offices have reference files on specific careers and employers. They also introduce students to the job-search process, helping them learn to write a résumé and cover letter and use the Internet to find job opportunities. Career offices often invite employers to interview students on campus and hold career fairs to introduce different companies and organizations. Summer internships and jobs are snapped up quickly, so check the office early and often to improve your chances. Visit the career office during your first year to begin developing an effective long-term career strategy.

Services for students with disabilities. Colleges and universities must provide disabled students with full access to facilities and programs. For students with documented disabilities, federal law requires that assistance be provided in the form of appropriate accommodations and aids. These range from interpreters for the hearing-impaired to readers and note-takers for the visually impaired to ramps for students in wheelchairs. If you have a disability, visit the Office of Students with Disabilities to learn what is offered. Remember, also, that this office is your advocate if you encounter problems.

Parking. Campus parking spaces can be scarce, with the best choices often going to students with seniority. (Disabled students are always given priority privileges.) Students with cars are generally required to register vehicles annually with campus security and get a parking sticker.

How to get academic *help*

Attending college or university is one of the best decisions you've made. However, deadlines, academic and social pressures, and simply being in new surroundings can make the experience stressful at times. (Chapter 10 talks more about stress management.) Understanding that help is available is the first step in helping yourself. Step two is actually *seeking* help from those who can give it. This requires knowing where to go and what assistance you can reasonably expect.

Before turning to others, try to find the answers you need on your own. For general guidance, check your college calendar, handbook, and website.

Help from instructors and teaching assistants

When you want to speak personally with an instructor for longer than a minute or two, choose your time carefully. Before or after class is usually not the best time for anything more than a quick question—instructors may be thinking about their lecture or be surrounded by other students with questions. When you need your instructor's full attention, there are three ways to communicate effectively—make an appointment during office hours, send email, and leave voice-mail messages.

Office hours. Instructors are required to keep regular office hours during which students can schedule personal conferences. Generally, these are posted during the first class, on instructors' office doors, and on instructors' or departmental websites. Always make an appointment for a conference; if you show up unannounced, there's a good chance your instructor will be busy. Face-to-face conferences are ideal for working through ideas and problems—for example, deciding on a term paper topic. Conferences are also the best setting to ask for advice—if, for example, you are considering majoring in the instructor's field and need guidance on courses.

Email. Use email to clarify assignments and assignment deadlines, to ask specific questions about lectures or readings, and to clarify what will be covered on a test. Try not to wait until the last minute to ask test-related questions; your instructor may not have time to respond. Instructors' email addresses are generally posted on the first day of class and may also be found in your student handbook or syllabus, which is a detailed description of what you will learn in the course. Links may also be available on your school's homepage. Some instructors also have ICQ or Windows Messenger in order to communicate with students.

Voice mail. If something comes up at the last minute, you can also leave a message in your instructor's office voice-mail box. Make your message short, but specific. Tell the instructor your reason for calling (*"This is Rick Jones from your ten o'clock Intro to Psychology class. I'm supposed to present my project today, but I'm sick in bed with a fever."*) and avoid general messages (*"This is Rick Jones from your ten o'clock class. Please call me at 555-5555."*). Avoid calling instructors at home unless they give specific permission to do so.

If you are taking a large lecture course, you may have a primary instructor plus a teaching assistant (TA) who meets with a small group of students on a regular basis. It is a good idea to approach your TA with course-related questions and problems before approaching the instructor. Because TAs deal with fewer students, they have more time to devote to specific issues.

Help from academic advisors

In most colleges and some universities, every student is assigned an advisor who is the student's personal liaison with the institution. (At some schools, students receive help at an advising centre.) Your advisor will help you choose courses every semester, plan your overall academic program, and understand college regulations including graduation requirements. He or she will point out possible consequences of your decisions (*"If you put off taking biology this semester, you're facing two lab courses next semester."*), help you shape your educational goals, and monitor your academic progress. Your advisor also knows about tutoring and personal counselling programs and may write recommendations when you are searching for a job.

It is important to remember that you, not your advisor, are responsible for your progress—for fully understanding graduation requirements, including credit requirements, and choosing the courses you need. Your advisor is there to help you with these critical decisions.

Help from a mentor

If you are fortunate, you will find a mentor at school—a trusted counsellor or guide who takes a special interest in helping you reach your goals. Mentoring relationships demand time and energy on both sides. A mentor can give you a private audience for questions and problems, advice tailored to your needs, support, guidance, and trust. A mentor cares about you enough to be devoted to your development. In return, you owe it to a mentor to be open to his or her ideas and, respectfully, to take advice into consideration. You and your mentor can learn from each other, receive positive energy from your relationship, and grow together.

Your mentor might be your faculty advisor, an instructor in your major or minor field of study, or an academic support instructor. You may also be drawn to someone outside school—a long-time friend whose judgment and experience you admire or a supervisor at work. Some schools have faculty or peer mentoring programs to match students with people who can help them. Check your student handbook or website or ask your faculty advisor if this is offered at your school.

Help from learning specialists

Almost everyone has difficulty in some aspect of learning, and you may view your struggles as simply an area of weakness. In contrast, people with diagnosed learning differences have conditions that make certain kinds of learning difficult. Some learning disabilities cause reading problems, some create difficulties in math, and still others make it difficult for students to process the language they hear.

If you have a learning disability, know that you are one of many. Colleges and universities are filled with students with diagnosed learning problems who get help, develop coping skills, and excel in their chosen fields. To succeed on your own terms, you have a responsibility to understand your disability, to become an advocate for your rights as a student with special needs, and to do your best to overcome your condition.

Identify your needs and seek assistance. If you are officially diagnosed with a learning disability, you are legally entitled to aid, and, in fact, the law requires schools to hire specialists to help you one-on-one. Armed with your test results and documentation, speak with your advisor about getting support that will help you learn. Among the services that may be available are testing accommodations (e.g., having extended time, working on a computer, or taking oral rather than written exams); books on tape; note-taking assistance (e.g., having a fellow student take notes for you or having access to the instructor's notes); taking a reduced course load; and auditing a course before you take it for credit.

What your school *expects* of you

You are a full participant in your relationship with your post-secondary education. Much is expected of you, and you have the right to expect much in return. The specific expectations described in this section involve understanding financial aid, curriculum, and graduation requirements; choosing and registering for classes; following procedures; pursuing academic excellence; understanding and following your school's academic integrity policy or honour code; learning your school's computer system; and getting involved in extracurricular activities. Do your best to understand how to proceed in all these areas and, if you still have problems, ask for help—from instructors, administrators, advisors, mentors, experienced classmates, and family members.

Understand and apply for financial aid

Let's face it: post-secondary education in Canada isn't cheap. As a result, many students need some sort of financial help. Most sources of financial aid don't seek out recipients. It is up to you to learn how you (or you and your parents, if they currently help to support you) can finance your education. Visit your school's financial aid office, research what's available, weigh the pros and cons of each option, decide what works best, then apply early. Above all, think critically. Never assume that you are *not* eligible for aid. The types of aid available are student loans, grants, and scholarships.

Student loans

As the recipient of a student loan, you are responsible for paying back the amount you borrow, plus interest, according to a predetermined payment schedule that may stretch over a number of years. The amount you borrow is known as the loan *principal*, and *interest* is the fee that you pay for the privilege of using money that belongs to someone else.

The federal government administers or oversees most student loans. To receive aid from any federal program, you must be a citizen or eligible non-citizen and be enrolled in a program that meets government requirements. The federal government recently took over control of the Canada Student Loans Program. Applying for assistance, no matter what province you live in, is done with a single application form. Your application is evaluated for eligibility for several programs, including the Canada Millennium Scholarship Program, provincial loans, plus any bursaries and grants you may be entitled to. For information regarding student loans in Canada, get an application form from your school. You can also contact the Canada Student Loans Program, administered through Human Resources Development Canada at

> Canada Student Loans Program
> Human Resources Development Canada
> P.O. Box 2090, Station "D"
> Ottawa, ON K1P 6C6

You can also call them at 1-800-O CANADA (1-800-622-6232) or you can go to http://www.hrsdc.gc.ca/en/gateways/topics/cxp-gxr.shtml for the latest information available. There are many helpful online references for student loans, some of which enable you to apply online. Be sure to apply early. Get your application at least 2–3 months prior to the start of your studies to ensure it will have time to be processed.

Grants and scholarships Unlike student loans, neither grants nor scholarships require repayment. Grants, funded by governments as well as private organizations, are awarded to students who show financial need. Scholarships may be financed by government or private organizations, schools, or individuals, and are awarded to students who show talent or ability in specified areas.

Even if you did not receive a grant or scholarship in your first year, you may be eligible for opportunities in other years of study. These opportunities are often based on grades and campus leadership and may be given by individual departments.

If you are receiving aid from your school, follow all the rules and regulations, including meeting application deadlines and remaining in good academic standing. In most cases, you will be required to reapply for aid every year.

Scholarships. Scholarships are given for various abilities and talents. They may reward academic achievement, exceptional abilities in sports or the arts, citizenship, or leadership. Certain scholarships are sponsored by government agencies. If you display exceptional ability and are disabled, female, of an ethnic background classified as a minority, or a child of someone who draws government benefits, you might find federal scholarship opportunities geared toward you.

All kinds of organizations offer scholarships. You may receive scholarships from individual departments at your school or from your school's independent scholarship funds, local organizations such as the Rotary Club, or privately operated aid foundations. Labour unions and companies may offer scholarships for children of employees. Membership groups, such as Scouting organizations or the YMCA/YWCA, might offer scholarships, and religious organizations are another source of money.

Researching grants and scholarships. It can take work to locate scholarships and work-study programs because many aren't widely advertised. Start digging at your financial aid office and visit your library, bookstore, and the Internet. Two good places to start looking are www.studentawards.com and www.scholarshipscanada.ca.

Understand curriculum and graduation requirements

Every school has requirements for diplomas and/or degrees that are stated in the calendar or on a website. Among the requirements you may encounter at your school are the following:

- The number of credits needed to graduate, including credits required in major and minor fields.
- Curriculum requirements, including specific course requirements. Your school may require a specified number of course hours or credits in the humanities, social sciences, and natural sciences, plus a foreign language and a computer-literacy course.
- Departmental major requirements, including the cumulative average needed for acceptance as a major in the department. For example, you may be automatically accepted if your average is at least 60 per cent.

Those with a lower average may require special approval and may be turned down.

Your goal is to remain in *good academic standing* throughout your post-secondary career as you pursue your academic goal.

Choose and register for classes

Choosing and registering for classes is challenging, especially the first time. Among the things you should consider as you scan your school's calendar and make your course selections are the following:

- Core/general requirements for graduation. You have to take these classes no matter what your major or program.

- Your major or minor or courses in departments you are considering as a major or minor.

- Electives you want to take because they sound interesting, even though they are out of your field. These include classes and teachers that the grapevine says are not to be missed.

In most schools, you can choose to attend a class without earning academic credit by *auditing* the class. Because tuition and fees are generally the same and seats are given on a space-available basis, why would you make this choice? The main reason is to explore different areas without worrying about a grade.

Once you decide on courses, but before you register, create a schedule that shows daily class times. If the first class meets at 8 a.m., ask yourself if you will be at your best at that early hour. It is always a good idea to create a back-up schedule, or even several alternatives, because you may be closed out of some classes. Show your ideas to your advisor for input and approval.

Actual course registration varies from school to school. Registration may take place through your school's computer network, via touch-tone phone, or in the school gym or student union. When you register, you may be asked to pay your tuition and other fees. If you are receiving financial aid, it is up to you to make sure that cheques from all aid sources have arrived at the school before registration. If they haven't, you'll probably need to get on the phone to expedite the payment.

Follow procedures

Your school is a bureaucratic organization, which means that you have to follow established rules and regulations. Normally, procedures are clear and not excessively burdensome, but they can still seem stressful the first time you do them. Among the most common procedures you will encounter are the following:

- Adding or dropping a class. This should be done within the first few days of the semester if you find that a course is not right for you or that there are better choices. Your advisor can tell you how to follow your school's drop/add procedures, which involve completing a form. Late-semester unexcused withdrawals (i.e., any withdrawal after a predetermined date) receive a failing grade. However, course withdrawals that are approved for medical problems, a death in the family, or other special circumstances have no impact on your average.

- **Taking an Incomplete.** If you can't finish your work due to circumstances beyond your control—an illness or injury, for example—many colleges and universities allow you to take a grade of *Incomplete* and make the work up at a later, specified time. You'll need approval from your instructor, and you'll also need to commit to making up the work during vacation or semester break.

- **Transferring schools.** If you are a student at a community college and intend to transfer to a university, or vice versa, be sure to take the courses required for admission to that school. In addition, be sure all your courses are transferable, which means they will be counted toward your degree at the university or community college. Schools generally have advisors to help students work through this process.

- **Taking a leave of absence.** There are many reasons students take a leave of absence for a semester or a year and then return. You may want time away from academics to think through your long-term goals, or you may be needed for a family emergency. If you are in good standing at your school, leaves are generally granted in consultation with your dean and advisor. In contrast, students with academic or disciplinary problems who take a leave may have to reapply for admission when their leave is complete. Check with your advisor regarding details.

Read your school's handbook about the various procedures used at your school. If you still have questions, speak with your advisor.

Pursue academic excellence

Your instructors expect you to do your best in their classes. Doing your best means that you attend every class with a positive attitude, arrive on time, complete assignments on schedule, listen attentively and participate in discussions, value honest scholarship, and seek help if you need it. In return for your efforts, you will learn a great deal and you will receive a course grade. Think of your instructor as the manager of a company. If you want to get the best performance review and the highest pay raise, you'll need to over-deliver on his or her expectations of you.

It is important to remember that your *work*—and not *you*—receives the grades. A *D* or an *F* does not diminish you as a person, but rather tells you that your efforts or work products are below what the instructor expects. Similarly, an *A* does not inflate your value as a person, but recognizes the superb quality of your academic performance.

Have academic integrity

Your school's academic integrity policy should be printed in your student handbook. This code defines the standards of ethical behaviour that are expected of you in your academic work and in your relationships with faculty, administrators, and fellow students. As you will see in Chapter 2, academic integrity is a commitment to five fundamental values: honesty, trust, fairness, respect, and responsibility. As a student enrolled in your school, you have agreed to abide by your school's honour code.

You have also agreed to suffer the consequences should you be discovered violating a core value. Different schools have different ways of dealing with alleged violations. In most cases, students are brought before a committee of instructors or a jury of students to determine whether the offence actually occurred. What happens to a student found guilty varies from school to school. Some penalties include expulsion, suspension, grade reduction, or course failure, depending on the offence.

Master the school's computer system

A large part of the communication and work that you do in college or university involves the computer. Here are some examples:

- Registering for classes.
- Accessing a web-based course syllabus and required-readings list.
- Emailing instructors and students for assignment clarification; receiving email responses.
- Tapping into library databases and the Internet for research.
- Completing assignments and writing papers on your word processor.
- Submitting papers via email to instructors.
- Creating spreadsheets for math and science classes.
- Emailing classmates to schedule group/team meetings.
- Receiving school-wide announcements via the school's computer network.
- Taking interactive quizzes.
- Downloading the latest plane/train/bus schedule via the Internet as you plan your trip home during a school break.

In most colleges and universities, it is no longer possible to manage without a computer—either your own, one borrowed from school, or one accessed in computer labs. Most residence rooms are now wired for computers, which gives students access to the campus network, including the library database.

Here are some suggestions for using your computer effectively:

- **Get trained.** Start by getting help to connect to your school's network. Then, take training classes to master word processing, data and spreadsheets, and the Internet. In some schools, these classes are required. If your typing skills are weak, take a course or use a software program to develop your skills.
- **Use computers to get information.** If you have specific questions about your school, check for answers on your school's website. You may find the information or the email address of a contact person. You must also learn to use the Internet for academic library research (see Chapter 7 for more information).

- Be a safe and cautious user. Although computers seem to be the answer to everything, they sometimes fail. To safeguard your work, use your computer carefully and with respect, especially if it belongs to someone else or your school. Second, create regular backups by saving your work onto the computer hard drive every few minutes. In addition, don't just rely on the hard drive; periodically back up your work in a secondary location such as on a diskette, a CD, or your pocket size USB drive.

- Use computers for appropriate tasks. A quick diversion to internet surfing or a computer game can help refresh you, but it can get out of hand. Try to stay away from these distractions altogether during study time and set strict time limits at other times to keep your academic focus. Remaining focused is especially important when you are using the computer lab and others are waiting their turn.

- Protect yourself from trouble. The following strategies will help:
  - Run virus checks on your personal machine and install and update an anti-virus program.
  - Don't reveal personal data, including financial data, to strangers you meet on the Internet.
  - Be reluctant to take part in chat rooms that are not part of your school's network. Locate chat rooms made up of fellow students and spend downtime visiting with others in cyberspace.
  - If you encounter a technical problem, talk to technicians in the computer lab. Their help can save you hours of time and frustration.

A special word about email

You may be required to communicate with your instructor, submit homework, and even take exams via email. Every student who has access to email should spend time becoming proficient in electronic communication. Following are some important suggestions.

- Use your school's email system. Register for an email account at your school as soon as possible, even if you have a personal email address through another Internet service provider. Without this connection, you may not be able to receive school-wide emails or access electronic files at the school library.

- Be careful of miscommunication. Body language (vocal tone, facial expression, body position) can account for over 75 per cent of what you communicate face to face. With email, however, your words stand alone, forcing you to be careful about your content and tone. Try to be diplomatic and pleasant, and think before you respond to messages that upset you. If you write back too quickly, you may be sorry later.

- Use effective writing techniques. Your email tells a lot about you. To make the best impression—especially when communicating with an instructor or administrator—take the time to find the right words. Organize your thoughts and use proper spelling, punctuation, and grammar. Here are some additional tips that will make your emails easy to read: get to the point in the first paragraph, use short paragraphs, use headings to divide long emails into digestible sections, and use numbered and bulleted lists. Always proofread before hitting "send."

- **Rein in social emailing.** Prioritize your emailing. Respond to the most important and time-sensitive requests first, especially school-related ones. Save personal and conversational email for when you have down time.

The computer skills you learn in college or university will be invaluable at work and in your personal and community activities. Most of today's jobs require computer literacy, as well as the ability to continue to learn as technology changes.

Get involved

The post-secondary lifestyle gives you the opportunity to become involved in activities outside class. These activities enable you to meet people who share your interests and to develop teamwork and leadership skills. They also give you the chance to develop skills that may be important in your career. For example, you might join the Spanish Club to improve your language skills. Being connected to friends and a supportive network of people is one of the main reasons people stay in school instead of dropping out.

Choose activities you genuinely enjoy, and then decide on your level of involvement. Do you want to attend meetings from time to time or become a group leader? As a first-year student, you may want to try several activities before deciding on those that are right for you.

Some first-year students take on more than they can comfortably handle and neglect their studies. If you see that your grades are dropping, it may be time to reduce your activities and focus on your work. You should seek balance in your post-secondary life; too much of anything is not effective time management.

You are beginning the journey of your post-secondary education. The work you do in this course and in the remaining pages of *Keys to Success* will help you achieve your goals in your studies and in your personal life and career. As you move forward, think about the words Josh Billings, a 19th-century American writer, said over 100 years ago: *"Everyone who does the best he can do is a hero."* From this day forward, be your own personal hero.

CHOOSE

1

IN THIS CHAPTER

In this chapter you will explore answers to the following questions: • Where are you now—and where can your education take you? • How do you make a successful transition to college or university? • How can successful intelligence help you achieve your goals? • How will *Keys to Success* help you build successful intelligence? • How can you get motivated? • How do you go about making and keeping a commitment? • How can what you learn now help you succeed in school, work, and life?

Welcome to your post-secondary career

WELCOME—or welcome back—to your education. You are embarking on a new phase of life that may bring all kinds of questions and concerns. This chapter will preview the changes ahead and inspire you to manage your transition successfully. As you contemplate the course of the next two to five years of your post-secondary life, you may wonder: How am I going to get from first-year orientation to graduation? How am I going to make it?

Here's one important part of the answer to that question: *With the help of this book.* Why? Because it will make your life easier. This book, and the course for which you are reading it, have a primary goal: To help you learn successfully, graduate, and reap the personal and professional rewards of a solid education. This chapter gives you an overview of how that will happen—how being a successfully intelligent, motivated, and forward-thinking student will help you face the challenges of post-secondary life and achieve more than you could have imagined.

opening doors

Where are you now—and where can your education take you?

You are standing at the gateway to a new phase of life. Before you think about moving forward, though, take a look at the road that brought you here. You completed high school or its equivalent. You may have built life skills from experience as a partner or parent. You may have been employed in one or more jobs. You have enrolled in university or college, found a way to pay for it, signed up for courses, and shown up for class. You made the choice to believe in your ability to accomplish important goals. You have earned this opportunity to be a post-secondary student!

What education can do for you

Begin to realize what education will mean for you by looking at your reasons for starting, or returning to, post-secondary education. These are just some of the many possibilities:

- I want to earn a better living.
- I want to get a diploma/degree so that I can move ahead in a career.
- I want to spend time learning new subjects.
- I just lost my job, so I want to learn new skills.
- Everybody in my family goes to college or university; it's expected.
- I really don't know why I'm here.

All of these answers are legitimate. It isn't easy to enrol in a program, cover tuition, sign up for classes, and show up at class. Your reasons have been compelling enough to get you here. Be honest with yourself about why you are here, and you will have a realistic picture about your expectations as you begin.

Next, begin to think about your educational goals in more detail. You don't need answers right now—what's important is that you start thinking. What courses do you want to take? What kind of schedule do you want? What degree or certificate are you shooting for? Think also about academic excellence and whether honours and awards are important goals. If you are aiming for a particular career, consider what may be required (e.g., degrees, certificates, post-graduate education, internships). Finally, and most importantly, think about what you want in terms of learning, relationships, and personal growth.

After you have a solid idea of what you want out of your post-secondary experience, you can begin your biggest and most rewarding job—to stick with it and reap the benefits.

How education promotes life success

If your work in college or university only helped you succeed in the classroom, the benefit of your learning wouldn't last beyond graduation day. However, learning is a tool for life, and a college education is designed to

serve you far beyond the classroom. Here are a few important "life success goals" that college can help you achieve:

Life Success Goal: Increased employability and earning potential. Getting a degree greatly increases your chances of finding and keeping a high-level, well-paying job. According to Statistics Canada, "higher education is a gateway to higher earnings."[1] Statistically speaking, the more education you have, the more you earn. (see Key 1.1).

Life Success Goal: Preparation for career success. Your course work will give you the knowledge and hands-on skills you need to achieve your career goals. It will also expose you to a variety of careers related to your major, many of which you may not have even heard of. Completing college and/or university will open career doors that are otherwise closed.

This book will frequently refer to the Employability Skills 2000+ Profile developed by the Conference Board of Canada. The Conference Board is a research organization whose members include Canadian corporations and the government. "Employability skills" are defined as "the skills you need to enter, stay in, and progress in the world of work—whether you work on your own or as part of a team."[2] Many Canadian companies helped to determine which skills were preferred by Canadian businesses. These were broken down into three categories: fundamental skills, personal management skills, and teamwork skills (see Key 1.2). This book will put skills learned in the classroom into the broader context of employability skills.

Education and income.

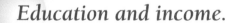

Median annual income of persons by their highest degree attained, 2000

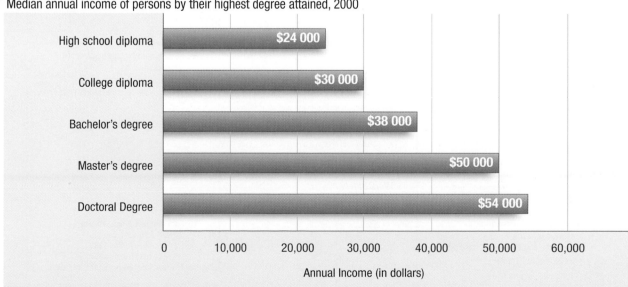

Source: Statistics Canada, "Education in Canada 2000," p. 124.

Employability skills 2000+.

The skills you need to enter, stay in, and progress in the world of work—whether you work on your own or as a part of a team.

These skills can also be applied and used beyond the workplace in a range of daily activities.

Fundamental Skills The skills needed as a base for further development	**Personal Management Skills** The personal skills, attitudes, and behaviours that drive one's potential for growth	**Teamwork Skills** The skills and attributes needed to contribute productively
You will be better prepared to progress in the world of work when you can:	*You will be able to offer yourself greater possibilities for achievement when you can:*	*You will be better prepared to add value to the outcomes of a task, project, or team when you can:*

Communicate
- read and understand information presented in a variety of forms (e. g., words, graphs, charts, diagrams)
- write and speak so others pay attention and understand
- listen and ask questions to understand and appreciate the points of view of others
- share information using a range of information and communications technologies (e. g., voice, e- mail, computers)
- use relevant scientific, technological, and mathematical knowledge and skills to explain or clarify ideas

Manage Information
- locate, gather, and organize information using appropriate technology and information systems
- access, analyze, and apply knowledge and skills from various disciplines (e. g., the arts, languages, science, technology, mathematics, social sciences, and the humanities)

Use Numbers
- decide what needs to be measured or calculated
- observe and record data using appropriate methods, tools, and technology
- make estimates and verify calculations

Think & Solve Problems
- assess situations and identify problems
- seek different points of view and evaluate them based on facts
- recognize the human, interpersonal, technical, scientific, and mathematical dimensions of a problem
- identify the root cause of a problem
- be creative and innovative in exploring possible solutions
- readily use science, technology, and mathematics as ways to think, gain, and share knowledge, solve problems, and make decisions
- evaluate solutions to make recommendations or decisions
- implement solutions
- check to see if a solution works, and act on opportunities for improvement

Demonstrate Positive Attitudes & Behaviours
- feel good about yourself and be confident
- deal with people, problems, and situations with honesty, integrity, and personal ethics
- recognize your own and other people's good efforts
- take care of your personal health
- show interest, initiative, and effort

Be Responsible
- set goals and priorities balancing work and personal life
- plan and manage time, money, and other resources to achieve goals
- assess, weigh, and manage risk
- be accountable for your actions and the actions of your group
- be socially responsible and contribute to your community

Be Adaptable
- work independently or as a part of a team
- carry out multiple tasks or projects
- be innovative and resourceful: identify and suggest alternative ways to achieve goals and get the job done
- be open and respond constructively to change
- learn from your mistakes and accept feedback
- cope with uncertainty

Learn Continuously
- be willing to learn and grow continuously
- assess personal strengths and areas for development
- set your own learning goals
- identify and access learning sources and opportunities
- plan for and achieve your learning goals

Work Safely
- be aware of personal and group health and safety practices and procedures, and act in accordance with these

Work with Others
- understand and work within the dynamics of a group
- ensure that a team's purpose and objectives are clear
- be flexible: respect and be open to and supportive of the thoughts, opinions, and contributions of others in a group
- recognize and respect people's diversity, individual differences, and perspectives
- accept and provide feedback in a constructive and considerate manner
- contribute to a team by sharing information and expertise
- lead or support when appropriate, motivating a group for high performance
- understand the role of conflict in a group to reach solutions
- manage and resolve conflict when appropriate

Participate in Projects & Tasks
- plan, design, or carry out a project or task from start to finish with well-defined objectives and outcomes
- develop a plan, seek feedback, test, revise, and implement
- work to agreed quality standards and specifications
- select and use appropriate tools and technology for a task or project
- adapt to changing requirements and information
- continuously monitor the success of a project or task and identify ways to improve

255 Smyth Road, Ottawa
ON K1H 8M7 Canada
Tel. (613) 526- 3280
Fax (613) 526- 4857
Internet: www. conferenceboard. ca/ nbec

Source: Conference Board of Canada, Employability Skills 2000+ Profile, **www.conferenceboard.ca/education/learning-tools/esp2000.pdf.**

Life Success Goal: Smart personal health choices. The more educated you are, the more likely you are to take care of your physical and mental health. A post-secondary education prepares you with health-related information that you will use over your lifetime, helping you to practise wellness through positive actions and to avoid practices with the potential to harm.

Life Success Goal: Active community involvement and an appreciation of different cultures. Going to college prepares you to understand complex political, economic, and social forces that affect you and others. This understanding is the basis for good citizenship and encourages community involvement. Your education also exposes you to the ways in which people and cultures are different and how these differences affect world affairs.

Thinking about these big-picture goals should help you begin to brainstorm, in more detail, what you want out of your post-secondary experience. What courses do you want to take? What kind of schedule do you want? What degree, diploma, or certificate are you shooting for? Think about academic excellence and whether honours and awards are important goals. If you have a particular career in mind, then consider the degrees and experience it may require. Finally, consider personal growth, and think about the importance of developing friendships with people who will motivate and inspire you.

How do you make a *successful transition* to college or university?

Beginning college is a significant transition for anyone. Introducing such a responsibility into your life is both exciting and stressful. For most students, it takes time to feel comfortable. To begin, spend some energy knowing your situation and connecting with others.

How can *successful intelligence* help you achieve your goals?

Think about how you would define *intelligence*. Chances are, like many people, you believe that people are born with a certain, unchangeable amount of intelligence and that this has a significant effect on the ability to succeed. Another fairly common belief is that standardized tests, such as IQ (intelligence quotient) tests, accurately measure a person's intelligence and are predictors of success.

Psychologist and Yale professor Robert J. Sternberg views intelligence differently. His life experiences convinced him that traditional intelligence measurements lock people into poor performances and often do not accurately reflect their potential for life success. When test anxiety caused Sternberg to score poorly on IQ and other standardized tests during elementary school, he delivered exactly what was expected of him—very little. In Grade 4, a teacher saw something in him. By letting him know that she expected more than he had ever shown he could give, she provided a spark that turned his life around.

According to Sternberg, standardized tests measure *inert intelligence*—that is, they require passive repetition rather than goal-directed thinking. He further explains that those who score well on tests may have strong recall and analytical skills but do not necessarily have the power to make things happen in the real world.[3] That power to put information to work is critical to your success. No matter how high you score on a library science test, for example, your knowledge won't serve you unless you can use it to research a topic successfully.

Defining successful intelligence

In Sternberg's view, intelligence is not a fixed quantity; people have the capacity to increase intelligence as they learn and grow. In his book *Successful Intelligence: How Practical and Creative Intelligence Determine Success in Life*, Sternberg focuses on what he calls *successful intelligence*—"the kind of intelligence used to achieve important goals."[4] Successful intelligence better predicts life success than any IQ test because it focuses on actions—what you *do* to achieve your goals—instead of just on recall and analysis.

Everyone knows people who fit the conventional definition of "smart." They score well on tests and get good grades. Teachers expect them to achieve academically, and they do. However, these students may have limited success outside the classroom if they can't translate their "smarts" into real-world actions.

In contrast, other students have a hard time making the grade but are seen as "offbeat," "creative," or "street smart." Some of these students use their practical or creative intelligence to lift themselves above the crowd. Successful people such as Bill Gates, Ellen DeGeneres, and Woody Allen, despite difficulties in school, built extraordinary success by creatively using their strengths and developing practical ways to reach their goals. Think about people you know who consistently achieve what they're after, whether they do so in a traditional or non-traditional way. These people demonstrate successful intelligence.

Sternberg breaks successful intelligence into three parts or abilities: *Analytical* thinking, *creative* thinking, and *practical* thinking.

- *Analytical thinking*—commonly known as critical thinking—involves analyzing and evaluating information, often in order to work through a problem or decision. Analytical thinking is largely responsible for school success and is recognized and measured through traditional testing methods.

- *Creative thinking* involves generating new and different ideas and approaches to problems, and, often, viewing the world in ways that disregard convention.

- *Practical thinking* means putting what you've learned into action in order to solve a problem or make a decision. Practical thinking enables you to accomplish goals despite real-world obstacles.

These ways of thinking work together to move you toward a goal, as Sternberg describes:

Analytical thinking is required to solve problems and to judge the quality of ideas. Creative intelligence is required to formulate good problems and ideas in the first place. Practical intelligence is needed to use the ideas and their analysis in an effective way in one's everyday life.[5]

Here are two examples that illustrate how this works.

Successful intelligence in a study group—reaching for the goal of helping each other learn.

- **Analyze** the concepts you must learn, including how they relate to what you already know.
- **Create** humorous memory games to help you remember key concepts.
- **Think practically** about whom in the group does what best, and assign tasks according to what you discover.

Successful intelligence in considering an academic path—reaching for the goal of declaring a major.

- **Analyze** what you do well, what you like to do. Then analyze the course offerings in your college catalogue until you come up with one or more that seem to match up with your strengths.
- **Create** a dream career, then work backward to come up with majors that might support it. For example, if you want to be a science writer, consider majoring in biology and minoring in journalism.
- **Think practically** about your major by talking with students and instructors in the department, looking at course requirements, and interviewing professionals in the fields that interest you.

Why successful intelligence is your key to success

When you understand how learning helps you achieve goals that are important to you, you want to learn. When you want to learn, you work hard to make it happen. When you make the effort to learn, you are most likely to succeed.

Successful intelligence powers this entire process, from understanding to success. By helping you to focus on how your learning propels you toward specific goals, it boosts your desire to learn. By giving you an action plan with which you can think through problems or pursue goals, successful intelligence inspires you to work hard and aim high. By helping you to make the most of your strengths and compensate for or correct your weaknesses, it helps you capitalize on who you are and what you can do.

More good news for all kinds of learners lies in the fact that successful intelligence has three equally important elements. Students who have had trouble with tests and other traditional analytical skills can take heart, knowing that creative and practical thinking can help them forge new paths to success. Students who test well can turn their analytical skills into real tools for success through creative thinking and practical action plans.

How will *Keys to Success* help you build *successful intelligence?*

The goal of *Keys to Success* is to help you build the analytical, creative, and practical thinking skills that will get you where you want to go in school and in life. Each element of the book contributes to this goal.

The chapter material

Through your exploration of the various topics in *Keys to Success*, you will develop all three aspects of successful intelligence. The material will often connect a topic to analytical, creative, or practical thinking. Accounts and examples from students, professors, and professionals show how people use various analytical, creative, and practical skills to accomplish personal goals. In addition, Chapter 4—the chapter on thinking—goes into detail about how you can evaluate and build analytical, creative, and practical skills.

Key 1.3 provides some examples of the practical, analytical, and creative thinking skills that lie within chapter topics.

The in-chapter activities

As you work through each chapter, you will find three activities designed to help you turn ideas you read into news you can use.

- *Get Analytical* gives you an opportunity to analyze a chapter topic.
- *Get Creative* prompts you to think creatively about chapter material.
- *Get Practical* provides a chance to consider a practical application of a chapter idea.

Working through these activities gives you a double benefit. While building successful intelligence skills, you are also deepening your understanding of chapter material, making it more useful to you in pursuing your goals.

The end-of-chapter exercises

The end-of-chapter exercises give you several opportunities to combine what you have learned and apply it to important tasks.

- *Developing Successful Intelligence: Putting It All Together* unites analytical thinking ("Think it through"), creative thinking ("Think out of the box"), and practical thinking ("Make it happen"). This exercise builds your understanding of successful intelligence as an active process and strengthens your ability to direct its elements toward a goal.
- *Team Building: Collaborative Solutions* encourages you to apply various successful intelligence elements to a group setting, building both thinking skills and your ability to work successfully with others.
- *Writing: Discovery Through Journaling* provides an opportunity to put your analysis, creative thoughts, and practical ideas down in words, building writing skills as well as thinking skills.

Keys to Success *chapters develop successful intelligence.*

CHAPTER	ANALYTICAL SKILLS	CREATIVE SKILLS	PRACTICAL SKILLS
2	• Thinking about whether your values reflect who you are or want to be • Analyzing how successful a time manager you are	• Coming up with creative ways to manage stress • Thinking about different paths toward a goal	• Planning steps toward a goal • Keeping an effective calendar
3	• Examining how you learn • Matching your learning style to courses, skills, and environments	• When thinking about a major, considering departments or types of majors that are off the beaten path • Opening your mind to new perceptions of you as a learner	• Creating a step-by-step plan toward declaring a major • Linking your learning style to study skills that will help you most
4	• Distinguishing fact from opinion • Evaluating assumptions	• Brainstorming • Using strategies that enhance creative abilities	• Practical problem solving • Making a well-considered decision
5	• Evaluating arguments • Analyzing the hidden perspectives found in all media messages	• Thinking of different ways to review reading material • Finding innovative ways to work with study group members	• Using a practical plan— SQ3R—for maximizing reading comprehension • Expanding your vocabulary
6	• Deciding which information is important enough to record in notes • Examining your particular listening challenges	• Coming up with interesting mnemonic devices • Brainstorming ways to listen more effectively when you don't agree with the speaker	• Memorizing by grouping information • Knowing when and how to use different note-taking systems
7	• Examining the credibility of research sources • Evaluating how well you support your thesis statement with examples	• Thinking up essay topics • Freewriting to generate a flow of ideas	• Going through a writing process—plan, draft, revise, edit • Using a basic research strategy
8	• Analyzing why you made a particular mistake on a test • Selecting the most important material to study for a test	• Brainstorming a study schedule • Coming up with a variety of review techniques	• Knowing how to handle different types of test questions • Combating test anxiety
9	• Examining how prejudice leads to discrimination • Evaluating the accuracy of your judgments of others	• Finding ways to think expansively about diversity • Brainstorming methods for managing anger	• Making connections with diverse people • Adjusting to different communication styles

CHAPTER	ANALYTICAL SKILLS	CREATIVE SKILLS	PRACTICAL SKILLS
10	• Thinking through the consequences of drugs and alcohol • Evaluating options for sexual decisions	• Coming up with ways you can use resources if you need help • Thinking of activities that reduce stress for you	• Facing and conquering addiction • Staying disease-free
11	• Analyzing how effectively you spend your money • Linking your learning style to related career areas	• Brainstorming careers that interest you and suit your talents • Coming up with people with whom you can network	• Keeping credit card use under control • Juggling work and school
12	• Reevaluating and modifying goals • Considering the effect you can have when you help others	• Engaging creative talents as a way to learn through life • Facing change with flexibility and creative options	• Getting involved in your community and environment • Living your personal mission

- *Career Portfolio: Plan for Success* is a chance to see how your analytical, creative, and practical skills will help you prepare for workplace success. Through the chapters you will build a tangible and useful portfolio—analyzing workplace opportunities, coming up with creative ideas about careers, and creating practical items that you will use in your job search.

get creative!   SEE YOURSELF AT YOUR BEST

Use your creative powers to improve your opinion of yourself and inspire action.

You probably have some idea of where you fit into the diverse Canadian student body—your age, stage of life, and educational background. However, your "student status" is only a small part of who you are.

    Imagine that students gained entry into college by writing personal ads and posting them on the admissions Web site. Write a personal ad that you feel would give you the best possible chance to get in. In it, talk about

- what makes you unique and anything but "average."
- what is special about you that will make your school a better place.
- how your post-secondary education will bring you personal and professional success.

_____

_____

_____

_____

_____

With the power of your mind and the tools waiting for you in this book, you possess the keys to success. What remains is to turn the key and get moving toward your goals—and this requires motivation. Here are some ways to find that motivation and put it to work.

How can you get *motivated*?

Success is a process, not a fixed mark—and **motivation** is what keeps the process in motion. Motivation is the energy that fuels your drive to achieve. Successful people are those who can consistently motivate themselves to learn, grow, and work toward goals.

Post-secondary education provides an opportunity for you to discover the goals most important to you and build the motivation it takes to achieve them. Wherever you start, and whatever obstacles you encounter on the way, your motivation can help lead you to the future you envision.

What motivates you? People have all kinds of different *motivators*—goals or ideas that move them forward. For example, some potential motivators for attending school could be learning a marketable skill, supporting a family, or self-improvement. Furthermore, motivators can change with time or with different situations. A student might begin work on a course feeling motivated by a desire to earn a particular grade, and later, becoming interested in the subject, he or she becomes motivated by a desire to master the material.

From time to time, everyone experiences a loss of motivation, whether in the short term or for a longer spell. How can you build motivation or renew lost motivation? First, start on the path. Just beginning makes you feel better as you work toward your goals. Newton's first law of motion, a law of physics, says that things in motion tend to stay in motion and things at rest tend to stay at rest. Be a thing in motion.

MOTIVATION

A force that moves a person to action; often inspired by an idea, a fact, an event, a goal.

A journey of a thousand miles begins with a single step.

LAO TZU

Second, explore the following motivation-boosting strategies—making a commitment, developing positive habits, being responsible, building self-esteem, and facing your fears. Explore them, and experiment to see what helps most. You might use them in combination, focus on the ones that have the most positive effects on you, or try them out one by one.

Finally, reading and thinking about the Stressbuster stories in each chapter will give you real-world insight into what it takes to sustain motivation in the face of difficult obstacles. Even if you have never experienced such obstacles, let the courage of the people profiled inspire you to confidence about your own life. If they can leap their hurdles successfully, so can you.

Make a Commitment

COMMITMENT

1. A pledge or promise to do something, or
2. dedication to a long-term course of action.

How do you focus the energy of motivation? Make a **commitment**. Commitment means that you do what you say you will do. When you honour a commitment to an academic goal, a career dream, or a self-improvement task, you prove to yourself and others that your intentions can be trusted. Commitment often stretches over a period of time; you hold yourself to a promise for as long as necessary to reach your goal.

How do you go about making and keeping a commitment?

- **State your commitment concretely.** Set a clear goal and break it into manageable pieces. Be specific; for example, "I'm going to turn in the weekly essay assignments on time," rather than "I'm going to do my best work in this course." Emphasize to yourself what you will gain from this commitment.

- **Take the first step.** Sometimes, feeling overwhelmed can immobilize you. Decide on the first step of your commitment and take it today. Then continue a day at a time, breaking tasks into small steps.

- **Stay aware of each commitment.** Keep a list of commitments in your planner, on your refrigerator, or on your computer. If they involve events or projects that take place on specific dates, note them on a calendar. Talk about them with someone you trust to help you stay on track.

- **Keep an eye on your progress.** You're not a failure if you lose steam; it's normal. Recharge by reflecting on the positive effects of your commitment and what you have already achieved.

- **Reward yourself as you move ahead.** Rewards help you feel good about what you've accomplished so far and can help keep you going. Treat yourself to dinner with a friend, a new CD or DVD, or a movie night.

For example, you might make this commitment: "I will write in my journal every night before going to sleep." You make journal entries for two weeks and then evaluate what positive effects this daily practice has had on your writing ability. If you stop writing for a time, you can renew your commitment by reminding yourself of how keeping a journal has improved your writing ability and relieved stress. You might boost your commitment by telling a partner or housemate to check on you.

Making commitments helps you keep a steady focus on your most important goals. It gives you a sense of accomplishment as you experience gradual growth and progress.

Develop Positive Habits

HABIT

A preference for a particular action that you do a certain way, and often on a regular basis or at certain times.

People have all kinds of **habits**; some you may consider "bad" and others "good." Bad habits stall motivation and prevent you from reaching important goals. Some bad habits, such as chronic lateness, cause obvious problems. Other habits, such as surfing the Internet, may not seem bad until you realize that you needed to spend those hours studying.

Good habits are those that bring the kind of positive effects that keep motivation high. You often have to wait longer and work harder to see a reward for good habits, which makes them harder to maintain. If you reduce your nights out to gain study time, for example, your marks won't improve in a week. Changing a habit is a process; trust that the rewards are somewhere down the road.

Look at the positive and negative effects of your habits to decide which you want to keep and which you need to change or improve. Take the following steps to evaluate a habit and, if necessary, make a change (if the habit has more negative effects than positive ones). Don't try to change more than one habit at a time—trying to reach perfection in everything all at once can overwhelm you.

1. *Define and evaluate the habit.* Name your habit and look at the negative and positive effects. If there are more negatives than positives, it is most likely a habit worth changing.

2. *Decide to keep or change the habit.* Until you are convinced that you will receive a benefit, efforts to change will not get you far. Commit to a change if you see too many negative effects.

3. *Start today—and keep it up.* Don't put it off until after this week, after the family reunion, or after the semester. Each day gained is a day you can benefit from a new lifestyle. To have the best chance at changing a habit, be consistent for at least three weeks so that you become accustomed to the new habit.

4. *Reward positive steps.* Choose a reward that encourages you to stay on target. If you earn a good grade, for example, treat yourself to one night out instead of slacking off on studying the following week.

Finally, don't get too discouraged if the process seems difficult. Rarely does someone make the decision to change and do so without a setback or two. Take it one step at a time; when you lose steam, reflect on what you stand to gain. With persistence and positive thinking, you can reach your goal.

Be Responsible

In your post-secondary career, you are in charge of your life in a way that you may never have been before. Even if you have lived on your own and held a job, helped raise a family, or both, post-secondary education adds greatly to that responsibility. You are responsible for making decisions that keep you in motion and avoiding choices that stall you in your tracks. You are your own manager.

Taking responsibility is all about living up to your obligations, both those that are imposed on you and those that you impose on yourself. Through action, you prove that you are responsible—"response-able"—able to respond. When something has to be done, a responsible person does it—as efficiently as possible and to the best of his or her ability.

Responsibility Means Action. Taking responsibility is taking action—and doing it reliably. In college or university, responsible people can be trusted to live up to obligations like these:

- Attending class and participating in activities and discussions
- Completing reading and assignments on time
- Communicating with instructors and fellow students

These actions may sound mundane to you, everyday requirements that don't have much bearing on the greater goals in your life. However, they are the building blocks of responsibility that get you where you want to go. Here's why:

- **Everyday responsibilities get you in the action habit.** As with any other habit, the more you do something, the more it becomes second nature. The more often you complete and turn in assignments on time, for example, the more likely you are to stay on top of your job tasks down the road when you are on a tight deadline.

- **The small accomplishments make a big impression.** When you show up to class, pay attention, contribute, and work hard, you send a message. An instructor who observes these behaviours is more likely to trust and respect you. People who trust you may give you increasing power and opportunities for growth because you have shown that you are capable of making the best of both.

- **Fulfilling day-to-day responsibilities gives you freedom.** The more responsible you are, and the more responsibilities you take on, the more those around you will give you the freedom to handle situations and problems on your own. You will be perceived as a fully functioning team member who can be counted on to pull his or her share of the load, no matter what the circumstances.

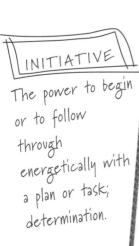

INITIATIVE

The power to begin or to follow through energetically with a plan or task; determination.

Responsibility Means Initiative. When you show **initiative**, you push yourself to take that first, often difficult, step. Initiative is the spark plug of responsibility—it jump-starts you into action. By taking initiative, you respond quickly and continually to changes that occur.

Initiative means that you make a move on your own instead of waiting for people, rules, requirements, or circumstances to push you. You show initiative when you go to a counsellor for help with a problem, make an appointment with an instructor to discuss a paper, talk to a friend about a conflict, speak up in class, find a better way to do a task at work, vote, or start an exercise program. Once you take that first step, it is often easier to keep your momentum going and continue to act responsibly.

Responsibility can take enormous effort. Remember that you gain self-respect when you prove that you can live up to your promises.

Face Your Fears

Everyone experiences fear. Anything unknown—new people, experiences, challenges, situations—can be frightening. The changes involved in pursuing an education, for example, can inspire fear. You may wonder if you can handle the work, if you have chosen the right school or program, or if your education will prepare you to find a job you like and that pays well.

If your fears become overwhelming, they can derail your motivation. Some people give in to fear because they feel safer with the familiar, even if it doesn't make them happy. Ultimately, though, giving in to fear by giving up on your motivation may keep you from living the life you have envisioned.

FACE YOUR FEARS[6]

Use practical skills to conquer a fear of yours that stems from the experience of starting college. First, describe your fear—and be specific.

_____

_____

Now, list three small activities that get you closer to working through that fear. If you don't want to start a project because you fear failure, for example, you can begin by reading a book on the subject, brainstorming what you already know about it, or making up a project schedule.

1. _____
2. _____
3. _____

Commit yourself to one step that you will take within the next two days. State it here. Include the time and date you will begin and how much time you will spend.

_____

_____

What reward will you give yourself for taking this step?

_____

Did taking this step help ease your fear? If so, describe how.

_____

_____

Affirm that you have taken that first step and are on the way to success by signing your name here and writing the date.

Name _____   Date _____

The challenges you face as you work toward your goals demand a willingness to face your fears and push your limits. The following steps will help you work through fear with courage:

1. *Acknowledge fears.* The act of naming your fear begins to lessen its hold on you. Be specific. Knowing that you fear taking a biology course may not inspire you to action, whereas focusing on your fear of working with live mice in biology lab gives you something tangible to deal with.

2. *Examine fears.* Sometimes one fear hides a larger one. If you fear a test, determine whether you fear the test itself or the fact that if you pass it, you will have to take a tougher class next. If you fear the test, take steps to prepare for it. If you fear the next class, you might talk with your instructor about it.

3. *Develop a plan of attack.* Evaluate what will help you overcome your fear. For example, if you are scared of reading Shakespeare, help yourself by asking your instructor for advice, going over assigned plays with a study group, and watching a Shakespearean movie.

4. *Move ahead with your plan.* Courage is the key to moving ahead. Take the steps that help you to confront and move beyond your fears.

He has not learned the lesson of life who does not every day surmount a fear.

RALPH WALDO EMERSON

As you work through your fears, talk about them with people you trust. Everyone has fears, and when people share strategies, everyone benefits.

Build Self-Esteem

SELF-ESTEEM
A strong and deeply felt belief that you as a person have value in the world.

When people believe in their value and capabilities, their **self-esteem** fuels their motivation to succeed. Belief, though, is only half the game. The other half is the action and effort that help you feel that you have earned your self-esteem. Rick Pitino, a highly successful basketball coach, discusses developing self-esteem in his book *Success Is a Choice*: "Self-esteem is directly linked to deserving success. If you have established a great work ethic and have begun the discipline that is inherent with that, you will automatically begin to feel better about yourself. It's all interrelated. You must deserve victory to feel good about yourself."[7]

Building self-esteem, therefore, involves both *thinking positively* and *taking action*. Together, they help you generate the belief in yourself that keeps you motivated.

Think Positively. Attitudes influence your choices and affect how you perceive and relate to others. A positive attitude can open your mind to learning experiences and inspire you to action. If, for example, you keep an open mind in a course that at first seems like a waste of time, you might discover that the course teaches you something valuable. You have the power to create your own reality, and with a positive attitude you can make that reality a positive one.

POSITIVE
SELF-TALK

Supportive and positive thoughts and ideas that a person communicates to himself or herself.

One way to create a positive attitude is through **positive self-talk**. When you hear negative thoughts in your mind ("I'm not very smart"), replace them with positive ones ("It won't be easy, but I'm smart enough to figure it out"). You would probably never criticize a good friend in the same way that you sometimes criticize yourself. These hints will help you put positive self-talk into action:

- **Stop negative talk in its tracks.** If you catch yourself thinking, "I can never write a decent paper," stop and say to yourself, "I can write better than that and next time I will." Then think about some specific steps you can take to improve your writing.

- **Pay yourself a compliment.** Note your successes. Be specific: "I have really improved my spelling and proofreading." Some people keep a list of positive statements about themselves in a notebook or use calendars with daily affirmations. These are great reminders of positive self-talk.

- Replace words of obligation with words of personal intent.

  I should *becomes* I choose to.

  I'll try *becomes* I will.

Words of intent give you power and control because they imply a personal decision to act. For example, when you say, "I have to be in class by nine o'clock," you're saying that someone else has power over you and has handed you a required obligation. When you say, "I want to be in class by nine o'clock because I don't want to miss anything I need to learn," you're saying that the choice is yours.

It can sometimes be difficult to think positively. If you have a deep-rooted feeling of unworthiness, you may want to see a counsellor. Many people have benefited from skilled professional advice.

Take Action. Although thinking positively sets the tone for success, it cannot get you there by itself. You have to take action. Without action, positive thoughts become empty statements or even lies.

Consider, for example, a student in a first year English writing class. This student thinks every possible positive thought: "I am a great student. I know how to write well. I can get a B in this class. I will succeed in school." And so on. She even writes her thoughts down on notes and posts them where she can see them. Then, during the semester, she misses about one-third of the class meetings, turns in some of her papers late, and completely forgets a couple of assignments. She doesn't make use of opportunities to work with her study partner. At the end of the course, when she barely passes, she wonders how things went so wrong when she had such a positive attitude.

This student did not succeed because she did not earn her belief in herself through action and effort. By the end of a semester like this, positive thoughts look like lies. "If I can get a B, why did I get a D? If I am such a great student, why did I barely make it through this course?" Eventually, with nothing to support them, the positive thoughts disappear, and with neither positive thoughts nor action, a student will have a hard time achieving any level of success.

Following are some ways to get moving in a positive direction:

- **Build your own code of discipline.** Develop general guidelines to follow, based on what actions are important to your success. Perhaps your top priorities are personal relationships and achievement in school. Construct each day's goals and actions so that they help you achieve your larger objectives.

- **Make action plans and follow through.** Figure out how you plan to take action for any situation, so that, for example, "I am a great student" is backed up by specific actions to ensure success. When you have a plan, just do it. Only after taking action can you reap the benefit.

- **Acknowledge every step.** Even the smallest action is worth your attention because every action reinforces a positive thought and builds self-esteem. First you believe that you are a good student, then you work hard in class, then you do well on a test, then you believe more emphatically that you are a good student, then you complete a successful group project, then you feel even better about yourself, and so on.

The process of building and maintaining self-esteem involves many successes and disappointments. Only by having a true sense of self-esteem, though, can you achieve your dreams. You are in control of your self-esteem because you alone are ultimately responsible for your thoughts and actions. Do what it takes to both believe in yourself and take the action that anchors and inspires that belief.

Believing in yourself helps you make good choices. When your self-esteem is strong, you are more likely to choose actions that you can be proud of.

How can *what you learn now* help you succeed in school, work, and life?

In his book *TechnoTrends—24 Technologies That Will Revolutionize Our Lives*, futurist Daniel Burns describes a tomorrow that is linked to continuing education: "The future belongs to those who are capable of being retrained again and again," he says. "Think of it as periodically upgrading your human assets throughout your career.... Humans are infinitely upgradeable, but it does require an investment" in lifelong learning.[8] In *Boom, Bust and Echo 2000*, David Foot and Daniel Stoffman claim that jobs for Canadians without college or university education will continue to disappear.[9] Colleges and universities are the ideal training grounds for learning skills that will serve you throughout your life.

Education Prepares You to Learn from Failure and Celebrate Success

Every life has problems to be solved and difficult decisions to be made. Even the most successful people and organizations make mistakes and experience failures. There is a lot to be gained from failing. In fact, failure is one of the greatest teachers. Failure is an opportunity to realize what you didn't know so that you can learn and improve. What you learn from a failure will most likely stay with you more intensely and guide you more effectively than many other things you learn.

Post-secondary education brings new challenges, and with them come situations in which you may fail. When you face difficult obstacles, let yourself down or disappoint others, or make mistakes, what is important is how you deal with the situation. Although it's human to pretend a failure didn't happen, to blame yourself or blame someone else, choices like these can deny you valuable lessons. If you can accept failure as part of life, forgive yourself, and learn from it, you will be able to pick yourself up and keep improving.

Learning from Failure. Learning from your failures and mistakes involves careful thinking. One useful course of action is to first look at what happened, make any improvements that you can, and finally decide how to change your action or approach in the future. For example, imagine that,

LEARN FROM A MISTAKE

Analyze what happened when you made a mistake in order to avoid the same mistake next time.

Describe an academic situation—you didn't study enough for a test, you didn't complete an assignment on time, you didn't listen carefully enough to a lecture and missed important information—where you made a mistake. What happened?

_____

_____

_____

What were the consequences of the mistake?

_____

_____

_____

What, if anything, did you learn from your mistake that you will use in similar situations?

_____

_____

_____

_____

after a long night of studying for a test, you forgot that you had a deadline for a five-page paper the next day.

Look at what happened. Your exhaustion and concern about the test caused you to forget to check your planner to see what else was on your plate. Now you may face a lower mark on your paper if you turn it in late, plus you may be inclined to rush it and quickly turn in a paper that isn't as good as it could be.

Make any possible improvements on the situation. You could visit your instructor during office hours, or send an email, explain the situation and ask if you can have a brief extension on the paper.

Make changes for the future. You can set a goal to note deadlines in a bright colour and to check your planner more often. You can also try arranging your study schedule so that you will be less exhausted.

Facing failure can be hard. Here are some ways to boost your outlook when failure gets you down:

- *Stay aware of the fact that you are a capable, valuable person.* Focus your energy on your best abilities and know that you have the strength to try again.

- *Share your thoughts and disappointment with others.* Exchange creative energy that can help you learn from failures rather than having a mutual gripe session.

- *Look on the bright side.* At worst, you flunk the test or paper. At best, you have learned a lesson that will help you avoid similar situations in the future. There might even be other positive results.

Finally, remember that your value as a human being does not diminish when you make a mistake. Expect that you always will do the best that you can, knowing that just getting through another day as a student, employee, or parent is a success. In addition, because failure is a frequent result of risk taking, people who can manage failure show that they have the courage to take risks and learn. Employers often value risk takers who sometimes fail more than they value people who avoid failure by never going beyond the status quo.

Celebrating Success. Success is being who you want to be and doing what you want to do. You may not feel successful until you reach an important goal you have set for yourself. However, success is a process. Each step along the way to improvement and growth, no matter how small, is a success worth acknowledging. If you received a C on a paper and then earned a B on the next one, for example, your advancement is successful. When you are trying to drop a harmful habit, each day you stay on course is a victory.

Education Builds a Foundation for Learning Throughout Life

As a student just beginning a post-secondary career, you may have so much on your plate that you can't imagine thinking past next month, never mind what you need to learn throughout life. However, you are investing time, money, and energy in your education—and you should know that the learning skills you are developing now will bring you success far beyond graduation.

The importance of being a lifelong learner is linked to the enormous changes taking place in the world. Changes such as the following demand continued learning in the years ahead.

- **Knowledge in nearly every field is doubling every two to three years.** That means that if you stop learning for even a few years, your knowledge base will be inadequate to keep up with the changes in your career.

- **Technology is changing how you live and work.** The Internet and technology will shape communications and improve knowledge and productivity during the next 20 years—and will require continual learning.

- **The global economy is moving from a product and service base to a knowledge and talent base.** Jobs of the past are being replaced by knowledge-based jobs that ask workers to think critically to come up with solutions. Statistics Canada says that the 2001 Census echoes this finding: They maintain that "average annual earnings surpassed $30,000 for the first time in 2000, as working Canadians began reaping the benefits of globalization and the knowledge based economy."[10] They also report that "Canada is better educated than ever. In the years between 1991 and 2001 the number of adults 25 and over with trade, college or university credentials increased by 2.7 million, an increase of 39%."[11]

- **Workers are changing jobs and careers more frequently.** The U.S. National Research Bureau reports that currently the average employee changes jobs every three to four years, and it is estimated that a 22-year-old graduate in the year 2000 will have an average of eight employers in his or her first ten years in the workplace.[12] Every time

STRESSBUSTER

ALEJANDRA GONZALEZ   Seneca College, Toronto, Ontario

Different students face different challenges when they begin their post-secondary education. What challenges do you face? How do you intend to overcome these challenges in a constructive way?

As a mature student, I'm confronted with many stressful situations daily such as driving to work, maintaining my job, and paying for tuition. I live about 40 to 50 km away from school, so taking the bus is not an option. I also work every day when I'm not in school, so commuting takes up much of my day. Driving to school and work is followed by the responsibility of paying for my car, gas, and insurance, as well as maintaining my car. I also pay for my own tuition and books, which can be very costly. On top of everything, I am striving to do very well in school and reach all the goals that I have set for myself.

It's definitely fair to say that money and time are the two major issues that I have to overcome in order to be successful in my school studies. There are many ways of dealing with the money situation, such as school bursaries and/or loans. Time management is very critical. Without time management it would be very difficult to be organized and keep up with school and workload. Procrastination is definitely not an option!

The only way that I can stay organized without falling behind is by keeping a weekly schedule, as opposed to a monthly or yearly one. It can be very overwhelming to look at the amount of work that needs to be done in a month. A weekly planner helps me accomplish many tasks without feeling overwhelmed. Procrastinating and being disorganized can make it even harder to cope with schoolwork, which often leads to failing marks or just dropping out because of stress. I feel that managing my time and staying organized will be the key to my success at Seneca College.

you decide to start a new career, you need new knowledge and skills. Coming back to school is a good place to learn new skills and to evaluate the employability skills you already have.

All of these signs point to the need to become a lifelong learner—an individual who continues to build knowledge and intelligence as a mechanism for improving life and career. Through successful intelligence, you will maintain the kind of flexibility that will enable you to adapt to the demands of the twenty-first century. If you analyze what is happening, come up with creative approaches for handling it, and make a practical plan to put your ideas into motion, you can stay on track toward your goals. Or, you may decide to shift direction toward a new goal that never occurred to you before the change.

Facing change means taking risks. When you enter college, you accept certain challenges and risks as necessary hurdles on the path toward success. As a successfully intelligent lifelong learner, you will find ways to continue to learn and strive toward what you want. Welcome to the beginning of the road to your dreams.

In Chinese writing, this character has two meanings: One is "chaos"; the other, "opportunity." The character communicates the belief that every chaotic, challenging situation in life also presents an opportunity. By responding to challenges actively, you can discover the opportunity within the chaos.

Let this concept reassure you as you begin college or university. You may feel that you are going through a time of chaos and change. Remember that no matter how difficult the obstacles, you have the ability to persevere. You can create opportunities for yourself to learn, grow, and improve.

BUILDING SKILLS

Developing Successful Intelligence

PUTTING IT ALL TOGETHER

Make your first semester count. Going to class is only part of your college or university experience. Campus resources, clubs, student activity groups, and other organizations can enrich your time at school. Remember that students who make social connections tend to do better. Put a toe in the water sooner rather than later and you will begin to benefit from what your school has to offer.

Step 1. Think it through: *Analyze yourself.* On a separate piece of paper, describe who you are as a student—your identity, interests, challenges, and goals—in a short paragraph. Here are some questions to inspire thought:

- How would you describe your culture, ethnicity, gender, age, lifestyle?
- How long are you planning to be in college?
- What family and work obligations do you have?
- What is your current living situation?
- What do you feel are your biggest challenges in college?
- What do you like to study, and why does it interest you?

Step 2. Think out of the box: *Brainstorm your ideal extracurriculars.* On a second piece of paper, write ideas about how you want to spend your time outside of class. To inspire creative ideas, try using one or more of the following questions as a starting point:

- If you had no fear, what horizon-broadening experience would you sign up for?
- When you were in elementary school, what were your favourite activities? Which activities might translate into current interests and pursuits?

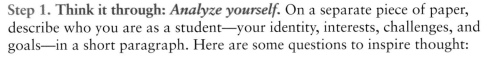

- What kinds of organizations, activities, groups, experiences, or people make you think, "Wow, I want to do that"?
- Think about the people that you feel bring out the best in you. What do you like to do with them? What kinds of things are they involved with?
- Who are the people with whom you have little in common? How could you benefit from getting to know them?

Step 3. Make it happen: *Take practical steps toward the activities you like.* Thinking about how you have described yourself in terms of both academics and extracurricular pursuits, look in your student handbook at the resources and organizations your school offers. These may include some or all of the following:

Academic centres (reading, writing, etc.)	Organizations for disabled students
Academic organizations	Religious organizations
Adult education centre	School publications
Arts clubs (music, drama, dance, etc.)	School TV/Radio stations
Fraternities/Sororities	Sports clubs
International student groups	Student associations
Minority student groups	Student government
On-campus work opportunities	Volunteer groups

In the left-hand column on the grid that follows, list the five offices or organizations you most want to check out this semester. Then—through your school publications (campus newspapers, student handbook) and/or a little legwork—fill in the information on the grid, answering the questions shown across the top for each item you listed. Notice that the last column requires action—fill it in when you have made initial contact with each office or organization.

Office or Organization	Location	Hours or times of meetings	What it offers	Phone number or e-mail	Initial contact— date and what happened

Let this exercise be a jumping-off point for real involvement this semester. If after your initial contact you wish to become more involved, go for it. Remember that the activities that inspire you are often a clue to your career path—and that knowing how to work with others is one of the most important skills you will build in college and university.

Team Building

Motivators. Gather in a group of three to five. Together, brainstorm school motivation blockers—situations or things that most often kill your motivation to succeed in school. When you have as many problems as you have group members, each person should choose one problem and write it at the top of a blank sheet of paper.

Look at the motivation blocker on your page. Under it, write one practical idea you have about how to overcome it. When everyone is finished, pass the pages one person to the left. Then write an idea about the new blocker at the top of the page you've received. If you can't think of anything, pass the page as is. Continue this way until your page comes back to you. Then discuss the ideas as a group, analyzing which ideas might work better than others. Add other ideas to the lists if you think of them.

The last step: On your own, keeping in mind your group discussion, list three specific actions that you commit to taking in order to keep motivation high when the going gets rough.

1. _____

2. _____

3. _____

Writing

Record your thoughts on a separate piece of paper or in a journal.

Reasons for college. People attend a post-secondary institution for numerous reasons: for technical training, the sake of learning, increased earning power, and more. Think about your own reasons. Why are you here, and what do you want out of the experience? On a scale of 1 (lowest) to 10 (highest), rank your commitment to succeeding in college. What sacrifices—in terms of time, hard work, finances—are you willing to make to get what you want and to persevere in your quest for success?

Career Portfolio

This is the first of 12 career portfolio assignments you will complete, one for each chapter. By the end of the semester, you will have compiled a portfolio of documents that will help you achieve your career goals.

Type your career portfolio work on a computer and store the documents electronically, on a disk or in a specific file on your hard drive. If you do not have access to a computer, type or write your work on sheets of paper and keep them together in one file folder. Use paper for assignments that ask you to draw or make collages.

Setting career goals. Whether you have a current career, have held a few different jobs, or have not yet entered the workplace, college is an ideal time to take stock of your career goals. The earlier in your post-secondary education that you consider career goals, the more you can take advantage of how college can help prepare you for work, in both job-specific and general ways. Having a strong vision of where you wish to go will also be a powerful motivator as you face some of the inevitable challenges of the next few years.

Take some time to think about your working life. Spend 15 minutes brainstorming everything that you wish you could be, do, have, or experience in your career 10 years from now—the skills you want to have, money you want to earn, benefits, experiences, travel—anything you can think of. List your wishes, draw them, depict them using cut-outs from magazines, or combine these ideas—whatever you like best.

Now, look at your list. To discover how your wishes relate to one another, group them in order of priority. Label three computer "pages" or three pieces of paper Priority 1, Priority 2, and Priority 3. Write each wish where it fits, with Priority 1 being the most important, Priority 2 the second most important, and Priority 3 the third.

Look at your priority lists. What do they tell you about what is most important to you? What wishes are you ready to work toward right now? Circle or highlight the three highest-priority wishes. Write down the trade-offs you will have to make today to make these wishes come true. Don't let yourself off the hook—be realistic and direct.

SUGGESTED READINGS

Evers, Frederick T., James Cameron Rush, and Iris Berdow. *The Bases of Competence: Skills for Lifelong Learning and Employability*. San Francisco, CA: Jossey-Bass, 1998.

Foot, David, and Daniel Stoffman. *Boom, Bust and Echo 2000*. Toronto: McFarlane, Walter and Ross, 1998.

Jeffers, Susan. *Feel the Fear... And Beyond: Mastering the Techniques for Doing It Anyway*. New York: Ballantine, 1998.

Lombardo, Alison. *Navigating Your Freshman Year*. New York: Natavi Guides, 2003.

Simon, Linda. *New Beginnings: A Guide for Adult Learners and Returning Students*, 2nd ed. Upper Saddle River, NJ: Prentice Hall.

Sternberg, Robert. *Successful Intelligence: How Practical and Creative Intelligence Determine Success in Life*. New York: Plume, 1997.

Tyler, Suzette. *Been There, Should've Done That II: More Tips for Making the Most of College*. Lansing, MI: Front Porch Press, 2001.

Weinberg, Carol. *The Complete Handbook for College Women: Making the Most of Your College Experience*. New York: New York University Press, 1994.

INTERNET RESOURCES

Campus Access, an online guide to everything you ever wanted to know about college and university life in Canada: www.campusaccess.com

Career Prospects, an online guide to career planning for everyone: www.canadaprospects.com

Conference Board of Canada: www.conferenceboard.ca

Association of Canadian Community Colleges: www.accc.ca

Association of Universities and Colleges of Canada: www.aucc.ca

1. Census of Population: Earnings, levels of schooling, field of study and school attendance, www.statcan.ca/daily, March 11, 2003.

2. Conference Board of Canada, http://www.conferenceboard.ca/education/learning-tools/pdfs/esp2000.pdf.

3. Robert J. Sternberg, *Successful Intelligence*. New York: Plume, 1997, p. 11.

4. Ibid, p. 12.

5. Ibid, pp. 127–128.

6. Rita Lenken Hawkins, Baltimore City Community College, 1997.

7. Rick Pitino, *Success Is a Choice*. New York: Broadway Books, 1997, p. 40.

8. Cited in Colin Rise and Malcolm J. Nicholl, *Accelerated Learning for the 21st Century*. New York: Dell, 1997, pp. 5–6.

9. David K. Foot and Daniel Stoffman, *Boom, Bust and Echo 2000: Profiting from the Demographic Shift in the New Millennium*. Toronto: MacFarlane, Walter and Ross, 1998.

10. Census of Population: Earnings, levels of schooling, field of study and school attendance, www.statcan.ca/daily, March 11, 2003.

11. Ibid.

12. Jay Palmer, "Marry Me a Little," *Barron's*, July 24, 2000, p. 25.

ASPIRE

2

IN THIS CHAPTER

In this chapter you will explore answers to the following questions: • Why is it important to know what you value? • How do you set and achieve goals? • How can you effectively manage your time? • How do you cope with the stress of college life?

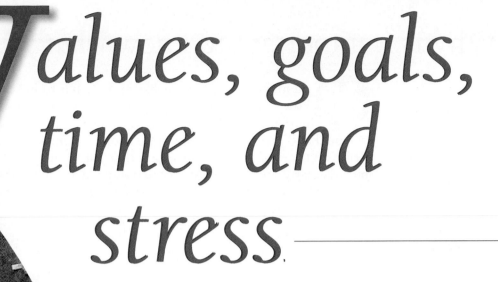

Values, goals, time, and stress.

ACHIEVING your most important goals depends on your ability to manage yourself. As an effective self-manager, you take charge of your life much like a CEO heads up a top-performing business. This chapter divides the indispensable skill of self-management into four parts: using values to guide your goal setting; working through a process to achieve goals; managing time in a way that propels you toward your goals; and, throughout the journey, managing the stress that will often arise.

The realities of school, workplace, and personal life will often create obstacles and produce stress. Everyone has problems; what counts is how you handle them. Your ability to manage yourself—accompanied by a generous dose of motivation—will help you cope with what you encounter, achieve your goals, and learn lasting lessons in the process. Goal setting and time management are just two ways to take responsibility for your life and actions and are two keys to success listed in the Conference Board of Canada's Employability Skills 2000+ report.

managing yourself.

Why is it important to know *what you value?*

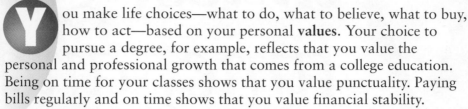

VALUES

Principles or qualities that one considers important.

You make life choices—what to do, what to believe, what to buy, how to act—based on your personal **values**. Your choice to pursue a degree, for example, reflects that you value the personal and professional growth that comes from a college education. Being on time for your classes shows that you value punctuality. Paying bills regularly and on time shows that you value financial stability.

Values play a key role in your drive to achieve important goals, because they help you to:

- **Understand what you want out of life.** Your most meaningful goals should reflect what you value most.
- **Build "rules for life."** Your values form the foundation for your decisions. You will return repeatedly to them for guidance, especially when you find yourself in unfamiliar territory.
- **Find people who inspire you.** Spending time with people who share similar values will help you clarify how you want to live and to find support as you work toward what's important to you.

Now that you have an idea of how you can use values, focus on how to identify yours.

Identifying and evaluating values

Ask yourself questions: What do you focus on in a given day? What do you consider important to be, to do, or to have? What do you wish to accomplish in your life? Answers to questions like these will point you toward your values. The exercise on page 34 will help you think through your values in more detail.

After you determine your values, evaluate them to see if they make sense for you. Many forces affect your values—family, friends, culture, media, school, work, neighbourhood, religious beliefs, world events. No matter how powerful these external influences may be, whether a value feels right should be your primary consideration in deciding to adopt it.

Answering the following questions about a value will help you decide if it "feels right."

- Where did the value come from?
- What other different values could I consider?
- What might happen as a result of adopting this value?
- Have I made a personal commitment to this choice? Have I told others about it?
- Do my life goals and day-to-day actions reflect this value?

Even the most solid set of values needs a re-evaluation from time to time. Why? Because values often change. Life experience and education give you new perspectives that may alter what you consider important. For example, a fun-loving student who is seriously injured in an auto accident may place greater value on friends and family after the accident than he did before. If you let your values shift to fit you as you grow, you will always have a base on which to build achievable goals and wise decisions.

How values affect your educational experience

Well-considered values can lead to smart choices while you are in school. Your values will help you:

- **Keep going when the going gets tough.** Translate your value of education into specific actions. Remember that success takes hard work and dedication. If you have trouble in one particular course, set aside some extra time to work on it.

- **Choose your major and a career direction.** If you've always been an environmentalist, then you may choose to major in environmental science. If you feel fulfilled when you help people, then you might consider a career in social work.

- **Choose friends and activities that enrich your life.** Having friends who share your desire to succeed in school will increase your motivation and reduce your stress. Joining organizations whose activities support your values will broaden your educational experience.

- **Choose what you want out of school and how hard you want to work.** What kinds of skills and knowledge do you wish to build? Do you want to focus on course work that will lead to career success? Do you want to learn about Egyptian archaeology simply because it interests you? Do you want to read every novel Margaret Atwood ever wrote? Decide also how hard you are willing to work to achieve your goals. Going above and beyond will build your drive to succeed and hone your work habits—two items that will be useful in a competitive job market.

Great minds have purposes; others have wishes.

WASHINGTON IRVING

Finally, your values affect your success at school and beyond, because the more ethical a student you are, the more likely you are to stay in school and to build lasting knowledge and skills.

Academic integrity: How ethical values promote success at school

Having **academic integrity** promotes learning and ensures a quality education based on ethics and hard work. Read your school's code of honour or academic integrity policy in your student handbook. When you enrolled, you agreed to abide by it.

Defining academic integrity

The Center for Academic Integrity, part of the Kenan Institute for Ethics at Duke University, defines academic integrity as a commitment to five fundamental values: honesty, trust, fairness, respect, and responsibility.[1] These values are the positive actions that define academic integrity.

ACADEMIC
INTEGRITY
Following a code of moral values, prizing honesty and fairness in all aspects of academic life—classes, assignments, tests, papers, projects, and relationships with students and faculty.

get analytical! EXPLORE YOUR VALUES

Evaluate what you think is most important to you, and connect educational goals to your top values.

Rate each of the values in the list on a scale from 1 to 5, 1 being least important to you and 5 being most important.

____ Knowing yourself	____ Being liked by others	____ Reading
____ Self-improvement	____ Taking risks	____ Time to yourself
____ Improving physical/mental health	____ Time for fun/relaxation	____ Lifelong learning
____ Staying fit through exercise	____ Competing and winning	____ Getting a good job
____ Pursuing an education	____ Spiritual/religious life	____ Making a lot of money
____ Good relationships with family	____ Community involvement	____ Creative/artistic pursuits
____ Helping others	____ Keeping up with the news	____ Other (write below)
____ Being organized	____ Financial stability	_____

Write your top three values here:

1. _____

2. _____

3. _____

Values often affect your educational choices. Choose one top value that is a factor in an educational choice that you have made. Explain the choice and how the value is involved. Example: A student who values mental health makes a choice to pursue a degree in psychology with a future plan to work as a school counsellor.

_____

_____

_____

_____

Name an area of study that you think would help you live according to this value.

_____

_____

- **Honesty.** Honesty defines the pursuit of knowledge and implies a search for truth in your class work, papers and lab reports, and team-work with other students.

- **Trust.** Mutual trust—between instructor and student, as well as among students—makes possible the free exchange of ideas that is fundamental to learning. Trust means being true to your word.

- **Fairness.** Instructors must create a fair academic environment where students are judged against clear standards and in which procedures are well defined.

- **Respect.** In a respectful academic environment, both students and instructors accept and honour a wide range of opinions, even if the opinions are contrary to core beliefs.

- **Responsibility.** You are responsible for making choices that will provide you with the best education—choices that reflect fairness and honesty.

Unfortunately, the principles of academic integrity are frequently violated on college campuses. In a recent survey, three out of four college students admitted to cheating at least once during their undergraduate careers.[2] Violations of academic integrity—turning in previously submitted work, using unauthorized devices during an exam, providing unethical aid to another student, or getting unauthorized help with a project—constitute a sacrifice of ethics that isn't worth the price.

Students who are discovered violating school policies experience a variety of consequences. In most cases, students are brought before a chair, dean or committee of instructors to determine whether the offence has occurred. Consequences vary from school to school and include participation in academic integrity seminars, grade reduction or course failure, suspension, or expulsion.

Why academic integrity is worth it

Choosing to act with integrity has the following positive consequences:

- **Increased self-esteem.** Self-esteem is tied to action. The more you act in respectful and honourable ways, the better you feel about yourself, and the more likely you are to succeed.
- **Acquired knowledge.** If you cheat you might pass a test—and a course—but chances are you won't retain the knowledge and skills you need for success. Honest work is more likely to result in knowledge that lasts—and that you can use to accomplish career and life goals.
- **Effective behavioural patterns.** When you condition yourself to play fair now, you set a pattern for your behaviour at work and with friends and family.
- **Mutual respect.** Respecting the work of others will lead others to respect your work.

The last two bullet points reflect the positive effect that integrity has on your relationships. This is only one way in which values help you to successfully relate to, work with, and understand the people around you. Here's another way: Being open to different values, often linked with different cultures, can enhance your understanding of cultural diversity.

Values and cultural diversity

At college, you may meet people who seem different in ways that you may not expect. Many of these differences stem from attitudes and behaviours that are unfamiliar to you. These attitudes and behaviours are rooted in the values that people acquire from their **culture**, either from the continuing influence of family and community here in Canada or from their homeland.

CULTURE
A set of values, behaviours, tastes, knowledge, attitudes, and habits shared by a group of people.

Cultural competence

In a multicultural country like Canada, the ability to understand and appreciate differences and to respond to people of all cultures in a way that values their worth, means respecting their beliefs and practices, and building communication and relationships.

Cultural misunderstandings can interfere with the relationships and friendships you form in school, career, and life. As someone who accepts and appreciates diversity, your goal is to develop the cultural competence to understand and appreciate these differences so that they enhance—rather than hinder—communication.[3]

A simple model to help you avoid communication problems with people from other cultures was developed by Edward Hall, an anthropologist and an authority on cross-cultural communication. Hall linked communication styles to what he called high-context and low-context cultures:[4]

- People from *high-context* cultures rely heavily in their communication on context and situation, as well as on body language and eye contact. Time (past, present, and future), fate, personal relationships and status, gender roles, trust, gestures, and sense of self and space are just some of the factors that influence communication in these cultures. High-context countries span the world and include China, Japan, Brazil, Saudi Arabia, Italy, and France.

- In contrast, people from *low-context* cultures focus on what is explicitly said or written and pay little attention to context and nonverbal cues. Countries with low-context cultures include Canada, the United States, England, Australia, Germany, and the Scandinavian countries.

As you continue to read *Keys to Success*, look for examples of how cultural diversity impacts everything from teamwork and relationships, to listening, questioning, and more. Then think of the wisdom of cultural diversity consultant Helen Turnbull on turning differences into strengths:

> We must suspend our judgment. We should not judge others negatively because they are indirect, or their accents aren't clear, or their tone of voice is tentative, or they avoid eye contact. We must learn patience and suspend judgment long enough to realize these differences don't make one of us right and the other wrong. They simply mean that we approach communication from a different frame of reference and, many times, a different value system.[5]

Although clarifying your values will help you choose your educational path, goal-setting and goal-achievement skills will help you travel that path to the end. Goals turn values into tools and put them to practical use.

How do you set and *achieve goals*?

GOAL
An end toward which effort is directed; an aim or intention.

When you identify something that you want, you set a **goal**. Actually *getting* what you want—from college, career, or life—demands working to *achieve* your goals. Achieving goals, whether they are short term or long term, involves following a goal-achievement plan. Think of the plan you are about to read as a map; with it helping you to establish each segment of the trip, you will be able to define your route and follow it successfully.

Set long-term goals

Start by establishing the goals that have the largest scope, the *long-term goals* that you aim to attain over a period of six months, a year, or more. As a student, your long-term goals include attending school and earning a degree or certificate. Getting an education is a significant goal that often takes years to reach.

Some long-term goals have an open-ended time frame. (For example, if your goal is to become a better musician, you may work at it over a lifetime.) These goals also invite more creative thinking; you have more time and freedom to consider all sorts of paths to your goal. Other goals, such as completing all the courses in your major, have a shorter scope, a more definite end, and often fewer options for how to get from A to Z.

The following long-term goal statement, written by Carol Carter, a *Keys to Success* author, may take years to complete:

> My goal is to build my own business in which I create opportunities for students to maximize their talents. In this business, I will reach thousands of students and teachers through books, the Internet, teacher seminars, and student-oriented programs.

Carol also has long-term goals that she hopes to accomplish in no more than a year:

> Develop and publish one book. Design three seminars for teachers with accompanying PowerPoints and other materials. Create Internet-based materials that encourage student success and use them in student seminars.

Just as Carol's goals are tailored to her personality, abilities, and interests, your goals should reflect your uniqueness. To determine your long-term goals, think about what you want to accomplish while you are in school and after you graduate. Think of ways you can link your personal values and professional aims, as in the following examples:

- **Values:** Health and fitness, helping others
  Goal: To become a physical therapist
- **Values:** Independence, financial success
  Goal: To obtain a degree in business and start a company

Basing your long-term goals on values increases your motivation. The more your goals focus on what is most important to you, the greater your drive to reach them.

Set short-term goals

Short-term goals are smaller steps that move you toward a long-term goal. Lasting as little as a few hours or as long as a few months, these goals help you manage your broader aspirations as they narrow your focus and encourage progress. If you had a long-term goal of graduating with a degree in nursing, for example, you may want to accomplish the following short-term goals in the next six months:

- I will learn the names, locations, and functions of every human bone and muscle.
- I will work with a study group to understand the musculoskeletal system.

These same goals can be broken down into even smaller parts, such as the following one-month goals:

- I will work with on-screen tutorials of the musculoskeletal system until I understand and memorize the material.
- I will spend three hours a week with my study partners.

In addition to monthly goals, you may have short-term goals that extend for a week, a day, or even a couple of hours in a given day. To support your month-long goal of regularly meeting with your study partners, you may wish to set the following short-term goals:

- **By the end of today:** Call study partners to ask them about when they might be able to meet.
- **One week from now:** Have scheduled each of our weekly meetings this month.
- **Two weeks from now:** Have had our first meeting.
- **Three weeks from now:** Type up and send around notes from the first meeting; have the second meeting.

Try to pay special attention to goals that are intermediate in length—for example, one-month or one-semester goals on the way to a year-long goal. Why? Because your motivation is at its peak when you begin to move toward a goal and when you are about to achieve that goal. If you work hard to stay motivated in the middle, you will have a more successful journey and a better result.

As you consider your long- and short-term goals, notice how all of your goals are linked to one another. As Key 2.1 shows, your long-term goals establish a context for the short-term goals. In turn, your short-term goals make the long-term goals seem clearer and more reachable.

At any given time, you will be working toward goals of varying importance. Setting priorities helps you decide where and when to focus your energy and time.

Reviewing animal physiology while caring for her son is just part of how this single parent and pre-med student juggles responsibilities on a daily basis.

Prioritize goals

When you **prioritize**, you evaluate everything you are working toward, decide which goals are most important, and focus your time and energy on them. What should you consider as you evaluate?

- **Your values.** Thinking about what you value will help you establish the goals that take top priority—for example, graduating in the top 25 per cent of your class or developing a strong network of personal contacts.
- **Your personal situation.** Are you going to school and working part-time? Are you a parent with young children who need your attention?

PRIORITIZE
To arrange or deal with in order of importance.

Goals reinforce one another.

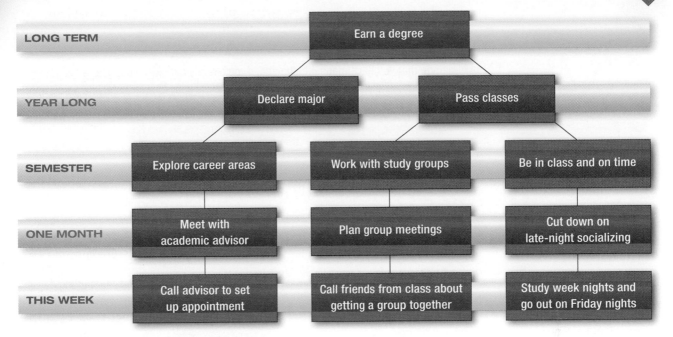

LONG TERM		Earn a degree	
YEAR LONG		Declare major	Pass classes
SEMESTER	Explore career areas	Work with study groups	Be in class and on time
ONE MONTH	Meet with academic advisor	Plan group meetings	Cut down on late-night socializing
THIS WEEK	Call advisor to set up appointment	Call friends from class about getting a group together	Study week nights and go out on Friday nights

Are you an athlete on a sports team? Are you a student with identified special needs? Every individual situation requires unique priorities and scheduling.

- **Your time commitments.** Hours of your day may already be committed to class, team practices, a part-time job, or sleep. Your challenge is to make sure these commitments reflect what you value and to establish priorities for the remaining hours.

As you will see later in the chapter, setting clear priorities will help you manage your time and accomplish more.

Goals are dreams with deadlines.

DIANA SCHARF HUNT

Work to achieve goals

When you've done all the work to think through a goal you want to achieve, these practical steps will help you achieve it. Remember, the more specific your plans, the more likely you are to fulfill them.

- **Define your goal-setting strategy:** *How do you plan to reach your goal?* Brainstorm different paths that might get you there. Choose one; then map out its steps and strategies. Focus on specific behaviours and events that are under your control and that are measurable.

- **Set a timetable:** *When do you want to accomplish your goal?* Set a realistic timeline that includes specific deadlines for each step and strategy you have defined. Charting your progress will help you stay on track.

get creative!

MAP OUT A PERSONAL GOAL

Work backwards to find an interesting path toward an important goal.

Name one important personal goal you have for this year.

_____

Now imagine that you have made it to the end—you already achieved your goal—and an impressed friend asks you to describe how you did it. Write your answer here, in a paragraph, as though you were telling this person about the specific steps you took to achieve your goal.

_____

_____

_____

_____

_____

_____

Finally, examine what you've written. You just created a potential plan! Consider putting it—or a plan similar to it—to work. As you begin, let the image of the success you created in this exercise motivate and inspire you.

- **Be accountable for your progress:** *What safeguards will keep you on track?* Define a personal reporting or buddy system that makes accountability a priority.
- **Get unstuck:** *What will you do if you hit a roadblock?* Define two ways to get help with your efforts if you run into trouble. Be ready to pursue more creative ideas if those don't work.

Through this process, you will continually be thinking about how well you are using your time. In fact, goal achievement is directly linked to effective time management.

How can you effectively *manage your time?*

Time is a universal resource; everyone has the same 24 hours in a day, every day. Depending on what's happening in your life, however, your sense of time may change. On some days you feel like you have hours to spare, while on others the clock becomes your worst enemy.

Your challenge is to turn time into a goal-achievement tool by making smart choices about how to use it. Think of each day as a jigsaw puzzle: You have all of the pieces in a pile, and your task is to form a picture of how you want your day to look. Successful time management starts with identifying your time-related needs and preferences. This self-knowledge sets the stage for building and managing your schedule, avoiding procrastination, and being flexible in the face of change.

Identify your time-related needs and preferences

Body rhythms and habits affect how each person deals with time. Some people are night owls; others are at their best in the morning. Some people are chronically late; others get everything done with time to spare. Individual tendencies become clear as people build up "records" of behaviour.

A mismatch between your habits and your schedule causes stress and drains energy. For example, a person who loses steam in the mid-afternoon may struggle in classes that meet between 3:00 and 5:00 p.m. However, an awareness of your needs and preferences will help you create a schedule that maximizes your strengths and cuts down on stress. If you are a morning person, for example, look for sections of required courses that meet early in the day. If you work best at night, schedule most of your study time at a library that stays open late.

Take the following steps to identify your time-related needs and preferences:

Create a personal time "profile." Ask yourself these questions: At what time of day do I have the most energy? The least energy? Do I tend to be early, on time, or late? Do I focus well for long stretches or need regular breaks? Your answers will help you find the schedule set-up that works best for you.

Evaluate the effects of your profile. Which of your time-related habits and preferences will have a positive impact on your success at school? Which are likely to cause problems?

Establish what schedule preferences suit your profile best. Make a list of these preferences—or even map out an ideal schedule as a way of illustrating them. For example, one student's preference list might read: "Classes bunched together on Mondays, Wednesdays, and Fridays. Tuesdays and Thursdays free for studying and research. Study time primarily during the day."

Next, it's time to build the schedule that takes all of this information into account, helping you maximize your strengths and compensate for your weaker time-management areas.

Build a schedule

You've set up your "goal map," with all of the steps that you need to accomplish to reach your destination. With a schedule you place each step in time and, by doing so, commit to making it happen. Schedules help you gain control of your life in two ways: They provide segments of time for tasks related to the fulfillment of your goals, and they remind you of tasks, events, due dates, responsibilities, and deadlines.

Use a planner

A planner is the ideal practical tool for managing your time. With it, you can keep track of events and commitments, schedule goal-related tasks, and rank tasks according to priority. Time-management expert Paul Timm says that "rule number one in a thoughtful planning process is: Use some form of a planner where you can write things down."[6]

There are two major types of planners. One is a book or notebook in which to note commitments. If you write detailed daily plans, look for the kind that devotes a page to each day. If you prefer to see more days at a glance, try the kind that shows a week's schedule on a two-page spread. Some planners contain sections for monthly and yearly goals.

The other option is an electronic planner or personal digital assistant (PDA). Basic PDA functions allow you to schedule days and weeks, note due dates, make to-do lists, perform mathematical calculations, and create and store an address book. You can enter information with an on-screen or attachable keyboard or hand write with a stylus. You can also transfer information to and from a computer.

Though electronic planners are handy and have a large data capacity, they cost more than the paper versions, and their small size means they can be easy to lose. Analyze your preferences and options, and decide which tool you are most likely to use every day. A simple notebook will work as well as a top-of-the-line PDA as long as you use it conscientiously.

STRESSBUSTER

KEVIN FORSETH Sprott-Shaw Community College, Duncan, BC

Time management can be the source of a lot of stress. Having too much to do and too little time is a common student experience. What techniques do you use to reduce schedule overloads and thereby reduce stress? How do you deal with stress when your schedule becomes too full?

Stress plays a major factor in the way you live and the way you plan your life. I am the father of four children. I work full time and go to school full time, so I have my fair share of stress. I have had to learn how to schedule my time and my finances. Being able to accommodate school and work while trying to spend quality time with my family gives me a feeling of victory. When I started out, however, if someone had asked me if I could handle it, I would have laughed and said, "Not in your lifetime!"

I have purchased a daily planner that helps me to keep on top of things. With so much on the go all the time, it's hard to keep everything in your head. You have to remember appointments, assignments, and bills, and you can't forget to plan some quality time with your family.

If I could give you one word of advice, it would be this: If stress gets the better of you, sit down, relax, and make a schedule. It will make your life more enjoyable during the tough times instead of having to live through the complete agony of stress.

Keep track of events and commitments

Your planner is designed to help you schedule and remember events and commitments. A quick look at your notations will remind you when items are approaching.

Putting your schedule in writing will help you anticipate and prepare for crunch times. For example, if you see that you have three tests and a presentation coming up all in one week, you may have to rearrange your schedule during the preceding week to create extra study time.

Among the events and commitments worth noting in your planner are:

- test and quiz dates; due dates for papers, projects, and presentations.
- details of your academic schedule, including semester and holiday breaks.
- club and organizational meetings.
- personal items—medical appointments, due dates for bills, birthdays, social events.
- milestones toward a goal, such as due dates for sections of a project.

Although many students don't think to do so, it's important to include class prep time—reading and studying, writing and working on assignments and projects—in the planner. According to one reasonable formula, you should schedule at least two hours of preparation for every hour of class—that is, if you take 15 credits, you should study about 30 hours a week, making your total classroom and preparation time 45 hours. Surveys have shown, however, that most students study 15 or fewer hours per week, and some study even less—often not enough to master the material.

Schedule tasks and activities that support your goals

Linking the events in your planner to your goals will give meaning to your efforts and bring order to your schedule. Planning study time for an economics test, for example, will mean more to you if you link the hours you spend studying to your goal of being accepted into business school. The simple act of relating what you do every day to what you want in your future has enormous power to move you forward.

Here is how a student might translate his goal of entering business school into action steps over a year's time:

Monday	Tuesday	Wednesday	Thursday	Friday	Saturday	Sunday
9 AM: Economics class Talk with study group members to schedule meeting.	3–5 PM: Study econ chapter 3.	9 AM: Economics class Drop by instructor's office hours to ask question about test	6 PM: Go over chapter 3 7–9 PM: Study group meeting.	9 AM: Economics class—Test 3:30 PM: Meet w/advisor to discuss GMAT and other business school requirements	Sleep in—schedule some down time	5 PM: Go over quiz questions with study partner

This year: Complete enough courses to meet curriculum requirements for business school.

This semester: Complete my economics class with a B average or higher.

This month: Set up economics study group schedule to coincide with quizzes and tests.

This week: Meet with study group; go over material for Friday's test.

Today: Go over Chapter 3 in econ text.

The student can then arrange his time to move him toward his goal. He schedules activities that support his short-term goal of doing well on the test and writes them in his planner, as shown in the example above. Achieving his overarching long-term goal of doing well in a course he needs for business school is the source of his motivation.

Before each week begins, remind yourself of your long-term goals and what you can accomplish over the next seven days to move you closer to them. Key 2.2 shows parts of a daily schedule and a weekly schedule.

Note daily and weekly tasks.

key 2.2

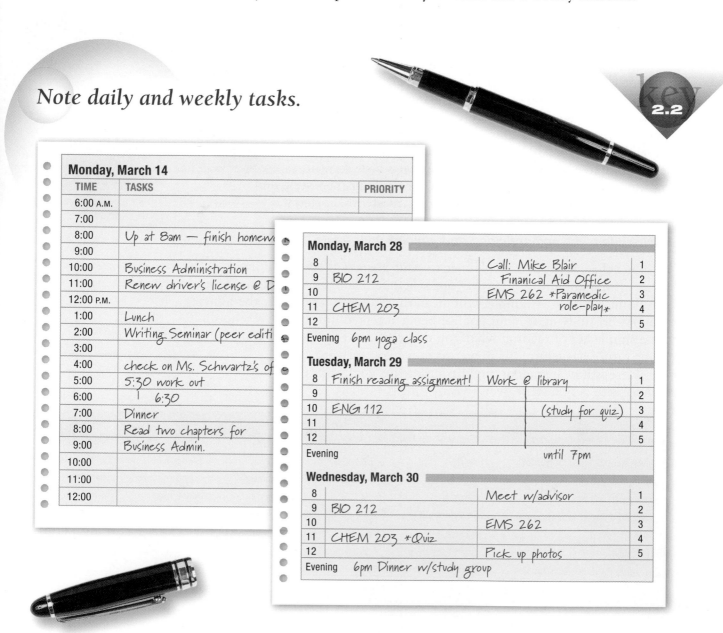

Monday, March 14

TIME	TASKS	PRIORITY
6:00 A.M.		
7:00		
8:00	Up at 8am — finish homew	
9:00		
10:00	Business Administration	
11:00	Renew driver's license @ D	
12:00 P.M.		
1:00	Lunch	
2:00	Writing Seminar (peer editi	
3:00		
4:00	check on Ms. Schwartz's of	
5:00	5:30 work out	
6:00	6:30	
7:00	Dinner	
8:00	Read two chapters for	
9:00	Business Admin.	
10:00		
11:00		
12:00		

Monday, March 28

8		Call: Mike Blair	1
9	BIO 212	Finanical Aid Office	2
10		EMS 262 *Paramedic	3
11	CHEM 203	role-play*	4
12			5
Evening	6pm yoga class		

Tuesday, March 29

8	Finish reading assignment!	Work @ library	1
9			2
10	ENG 112	(study for quiz)	3
11			4
12			5
Evening		until 7pm	

Wednesday, March 30

8		Meet w/advisor	1
9	BIO 212		2
10		EMS 262	3
11	CHEM 203 *Quiz		4
12		Pick up photos	5
Evening	6pm Dinner w/study group		

Indicate priority levels

On any given day, the items on your schedule have varying degrees of importance. Prioritizing these items boosts scheduling success in two ways. First, it helps you to identify your most important tasks and to focus the bulk of your energy and time on them. Second, it helps you plan when in your day to get things done. Since many top-priority items (classes, work) occur at designated times, prioritizing helps you lock in these activities and schedule less urgent items around them.

Indicate an item's level of importance by using three different categories. Identify these categories by using any code that makes sense to you. Some people use numbers, some use letters (A, B, C), and some use different-coloured pens. The three categories are as follows:

- *Priority 1* items are the most crucial. They may include attending class, completing school assignments, working at a job, picking up a child from day care, and paying bills. Enter Priority 1 items on your planner first, before scheduling anything else.

- *Priority 2* items are important but more flexible parts of your routine. Examples include library study time, completing an assignment for a school club, and working out. Schedule these around Priority 1 items.

- *Priority 3* items are least important—the "it would be nice if I could get to that" items. Examples include making a social phone call, stocking up on birthday cards, and cleaning out a closet. Many people don't enter Priority 3 tasks in their planners until they know they have time for them. Others keep a separate list of these tasks so that when they have free time they can consult it and choose what they want to accomplish.

Use scheduling techniques

The following strategies will help you turn your scheduling activities into tools that move you closer to your goals:

Plan regularly. Spending time planning your schedule will reduce stress and save you from the hours of work that might result if you forget something important. At the beginning of each week, write down specific time commitments as well as your goals and priorities. Decide where to fit activities like studying and Priority 3 items. For example, if you have a test on Thursday, you can plan study sessions on the preceding days. If you have more free time on Tuesday and Friday, you can plan workouts or other low-priority tasks. Your planner only helps you when you use it—keep it with you and check it throughout the day.

Make and use to-do lists. Use a to-do list to record the things you want to accomplish on a given day or week. Write your to-do items on a separate piece of paper so you can set priorities. Then transfer the items you plan to accomplish each day to open time periods in your planner.

To-do lists are critical time-management tools during exam week and when major projects are due. They will help you rank your responsibilities so that you get things done in order of importance.

Post monthly and yearly calendars at home. Keeping track of your major commitments on a monthly wall calendar will give you the overview you need to focus on responsibilities and upcoming events. Key 2.3 shows a monthly calendar. If you live with family or friends, create a group calendar to stay aware of each other's plans and avoid scheduling conflicts.

Avoid time traps. Try to stay away from situations that eat up time unnecessarily. Say "no" graciously if you don't have time for a project; curb excess social time that interferes with academics; delegate chores if you find yourself overloaded. Pay special attention to how much time you spend surfing the Internet and chatting on-line, because these activities can waste hours.

DOWN TIME
Quiet time set aside for relaxation and low-key activity.

Schedule down time. Leisure time is more than just a nice break—it's essential to your health and success. A little **down time** will refresh you and actually improve your productivity when you get back on task. Even half an hour a day helps. Fill the time with whatever relaxes you—reading, watching television, chatting on-line, playing a game or sport, walking, writing, or just doing nothing.

Keep track of your time with a monthly calendar.

key 2.3

MARCH						
SUNDAY	MONDAY	TUESDAY	WEDNESDAY	THURSDAY	FRIDAY	SATURDAY
	1 WORK	**2** Turn in English paper topic	**3** Dentist 2pm	**4** WORK	**5**	**6**
7 Frank's birthday	**8** Psych Test 9am WORK	**9**	**10** 6:30 pm Meeting @ Student Ctr.	**11** WORK	**12**	**13** Dinner @ Ryan's
14	**15** English paper due WORK	**16** Western Civ paper—Library research	**17**	**18** Library 6 p.m. WORK	**19** Western Civ makeup class	**20**
21	**22** WORK	**23** 2 p.m. meeting, psych group project	**20** Start running program: 3 km	**25**	**26** WORK Run 3 km	**27**
28 Run 5 km	**29** WORK	**30** Western Civ paper due	**31** Run 3 km			

MAKE A TO-DO LIST

Accomplish practical goals with a to-do list and reduce stress as a result.

Make a to-do list for what you have to do on your busiest day this week. Include all the tasks and events you know about, including attending class and study time, and the activities you would like to do (working out at the gym, watching your favourite TV show) if you have extra time. Then prioritize your list using the coding system of your choice.

Date: _____

1. _____   7. _____
2. _____   8. _____
3. _____   9. _____
4. _____   10. _____
5. _____   11. _____
6. _____   12. _____

After examining this list, record your daily schedule in your planner. Include a separate list for Priority 3 items that you can fit into empty time blocks if you finish all your higher priority commitments. At the end of the day, evaluate this system. Did the list make a difference? If you liked it, use this exercise as a guide for using to-do lists regularly.

Fight procrastination

It's human, and common for busy students, to put off difficult or undesirable tasks until later. If taken to the extreme, however, **procrastination** can develop into a habit that causes serious problems. This excerpt from the Study Skills Library at California Polytechnic State University at San Luis Obispo illustrates how procrastination can quickly turn into a destructive pattern.

PROCRASTINATION

The act of putting off a task until another time.

> The procrastinator is often remarkably optimistic about his ability to complete a task on a tight deadline.... For example, he may estimate that a paper will take only five days to write; he has fifteen days; there is plenty of time, no need to start. Lulled by a false sense of security, time passes. At some point, he crosses over an imaginary starting time and suddenly realizes, "Oh no! I am not in control! There isn't enough time!"
>
> At this point, considerable effort is directed toward completing the task, and work progresses. This sudden spurt of energy is the source of the erroneous feeling that "I work well only under pressure." Actually, at this point you are making progress only because you haven't any choice.... Progress is being made, but you have lost your freedom.
>
> Barely completed in time, the paper may actually earn a fairly good grade; whereupon the student experiences mixed feelings: pride of accomplishment (sort of), scorn for the professor who cannot recognize substandard work, and guilt for getting an undeserved grade. But the net result is reinforcement: The procrastinator is rewarded positively for his poor behavior ("Look what a decent grade I got after all!"). As a result, the counterproductive behavior is repeated time and time again.[7]

Among the reasons people procrastinate are:

Perfectionism. According to Jane B. Burka and Lenora M. Yuen, authors of *Procrastination: Why You Do It and What to Do About It*, habitual procrastinators often gauge their self-worth solely by their ability to achieve. In other words, "an outstanding performance means an outstanding person; a mediocre performance means a mediocre person."[8] To the perfectionist procrastinator, not trying at all is better than an attempt that falls short of perfection.

Fear of limitations. Some people procrastinate in order to avoid the truth about what they can achieve. "As long as you procrastinate, you never have to confront the real limits of your ability, whatever those limits are,"[9] say Burka and Yuen. If you procrastinate and fail, you can blame the failure on waiting too long, not on any personal shortcoming.

Being unsure of the next step. If you get stuck and don't know what to do, sometimes it seems easier to procrastinate than to make the leap to the next level of your goal.

Even if you're on the right track, you'll get run over if you just sit there.

WILL ROGERS

Facing an overwhelming task. Some projects are so big that they create immobilizing fear. If a person facing such a task fears failure, she may procrastinate in order to avoid confronting the fear.

Avoiding procrastination

Although it can bring relief in the short term, avoiding tasks almost always causes problems, such as a buildup of responsibilities and less time to complete them; work that is not up to par; the disappointment of others who are depending on your work; and stress brought on by the weight of the unfinished tasks. Particular strategies can help you avoid procrastination and the problems associated with it.

Analyze the effects of procrastinating. What may happen if you continue to put off a responsibility? Chances are you will benefit more in the long term from facing the task head-on.

Set reasonable goals. Unreasonable goals can intimidate and immobilize you. Set manageable goals and allow enough time to complete them.

Break tasks into smaller parts. If you concentrate on achieving one small step at a time, the task may become less burdensome. Setting concrete time limits for each task may help you feel more in control.

Get started whether or not you "feel like it." The motivation techniques from Chapter 1 might help you take the first step. Once you start, you may find it easier to continue.

Ask for help. You don't have to go it alone. Once you identify what's holding you up, see who can help you face the task. Another person may come up with an innovative way that can get you moving.

Don't expect perfection. No one is perfect. Most people learn by starting at the beginning, making mistakes, and learning from those mistakes. It's better to try your best than to do nothing at all.

Reward yourself. Find ways to boost your confidence when you accomplish a particular task. Remind yourself—with a break, a movie, some kind of treat—that you are making progress.

Be flexible

No matter how well you plan your time, sudden changes can upend your plans. Any change, whether minor (a room change for a class) or major (a medical emergency), can cause stress. As your stress level rises, your sense of control dwindles.

Although you can't always choose your circumstances, you have some control over how you handle them. Your ability to evaluate situations, come up with creative options, and put practical plans to work will help you manage the changes that you will inevitably encounter. Think of change as part of life, and you will be better prepared to brainstorm solutions when dilemmas arise.

Small changes—the need to work an hour overtime at your after-school job, a meeting that runs late—can result in priority shifts that jumble your schedule. For changes that occur frequently, think through a backup plan ahead of time. For surprises, the best you can do is to keep an open mind about possibilities and rely on your internal and external resources.

When change involves serious problems—your car breaks down and you have no way to get to school; you fail a class and have to consider summer school; a family member develops a medical problem and needs you more at home—use problem-solving skills to help you through. As you will see in Chapter 4, problem solving involves identifying and analyzing the problem, brainstorming and exploring possible solutions, and choosing the solution you decide is best. There are resources available at your college to help you throughout this process. Your academic advisor, counsellor, dean, financial aid advisor, and instructors may have ideas and assistance.

Change is one of many factors associated with stress. In fact, stress is part of the normal college experience. If you take charge of how you manage stress, then you can keep it from taking charge of you.

How do you *cope with the stress* of college life?

I f you are feeling more stress in your everyday life as a student, you are not alone.[10] Stress levels among college students have increased dramatically. Today, more than 30 per cent of first year students report that they frequently feel overwhelmed, almost double the rate in 1985. Stress factors for college and university students include being in a new environment; facing increased work and difficult decisions; and juggling school, work, and personal responsibilities.

Hans Selye (1907–1982), a Canadian who was a professor at McGill University in Montreal, is considered by many to be the father of stress research. He once said, "To be totally without stress is to be dead." What Selye meant was that we won't ever be able to eliminate stress from our lives, but we can be taught to manage it effectively. Selye defined stress as our reaction to an outside stimulus. This reaction can be positive (eustress) or negative (distress).[11] Most of the time, when we think of stress we think of the negative *distress*. In a survey commissioned by the Canadian National Mental Health Association, 50 per cent of Canadians felt "really stressed" a few times each week.[12]

Stress refers to the way in which your mind and body react to pressure. Pressure comes from situations like heavy workloads (final exam week), excitement (being a finalist for the lead in a play), change (new school, new courses), being short on time (working 20 hours a week at a job and finding time to study), or illness (having a head cold that wipes you out for a week).

The Social Readjustment Scale, developed by psychologists T. H. Holmes and R. H. Rahe, measures the intensity of people's reaction to change and the level of stress related to it (see Key 2.4). Holmes and Rahe

Use the Holmes-Rahe scale to find your "stress score."

key
2.4

To find your current "stress score," add the values of the events that you experienced in the past year. The higher the number, the greater the stress. Scoring over 300 points puts you at high risk for developing a stress-related health problem. A score between 150 and 299 reduces your risk by 30 percent, and a score under 150 means that you have only a small chance of a problem.

EVENT	VALUE	EVENT	VALUE
Death of spouse or partner	100	Son or daughter leaving home	29
Divorce	73	Trouble with in-laws	29
Marital separation	65	Outstanding personal achievement	28
Jail term	63	Spouse begins or stops work	26
Personal injury	53	Starting or finishing school	26
Marriage	50	Change in living conditions	25
Fired from work	47	Revision of personal habits	24
Marital reconciliation	45	Trouble with boss	23
Retirement	45	Change in work hours, conditions	20
Changes in family member's health	44	Change in residence	20
Pregnancy	40	Change in schools	20
Sex difficulties	39	Change in recreational habits	19
Addition to family	39	Change in religious activities	19
Business readjustment	39	Change in social activities	18
Change in financial status	38	Mortgage or loan under $10,000	17
Death of a close friend	37	Change in sleeping habits	16
Change to different line of work	36	Change in # of family gatherings	15
Change in # of marital arguments	35	Change in eating habits	15
Mortgage or loan over $10,000	31	Vacation	13
Foreclosure of mortgage or loan	30	Christmas season	12
Change in work responsibilities	29	Minor violation of the law	11

Source: Reprinted from *Journal of Psychosomatic Research,* 11(2), T. H. Holmes and R. H. Rahe, "The social readjustment rating scale," 1967, with permission from Elsevier.

Stress levels can help or hinder performance.

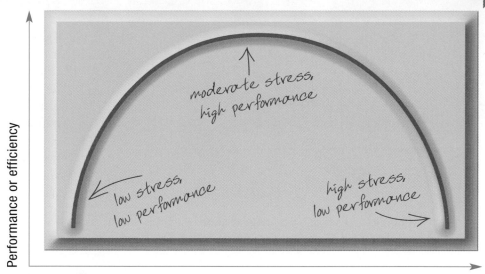

Performance or efficiency

moderate stress, high performance

low stress, low performance

high stress, low performance

Stress or anxiety

Source: From *Your Maximum Mind* by Herbert Benson, M.D., copyright © 1987 by Random House, Inc. Used by permission of Time Books, a division of Random House, Inc.

found that people experience both positive and negative events as stressors. For example, whereas some events like the death of a relative are clearly negative, other stressors, like moving to a new house or even taking a vacation, are generally positive.

At their worst, stress reactions can make you physically ill (Chapter 10 will examine stress-related health issues—situations in which stress goes beyond normal levels, causing physical and emotional problems). But stress can also supply the heightened readiness you need to do well on tests, finish assignments on time, prepare for a class presentation, or meet new people. Your goal is to find a manageable balance. Key 2.5, based on research conducted by Drs. Robert M. Yerkes and John E. Dodson, shows that stress can be helpful or harmful, depending on how much you experience.

Successful time management and goal setting relieve stress

Dealing with the stress of college life is, and will continue to be, one of your biggest challenges. But here's a piece of good news: Every goal-achievement and time-management strategy you have read in this chapter contributes to your ability to cope with stress. Remember that stress refers to how you react to pressure. When you set up effective plans to move toward goals, you reduce pressure. When you set a schedule that works for you and stick to it, you reduce pressure. Less pressure, less stress.

Carefully analyze the relationship between stress and your time-management habits. Often, people create extra stress for themselves without realizing it. For example, say you're a night person but have a habit of scheduling early classes. You are consistently stressed about waking up

in time for them. What's wrong with this picture? Reduce your stress by finding practical ways to change your scheduling. Taking later classes will help, but if that isn't possible, cope in other ways. Get to bed earlier a few nights a week, nap in the afternoon, and exercise briefly before class to restore your energy. Make sure that you are not expending energy coping with stress that you can avoid with thought and planning.

Extracurricular activities can provide relaxation and stress relief, as these students have found in their work with the Dynamics, an a cappella group at Skidmore College.

Stress-management strategies

Here are some practical strategies for coping with the day-to-day stress of being a college student.

- **Eat right.** The healthier you are, the stronger you are—and the more able you will be to weather tough situations like all-nighters, illnesses, and challenging academic work. Try to eat a balanced, low-fat diet and avoid overloading on junk food. Try also to maintain a healthy weight.

- **Exercise.** Physical exercise will help you manage your stress. Find a type of exercise you like and make it a regular part of your life.

- **Get sleep.** Avoid the system-wide dysfunction that sleep deprivation can create. Figure out how much sleep you need and do your best to get it. When you pull an all-nighter, make sure you play catch-up over the next couple of days.

- **Think positively.** Try to think of the things you have to do as challenges, not problems.

- **Seek balance.** A balanced life includes time by yourself—for your thoughts, hopes, and plans—and time for relaxation, in whatever form you choose.

- **Address issues.** Try not to let things lie too long. Analyze stressful situations and use problem-solving strategies (see Chapter 4) to decide on a specific plan of action.

- **Set boundaries and learn to say no.** Try to delegate. Review obligations regularly; if you find that something has become a burden, then consider dropping it from your roster of activities.

- **Surround yourself with people who are good for you.** Focus on friends who are good listeners and who will support you when things get rough. Friendship and humour go a long way toward reducing stress.

Sometimes you'll be able to pull out the strategies that fit the situation, finding ways to cope with the stress you encounter. Sometimes stress will make you feel frozen, not knowing where to turn to work your way out of it. At those times, remember: *Any step toward a goal is a stress-management strategy because it reduces pressure.* In that sense, this entire book is a stress-management strategy. Every useful tool, from test-taking hints to job-hunting strategies, will help you reduce the pressure and cover the distance toward your dreams.

חַי

In Hebrew, this word, pronounced "chai," means "life," representing all aspects of life—spiritual, emotional, family, educational, and career. Individual Hebrew characters have number values. Because the characters in the word *chai* add up to 18, the number 18 has come to be associated with good luck. The word *chai* is often worn as a good luck charm. The phrase *l'chaim* means "to life" and good luck.

As you plan your goals, think about the role luck may play in your success. If you work hard and are open to new opportunities, you may find yourself in the right place at the right time to benefit from a "lucky break." Because you are prepared, you may find a teacher who is so impressed by your tenacity and focus that she offers to become your mentor. Or, after you graduate, you may meet someone with a business opportunity that is a perfect match for your skills and who hires you on the spot. All your hard work in the direction of your goal will prepare you to take advantage of lucky breaks that come your way.

BUILDING SKILLS

FOR ACADEMIC, CAREER, AND LIFE SUCCESS

Developing Successful Intelligence

PUTTING IT ALL TOGETHER

The Wheel of Life. This exercise uses a wheel—an image that has been used for centuries to promote understanding of the self and the world—to help you think about your strength and weakness in eight important goal areas. Assess your level of proficiency in self-knowledge, study skills, personal life goals, finances, health and stress management, relationships, career, and time management by filling out the wheel as directed in Key 2.6 on p. 55.

Let this self-assessment help you make decisions about how you approach the material in this course. If you wish to improve your career preparation, for example, pay special attention to Chapter 11. If you need work on study skills, then focus specifically on the reading, note-taking, and test-taking chapters. If you work hard in this course, you should sense improvement in your weaker goal areas over the course of the semester. Plus, you will have developed your ability to evaluate and manage yourself—a skill that is crucial to your success in school and at work.

Team Building

COLLABORATIVE SOLUTIONS

Multiple paths to a goal. In a group of three or four, brainstorm goals that focus on building a life skill—for example, leadership, teamwork, or learning a foreign language. Write your ideas on a piece of paper. From that list, pick out one goal to explore together.

Each group member takes two minutes alone to think about this goal in terms of the first goal-achievement step on page 39—defining a strategy. In other words, answer the question: "How would I do it?" Each person writes down all of the paths he or she can think of.

create your future

Build self-knowledge with the Wheel of Life.

Rate yourself in each area of the wheel on a scale of 1 to 10, 1 being least developed (near the center of the wheel) and 10 being most developed (the outer edge of the wheel). In each area, at the level of the number you choose, draw a curved line and fill in the wedge below that line. Be honest—this is for your benefit only. Finally, look at what your wheel says about the balance in your life. If this were a real wheel, how well would it roll?

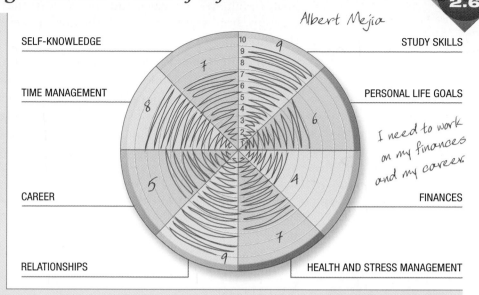

Albert Mejia

SELF-KNOWLEDGE

STUDY SKILLS

TIME MANAGEMENT

PERSONAL LIFE GOALS

I need to work on my finances and my career.

CAREER

FINANCES

RELATIONSHIPS

HEALTH AND STRESS MANAGEMENT

Sample Wheel

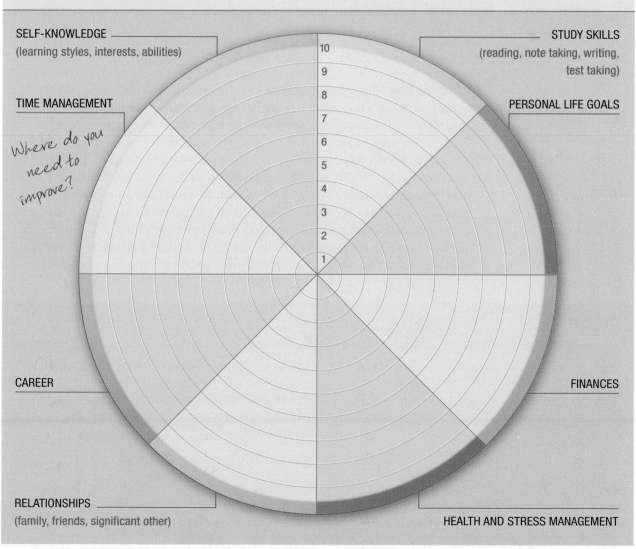

SELF-KNOWLEDGE
(learning styles, interests, abilities)

STUDY SKILLS
(reading, note taking, writing, test taking)

TIME MANAGEMENT

PERSONAL LIFE GOALS

Where do you need to improve?

CAREER

FINANCES

RELATIONSHIPS
(family, friends, significant other)

HEALTH AND STRESS MANAGEMENT

Source: Based on "The Wheel of Life" model developed by the Coaches Training Institute. © Co-Active Space 2000.

The group then gathers and everyone shares their strategies. The group evaluates strategies and chooses one that seems effective. Finally, as a group, brainstorm the rest of the goal-achievement process, based on the chosen strategy or path:

- **Set a timetable.** When do you plan to reach your goal? Discuss different time frames and how each might change the path.

- **Be accountable.** What safeguards will keep you on track? Talk about different ways to make sure you are moving ahead consistently.

- **Get unstuck.** What will you do if you hit a roadblock? Brainstorm the kinds of roadblocks that could get in the way of this particular goal. Come up with ways to overcome each obstacle.

At the end of the process, you should have a wealth of ideas for how to approach one particular goal—and an appreciation for how many paths you could take in order to get there.

Writing

DISCOVERY THROUGH JOURNALING

Use the tables here to record data; answer questions and write additional thoughts on a separate piece of paper or in a journal.

Discover how you spend your time. In the table below, estimate the total time you think you spend per week on each listed activity. Then, add the hours. If your number is over 168 (the number of hours in a week), rethink your estimates and recalculate so that the total is equal to 168.

Now, spend a week recording exactly how you spend your time. The chart on pages 57–58 has blocks showing half-hour increments. As you go through the week, write in what you do each hour, indicating when you started and when you stopped. Don't forget activities that don't feel like "activities" such as sleeping, relaxing, and watching TV. Finally, be sure to record your actual activities instead of how you want to have, or think you should have, spent your time. There are no wrong answers.

Activity	Estimated Time Spent	Activity	Estimated Time Spent
Class	24	Chores and personal business	10
Work	12	Friends and important relationships	30
Studying	6	Telephone time	1
Sleeping	49	Leisure/entertainment	10
Eating	4	Spiritual life	0
Family time/child care	4	Other	0
Commuting/travelling	6	**TOTAL**	156

Monday		Tuesday		Wednesday		Thursday	
TIME	ACTIVITY	TIME	ACTIVITY	TIME	ACTIVITY	TIME	ACTIVITY
6:00 A.M.	Sleep	6:00 A.M.	Sleep	6:00 A.M.	Sleep	6:00 A.M.	Sleep
6:30 A.M.	sleep	6:30 A.M.		6:30 A.M.	sleep	6:30 A.M.	sleep
7:00 A.M.	sleep	7:00 A.M.		7:00 A.M.	Breakfast	7:00 A.M.	Breakfast
7:30 A.M.	sleep	7:30 A.M.		7:30 A.M.	shower	7:30 A.M.	shower
8:00 A.M.	Sleep	8:00 A.M.		8:00 A.M.	class	8:00 A.M.	class
8:30 A.M.	sleep	8:30 A.M.		8:30 A.M.		8:30 A.M.	
9:00 A.M.	Sleep	9:00 A.M.		9:00 A.M.		9:00 A.M.	
9:30 A.M.	Sleep	9:30 A.M.		9:30 A.M.		9:30 A.M.	
10:00 A.M.	sleep	10:00 A.M.		10:00 A.M.	Lunch	10:00 A.M.	
10:30 A.M.	Getting Ready	10:30 A.M.	Breakfast	10:30 A.M.	Lunch	10:30 A.M.	
11:00 A.M.	class	11:00 A.M.	class	11:00 A.M.	class	11:00 A.M.	
11:30 A.M.	Class	11:30 A.M.	class	11:30 A.M.		11:30 A.M.	
12:00 P.M.	class	12:00 P.M.	lunch	12:00 P.M.		12:00 P.M.	
12:30 P.M.	class	12:30 P.M.		12:30 P.M.		12:30 P.M.	
1:00 P.M.	Class	1:00 P.M.		1:00 P.M.		1:00 P.M.	
1:30 P.M.	class	1:30 P.M.		1:30 P.M.		1:30 P.M.	
2:00 P.M.	Lunch	2:00 P.M.	Class	2:00 P.M.	Homework	2:00 P.M.	Homework
2:30 P.M.	lunch	2:30 P.M.	class	2:30 P.M.	Homwork	2:30 P.M.	
3:00 P.M.	Class	3:00 P.M.	Homework	3:00 P.M.	class	3:00 P.M.	
3:30 P.M.	class	3:30 P.M.	Homework	3:30 P.M.		3:30 P.M.	
4:00 P.M.	class	4:00 P.M.	class	4:00 P.M.		4:00 P.M.	
4:30 P.M.	class	4:30 P.M.	class	4:30 P.M.		4:30 P.M.	
5:00 P.M.	Dinner	5:00 P.M.	Dinner	5:00 P.M.		5:00 P.M.	Dinner
5:30 P.M.	homework	5:30 P.M.	Driving	5:30 P.M.	Homework	5:30 P.M.	Driving
6:00 P.M.	homework	6:00 P.M.	Work	6:00 P.M.	Homework	6:00 P.M.	Work
6:30 P.M.	homework	6:30 P.M.		6:30 P.M.	Wingshack	6:30 P.M.	
7:00 P.M.	homework	7:00 P.M.		7:00 P.M.		7:00 P.M.	
7:30 P.M.	homework	7:30 P.M.		7:30 P.M.		7:30 P.M.	
8:00 P.M.	tv	8:00 P.M.		8:00 P.M.		8:00 P.M.	
8:30 P.M.	tv	8:30 P.M.		8:30 P.M.		8:30 P.M.	
9:00 P.M.	Computer	9:00 P.M.		9:00 P.M.		9:00 P.M.	
9:30 P.M.	computer	9:30 P.M.		9:30 P.M.	TV	9:30 P.M.	
10:00 P.M.	Computer	10:00 P.M.		10:00 P.M.	TV	10:00 P.M.	
10:30 P.M.	Computer	10:30 P.M.		10:30 P.M.	computer	10:30 P.M.	
11:00 P.M.	Sleep	11:00 P.M.		11:00 P.M.	sleep	11:00 P.M.	
11:30 P.M.	sleep	11:30 P.M.		11:30 P.M.	sleep	11:30 P.M.	
12–6 A.M.	Sleep	12–6 A.M.	Sleep	12–6 A.M.	sleep	12–6 A.M.	sleep

Friday		Saturday		Sunday		Notes
TIME	ACTIVITY	TIME	ACTIVITY	TIME	ACTIVITY	
6:00 A.M.	Sleep	6:00 A.M.	Sleep	6:00 A.M.	Sleep	
6:30 A.M.		6:30 A.M.		6:30 A.M.		
7:00 A.M.		7:00 A.M.		7:00 A.M.		
7:30 A.M.		7:30 A.M.		7:30 A.M.		
8:00 A.M.		8:00 A.M.		8:00 A.M.		
8:30 A.M.		8:30 A.M.		8:30 A.M.		
9:00 A.M.	Breakfast	9:00 A.M.		9:00 A.M.		
9:30 A.M.	shower	9:30 A.M.		9:30 A.M.		
10:00 A.M.	class	10:00 A.M.		10:00 A.M.		
10:30 A.M.		10:30 A.M.		10:30 A.M.		
11:00 A.M.		11:00 A.M.		11:00 A.M.		
11:30 A.M.		11:30 A.M.		11:30 A.M.		
12:00 P.M.		12:00 P.M.		12:00 P.M.		
12:30 P.M.	Lunch	12:30 P.M.	Breakfast	12:30 P.M.	Breakfast	
1:00 P.M.	Lunch	1:00 P.M.	Chores	1:00 P.M.	Homework	
1:30 P.M.	class!	1:30 P.M.		1:30 P.M.		
2:00 P.M.		2:00 P.M.		2:00 P.M.		
2:30 P.M.		2:30 P.M.		2:30 P.M.		
3:00 P.M.		3:00 P.M.		3:00 P.M.		
3:30 P.M.	Homework	3:30 P.M.	Homework	3:30 P.M.		
4:00 P.M.		4:00 P.M.		4:00 P.M.		
4:30 P.M.		4:30 P.M.		4:30 P.M.	TV	
5:00 P.M.		5:00 P.M.		5:00 P.M.	Dinner	
5:30 P.M.	Dinner	5:30 P.M.		5:30 P.M.	Dinner	
6:00 P.M.	out w/friends	6:00 P.M.	Dinner	6:00 P.M.	Homework	
6:30 P.M.		6:30 P.M.	Out w/friends	6:30 P.M.		
7:00 P.M.		7:00 P.M.		7:00 P.M.		
7:30 P.M.		7:30 P.M.		7:30 P.M.		
8:00 P.M.		8:00 P.M.		8:00 P.M.	TV	
8:30 P.M.		8:30 P.M.		8:30 P.M.		
9:00 P.M.		9:00 P.M.		9:00 P.M.		
9:30 P.M.		9:30 P.M.		9:30 P.M.		
10:00 P.M.		10:00 P.M.		10:00 P.M.		
10:30 P.M.		10:30 P.M.		10:30 P.M.		
11:00 P.M.		11:00 P.M.		11:00 P.M.	sleep	
11:30 P.M.		11:30 P.M.		11:30 P.M.	sleep	
12–6 A.M.	Sleep	12–6 A.M.	Sleep	12–6 A.M.	sleep	

After a week, go through the chart below and add up how many hours you spent on the activities for which you previously estimated your hours. Tally the hours in the boxes in the following table using straight tally marks; round off to half hours and use a short tally mark for each half hour. In the third column, total the hours for each activity. Leave the "Ideal Time in Hours" column blank for now.

Activity	Time Tallied Over One-Week Period	Total Time in Hours	Ideal Time in Hours
Example: Class	IHt LHt LHt Iı	165	
Class		24	18
Work		12	12
Studying		15	13
Sleeping		49	49
Eating		4.5	4
Family time/child care	0	0	0
Commuting/travelling		1	.5
Chores and personal business		10	7
Friends and important relationships		15	15
Telephone time	0	0	0
Leisure/entertainment		13	13
Spiritual life	0	0	0
Other			

Add the totals in the third column to find your grand total. Compare your grand total to your estimated grand total; compare your actual activity hour totals to your estimated activity hour totals. Use a separate sheet of paper to answer the following questions:

- What matches and what doesn't? Describe the most interesting similarities and differences.
- Where do you waste the most time? What do you think that is costing you?

Now evaluate what kinds of changes might improve your ability to achieve goals. Analyze what you do daily, weekly, and monthly. Go back to the chart above and fill in the "Ideal Time in Hours" column. Consider the difference between actual hours and ideal hours. Ask questions:

- On what activities do you think you should spend more or less time?
- What are you willing to do to change, and why?

Finally, write a short paragraph describing two key time-management changes in detail. Describe what goal you are aiming for, and map out how you plan to put the changes into action.

Career Portfolio

PLAN FOR SUCCESS

Complete the following in your electronic portfolio or on separate sheets of paper.

Career goals—knowledge and skills. No matter what career goals you ultimately pursue, certain knowledge and skills are useful in any career area. Consider this list of the general skills employers look for in people they hire:

Acceptance	Critical thinking	Leadership
Communication	Flexibility	Positive attitude
Continual learning	Goal setting	Teamwork
Creativity	Integrity	

Choose and circle three of these that you want to focus on developing this year.

Map out a plan for your progress by indicating a series of smaller goals—from short-term to long-term—that will lead you toward developing these skills. For each of the three skills, write what you hope to accomplish in the next year, the next six months, and the next month. For example:

Skill: Leadership

Next month: I will volunteer to lead a session with my economics study group.

In six months: I will look into leadership positions on the college newspaper.

By the end of the year: I will have joined the newspaper team and expressed my interest in a leadership position.

SUGGESTED READINGS

Allen, David. *Getting Things Done: The Art of Stress-Free Productivity.* New York: Penguin Books, 2003.

Burka, Jane B., Ph.D., and Lenora M. Yuen, Ph.D. *Procrastination.* Reading, MA: Perseus Books, 1983.

Covey, Stephen. *The Seven Habits of Highly Effective People.* New York: Simon & Schuster, 1995.

Emmett, Rita. *The Procrastinator's Handbook: Mastering the Art of Doing It Now.* New York: Walker & Co., 2000.

Gleeson, Kerry. *The Personal Efficiency Program: How to Get Organized to Do More Work in Less Time,* 2nd ed. New York: John Wiley & Sons, 2000.

Lakein, Alan. *How to Get Control of Your Time and Your Life.* New York: New American Library, 1996.

Leyden-Rubenstein, Lori. *The Stress Management Handbook.* New York: McGraw-Hill, 1999.

Sapadin, Linda, and Jack Maguire. *Beat Procrastination and Make the Grade: The Six Styles of Procrastination and How Students Can Overcome Them.* New York: Penguin USA, 1999.

Timm, Paul R. *Successful Self-Management: A Psychologically Sound Approach to Personal Effectiveness.* Los Altos, CA: Crisp Publications, 1996.

Jim Blakley, a counsellor for Loyalist College in Belleville, Ontario, offers students many tips on time management: http://www.loyalistc.on.ca/loyalist/index_e.aspx?DetailID=125

The University of Toronto offers this on-line handbook for their students. It includes tips on stress and time management: http://www.sa.utoronto.ca/handbook

Top Achievement—goal-setting and self-improvement resources are available at www.topachievement.com

ENDNOTES

1. *A Report from the Center for Academic Integrity*, Center for Academic Integrity, Kenan Institute for Ethics, Duke University, October 1999 [on-line]. Available at www.academicintegrity.org (March 2001).

2. Ibid.

3. Background information for information on cultural diversity from Afsaneh Nahavandi and Ali Malekzadeh, *Organizational Behavior: The Person-Organization Fit*. Upper Saddle River, NJ: Prentice Hall, 1999.

4. Louis E. Boone, David L. Kurtz, and Judy R. Block, *Contemporary Business Communication*, 2nd ed. Upper Saddle River, NJ: Prentice Hall, 1997, pp. 68–72.

5. Louis E. Boone and David L. Kurtz, *Contemporary Business Communication*. Englewood Cliffs, NJ: Prentice Hall, 1994, p. 643.

6. Paul Timm, *Successful Self-Management: A Psychologically Sound Approach to Personal Effectiveness*. Los Altos, CA: Crisp Publications, 1987, pp. 22–41.

7. William E. Sydnor, "Procrastination," from the California Polytechnic State University Study Skills Library [on-line]. Based on *Overcoming Procrastination* by Albert Ellis. Available at www.sas.calpoly.edu/asc/ssl/procrastination.html (May 2003). Used with permission.

8. Jane B. Burka, Ph.D. and Lenora M. Yuen, Ph.D., *Procrastination*. Reading, MA: Perseus Books, 1983, pp. 21–22.

9. Ibid.

10. The following articles were used as sources in this section: Glenn C. Altschuler, "Adapting to College Life in an Era of Heightened Stress," *New York Times*, Education Life, Section 4A, August 6, 2000, p. 12; Carol Hymowitz and Rachel Emma Silverman, "Can Workplace Stress Get Worse?" *Wall Street Journal*, January 16, 2001, p. B1; Robert M. Sapolsky, "Best Ways to Reduce Everyday Levels of Stress... Bad Ol' Stress," *Bottom Line Personal*, January 15, 2000, p. 13; Kate Slaboch, "Stress and the College Student: A Debate" [on-line]. Available at www.jour.unr.edu/outpost/voices/voi.slaboch.stress.html (April 4, 2001); University of South Florida, The Counseling Center for Human Development, "Coping with Stress in College" [on-line]. Available: http://usfweb.usf.edu/counsel/self-hlp/stress.htm (April 4, 2001); Jodi Wilgoren, "Survey Shows High Stress Levels in College Freshmen," *New York Times*, January 23, 2000, p. NA.

11. Hans Selye, *The Stress of Life*. New York: McGraw-Hill, 1976.

12. Patricia Chisholm, "Coping with Stress," *Macleans*, January 8, 1996, pp. 33–36.

EXPLORE

3

In this chapter you will explore answers to the following questions: • What is a learning style? • How can you discover how you learn? • Why is it important to know how you learn? • How can you choose a major? • How can multiple intelligences help you explore majors and careers? • How can you identify and manage learning disabilities?

Learning styles, majors, and careers

AS A COLLEGE STUDENT, you are investing valuable resources—time, effort, and money—in your education. Learning is the return on your investment. How well you learn, and therefore how good a return you receive, depends in part on knowing yourself in two ways: knowing *how* you learn and knowing what you want to *do* with what you learn.

This chapter focuses first on helping you identify your learning styles, because when you understand how you learn, you will be a more effective student. Then you will read about majors and careers, because knowing where you want your education to take you will motivate you toward a goal.

Learning is not something you do just in college or university. In its report entitled Employability Skills 2000+, the Conference Board of Canada recognizes the need for employees to "learn and grow continuously." It also stresses the importance of assessing one's own strengths and weaknesses as well as setting goals for learning on your own terms. In other words, it is important in the "real world" to know what your learning style is.

knowing your talents and finding your direction

What is a *learning style?*

It happens in nearly every college or university course: Students listen to lectures throughout the semester. Each student hears the same words at exactly the same time and completes the same assignments. However, after finals, student experiences with the course range from fulfillment and high grades to complete disconnection and low grades or withdrawals. Many causes may be involved—different levels of interest and effort, different levels of ability, outside stresses. Another major factor that often is not considered is **learning style**.

Although presentation styles vary, the standard lecture is still the norm in many classrooms. This might lead you to assume that most students learn best in a lecture setting. Unfortunately, this is not the case, and students who don't learn as well from a lecture course may develop doubts about their competence. However, there are many different and equally valuable ways to learn. To succeed in any kind of course—and in life—you have to know how you learn, understand the strategies that heighten your strengths and boost your weaknesses, and know when to use them.

The Two Parts of Learning Style

Students process information in different ways and have varied styles of interaction with others. Say, for example, that a group of students is taking an English course that is broken up into study groups during two out of three class meetings. Students who are comfortable working with words or happy when engaged in discussion with a study group may do well in the course. Students who are more mathematical than verbal, or who prefer to work alone, might not do as well. The learning-style factor results in different levels of success with the course.

This example shows that learning style is about more than just what kinds of courses or topics you prefer. Learning style can be seen as having two equally important aspects:

- Learning preferences—what abilities and areas of learning interest you and come most easily to you
- Personality traits—how you interact with information and with others

These two aspects are important partners in defining how you learn—and how you succeed in college and beyond. Neither one gives you a complete picture without the other. Imagine that a first-year English instructor discovers that her entire class has strong verbal learning preferences. Thrilled, she proceeds with her group discussion-based course, figuring that the students will continue to do well. After finals, she is surprised to find a wide array of grades. A possible reason: Not everyone functions well in small group discussions.

Likewise, suppose another instructor chances on a course section composed entirely of students who love the experience-based, hands-on style of his biology course. He assumes that everyone will pass with flying colours. They don't, however—because, of course, not everyone has a natural learning preference in the sciences, no matter how much they like the style of interacting with the course material.

LEARNING STYLE

A particular way in which the mind receives and processes information.

Getting Perspective on Learning Style

What you find out about your learning style through the assessments in this chapter can help you manage your-self effectively at school, work, and home. However, no assessment has the final word on who you are and what you can and cannot do. It's human to want an easy answer—a one-page printout revealing the secrets of your identity—but this kind of quick fix does not exist.

Your thinking skills—your ability to evaluate information—enable you to see yourself as a whole, including your strengths and weaknesses. Your job is to analyze the information you gain from the assessments in this chapter to arrive at an accurate self-portrait. Before you get into the heart of the assessments and what they mean, consider how to best use what you learn from them.

Using Assessments for Reference. Approach any assessment as a tool with which you can expand your idea of yourself. There are no "right" answers, no "best" set of scores. Think of it in the same way you would a new set of eyeglasses for a person with somewhat blurred vision. The glasses will not create new paths and possibilities, but will help you see more clearly the ones that already exist.

You continually learn, change, and grow throughout your life. Any evaluation is simply a snapshot, a look at who you are in a given moment. Your answers can, and will, change as you change and as circumstances change. They provide an opportunity for you to look at the present moment by asking questions: Who am I right now? How does this compare to who I want to be?

Using Assessments for Understanding. Understanding your preferred learn-ing styles helps to prevent you from boxing yourself into categories that limit your life. Instead of saying, "I'm no good in math," someone who is not a natural in math can make the subject easier by tapping into learning style-related strategies. For example, a learner who responds to visuals can learn better by drawing diagrams of math problems; a learner who benefits from discussing material with others can improve compre-hension by talking out problems with a study partner.

Most people have one or two dominant learning styles. In addition, you may change which abilities you emphasize, depending on the situa-tion. For example, a student with a highly developed visual sense might find it easy to take notes in think link style (see Chapter 6 for an explana-tion of different note-taking styles). However, if an instructor writes an outline on the board as a guide to a detailed topic, the same student might work with the outline. The more you know yourself, the more you are able to assess and adapt to any situation.

Facing Challenges Realistically. Any assessment reveals areas of challenge as well as ability. Rather than dwelling on limitations (which often results in a negative self-image) or ignoring them (which often leads to unproductive choices), use what you know from the assessment to face your limitations and work to improve them.

To be what we are, and to become what we are capable of becoming, is the only end of life.

ROBERT LOUIS STEVENSON

In any area of challenge, look at where you are and set goals that help you reach where you want to be. If a class is difficult, examine what improvements to make in order to succeed. If a work project involves tasks that give you trouble, face your limitations head-on and ask for help. Exploring what you gain from working on a limitation helps you build the motivation you need to move ahead.

How can you *discover* how you learn?

This chapter presents two assessments that help you discover your style of learning and personality traits. View these as two equally important halves that help you form a whole picture of who you are as a learner.

The first assessment, which focuses on learning preferences, is called *Multiple Pathways to Learning*. It is based on the Multiple Intelligences Theory developed by Howard Gardner.

The second assessment is geared toward personality analysis and is based on the Myers-Briggs Type Inventory® (MBTI). The assessment is called *Personality Spectrum* and helps you evaluate how you react to people and situations.

Multiple Intelligences

There is a saying, "It is not how smart you are, but how you are smart." In 1983, Howard Gardner, a Harvard University professor, changed the way people perceive intelligence and learning with his theory of Multiple Intelligences. This theory holds that there are at least eight distinct **intelligences** possessed by all people, and that every person has developed some intelligences more fully than others. According to the Multiple Intelligences Theory, when you find a task or subject easy, you are probably using a more fully developed intelligence; when you have more trouble, you may be using a less developed intelligence.[1]

Gardner believes that the way you learn is a unique blend of intelligences that result from your distinctive abilities, challenges, experiences, and training. In addition, how you learn isn't necessarily set in stone—particular levels of ability in the intelligences may develop or recede based on changes in your life. Traditionally, the notion of intelligence has been linked to tests such as the Stanford-Binet IQ test and others like it that rely on mathematical, logical, and verbal measurements. Gardner, however, thinks that this doesn't accurately reflect the entire spectrum of human ability:

> I believe that we should... look... at more naturalistic sources of information about how peoples around the world develop skills important

INTELLIGENCE

As defined by H. Gardner, an ability to solve problems or fashion products that are useful in a particular cultural setting or community.

to their way of life. Think, for example, of sailors in the South Seas, who find their way around hundreds, or even thousands, of islands by looking at the constellations of stars in the sky, feeling the way a boat passes over the water, and noticing a few scattered landmarks. A word for intelligence in a society of these sailors would probably refer to that kind of navigational ability.[2]

Key 3.1 offers brief descriptions of the focus of each of the intelligences. You can find information on related skills and study techniques in Key 3.2 on page 72. The Multiple Pathways to Learning assessment helps you determine the levels to which your intelligences are developed.

Personality Spectrum

Personality assessments indicate how you respond to both internal and external situations—in other words, how you react to information, thoughts, and feelings, as well as to people and events. Employers may give such assessments to employees and use the results to set up and evaluate teams.

The Myers-Briggs Type Inventory is one of the most widely used personality inventories in both psychology and business, and was one of the first instruments to measure psychological types. Katharine Briggs and

Multiple intelligences.

INTELLIGENCE	DESCRIPTION
Verbal–Linguistic	Ability to communicate through language (listening, reading, writing, speaking)
Logical–Mathematical	Ability to understand logical reasoning and problem solving (math, science, patterns, sequences)
Bodily–Kinesthetic	Ability to use the physical body skilfully and to take in knowledge through bodily sensation (coordination, working with hands)
Visual–Spatial	Ability to understand spatial relationships and to perceive and create images (visual art, graphic design, charts and maps)
Interpersonal	Ability to relate to others, noticing their moods, motivations, and feelings (social activity, co-operative learning, teamwork)
Intrapersonal	Ability to understand one's own behaviour and feelings (self-awareness, independence, time spent alone)
Musical	Ability to comprehend and create meaningful sound and recognize patterns (music, sensitivity to sound and patterns)
Naturalistic	Ability to understand features of the environment (interest in nature, environmental balance, ecosystem, stress relief brought by natural environments)

her daughter, Isabel Briggs Myers, together designed the MBTI. Later, David Keirsey and Marilyn Bates combined the 16 Myers-Briggs types into four temperaments and developed an assessment called the Keirsey Sorter based on those temperaments.

Derived in part from the Myers-Briggs and Keirsey theories, the Personality Spectrum assessment adapts and simplifies their material into four personality types—Thinker, Organizer, Giver, and Adventurer—and was developed by Dr. Joyce Bishop in 1997. The Personality Spectrum gives you a personality perspective on how you can maximize your functioning at school and work. For each personality type, you'll see techniques that improve work and school performance, learning strategies, and ways of relating to others. Page 70 gives you more details about each type.

Scoring the Assessments

The assessments follow this section of text. As you complete them, try to answer the questions objectively—in other words, answer the questions to best indicate who you are, not who you want to be (or who your parents or instructors want you to be). Then, enter your scores on page 69. Don't be concerned if some of your scores are low—that is true for almost everyone.

Following each assessment is information about the typical traits of, and appropriate study strategies for, each intelligence or spectrum dimension. You have abilities in all areas, though some are more developed than others. Therefore, you may encounter useful suggestions under any of the headings. During this course, try a large number of new study techniques and keep what works for you.

Remember also that knowing your learning style is not only about guiding your life toward your strongest abilities, it is also about using other strategies when you face challenges. No one goes through life always able to find situations where strengths are in demand and weaknesses are uninvolved. Use the strategies for your weaker areas when what is required of you involves tasks and academic areas that you find difficult. For example, if you are not characteristically strong in logical–mathematical intelligence and have to take a required math or science course, the suggestions geared toward logical–mathematical learners may help you build what skill you have.

> **IMPORTANT NOTE** *about scoring...*
>
> The two assessments that follow are scored *differently.* For *Multiple Pathways to Learning,* each intelligence has a set of numbered statements, and you consider each numbered statement on its own, giving it the number you feel best suits your response to it. You will, therefore, have any combination of numbers for each intelligence, from all 4s to all 1s or anywhere in between.
>
> For *Personality Spectrum,* you rank the four statements that complete each statement, giving a 4 to the one most like you, a 3 to the next most, a 2 to the next, and a 1 to the one least like you. You will, therefore, have a 4, 3, 2, and 1 for each of the eight numbered questions.

MULTIPLE PATHWAYS TO LEARNING

Directions: Rate each statement as follows. Write the number of your response (1–4) on the line next to the statement and total each set of six questions.

rarely	sometimes	usually	always
1	2	3	4

1. _____ I enjoy physical activities.
2. _____ I am uncomfortable sitting still.
3. _____ I prefer to learn through doing.
4. _____ When sitting, I move my legs or hands.
5. _____ I enjoy working with my hands.
6. _____ I like to pace when I'm thinking or studying.

_____ TOTAL for **BODILY–KINESTHETIC**

1. _____ I enjoy telling stories.
2. _____ I like to write.
3. _____ I like to read.
4. _____ I express myself clearly.
5. _____ I am good at negotiating.
6. _____ I like to discuss topics that interest me.

_____ TOTAL for **VERBAL–LINGUISTIC**

1. _____ I use maps easily.
2. _____ I draw pictures/diagrams when explaining ideas.
3. _____ I can assemble items easily from diagrams.
4. _____ I enjoy drawing or photography.
5. _____ I do not like to read long paragraphs.
6. _____ I prefer a drawn map over written directions.

_____ TOTAL for **VISUAL–SPATIAL**

1. _____ I like math.
2. _____ I like science.
3. _____ I problem-solve well.
4. _____ I question how things work.
5. _____ I enjoy planning or designing something new.
6. _____ I am able to fix things.

_____ TOTAL for **LOGICAL–MATHEMATICAL**

1. _____ I listen to music.
2. _____ I move my fingers or feet when I hear music.
3. _____ I have good rhythm.
4. _____ I like to sing along with music.
5. _____ People have said I have musical talent.
6. _____ I like to express my ideas through music.

_____ TOTAL for **MUSICAL**

1. _____ I need quiet time to think.
2. _____ I think about issues before I want to talk.
3. _____ I am interested in self-improvement.
4. _____ I understand my thoughts and feelings.
5. _____ I know what I want out of life.
6. _____ I prefer to work on projects alone.

_____ TOTAL for **INTRAPERSONAL**

1. _____ I like doing a project with other people.
2. _____ People come to me to help settle conflicts.
3. _____ I like to spend time with friends.
4. _____ I am good at understanding people.
5. _____ I am good at making people feel comfortable.
6. _____ I enjoy helping others.

_____ TOTAL for **INTERPERSONAL**

1. _____ I enjoy nature whenever possible.
2. _____ I think about having a career involving nature.
3. _____ I enjoy studying plants, animals, or oceans.
4. _____ I avoid being indoors except when I sleep.
5. _____ As a child I played with bugs and leaves.
6. _____ When I feel stressed I want to be out in nature.

_____ TOTAL for **NATURALISTIC**

Developed by Joyce Bishop, Ph.D., and based upon Howard Gardner's *Frames of Mind: The Theory of Multiple Intelligences*.[3]

Name: _____   Date: _____

PERSONALITY SPECTRUM

STEP 1. Rank order all four responses to each question from most like you (4) to least like you (1). Use the circles next to the responses to indicate your rankings.

4 most like me   **3** more like me   **2** less like me   **1** least like me

1. I like instructors who

   a. ☐ tell me exactly what is expected of me.
   b. ☐ make learning active and exciting.
   c. ☐ maintain a safe and supportive classroom.
   d. ☐ challenge me to think at higher levels.

2. I learn best when the material is

   a. ☐ well organized.
   b. ☐ something I can do hands-on.
   c. ☐ about understanding and improving the human condition.
   d. ☐ intellectually challenging.

3. A high priority in my life is to

   a. ☐ keep my commitments.
   b. ☐ experience as much of life as possible.
   c. ☐ make a difference in the lives of others.
   d. ☐ understand how things work.

4. Other people think of me as

   a. ☐ dependable and loyal.
   b. ☐ dynamic and creative.
   c. ☐ caring and honest.
   d. ☐ intelligent and inventive.

5. When I experience stress I would most likely

   a. ☐ do something to help me feel more in control of my life.
   b. ☐ do something physical and daring.
   c. ☐ talk with a friend.
   d. ☐ go off by myself and think about my situation.

6. I would probably not be a close friend with someone who is

   a. ☐ irresponsible.
   b. ☐ unwilling to try new things.
   c. ☐ selfish and unkind to others.
   d. ☐ an illogical thinker.

7. My vacations could be described as

   a. ☐ traditional.
   b. ☐ adventuresome.
   c. ☐ pleasing to others.
   d. ☐ a new learning experience.

8. One word that best describes me is

   a. ☐ sensible.
   b. ☐ spontaneous.
   c. ☐ giving.
   d. ☐ analytical.

STEP 2. Add up the total points for each letter.

TOTAL FOR **a.** ☐ Organizer   **b.** ☐ Adventurer   **c.** ☐ Giver   **d.** ☐ Thinker

STEP 3. Plot these numbers on the brain diagram on page 71.

Name: _____ Date: _____

Personality Spectrum: Place a dot on the appropriate number line in the brain diagram for each of your four scores from p. 70; connect the dots; then shade each section using a different colour. Write your scores in the four circles just outside the diagram. See information regarding scores below.

Multiple Pathways to Learning: In the vertical bars below the brain diagram, indicate your scores from p. 69 by shading from the bottom going up until you reach the number corresponding to your score for that intelligence. See information regarding scores below.

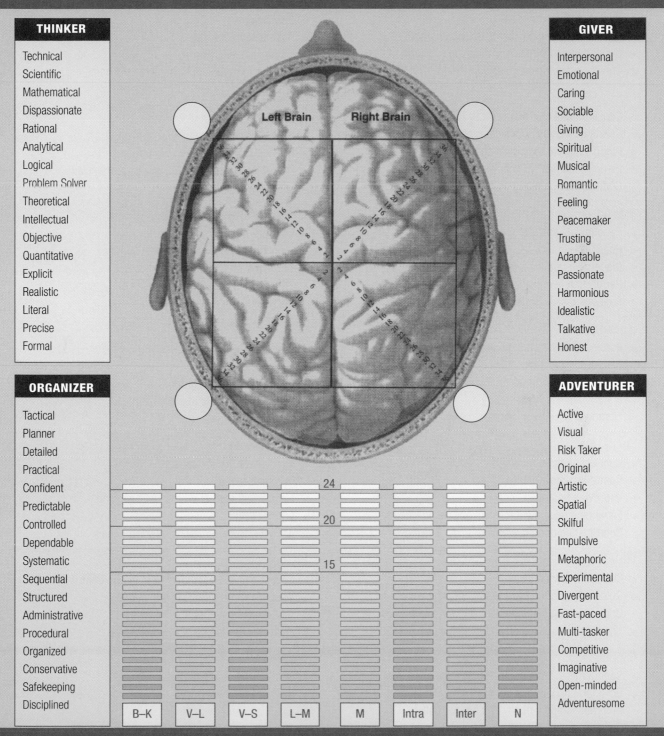

THINKER

Technical
Scientific
Mathematical
Dispassionate
Rational
Analytical
Logical
Problem Solver
Theoretical
Intellectual
Objective
Quantitative
Explicit
Realistic
Literal
Precise
Formal

Left Brain   Right Brain

GIVER

Interpersonal
Emotional
Caring
Sociable
Giving
Spiritual
Musical
Romantic
Feeling
Peacemaker
Trusting
Adaptable
Passionate
Harmonious
Idealistic
Talkative
Honest

ORGANIZER

Tactical
Planner
Detailed
Practical
Confident
Predictable
Controlled
Dependable
Systematic
Sequential
Structured
Administrative
Procedural
Organized
Conservative
Safekeeping
Disciplined

ADVENTURER

Active
Visual
Risk Taker
Original
Artistic
Spatial
Skilful
Impulsive
Metaphoric
Experimental
Divergent
Fast-paced
Multi-tasker
Competitive
Imaginative
Open-minded
Adventuresome

24

20

15

B–K   V–L   V–S   L–M   M   Intra   Inter   N

For the Personality Spectrum, 26–36 indicates a strong tendency in that dimension, 14–25 a moderate tendency, and below 14 a minimal tendency.

For Multiple Pathways to Learning, 21–24 indicates a high level of development in that particular type of intelligence, 15–20 a moderate level, and below 15 an underdeveloped intelligence.

Source for brain diagram: *Understanding Psychology*, 3rd ed., by Morris, © 1996. Adapted by permission of Prentice Hall, Inc., Upper Saddle River, NJ.

How to put your Multiple Intelligences to work for you.

ABILITIES AND SKILLS ASSOCIATED WITH EACH INTELLIGENCE

Verbal–Linguistic
- Analyzing own use of language
- Remembering terms easily
- Explaining, teaching, learning, using humour
- Understanding syntax and meaning of words
- Convincing someone to do something

Musical–Rhythmic
- Sensing tonal qualities
- Creating or enjoying melodies and rhythms
- Being sensitive to sounds and rhythms
- Using "schemas" to hear music
- Understanding the structure of music

Logical–Mathematical
- Recognizing abstract patterns
- Reasoning inductively and deductively
- Discerning relationships and connections
- Performing complex calculations
- Reasoning scientifically

Visual–Spatial
- Perceiving and forming objects accurately
- Recognizing relationships between objects
- Representing something graphically
- Manipulating images
- Finding one's way in space

Bodily–Kinesthetic
- Connecting mind and body
- Controlling movement
- Improving body functions
- Expanding body awareness to all senses
- Coordinating body movement

Intrapersonal
- Evaluating own thinking
- Being aware of and expressing feelings
- Understanding self in relationship to others
- Thinking and reasoning on higher levels

Interpersonal
- Seeing things from others' perspectives
- Co-operating within a group
- Communicating verbally and non-verbally
- Creating and maintaining relationships

Naturalist
- Deep understanding of nature
- Appreciation of the delicate balance in nature

STUDY TECHNIQUES TO MAXIMIZE EACH INTELLIGENCE

Verbal–Linguistic
- Read text and highlight no more than ten per cent
- Rewrite notes
- Outline chapters
- Teach someone else
- Recite information or write scripts/debates

Musical–Rhythmic
- Create rhythms out of words
- Beat out rhythms with hand or stick
- Play instrumental music, write raps
- Put new material to songs you already know
- Take music breaks

Logical–Mathematical
- Organize material logically
- Explain material sequentially to someone
- Develop systems and find patterns
- Write outlines and develop charts and graphs
- Analyze information

Visual–Spatial
- Develop graphic organizers for new material
- Draw mind maps
- Develop charts and graphs
- Use colour in notes to organize
- Visualize material

Bodily–Kinesthetic
- Move or rap while you learn
- Pace and recite
- Move fingers under words while reading
- Create "living sculptures"
- Act out scripts of material, design games

Intrapersonal
- Reflect on personal meaning of information
- Visualize information, keep a journal
- Study in quiet settings
- Imagine experiments

Interpersonal
- Study in a group
- Discuss information
- Use flash cards with others
- Teach someone else

Naturalist
- Connect with nature whenever possible
- Form study groups of people with like interests

Adapted by Dr. Joyce Bishop from David Lazear, *Seven Pathways of Learning*, 1994.

How to put your Personality Spectrum to work for you.

CHARACTERISTICS OF EACH PERSONALITY TYPE

Thinker

- Solving problems
- Developing models and systems
- Analytical and abstract thinking
- Exploring ideas and potentials
- Ingenuity
- Going beyond established boundaries
- Global thinking—seeking universal truth

Organizer

- Responsibility, reliability
- Operating successfully within social structures
- Sense of history, culture, and dignity
- Neatness and organization
- Loyalty
- Orientation to detail
- Comprehensive follow-through on tasks
- Efficiency

Giver

- Honesty, authenticity
- Successful, close relationships
- Making a difference in the world
- Cultivating your own potential and that of others
- Negotiation; promoting peace
- Communicating with others
- Openness
- Helping others

Adventurer

- High ability in a variety of fields
- Courage and daring
- Approaching problem-solving in a hands-on fashion
- Living in the present
- Spontaneity and action
- Ability to negotiate
- Non-traditional style
- Flexibility
- Zest for life

STUDY TECHNIQUES TO MAXIMIZE PERSONALITY TYPES

Thinker

- Find time to reflect independently on new information
- Learn through problem solving
- Design new ways of approaching issues
- Convert material into logical charts and graphs
- Try to minimize repetitive tasks
- Look for opportunities where you have the freedom to work independently

Organizer

- Try to have tasks defined in clear, concrete terms so that you know what is required
- Look for a well-structured, stable environment
- Request feedback
- Use a planner to schedule tasks and dates
- Organize material by rewriting and organizing class or text notes, making flash cards, or carefully highlighting

Giver

- Study with others
- Teach material to others
- Seek out tasks, groups, and subjects that involve helping people
- Find ways to express thoughts and feelings clearly and honestly
- Put energy into your most important relationships

Adventurer

- Look for environments that encourage non-traditional approaches
- Find hands-on ways to learn
- Seek people whom you find stimulating
- Use or develop games and puzzles to help memorize terms
- Fight boredom by asking if you can do something extra or perform a task in a more active way

Joyce Bishop, *Keys to Success,* © 2001

Why is it *important* to know *how* you learn?

The knowledge you have gained by taking the assessments in this chapter can guide you to smart choices that will bring success in your studies, the classroom, and the workplace.

Study Benefits

Knowing how you learn helps you choose study techniques that capitalize on your strengths. For example, if you learn successfully from a linear, logical presentation, you can look for order (for example, a chronology or a problem–solution structure) as you review notes. If you are a strong interpersonal learner, you can try to work in study groups whenever possible.

Learning style also points you toward strategies that help with tasks and topics that don't come so easily. An Adventurer who does *not* respond well to linear information, for example, has two choices when faced with logical presentations. She can apply her strengths to the material—for example, she might find a hands-on approach. Or she can work on her ability to handle the material by developing study skills that work well for linear learners.

When you study with others, an understanding of diverse learning styles will help you assign tasks effectively and learn more comprehensively. An Interpersonal learner might take the lead in teaching material to others; an Organizer might be the schedule coordinator for the group; a Musical learner might present information in a new way that helps to solidify concepts.

Classroom Benefits

Knowing your learning style can help you make the most of the teaching styles of your instructors (an instructor's teaching style often reflects his or her learning style). Your particular learning style may work well with the way some instructors teach—and be a mismatch with other instructors. Occasionally, you may be able to choose an instructor who teaches in a way that maximizes how you learn. Class schedules, however, usually don't make such choices possible.

After several class meetings, you should be able to assess the instructor's teaching styles (it's common for instructors to have more than one). Key 3.4 sets forth some common styles. If your style doesn't match up well with that of your instructor, you have a number of options.

Bring extra focus to your weaker areas. Working on your weaker points helps you break new ground in your learning. For example, if you're a verbal person in a math- and logic-oriented class, increase your focus and concentration during class so that you get as much as you can from the presentation. Then spend extra study time on the material, ask others from your class to help you, and search for additional supplemental materials and exercises to reinforce your knowledge.

Ask your instructor for additional help. For example, a visual person might ask an instructor to recommend visuals that help to illustrate the points made in class. Take advantage of your instructor's office hours to talk one-on-one about what's giving you trouble—especially in a large lecture, your instructor won't know what's going on with you unless you speak up.

"Convert" class material during study time. For example, an interpersonal learner takes a class with an instructor who presents big-picture information in lecture format. This student might organize study groups and talk through concepts with other group members while filling in the factual gaps. Likewise, a visual student might rewrite notes in different colours to add a visual element—for example, using one colour for central ideas, another for supporting examples.

Instructors are as unique as students, and no instructor can fulfill the particular needs of a whole classroom of individuals. You often have to shift elements of your habitual learning approach to better mesh with how your instructor presents material. Being flexible in this way benefits you throughout life. Just as you can't hand-pick your instructors, in the workplace you are rarely, if ever, able to choose your boss or change his or her style.

Workplace Benefits

Because different careers require different abilities, there is no one "best" learning style for the workplace. As the Conference Board of Canada

Teaching styles reflect instructor learning styles.

Lecture	Instructor speaks to the class for the entire period; little to no class interaction.
Group Discussion	Instructor presents material but encourages class discussion throughout.
Small Groups	Instructor presents material and then breaks class into small groups for discussion or project work.
Visual Focus	Instructor uses visual elements such as diagrams, photographs, drawings, and transparencies.
Verbal Focus	Instructor relies primarily on words, either spoken or written on the board or overhead projector.
Logical Presentation	Instructor organizes material in a logical sequence, such as by time or importance.
Random Presentation	Instructor tackles topics in no particular order, jumps around a lot, or digresses.

suggest in their Employability Skills 2000+, knowing how you learn brings you the following key benefits on the job:

- **Better performance.** Because so much of what you do at school (e.g., interacting with others, reading, taking notes) is what you do on the job, it follows that your learning style is essentially the same as your working style. If you know how you learn, you can look for a career, position, and environment that suit you best. You can perform at the top of your ability if you work at a job in which you feel competent and happy.

- **Better teamwork.** Teamwork is a primary feature of the modern workplace. The better your awareness of your abilities and personality traits, the better you are able to communicate with others and identify what tasks you can best perform in a team situation.

- **Better self-awareness.** Knowing how you learn helps you pinpoint roadblocks. This helps you to work on difficult areas; plus, when a task requires a skill that is tough for you, you can either take special care with it or suggest someone else whose style may be better suited to it.

They are able because they think they are able.

VIRGIL

STRESSBUSTER

MICHAEL MURRAY **University of British Columbia**

What techniques have you adopted to focus on your learning strengths and to address your weaknesses as a student? How has this reduced stress in your everyday life, and in your studies?

In order to complete my degree in geography, I need to balance a course load that includes both humanities and science classes. My learning style is more verbal-linguistic and when I first started my degree, I studied for each course in the same way: I rewrote my notes, highlighted text and drafted chapter outlines. I found this approach to be really effective for me.

Unfortunately, this study method didn't work as well for my science credits. No matter how hard I studied, I kept having the same problems with courses requiring complex calculations and analyses. I was stressed out and convinced that I would fail and never get my degree.

It wasn't until I changed my study techniques to suit the logical-mathematical skills these courses required, that things finally turned around. I used graphic organizers, charts, and maps to assist with my studying and it made a big difference.

Knowing my learning style and understanding how to adapt to take on those tougher courses helped to alleviate a lot of my stress. I now know the kinds of courses that I am better suited for and understand when certain science courses require more time and different study techniques.

How can you *choose a major?*

The **major:** It may not be around the corner, but it's probably not that far away. At some point in the future, you will be asked to declare an academic major. Through this act, you largely determine the courses you take, what you learn, with whom you spend your school time. Your major may also have a significant influence on your future career.

Taking a practical approach to declaring a major can help you avoid becoming overwhelmed by the task. Think of it as a long-term goal made up of multiple steps (short-term goals) that begin with knowing your learning styles, interests, and talents; exploring academic options; and establishing your academic schedule. You will be wise to start the process now, even though you probably don't need to decide right away—and even if, as is true of many students, you don't yet know what you want to study.

MAJOR

An academic subject chosen as a field of specialization, requiring a specific course of study.

Short-term goal #1: Use learning styles assessments to identify interests and talents

Considering what you like and what you do well can lead to a fulfilling area of study. When you identify your interests and talents and choose a major that focuses on them, you are likely to have a positive attitude and perform at your highest level.

Great minds have purposes; others have wishes.

WASHINGTON IRVING

To pinpoint the areas that spark your interest, use your Multiple Intelligences and Personality Spectrum assessment results to answer the following questions:

- What courses have I enjoyed the most in college and high school? What do these courses have in common?
- What subjects am I drawn to in my personal reading?
- What activities do I look forward to most?
- In what skills or academic areas do I perform best? Am I a "natural" in any area?
- What do people say I do well?
- What are my dominant learning styles?

Short-term goal #2: Explore academic options

Next, find out about the academic choices available at your school. Plan to achieve the following mini-goals in order to reach this short-term goal.

Learn what's possible. Consult your school's undergraduate calendar for guidelines on declaring (and changing) your major. Find answers to these questions:

- When do I have to declare a major?
- What are my options in majoring? (double majors, minors, interdisciplinary majors)
- What majors are offered at my school?

If a major looks interesting, explore it further by answering these questions:

- What are the minimum requirements?
- What overall average must I maintain in the courses included in the major?
- What preparatory courses (prerequisites) are required?
- What courses will I be required to take and in what sequence? How many credits do I need to graduate in the major?
- Will I have to write a thesis or complete a co-op to graduate?

Work closely with your advisor. Early on, begin discussing your major with your advisor; he or she can help you evaluate different options.

Visit the department. When considering a major, analyze your comfort with the academic department as well as with the material. To learn more about the department, ask the department secretary for information. Then sit in on several classes to get a feel for the instructors and the work. Consider asking an instructor for an appointment to discuss the program.

Speak to people with experience in the major. Ask students who are a year or two ahead of you to describe their experiences with the courses, the workload, and the instructors.

Consider creative options for majoring. Think beyond the traditional majoring path, and investigate the possibilities at your school. One or more of the following may be open to you:

- **Double majors.** If, for example, you want to major in English and philosophy, ask your academic advisor if it is possible to meet the requirements for both departments.
- **Interdisciplinary majors.** If your preferred major isn't in the undergraduate calendar, consult your advisor. Some schools allow students to design majors with guidance from advisors and instructors.
- **Minors.** A minor involves a concentration of departmental courses but has fewer requirements than a major. Many students choose a minor that is suited for a career.
- **Majors involving courses outside your school.** Some schools may offer study-abroad programs (in which students spend a semester or a year at an affiliated college in a different country) or opportunities to take courses at nearby schools. Such courses might apply to a major that interests you.

Short-term goal #3: Establish your academic schedule

Effective time management will enable you to fulfill the requirements of your major and complete all additional credits.

Look at your time frame. How many years do you plan to study? Do you plan on continuing your education once you've graduated? If so, do you plan to go there directly after graduation or take time off?

Set timing for short-term goals. Within your time frame, pinpoint when to accomplish the important short-term goals that lead to graduation. What are the deadlines for completing core requirements, declaring a major, completing your co-op, or writing a thesis? Although you won't need to plan out your entire college or university course load at the beginning of your first semester, drafting a tentative curriculum—both within and outside your major—can help clarify where you are heading.

Identify dates connected to your goal fulfillment. Pay attention to academic dates (you will find an academic calendar in each year's college catalogue and on the college's Web site). Such dates include registration dates, final date to declare a major, final date to drop a course, and so forth. Plan ahead so you don't miss a deadline.

Be flexible as you come to a decision

As with any serious challenge that involves defining your path flexibility is essential. Many students change their minds as they consider majors; some declare a major and then change it one or more times before finding a good fit. Just act on any change right away—once you have considered it carefully—by informing your advisor, completing any required paperwork, and redesigning your schedule to reflect your new choices.

get analytical, creative, and practical!

LINK YOUR INTERESTS TO INTRIGUING MAJORS

Looking at a list of the majors and programs your school offers, write down three that you want to consider.

1. _____
2. _____
3. _____

Now look at the list again. Other than what you wrote above, what majors catch your eye? Write down three intriguing majors or programs—without thinking about what you would do with them or whether they are practical choices.

1. _____
2. _____
3. _____

Choose one major or program from the second list and explore it. Talk to your advisor about the major. Read about it in your college catalogue. Consider a minor in the subject. Speak to an instructor in the department about related careers. You will have taken a casual interest and turned it into a viable academic option.

How can multiple intelligences help you *explore majors and careers?*

All that you have learned in this chapter about your learning styles and strengths has practical application as you begin thinking about your future at school and in the workplace. A strength in one or more intelligences may lead you to a major, an internship, and even a lifelong career.

Key 3.5 lists some possibilities for the eight intelligence types. This list is by no means complete. Rather, it represents only a fraction of the available opportunities. Use what you see here to inspire thought and spur investigation.

Career exploration strategies

Whatever your major, you will benefit from starting to think about careers early on. Use the following strategies to explore what's out there (later in the text, we will examine the topic of career exploration in depth).

Keep what you value in mind. Ask yourself what careers support the principles that guide your life. How important to you are service to others, financial security, a broad-based education, and time for family?

Follow your passion. Find something you love doing more than anything else in the world, and then find a way to make money doing it. If you are sure of what you love to do but cannot pinpoint a career niche, open yourself to your instructors' advice.

Use career resources. Visit your school's career centre to read current media, take an assessment, or explore the career areas that currently have good prospects. Check out careers, industries, and companies on the Internet. Talk with people who have jobs that interest you.

Explore educational requirements of careers. How much your choice of a major matters may depend on the career. For example, pursuing a career in medicine usually requires majoring in the biological sciences. In contrast, aiming for a career in law gives you more flexibility (political science, philosophy, and English are just a few possibilities for pre-law students).

Try hands-on exploration. Extracurricular activities and volunteering opportunities might provide experiences that help you decide. For example, a student interested in teaching may volunteer as a camp counsellor or an after-school tutor.

Although almost everyone faces challenges during their post-secondary career, people with diagnosed learning disabilities have unique challenges that may interfere with university or college success. Focused assistance can help students who are learning disabled to manage their conditions and excel in school.

Multiple Intelligences may open doors to majors, internships, and careers.

MULTIPLE INTELLIGENCE	CONSIDER MAJORING IN . . .	THINK ABOUT AN INTERNSHIP AT A . . .	LOOK INTO A CAREER AS . . .
Bodily–Kinesthetic	Massage Therapy Physical Therapy Kinesiology Construction Engineering Chiropractics Sports Medicine Anatomy Dance Theatre	Sports Physician's Office Athletic Club Physical Therapy Centre Chiropractor's Office Construction Company Surveying Company Dance Studio Athletic Trainer Drafting Firm Theatre Company	Carpenter Draftsman Recreational Therapist Physical Therapist Mechanical Engineer Massage Therapist Dancer or Acrobat Exercise Physiologist Actor
Intrapersonal	Psychology Sociology English Finance Liberal Arts Biology Computer Science Economics	Research and Development Firm Accounting Firm Computer Company Publishing House Pharmaceutical Company Engineering Firm Biology Lab	Research Scientist Motivational Speaker Engineer Physicist Sociologist Computer Scientist Economist Author Psychologist
Interpersonal	Psychology Sociology Education Real Estate Public Relations Nursing Business Hotel/Restaurant Management Rhetoric/Communications	Hotel or Restaurant Travel Agency Real Estate Agency Public Relations Firm Human Resources Customer Service Teaching Assistant Marketing/Sales Group Counselling Social Service	Social Worker PR Rep/Media Liaison Human Resources Travel Agent Sociologist Anthropologist Counsellor Therapist Teacher Nurse
Naturalistic	Forestry Astronomy Geology Biology Zoology Atmospheric Sciences Oceanography Agriculture Animal Husbandry Environmental Law Physics	Museum National Park Oil Company Botanical Gardens Environmental Law Firm Outward Bound Adventure Travel Agency Zoo Camp Counsellor Biological Research Firm	Forest Ranger Botanist or Herbalist Geologist Ecologist Marine Biologist Archaeologist Astronomer Adventure Travel Agent Wildlife Tour Guide Landscape Architect

(continued)

MULTIPLE INTELLIGENCE	CONSIDER MAJORING IN . . .	THINK ABOUT AN INTERNSHIP AT A . . .	LOOK INTO A CAREER AS . . .
Musical	Music Musical History Musical Theory Performing Arts Composition Voice Liberal Arts Entertainment Law	Performance Hall Radio Station Record Label Ballet or Theatre Company Recording Studio Children's Music Camp Orchestra or Opera Company Musical Talent Agency Entertainment Law Firm	Lyricist or Composer Singer or Musician Voice Coach Music Teacher or Critic Record Executive Conductor Radio DJ Sound Engineer Entertainment Lawyer
Logical–Mathematical	Math Accounting Physics Economics Medicine Banking/Finance Astronomy Computer Science Systems Theory Law Chemistry Engineering	Law Firm Health Care Office Real Estate Brokerage Accounting Firm Animal Hospital Science Lab Consulting Firm Pharmaceutical Firm Bank	Doctor, Dentist, or Veterinarian Accountant Pharmacist Chemist Physicist Systems Analyst Investment Banker Financial Analyst Computer Scientist
Verbal–Linguistic	Communications Marketing English/Literature Journalism Foreign Languages Linguistic Theory Political Science Advertising/PR	Newspaper/Magazine Network TV Affiliate Publishing House Law Firm PR/Marketing Firm Speech Therapist Ad Agency Training Company Human Resources Customer Service	Author Playwright Journalist TV/Radio Producer Literature Teacher Speech Pathologist Business Executive Copywriter or Editor
Visual–Spatial	Visual Arts Architecture Interior Design Multimedia Design Film Theory Photography Art History	Art Gallery Museum Photography Studio Design Firm Advertising Agency Theatrical Set Designer Multimedia Firm Architecture Firm Film Studio	Graphic Artist Photographer Architect Cinematographer Art Therapist Designer Cartoonist/Illustrator Art Museum Curator Art Teacher

How can you *identify and manage* learning disabilities?

Some learning disabilities cause reading problems, some create difficulties in math, and some make it difficult for students to process the language they hear. The following will help you understand learning disabilities and, should you be diagnosed with one, give you the tools to manage your disability successfully.

Identifying a learning disability

The National Center for Learning Disabilities (NCLD) defines learning disabilities in terms of what they are and what they are not:[4]

- They are neurological disorders that interfere with one's ability to store, process, and produce information.
- They do *not* include mental retardation, autism, behavioural disorders, impaired vision, hearing loss, or other physical disabilities.
- They do *not* include attention deficit disorder and attention deficit hyperactivity disorder (disorders involving consistent and problematic inattention, hyperactivity, and/or impulsivity), although these problems may accompany learning disabilities.[5]
- They often run in families and are lifelong, although learning-disabled people can use specific strategies to manage and even overcome areas of weakness.
- They must be diagnosed by professionals in order for the disabled person to receive federally funded aid.

How can you determine if you should be evaluated for a learning disability? According to the NCLD, persistent problems in any of the following areas may indicate a learning disability:[6]

- reading or reading comprehension
- math calculations, understanding language and concepts
- social skills or interpreting social cues
- following a schedule, being on time, meeting deadlines
- reading or following maps
- balancing a chequebook
- following directions, especially on multi-step tasks
- writing, sentence structure, spelling, and organizing written work

Details on specific learning disabilities appear in Key 3.6. For an evaluation, contact your school's learning centre or student health centre for a referral to a licensed professional.

Managing a learning disability

If you are diagnosed with a learning disability, focused action will help you manage it and maximize your ability to learn and succeed:

Be informed about your disability. Search the library and the Internet—try The Learning Disabilities Association of Canada at **www.ldac-taac.ca**, the NCLD at **www.ncld.org** or LD Online at **www.ldonline.org** (other Web sites are listed at the end of the chapter). Seek assistance from your school. Speak with your advisor about specific accommodations that will help you learn. Services mandated by law for students who are learning disabled include:

- extended time on tests
- note-taking assistance (for example, having a fellow student take notes for you)
- assistive technology devices (tape recorders or laptop computers)
- modified assignments
- alternative assessments and test formats

Other services are tutoring, study skills assistance, and counselling.

Be a dedicated student. Be on time and attend class. Read assignments before class. Sit where you can avoid distractions. Review notes soon after class. Spend extra time on assignments. Ask for help.

What different learning disabilities are and how to recognize them.

DISABILITY/CONDITION	WHAT ARE THE SIGNS?
Dyslexia and related reading disorders	Problems with reading (including spelling, word sequencing, and comprehension) and processing (translating written language to thought or thought to written language)
Dyscalculia (developmental arithmetic disorders)	Difficulties in recognizing numbers and symbols, memorizing facts, aligning numbers, understanding abstract concepts like fractions, and applying math to life skills (time management, gauging distance, handling money, etc.)
Developmental writing disorders	Difficulties in composing complete sentences, organizing a writing assignment, or translating thoughts coherently to the page
Handwriting disorders (dysgraphia)	Disorder characterized by writing disabilities, including writing that is distorted or incorrect. Sufferers have poor handwriting that is difficult to read because of inappropriately sized and spaced letters. The use of wrong or misspelled words is also common
Speech and language disorders	Problems with producing speech sounds, using spoken language to communicate, and/or understanding what others say
LD-related social issues	Problems in recognizing facial or vocal cues from others, controlling verbal and physical impulsivity, and respecting others' personal space
LD-related organizational issues	Difficulties in scheduling and in organizing personal, academic, and work-related materials

Source: LD Online: Learning Disabilities Information and Resources, www.ldonline.org (accessed March 17, 2004). © 2001 WETA.

Build a positive attitude. See your accomplishments in light of how far you have come. Rely on people who support you. Know that the help you receive will give you the best possible chance to learn and grow.

Sabiduría

In Spanish, the term *sabiduría* represents the two sides of learning: knowledge and wisdom. *Knowledge* involves gaining information, understanding concepts, building on what you know about how the world works. *Wisdom* is the collected meaning and significance gained from knowledge. The learning and life experiences you gain in college will build your personal *sabiduría*, which, in turn, will help you make wise personal, educational, and career choices.

Think of this concept as you acquire knowledge in your classes. Try to transform the facts and concepts you study into the building blocks of wisdom.

PERSONAL TRIUMPH

MICHAËLLE JEAN, Canada's Governor General

Former journalist Michaëlle Jean was installed as the 27th Governor General of Canada on September 27, 2005. She succeeded Adrienne Clarkson. She is the third woman to hold the position and the first black person to be appointed to the position. Prime Minister Paul Martin referred to Jean as "a woman of talent and achievement. Her personal story is nothing short of extraordinary. And extraordinary is precisely what we seek in a Governor General—who must after all represent all of Canada to all Canadians and to the rest of the world as well." Read this account of her life's journey; then use a separate piece of paper to answer the questions on page 87.

Rideau Hall in Ottawa is a long way from Port-au-Prince, Haïti, but that's where Michaëlle Jean's destiny led her.

Born on September 6, 1957, Michaëlle Jean and her family fled Haïti in 1968. Her father, a philosopher, was tortured by government officials under the rule of François "Baby Doc" Duvalier. While Canada was certainly a welcome destination for Jean's family, it wasn't without problems. She and her family experienced racism here in Canada. As a child, she was the target of racial slurs. When she was young, she remembers her classmates touching her black skin to see if it was real.

Despite the adversity she faced as a child, Jean worked to overcome these obstacles. At her swearing-in ceremony, Jean said "The story of that little girl, who watched her parents, her family, and her friends grappling with the horrors of a ruthless dictatorship, who became the woman standing before you today, is a lesson in learning to be free."

On the Personality Spectrum introduced earlier in this chapter, Jean is certainly an Adventurer and a Giver. It was that side of her personality that helped shape who she became. Her academic adventures have taken her to the University of Florence and The Catholic University of Milan. She is fluent in five languages: English, French, Haitian-Creole, Spanish, and Italian. While working on her Master's Degree in Comparative Literature at the University of Montreal, Jean was also making a difference in the community by helping those in need become free from abuse, violence and harm. Between 1979 and 1987, she worked at shelters for battered women and with immigrant aid organizations. In 1987, she helped coordinate a landmark study into abusive and violent relationships. She hopes to have given hope to those in need. "Hope has been a beacon for me since childhood and into my adult years. It is embodied in this country with its unlimited possibilities—this country that we sometimes take for granted."

She took her passion for social issues and put them on the national media agenda. For 18 years, Jean was a broadcast journalist on CBC Radio-Canada in Quebec. English-speaking Canadians recognize her as host of CBC Newsworld's documentary programs The Passionate Eye and Rough Cuts. She is also a social activist filmmaker. Her husband, Jean-Daniel Lafond, is a critically-acclaimed documentary filmmaker. Their films *L'heure de Cuba* (*Cuba's Hour*) and *Haïti dans tous nos rêves* (*Haiti In All Our Dreams*) have won critical acclaim around the world. Jean herself has won many awards for journalism, including the Amnesty International Journalism Award.

Despite some controversy when her appointment was announced, Jean summed up her philosophy on life and Canada in her inaugural speech, "I am determined that the position I occupy as of today will be more than ever a place where citizens' words will be heard, where the values of respect, tolerance and sharing that are essential to me and to all Canadians, will prevail. Those values, which are paramount to me, are linked inextricably with the Canada I love. We must eliminate the spectre of all solitudes and promote solidarity among all the citizens who make up the Canada of today."

BUILDING SKILLS
FOR ACADEMIC, CAREER, AND LIFE SUCCESS

SUCCESSFUL INTELLIGENCE
CREATIVE
PRACTICAL
ANALYTICAL
SUCCESSFUL INTELLIGENCE

Developing Successful Intelligence

Learn from the experiences of others. Look back to Michaëlle Jean's Personal Triumph on page 86. After you've read her story, relate her experience to your own life by completing the following:

Step 1. Think it through: Analyze your Learning Style or place on the Personality Spectrum. What is a passion for you as a student? As a person? How might this be explained by your learning styles or personality type?

Step 2. Think out of the box: Imagine ways of advising. You are an advisor to a student identical to yourself. Be a harsh advisor—how would you criticize your performance as a student? Then be a wise advisor, focused on tapping into learning styles information—how would you identify challenges and suggest ways to handle them?

Step 3. Make it happen: Head off your own challenges with practical strategies. You have identified your learning style and type of personality—and you have imagined what you would say as your own advisor. Now identify steps that will help you face your challenge (choosing particular courses, meeting with an advisor or instructor who can give you ideas, approaching work in particular ways, brainstorm some ways you can apply your particular style and gifts).

Team Building

Ideas about personality types. Divide into groups according to the four types of the Personality Spectrum—Thinker-dominant students in one group, Organizer-dominant students in another, Giver-dominant students in a

create your future

third, and Adventurer-dominant students in the fourth. If you have scored the same in more than one of these types, join whatever group is smaller. With your group, brainstorm the following lists for your type:

1. the strengths of this type
2. the struggles it brings
3. the stressors (things that cause stress) for this type
4. career areas that tend to suit this type
5. career areas that are a challenge for this type
6. people who annoy this type the most (often because they are strong in areas where this type needs to grow)

If there is time, each group can present this information to the entire class; this will boost understanding and acceptance of diverse ways of relating to information and people.

Writing

DISCOVERY THROUGH JOURNALING

Record your thoughts on a separate piece of paper or in a journal.

Strengths and weaknesses. What have the personal assessments in this chapter taught you about your strengths? Choose what you consider your greatest strength and discuss how you plan to use it to your advantage this semester. What areas of weakness did the assessments highlight? Choose a weakness that has given you difficulty in school and brainstorm ways to compensate for it this semester. Finally, brainstorm ideas for how you will deal this semester with the kinds of people who challenge you the most.

Career Portfolio

PLAN FOR SUCCESS

Complete the following. If you can, use a graphics program, or use a separate sheet of paper.

Self-portrait. Because self-knowledge helps you to make the best choices about your future, a self-portrait is an important step in your career exploration. Use this exercise to synthesize everything you have been exploring about yourself into one comprehensive "self-portrait." Design your portrait in "think link" style, using words and visual shapes to describe your dominant Multiple Intelligences and Personality Spectrum dimensions, values, abilities, career interests, and anything else that is an important part of who you are.

A "think link" is a visual construction of related ideas, similar to a map or web, that represents your thought process. Ideas are written inside geometric shapes, often boxes or circles, and related ideas and facts are attached to those ideas by lines that connect the shapes. See the note-taking section in Chapter 6 for more about think links.

Use the style shown in the example in Key 3.7 or create your own. For example, in this exercise you may want to create a "wheel" of ideas coming off your central shape, entitled "Me." Then, spreading out from each of those ideas (interests, learning style, etc.), draw lines connecting all of the thoughts that go along with that idea. Connected to "Interests," for example, might be "singing," "stock market," and "history."

You don't have to use the wheel image. You might want to design a treelike think link or a line of boxes with connecting thoughts written below the boxes, or anything else you like. Let your design reflect who you are, just as what you write does.

One example of a self-portrait.

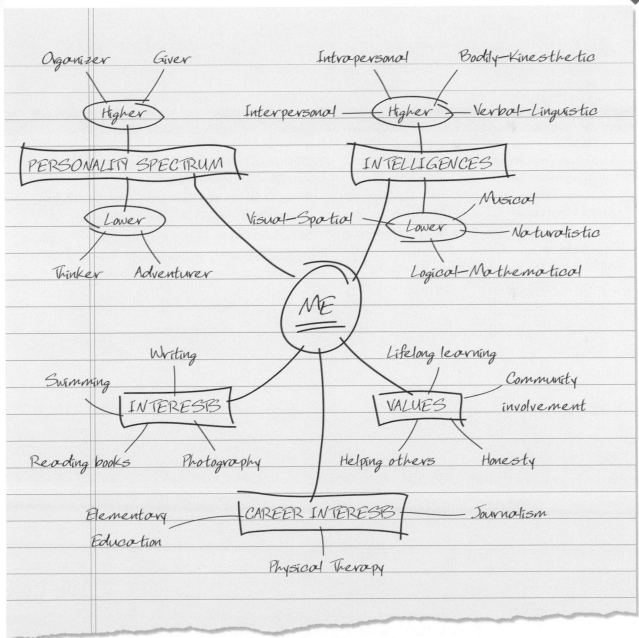

SUGGESTED READINGS

Cobb, Joyanne. *Learning How to Learn: A Guide for Getting into College with a Learning Disability, Staying in, and Staying Sane*. Washington, DC: Child Welfare League of America, 2001.

College Board, ed. *The College Board Index of Majors and Graduate Degrees 2001*. New York: College Entrance Examination Board, 2000.

Gardner, Howard. *Intelligence Reframed: Multiple Intelligences for the 21st Century*. New York: Basic Books, 2000.

Fogg, Neeta, et al. *The College Majors Handbook with Real Career Paths and Payoffs: The Actual Jobs, Earnings, and Trends for Graduates of 60 College Majors*. Indianapolis, IN: Jist Works, 2004.

Keirsey, David. *Please Understand Me II: Temperament, Character, Intelligence*. Del Mar, CA: Prometheus Nemesis Book Company, 1998.

Pearman, Roger R., and Sarah C. Albritton. *I'm Not Crazy, I'm Just Not You: The Real Meaning of the 16 Personality Types*. Palo Alto, CA: Consulting Psychologists Press, 1997.

Phifer, Paul. *College Majors and Careers: A Resource Guide for Effective Life Planning*, 4th ed. Chicago: Ferguson Publishing, 1999.

Sclafani, Annette. *College Guide for Students with Learning Disabilities*. New York: Laurel Publications, 2003.

INTERNET RESOURCES

If you think you may have a learning disorder, check out the following resources:

The Learning Disabilities Association of Canada: www.ldac-taac.ca

Canadian Learning Disabilities Resource Community: www.ldrc.ca

Attention Deficit Disorder Association: www.add.org

Children and Adults with Attention Deficit/Hyperactivity Disorder: www.chadd.org

International Dyslexia Association: www.interdys.org

Learning Disabilities Online: www.ldonline.org

National Center for Learning Disabilities: www.ncld.org

Find out more about your personality type with Myers & Briggs online: www.myersbriggs.org

1. Howard Gardner, *Multiple Intelligences: The Theory in Practice*. New York: HarperCollins, 1993, pp. 5–49.

2. Ibid, p. 7.

3. Developed by Joyce Bishop, Ph.D., Golden West College, Huntington Beach, CA. Based on Howard Gardner, *Frames of Mind: The Theory of Multiple Intelligences*. New York: HarperCollins, 1993.

4. National Center for Learning Disabilities. "LD at a Glance" [on-line]. Available at www.ncld.org/LDInfoZone/InfoZone_FactSheet_LD.cfm (May 2003).

5. National Center for Learning Disabilities. "Adult Learning Disabilities: A Learning Disability Isn't Something You Outgrow. It's Something You Learn to Master" [pamphlet]. New York: National Center for Learning Disabilities.

6. National Center for Learning Disabilities. "LD Advocates Guide" [on-line]. Available at www.ld.org/Advocacy/tutorial_talking_about.cfm (May 2003).

C R E A T E

4

IN THIS CHAPTER

In this chapter you will explore answers to the following questions: • What is successfully intelligent thinking? • How can you improve your analytical thinking skills? • How can you improve your creative thinking skills? • How can you improve your practical thinking skills? • How can you put *analytical, creative, and practical thinking together* to solve a problem or make a decision?

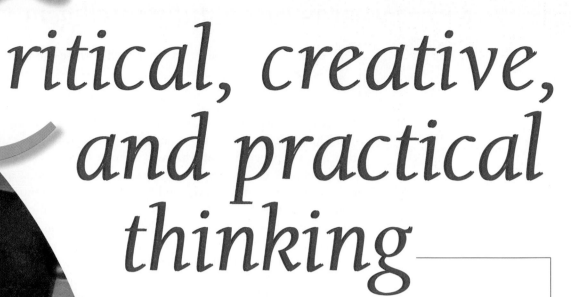

Critical, creative, and practical thinking

TO SURVIVE and to thrive in college and beyond, you will need to use your thinking power to do more than remember formulas for a test. When problems or decisions arise on the road toward goals large and small, how can you work through them successfully? The answer lies in how you combine your analytical, creative, and practical thinking skills—in other words, how you use your successful intelligence. As you remember from Chapter 1, successful intelligence is "the kind of intelligence used to achieve important goals."[1]

Thinking, like note taking or car repair, is a skill that can be developed with practice. This chapter will help you build your ability to analyze information, come up with creative ideas, and put a practical plan into action. With these skills you can become a better thinker, problem solver, and decision maker, able to reach the goals that mean the most to you. This ability is emphasized by the Conference Board of Canada's Employability Skills 2000+ report in which employers underline the significance of being able to "assess situations, identify problems and then evaluate and implement solutions."

solving problems and making decisions

What is *successfully intelligent* thinking?

Robert Sternberg uses this story to illustrate the impact of successful intelligence:

Two boys are walking in a forest. They are quite different. The first boy's teachers think he is smart, his parents think he is smart, and as a result, he thinks he is smart. He has good test scores, good grades, and other good paper credentials that will get him far in his scholastic life.

Few people consider the second boy smart. His test scores are nothing great, his grades aren't so good, and his other paper credentials are, in general, marginal. At best, people would call him shrewd or street smart.

As the two boys walk along in the forest, they encounter a problem—a huge, furious, hungry-looking grizzly bear, charging straight at them. The first boy, calculating that the grizzly bear will overtake them in 17.3 seconds, panics. In this state, he looks at the second boy, who is calmly taking off his hiking boots and putting on his jogging shoes.

The first boy says to the second boy, "You must be crazy. There is no way you are going to outrun that grizzly bear!"

The second boy replies, "That's true. But all I have to do is outrun you!"[2]

This story shows that successful problem solving and decision making require more than "book smarts." When confronted with a problem, using only analytical thinking put the first boy at a disadvantage. On the other hand, the second boy thought in different ways; he analyzed the situation, creatively considered the options, and took practical action. He asked and answered questions. He knew his purpose. And he lived to tell the tale.

Successfully intelligent thinking is balanced

Some tasks require only one thinking skill or ability at a time. You might use analytical thinking to complete a multiple-choice quiz, creative thinking to figure out how to get a paper done the same day you work a long shift, or practical thinking to put together a desk marked "some assembly required." However, when you need to solve a problem or make a decision, your analytical, creative, and practical thinking skills build upon one another to move you forward.[3] Envision it this way: Just as a pyramid needs three sides in order to stand, successful thinkers need all three thinking skills to develop the best solutions and decisions (see Key 4.1).

Each thinking skill adds an important dimension to accomplishing goals. Developing a balanced set of skills and knowing how and when to use each of them gives you more thinking power than having a strong aptitude in any one ability.[4] This kind of flexible thinking will help you connect your academic tasks to life goals—and show you where your hard work can take you (see Key 4.2).

Successful intelligence depends on three thinking skills.

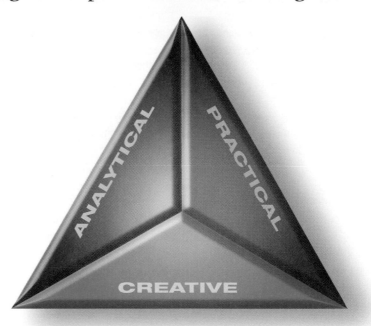

Successfully intelligent thinking means asking and answering questions

What is thinking? According to experts, it is what happens when you ask questions and move toward the answers.[5] "To think through or rethink anything," says Dr. Richard Paul, director of research at the Center for Critical Thinking and Moral Critique, "one must ask questions that stimulate our thought. Questions define tasks, express problems and delineate issues.... [O]nly students who have questions are really thinking and learning."[6]

As you answer questions, you transform raw data into information that you can use. A *Wall Street Journal* article entitled "The Best Innovations Are Those That Come from Smart Questions" relates the story of a cell biology student, William Hunter, whose professor told him that "the difference between good science and great science is the quality of the questions posed." Later, as a doctor and the president and CEO of a pharmaceutical company, Dr. Hunter asked questions about new ways to use drugs. His questions led to the development of a revolutionary product—a drug-coated coronary stent that prevents scar tissue from forming. Through seeking answers to probing questions, Dr. Hunter reached a significant goal.[7]

You use questions in order to analyze ("How bad is my money situation?"), come up with creative ideas ("What ways could I earn money?"), and apply practical solutions ("How can I get a job on campus?"). Later in the chapter, in the sections on analytical, creative, and practical thinking, you will find examples of the kinds of questions that drive each skill.

Like any aspect of thinking, questioning is not often a straightforward process. Sometimes the answer doesn't come right away. Often the answer leads to more—and more specific—questions.

DISCIPLINE	ANALYTICAL THINKING	CREATIVE THINKING	PRACTICAL THINKING
Behavioural Science	Comparing one theory of child development with another	Devising a new theory of child development	Applying child development theories to help parents and teachers understand and deal with children more effectively
Literature	Analyzing the development of the main character in a novel	Writing alternative endings to the novel	Using the experience of the main character to better understand and manage one's own life situations
History	Considering similarities and differences between WWI and WWII	Imagining yourself as a German citizen, dealing with economic depression after WWI	Seeing what WWI and WWII lessons can be applied to current Middle East conflicts
Sports	Analyzing the opposing team's strategy on the soccer field	Coming up with innovative ways to move the ball downfield	Using tactics to hide your strategy from an opposing team—or a competing company

Source: Adapted from Robert J. Sternberg, *Successful Intelligence*. Plume: New York, 1997, p. 149.

Successfully intelligent thinking requires knowing your purpose

In order to ask useful questions, you need to know *why* you are questioning. In other words, you need to define your purpose. Not knowing your purpose may lead you to ask questions that take you in irrelevant directions and waste your time. For example, if an assignment asks you to analyze the effectiveness of Canada's foreign policy during Jean Chrétien's tenure as prime minister, asking questions about his personal life may lead you off the track.

A general question can be your starting point for defining your purposes: "What am I trying to accomplish, and why?" Then, within each stage of the process, you will find more specific purposes or sub-goals that help you generate analytical, creative, or practical questions along the way.

Successfully intelligent thinking is yours to build

You can improve your ability to think, now and throughout your life. Studies have shown that the brain continues to develop throughout your life if you continue to learn new things.[8] Puzzle master Nob Yoshigahara has said, "As jogging is to the body, thinking is to the brain. The more we do it, the better we become."[9]

The mini-assessments within this chapter will help you to get an idea of how you perceive yourself as an analytical, creative, and practical thinker. Every other chapter's set of *Get Analytical*, *Get Creative*, and *Get Practical* exercises then helps you to build your skills in those areas. Finally, the *Developing Successful Intelligence*: *Putting It All Together* exercises at the ends of chapters encourage you to both build and combine your skills. *Your work throughout the book is geared toward building your successful intelligence.*

Begin by exploring the analytical thinking skills that you'll need in order to solve problems and make decisions effectively.

How can you improve your *analytical thinking skills?*

A nalytical thinking—also known as critical thinking—is the process of gathering information, analyzing it in different ways, and evaluating it for the purposes of gaining understanding, solving a problem, or making a decision. It is as essential for real-life problems and decisions as it is for thinking through the hypothetical questions on your chemistry homework.

The first step in analytical thinking, as with all aspects of successful intelligence, is to define your purpose. What do you want to analyze, and why? Perhaps you need to analyze the plot of a novel in order to determine its structure; maybe you want to analyze your schedule in order to figure out whether you are arranging your time and responsibilities effectively.

Once you define your purpose, the rest of the analytical process involves gathering the necessary information, analyzing and clarifying the ideas, and evaluating what you've found.

Gather information

Information is the raw material for thinking. Choosing what to gather requires a careful analysis of how much information you need, how much time to spend gathering it, and whether the information is relevant. Say, for instance, that your assignment is to write a paper on rock 'n' roll music in Canada. If you gathered every available resource on the topic, it might be next semester before you got to the writing stage.

Here's how you might use analysis to effectively gather information for that paper:

- Reviewing the assignment, you learn that the paper should be ten pages and cover at least three influential Canadian musicians.
- At the library and on-line, you find a lot of what appears to be relevant information.
- You choose Neil Young, Randy Bachman, and Joni Mitchell, and then select three in-depth sources on each of the three musicians and how they influenced the development of rock music in Canada.

In this way you achieve a sub-goal—a selection of useful materials—on the way to your larger goal of writing a well-crafted paper.

Analyze and clarify information

Once you've gathered the information, the next step is to analyze it to determine whether the information is reliable and useful in helping you answer your questions.

Break information into parts

When analyzing information, you break information into parts and examine the parts so that you can see how they relate to each other and to information you already know. The following strategies help you break information down into pieces and set aside what is unclear, unrelated, or unimportant, resulting in a deeper and more reliable understanding.

Separate the ideas. If you are reading about Neil Young, you might want to break down his career and significant contributions to music as a solo artist, and as a member of The Mynah Birds, Buffalo Springfield, and Crosby, Stills, Nash, and Young. You might also want to separate his contributions as a performer and as a songwriter.

Compare and contrast. Look at how things are similar to, or different from, each other. You might explore how these three musicians are similar in style. You might look at how they differ in what they want to communicate with their music.

Examine cause and effect. Look at the possible reasons why something happened (possible causes) and its consequences (effects, both positive and negative). You might also wish to examine which contemporary Canadian musicians were influenced by Neil Young or how the grunge movement of the 1990s was inspired by Young.

Look for themes, patterns, and categories. Note connections that arise out of how bits of information relate to one another. You may choose to write about the theme of social and political consciousness in the lyrics of Neil Young. What category would Neil Young's music best fit into: rock or folk?

> If one wants to be successful, one must think; one must think until it hurts.

ROY THOMSON

Once the ideas are broken down, you can examine whether examples support ideas, separate fact from opinion, consider perspective, and investigate hidden assumptions.

Examine whether examples support ideas

When you encounter an idea or claim, examine how it is supported with examples or evidence (facts, expert opinion, research findings, personal experience, and so on). Ideas that aren't backed up with solid evidence or made concrete with examples are not useful. Be critical of the information you gather; don't take it at face value.

For example, an advertisement for a weight-loss pill claiming that it allows users to drop a pound a day, quotes "Anne" who says that she lost 30 pounds in 30 days. The word of one person, who may or may not be telling the truth, is not adequate support. On the other hand, a claim that water once existed on Mars, backed up by measurements and photography from one of the Mars Exploration Rovers, may prove more reliable.

Distinguish fact from opinion

A *statement of fact* is information presented as objectively real and verifiable ("It's raining outside right now"). In contrast, a *statement of opinion* is a belief, conclusion, or judgment that is inherently difficult, and sometimes impossible, to verify ("This is the most miserable rainstorm ever"). Key 4.3 defines important characteristics of fact and opinion. Finding credible, reliable information with which to answer questions and come up with ideas enables you to separate fact from opinion. Even though facts may seem more solid, you can also make use of opinions if you determine that they are backed up with facts. However, it is important to examine opinions for their underlying perspectives and assumptions.

Examine perspectives and assumptions

Perspective is a characteristic way of thinking about people, situations, events, and ideas. Perspectives can be broad, such as a generally optimistic or pessimistic view of life. Or they can be more focused, such as an attitude about whether students should commute or live on campus.

Shifting your perspective helps you accept and understand different ways of living and interacting. Two students communicate via sign language while walking on campus.

Perspectives are associated with *assumptions*—judgments, generalizations, or biases influenced by experience and values. For example, the perspective that there are many different successful ways to be a family leads to assumptions such as "Single-parent homes can provide nurturing environments" and "Same-sex couples can rear well-adjusted children." Having a particular experience with single-parent homes or same-sex couples can build or reinforce a perspective.

Assumptions often hide within questions and statements, blocking you from considering information in different ways. Take this classic puzzler as an example: "Which came first, the chicken or the egg?" Thinking about this question, most people assume that the egg is a chicken egg. If you think past that assumption and come up with a new idea—such as, the egg is a dinosaur egg—then the obvious answer is that the egg came first!

Examining perspectives and assumptions is important for two reasons. First, they often affect your perception of the validity of materials you read and research. Second, your own perspectives and assumptions can cloud your interpretation of the information you encounter.

Perspectives and assumptions in information

Being able to determine the perspectives that underlie materials will help you separate **biased** from unbiased information. For example, the conclusions in two articles on federal versus provincial government control of education may differ radically if one appears in a politically conservative publication and one appears in a liberal publication. Comparing those articles will

BIASED
Leaning in a particular direction; influenced by a point of view.

OPINIONS INCLUDE STATEMENTS THAT . . .	FACTS INCLUDE STATEMENTS THAT . . .
. . . *show evaluation.* Any statement of value indicates an opinion. Words such as *bad, good, pointless,* and *beneficial* indicate value judgments. Example: "Bob Geldof is the most socially consious rock star ever."	. . . *deal with actual people, places, objects, or events.* Example: "In 1985, Bob Geldof organized Live Aid, which raised money and awareness for famine relief in Africa. In 2005, Live8 helped push the G8 Summit agenda into the mainstream."
. . . *use abstract words.* Words that are complicated to define, like *misery* or *success,* usually indicate a personal opinion. Example: "The charity event was a smashing success."	. . . *use concrete words or measurable statistics.* Example: "The charity event raised $5,862."
. . . *predict future events.* Statements that examine future occurrences are often opinions. Example: "Mr. Maurin's course is going to set a new environment record this year."	. . . *describe current events in exact terms.* Example: "Mr. Maurin's course has set a new enrolment record this semester."
. . . *use emotional words.* Emotions are by nature unverifiable. Chances are that statements using such words as *delightful* or *miserable* express an opinion. Example: "That class is a miserable experience."	. . . *avoid emotional words and focus on the verifiable.* Example: "Citing dissatisfaction with the instruction, 7 out of the 25 students in that class withdrew in September."
. . . *use absolutes.* Absolute *qualifiers,* such as *all, none, never,* and *always,* often point to an opinion. Example: "All students need to have a job while in school."	. . . *avoid absolutes.* Example: "Some students need to have a job while in school."

Source: Adapted from Ben E. Johnson, *Stirring Up Thinking.* New York: Houghton Mifflin, 1998, pp. 268–270.

require that you understand and take into account the conservative and liberal perspectives on government's role in education.

Assumptions often affect the validity of materials you read and research. A historical document that originated on-line at a conservative blog may assume that liberal policies on health care are flawed, but may also leave out information to the contrary. Clearly understanding such a document means separating the assumptions from the facts.

Personal perspectives and assumptions

Your own preferences, values, and prejudices—which influence your perspective—can affect how accurately you view information. A student who thinks that the death penalty is wrong, for example, may have a hard time analyzing the facts and arguments in an article that supports it. Or in a research situation, he might use only materials that agree with his perspective.

Consider the perspectives and assumptions that might follow from your values. Then when you have to analyze information, try to set them aside. "Anticipate your reactions and prejudices and then consciously resist their influence," says Colby Glass, professor of information research and philosophy.[10]

In addition to helping you analyze accurately, opening yourself to new perspectives will help you build knowledge. The more you know, the more information you have to work with as you move through life and encounter new problems and decisions. Come to school ready to hear and read about new ideas, think about their merits, and make informed decisions about what you believe. Says Sternberg, "We need to... see issues from a variety of viewpoints and, especially, to see how other people and other cultures view issues and problems facing the world."[11]

Evaluate information

You've gathered and analyzed your information. You have examined its components, its evidence, its validity, its perspective, and any underlying assumptions. Now, based on an examination of evidence and careful analysis, you *evaluate* whether an idea or piece of information is good or bad, important or unimportant, right or wrong. You then set aside what is not useful and use the rest to form an opinion, possible solution, or decision.

For example, you're working on a group presentation on the effects of television-watching on young children. You've gathered information that relates to your topic, come up with an idea, and analyzed whether the information supports this idea. Now you evaluate all of the evidence and present what's useful in an organized, persuasive way. Another example: In creating a résumé, you decide which information to include that will generate the most interest in potential employers and present you in the best light possible.

See Key 4.4 for some questions you can ask to build and use analytical thinking skills.

Analytical thinking is only part of the picture. Pursuing your goals in school and in the workplace requires not just analyzing information but also thinking creatively about how to use it.

ASSESS ANALYTICAL THINKING SKILLS

get analytical!

How do you perceive yourself as an analytical thinker? For each statement, circle the number that feels right to you, from 1 for "least like me" to 5 for "most like me."

1. I tend to perform well on objective tests.　　　　　　　　　　1　2　3　4　5
2. People say I'm a "thinker," "brainy," "studious."　　　　　　　1　2　3　4　5
3. I am not comfortable with grey areas—I prefer information to be laid out in black and white.　　　　　　　　　　　　　　　1　2　3　4　5
4. In a group setting, I like to tackle the details of a problem.　　1　2　3　4　5
5. I sometimes over-think things and miss my moment of opportunity.　1　2　3　4　5

Total your answers here: _____

If your total ranges from 5–12, you consider your analytical thinking skills to be weak.

If your total ranges from 13–19, you consider your analytical thinking skills to be average.

If your total ranges from 20–25, you consider your analytical thinking skills to be strong.

Ask questions like these in order to analyze.

To gather information, ask:	• What requirements does my goal have?
	• What kinds of information do I need to meet my goal?
	• What information is available?
	• Where and when is it available? Where and when can I access it?
	• Of the sources I found, which ones will best help me achieve my goal?

To analyze, ask:	• What are the parts of this information?
	• What is similar to this information? What is different?
	• What are the reasons for this? Why did this happen?
	• What ideas or themes emerge from this material?
	• How would you categorize this information?
	• What conclusions can you make about this information?

To see if examples support an idea, ask:	• What examples, or evidence, support the idea?
	• Does the evidence make sense?
	• Does the evidence support the idea/claim?
	• Is this evidence key information that I need to answer my question?
	• Are there examples that might disprove the idea/claim?

To distinguish fact from opinion, ask:	• Do the words in this information signal fact or opinion? (See Key 4.3)
	• What is the source of this information? Is the source reliable?
	• How does this information compare to other facts or opinions?
	• If this is an opinion, is it supported by facts?
	• How can I use this fact or opinion?

To examine perspectives and assumptions, ask:	• Who is the author? What perspectives might this person have?
	• What might be emphasized or left out as a result of the perspective?
	• How could I consider this information from a different perspective?
	• What assumptions might lie behind this statement or material?
	• How could I prove or disprove an assumption?
	• What contradictory assumptions might be equally valid?
	• How might a personal perspective or assumption affect the way I see this material?

To evaluate, ask:	• Do I agree with this information?
	• Does this information fit what I'm trying to prove or accomplish?
	• Is this information true or false, and why?
	• How important is this information?
	• Which ideas or pieces of information would I choose to focus on?

Adapted from www.ed.fnal.gov/trc/tutorial/taxonomy.html (Richard Paul, *Critical Thinking: How to Prepare Students for a Rapidly Changing World,* 1993) and from www.kcmetro.edu/longview/ctac/blooms.htm, Barbara Fowler, Longview Community College "Bloom's Taxonomy and Critical Thinking."

How can you improve your *creative thinking* skills?

Some researchers define creativity as combining existing elements in an innovative way to create a new purpose or result. For example, in 1970, 3M researcher Spencer Silver created a weak adhesive; four years later, another 3M scientist, Arthur Fry, used it for a hymnal marker. Post-it® Notes are now an office staple. Others see creativity as the art of generating ideas from taking a fresh look at how things are related (noting what ladybugs eat inspired organic farmers to bring them in to consume crop-destroying aphids).[12] Still others, including Sternberg, define it as the ability to make unusual connections—to view information in quirky ways that bring about unique results.

To think creatively is to generate new ideas that often go against conventional wisdom and may bring change. Consider how, in the 1940s, mathematician Grace Murray Hopper pioneered the effort to create computer languages that non-mathematicians could understand; her efforts opened the world of computers to a wide audience.

Creativity is not limited to inventions. For example, when she was in her first year of college, Meghan E. Taugher used her creative mind in two ways. First, she and her study group, as part of their class on electrical circuits, devised a solar-powered battery for a laptop computer. "We took the professor's laptop, put all the parts together, and sat outside watching it with a little device to see how much power it was saving. When it fully charged the battery, it was one of those times I felt that what I was learning was true, because I was putting it to use in real life."[13] Second, her experience led her to generate an idea of a new major and career plan—engineering.

Creativity forms a bridge between analytical and practical thinking (see Key 4.5). You need to think analytically to evaluate the quality of your creative ideas. You also need to think practically to implement them.

Where does creativity come from? Some people, through luck or natural inclination, seem to come up with inspired ideas more often than others. However, creative thinking, like analytical thinking, is a skill that can be developed. Creativity expert Roger von Oech says that mental flexibility is essential. "Like race-car drivers who shift in and out of different gears depending on where they are on the course," he says, you can enhance your creativity by learning to "shift in and out of different types of thinking depending on the needs of the situation at hand."[14]

The following strategies will help you make those shifts and build your ability to think creatively. Note that, because creative ideas often pop up at random, writing them down as they arise will help

These students, working through a problem for a course, demonstrate that successful problem solving often requires the input and teamwork of a group of people.

4.5

you remember them. Keep a pen and paper by your bed, your BlackBerry or your Palm Pilot in your pocket, and a notepad in your car so that you can grab ideas before they fade from your mind.

Brainstorm

Brainstorming—letting your mind free-associate to come up with different ideas or answers—is also referred to as *divergent thinking*: You start with a question and then let your mind diverge—go in many different directions—in search of solutions. Think of brainstorming as *deliberate* creative thinking—you go into it fully aware that you are attempting to create new ideas. When you brainstorm, generate ideas without thinking about how useful they are; evaluate their quality later. Brainstorming works well in groups because group members can become inspired by, and make creative use of, one another's ideas.[15]

One way to inspire ideas when brainstorming is to think of similar situations—in other words, to make analogies. For example, the discovery of Velcro is a product of **analogy:** When imagining how two pieces of fabric could stick to each other, the inventor thought of the similar situation of a burr sticking to clothing.

When you are brainstorming ideas, don't get hooked on finding the one right answer. Questions may have many "right answers"—or many answers that have degrees of usefulness. The more possibilities you generate, the better your chance of finding the best one. Also, don't stop the process when you think you have the best answer—keep going until you are out of steam. You never know what may come up in those last gasps of creative energy.[16]

Shift your perspective

Just because everyone believes something doesn't make it so; just because something "has always been that way" doesn't make it good. Changing

ANALOGY
A comparison based on a resemblance of things that are otherwise unalike.

Ask these questions to jump-start creativity.

To brainstorm, ask:	• What do I want to accomplish?
	• What are the craziest ideas I can think of?
	• What are ten ways that I can reach my goal?
	• What ideas or strategies have worked before and how can I apply them?
	• How else can this be done?
To shift your perspective, ask:	• How has this always been done—and what would be a different way?
	• What is another way to look at this situation?
	• How can I approach this task from a completely new angle?
	• How would others do this? How would they view this?
	• What if . . . ?
To set the stage for creativity, ask:	• Where and with whom do I feel relaxed and inspired?
	• What music helps me think out of the box?
	• When in the day or night am I most likely to experience a flow of creative ideas?
	• What do I think would be new and interesting to try, to see, to read?
	• What is the most outrageous outcome of a situation that I can imagine?
To take risks, ask:	• What is the conventional way of doing this? What would be a totally different way?
	• What would be a risky approach to this problem or question?
	• What choice would people caution me about and why?
	• What is the worst that can happen if I take this risk? What is the best?
	• What have I learned from this mistake?

Let mistakes be okay. Open yourself to the learning that comes from not being afraid to mess up. Sternberg reports that "in the course of their schooling... children learn that it's not all right to make mistakes. As a result, they become afraid to err and thus to risk the kind of independent, if sometimes flawed, thinking" that can promote creative ideas.[22] When Dr. Hunter—successful inventor of the drug-coated coronary stent—and his company failed to develop a particular treatment for multiple sclerosis, he said, "You have to celebrate the failures. If you send the message that the only road to career success is experiments that work, people won't ask risky questions, or get any dramatically new answers."[23]

As with analytical thinking, asking questions powers creative thinking. See Key 4.7 for examples of the kinds of questions you can ask to get your creative juices flowing.

When you are working to solve a problem or make a decision, creative thinking allows you to generate possible solutions and choices. However, choices aren't enough and potential solutions must be tried out. You need practical thinking in order to make the best solution or choice happen.

get creative!

ASSESS CREATIVE THINKING SKILLS

How do you perceive yourself as a creative thinker? For each statement, circle the number that feels right to you, from 1 for "least like me" to 5 for "most like me."

1. I tend to resist rules and regulations.   ① ② ③ ④ ⑤
2. People say I'm "expressive," "full of ideas," "innovative."   ① ② ③ ④ ⑤
3. I break out of my routine and find new experiences.   ① ② ③ ④ ⑤
4. In a group setting, I like to toss ideas into the ring.   ① ② ③ ④ ⑤
5. If you say something is too risky, I'm all for it.   ① ② ③ ④ ⑤

Total your answers here: _____

If your total ranges from 5–12, you consider your creative thinking skills to be weak.

If your total ranges from 13–19, you consider your creative thinking skills to be average.

If your total ranges from 20–25, you consider your creative thinking skills to be strong.

How can you improve your *practical thinking skills?*

Practical thinking—also called "common sense" or "street smarts"—refers to how you adapt to your environment, or shape or change your environment to adapt to you, in order to pursue important goals. A basic example: Your goal is to pass your required composition course. You are a visual learner in a verbally focused classroom. To achieve your goal, you can build your verbal skills (adapt to your environment) or ask the instructor and your study group to help you present information in visual terms (change your environment to adapt to you)—or both.

Why do you need to think practically? Since many academic problems can be solved with analytical thinking alone, it's easy to get the impression that strong analytical thinking skills translate into life success. However, real-world problems are different from many academic problems—they are often less clear, related closely to your life and needs, and answerable in more than one way. Plus, stakes are often higher—in other words, the way you solve a financial dilemma has a more significant impact on your life than how you work through a geometry proof. Successfully solving real-world problems demands a practical approach.[24]

Practical thinking allows you to bridge the gap between what makes a successful student and what brings real-world success. In other words, even if you ace the courses for your math and education double major, you also need to be able to apply what you learned in a specific job.

Experience helps develop practical thinking skills

You gain much of your ability to think practically—your common sense—from personal experience, rather than from formal lessons. This knowledge is an important tool in achieving goals.[25]

What you learn from experience answers "how" questions—how to talk, how to behave, how to proceed.[26] For example, after completing a few papers for a particular course, you may pick up cues about how to impress that instructor. Following a couple of conflicts with a partner, you may learn how to avoid sore spots when the conversation heats up. See Key 4.8 for ways in which this kind of knowledge can be shown in "if–then" statements.

There are two keys to making practical knowledge work for you. First, make an active choice to learn from experience—to pay attention to how things work at school, in personal relationships, and at work. Second, make sure you apply what you learn, assuring that you will not have to learn the same lessons over and over again. As Sternberg says, "What matters most is not how much experience you have had but rather how much you have profited from it—in other words, how well you apply what you have learned."[27]

The emotional intelligence connection

Part of what you learn from experience involves *emotional intelligence.* Based on the work of psychologist Daniel Goleman, your emotional

One way to map out what you learn from experience.

Goal: You want to talk to the soccer coach about your status on the team.

IF the team has had a good practice and IF you've played well during the scrimmage and IF the coach isn't rushing off some-where, THEN grab a moment with him right after practice ends.

IF the team is having a tough time and IF you've been sidelined and IF the coach is in a rush and stressed, THEN drop in on his office hours tomorrow.

intelligence quotient (EQ) is the set of personal and social competencies that involve knowing yourself, mastering your feelings, and developing social skills.[28] *Social competence*—involving skills such as sensing other people's feelings and needs, getting your message across to others, managing conflict, leading and bonding with people—usually is built through experience rather than by reading theory or a how-to manual.

Emotional intelligence has a significant effect on your ability to communicate and manoeuvre in a social environment in a way that helps you achieve your goals. It will be examined in greater detail in the section on communication and diversity in Chapter 9.

Practical thinking means action

Learning different ways to take action and stay in motion builds your practical thinking ability. Strategies you learn throughout this course will keep you moving toward your goals:[29]

- **Stay motivated.** Use techniques from Chapter 1 to persevere when you face a problem. Get started on achieving results instead of dwelling on exactly how to start. Translate thoughts into concrete actions instead of getting bogged down in "analysis paralysis."

- **Make the most of your personal strengths.** What you've learned in Chapter 2 will help you see what you do best—and use those strengths as you apply practical solutions.

- **When things go wrong, accept responsibility and reject self-pity.** You know from Chapter 1 that failure is an excellent teacher. Learn from what happened, act on what you have learned, and don't let self-pity stall your momentum.

- **Focus on the goal and avoid distractions.** Keep your eye on the big picture and complete what you've planned, rather than getting lost in the details. Don't let personal problems or other distractions take you off the track.

- **Manage time and tasks effectively.** Use what you know from Chapter 2 to plan your time in a way that promotes goal accomplishment. Avoid the pitfalls of procrastination. Accurately gauge what you can handle—don't take on too many projects, or too few.

- **Believe in yourself.** Have faith in your ability to achieve what you set out to do.

See Key 4.9 for some questions you can ask in order to apply practical thinking to your problems and decisions.

Ask questions like these to activate practical thinking.

To learn from experience, ask:	• What worked well, or not so well, about my approach? My timing? My tone? My wording?
	• What did others like or not like about what I did?
	• What did I learn from that experience, conversation, event?
	• How would I change things if I had to do it over again?
	• What do I know I would do again?
To apply what you learn, ask:	• What have I learned that would work here?
	• What have I seen others do, or heard about from them, that would be helpful here?
	• What does this situation have in common with past situations I've been involved in?
	• What has worked in similar situations in the past?
To boost your ability to take action, ask:	• How can I get motivated and remove limitations?
	• How can I, in this situation, make the most of what I do well?
	• If I fail, what can I learn from it?
	• What steps will get me to my goal, and what trade-offs are involved?
	• How can I manage my time more effectively?

ASSESS PRACTICAL THINKING SKILLS

get practical!

How do you perceive yourself as a practical thinker? For each statement, circle the number that feels right to you, from 1 for "least like me" to 5 for "most like me."

1. I can find a way around any obstacle.   1 2 3 4 5
3. When I have a vision, I translate it into steps from A to B to C.   1 2 3 4 5
4. In a group setting, I like to set up the plan.   1 2 3 4 5
5. I don't like to leave loose ends dangling—I'm a finisher.   1 2 3 4 5

Total your answers here: _____

If your total ranges from 5–12, you consider your practical thinking skills to be weak.

If your total ranges from 13–19, you consider your practical thinking skills to be average.

If your total ranges from 20–25, you consider your practical thinking skills to be strong.

Your skills at a glance: In the sections of the triangle, write your assessment scores from *Get Analytical*, *Get Creative*, and *Get Practical* from this chapter. Looking at the scores together will give you an idea of how you perceive your skills in all three aspects of successful intelligence, and will help you think about where you may want to build strength.

PROBLEM SOLVING	THINKING SKILL	DECISION MAKING
Define the problem—recognize that something needs to change, identify what's happening, look for true causes	**STEP 1** DEFINE	Define the decision—identify your goal (your need) and then construct a decision that will help you get it
Analyze the problem—gather information, break it down into pieces, verify facts, look at perspectives and assumptions, evaluate information	**STEP 2** ANALYZE	Examine needs and motives—consider the layers of needs carefully, and be honest about what you really want
Generate possible solutions—use creative strategies to think of ways you could address the causes of this problem	**STEP 3** CREATE	Name and/or generate different options—use creative questions to come up with choices that would fulfill your needs
Evaluate solutions—look carefully at potential pros and cons of each, and choose what seems best	**STEP 4** ANALYZE (EVALUATE)	Evaluate options—look carefully at potential pros and cons of each, and choose what seems best
Put the solution to work—persevere, focus on results, and believe in yourself as you go for your goal	**STEP 5** TAKE PRACTICAL ACTION	Act on your decision—go down the path and use practical strategies to stay on target
Evaluate how well the solution worked—look at the effects of what you did	**STEP 6** ANALYZE (RE-EVALUATE)	Evaluate the success of your decision—look at whether it accomplished what you had hoped
In the future, apply what you've learned—use this solution, or a better one, when a similar situation comes up again	**STEP 7** TAKE PRACTICAL ACTION	In the future, apply what you've learned—make this choice, or a better one, when a similar decision comes up again

How can you put *analytical, creative, and practical thinking together* to solve a problem or make a decision?

You have developed your understanding of what it means to think analytically, creatively, and practically. You have explored your perception of where your strengths and weaknesses lie. Now you will see how to put analytical, creative, and practical thinking together to solve problems and make decisions successfully—at school, in the workplace, or in your personal life.

Problem solving and decision making follow similar paths. Both require you to identify and analyze a situation, generate possibilities, choose one, follow through on it, and evaluate its success. Key 4.10 gives an overview of the paths, indicating how you think at each step.

How do you choose which path to follow? Understanding the differences will help. First of all, problem solving generally requires more focus on coming up with possible solutions; when you face a decision, your choices are often determined. Second, problem solving aims to remove or

Examine how problems and decisions differ.

SITUATION	YOU HAVE A PROBLEM IF . . .	YOU NEED TO MAKE A DECISION IF . . .
Planning summer activities	Your low GPA means you need to attend summer school—and you've already accepted a summer job.	You've been accepted into two summer abroad internship programs.
Declaring a major	It's time to declare but you don't have all the prerequisites for the major you want.	There are three majors that appeal to you and you qualify for them all.
Handling relationships with instructors	You are having trouble following the lecture style of a particular instructor.	Your psychology survey course has seven sections taught by different instructors; you have to choose one.

counteract negative effects; decision making aims to fulfill a need. See Key 4.11 for some examples. Remember too that, whereas all problem solving requires you to make a decision—when you decide on a solution—only some decision making requires you to solve a problem.

What approach may best help you to overcome barriers and achieve your goal? Talk to people who are where you want to be—professionally or personally—and ask them what you should anticipate.

Solving a problem

A problem exists when a situation has negative effects. Recognizing that there is a problem—being aware of those effects—is essential before you can begin to solve it. In other words, your first move is to go from the effects—"I'm unhappy/uneasy/angry"—to determining why: "My schedule is overwhelming me." "I'm over my head in this course." "My credit card debt is out of control." Then you begin the problem-solving process in earnest.

What happens if you *don't* act in a successfully intelligent way? Take, for example, a student having an issue with an instructor. He may get into an argument with the instructor during class time. He may stop showing up to class. He may not make an effort with assignments. All of these choices will most likely have bad consequences for him.

Now look at how this student might work through this problem using his analytical, creative, and practical thinking skills. Key 4.12 shows how his effort can pay off.

As you go through the problem-solving process, keep these tips in mind.

Use probing questions to define problems. Focus on causes. If you are not happy in a class, for example, you could ask questions like these:

- What do I think about when I feel unhappy?
- Do my feelings involve my instructor? My classmates?
- Is the subject matter difficult? The volume of work too much?

Chances are that how you answer one or more of these questions may lead to a clear definition—and ultimately to the right solution.

STRESSBUSTER

GABRIEL SCHROEDTER   Red River College, Winnipeg, Manitoba

Was there ever a time when you felt so stressed out that you just didn't know what to do? How did you get back on track?

Late last year I was running into a potential catastrophe. I had presentations and supporting material to work on, final exams, as well as writing and layout for five pages of a magazine project. My truck was leaking gas constantly, making any driving a stress that I didn't need. I felt like I was stuck between an immovable object, in the form of a mountain of work, and an unstoppable force, deadlines rushing towards me at the speed of light.

The problem was that I wasn't taking any time to get my bearings, and was just flailing about trying to grab hold of something. I felt like I needed something to clear my mind for at least an hour. Just one hour and then I'd be okay.

I thought video games might work. They didn't; neither did going out and partying. That kind of stuff doesn't clear your mind as much as cloud it up so you can't see the problems for a bit.

What I had to do was something that I had never thought of doing before, something so different from my routine that I'd use a totally different part of my brain. It's the novelty that relaxes you; learning becomes fun again. The best part for students is that they are good at learning.

What I came up with was Tai Chi, but it could be different things for different people. It could be learning to play an instrument, taking a cooking class, or something like that.

If you can't think of something don't worry; you could still be on the right track. Watch a couple of movies and wait until you see something that makes you say, "Wow, I'd like to do that. I think I will."

Yes, I know how it sounds, but think about it next time you feel stress start to creep in. You don't even really have to go so far as to take a class. Just do something that surprises you and you'll feel like you've created a little more distance between your unstoppable force and your immovable object.

Analyze carefully. Gather all the information you can, so that you can consider the situation comprehensively. Consider what you can learn from how the problem is similar to or different from other problems. Clarify facts. Note your own perspective, and ask others for theirs. Make sure you are not looking at the problem through the lens of an assumption.

No problem can stand the assault of sustained thinking.

VOLTAIRE

Generate possible solutions based on causes, not effects. Addressing a cause provides a lasting solution, whereas "fixing" an effect cannot. Say your shoulder hurts when you use your computer. Getting a friend to massage it is a nice but temporary solution, because the pain returns whenever you go back to work. Changing the height of your keyboard and mouse is a better idea, because it eliminates the cause of your pain.

Working through a problem relating to an instructor.

DEFINE PROBLEM HERE:	ANALYZE THE PROBLEM
I don't like my Composition instructor	We have different views and personality types— I don't feel respected or heard. I'm not interested in being there and my grades are suffering from my lack of motivation.

Use boxes below to list possible solutions:

POTENTIAL POSITIVE EFFECTS	SOLUTION #1	POTENTIAL NEGATIVE EFFECTS
List for each solution: Don't have to deal with that instructor Less stress	Drop the course	*List for each solution:* Grade gets entered on my transcript I'll have to take the course eventually; it's required for my major
Getting credit for the course Feeling like I've honoured a commitment	**SOLUTION #2** Put up with it until the end of the semester	Stress every time I'm there Lowered motivation Probably not such a good final grade
A chance to express myself Could get good advice An opportunity to ask direct questions of the instructor	**SOLUTION #3** Schedule meetings with advisor and instructor	Have to face instructor one-on-one Might just make things worse

Now choose the solution you think is best—circle it and make it happen.

ACTUAL POSITIVE EFFECTS	PRACTICAL ACTION	ACTUAL NEGATIVE EFFECTS
List for chosen solution: Got some helpful advice from advisor Talking in person with the instructor actually promoted a fairly honest discussion I won't have to take the course again	I scheduled and attended meetings with both advisor and instructor, and opted to stick with the course.	*List for chosen solution:* The discussion was difficult and sometimes tense I still don't know how much learning I'll retain from this course

FINAL EVALUATION: Was it a good or bad solution?

The solution has improved things. I'll finish the course, and even though the instructor and I aren't the best of friends, we have a mutual understanding now. I feel more respected and more willing to put my time into the course.

Making a decision

Psychologists who have studied decision making have learned that many random factors influence the choices people make. For example, you may choose a major not because you love the subject but because you think your parents will approve of it. The goal is to make considered decisions despite factors that may derail your thinking.

What happens when you make important decisions quickly, without using your analytical, creative, and practical thinking skills? Consider a student trying to work on a budget. Right now, she won't have enough money to continue in school next semester. If she drops out, that would mean she would lose her year and the time/money spent on her education. Does she drop down to part time? That might mean graduating at a later date. Now look at how this student might make a successfully intelligent decision. Key 4.13 shows how she worked through the analytical, creative, and practical parts of the process.

As you use the steps in Key 4.13 to make a decision, remember these hints.

Look at the given options—then try to think of more. Some decisions have a given set of options. For example, your school may allow you to major, double major, or major and minor. However, when you are making your decision, you may be able to brainstorm with an advisor to come up with more options—such as an interdisciplinary major you create on your own.

Think about how your decision affects others. For example, the student thinking about a transfer considers the impact on friends and family. What she concludes about that impact may inform when she transfers and even the school she chooses.

Gather perspectives. Talk with others who have made similar decisions. There are more ways of doing things than one brain can possibly imagine on its own.

Look at the long-term effects. For important decisions, do a short-term evaluation and another evaluation after a period of time. See whether your decision has sent you down a path that has continued to bring positive effects.

Keeping your balance

No one has equal strengths in analytical, creative, and practical thinking. Adjusting your expectations to match what you can accomplish is a key principle of successful intelligence. It requires that you

- use what you've learned in this chapter and the rest of the text to maximize your analytical, creative, and practical abilities.
- reflect on what you do well, and focus on strengthening weaker skills.
- combine all three thinking skills to accomplish your goals, knowing when and how to apply your analytical, creative, and practical abilities.
- believe in your skills as a thinker.

Walking through a problem . . . financing course work.

CAUSES OF PROBLEM	STATE PROBLEM HERE:	EFFECTS OF PROBLEM
Lost financial aid due to slipping grades Part-time job doesn't bring in much money	I don't have enough money to cover tuition next semester	Need to find money from a different source Might be unable to continue school right now

Use boxes below to list possible solutions:

POTENTIAL POSITIVE EFFECTS	SOLUTION #1	POTENTIAL NEGATIVE EFFECTS
List for each solution: Ability to stay on planned school schedule Ability to stay in school	Find new source of financial aid	List for each solution: Money might not be renewable like current grant Time and effort spent to find and qualify for new aid

	SOLUTION #2	
More money to pay for school More on-the-job experience	Find full-time, better-paying job	Less time for school May have to take classes part time, graduate later

	SOLUTION #3	
More time to study More ability to focus	Take classes part time next semester	Extends how long I'll be in school Could make me ineligible for certain kinds of aid

Now choose the solution you think is best—and try it.

ACTUAL POSITIVE EFFECTS	CHOSEN SOLUTION	ACTUAL NEGATIVE EFFECTS
List for chosen solution: More money earned More study time and ability to focus resulted in better grades	For next semester, take classes part time and work full time	List for chosen solution: Had to put off planned graduation date Ineligible this semester for most aid, had to use my own money for tuition

FINAL EVALUATION: WAS IT A GOOD OR BAD CHOICE?

It was tough but it worked out well. Even though I had to pay for courses myself, the full-time job and fewer classes allowed me to do that. Then, with better focus, I was able to raise my average back up so that next semester I'll requalify for aid and can go back to being a full-time student.

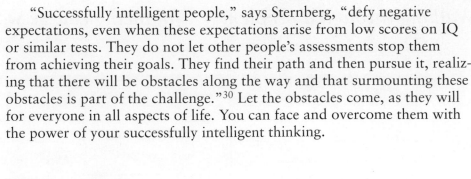

"Successfully intelligent people," says Sternberg, "defy negative expectations, even when these expectations arise from low scores on IQ or similar tests. They do not let other people's assessments stop them from achieving their goals. They find their path and then pursue it, realizing that there will be obstacles along the way and that surmounting these obstacles is part of the challenge."[30] Let the obstacles come, as they will for everyone in all aspects of life. You can face and overcome them with the power of your successfully intelligent thinking.

Κριvειv

The word "critical" is derived from the Greek word *krinein*, which means to separate in order to choose or select. Successful intelligence requires that you separate, evaluate, and select ideas and information as you think through problematic situations. Says Sternberg, "It is more important to know when and how to use these aspects of successful intelligence than just to have them."[31]

Think of this concept as you use your analytical, creative, and practical thinking skills to solve problems, make decisions, innovate, and question. Consider information carefully, and separate out and select the best approaches. Successful intelligence gives you the power to choose how to respond to information, people, and events in ways that help you reach your goals.

BUILDING SKILLS

FOR ACADEMIC, CAREER, AND LIFE SUCCESS

Developing Successful Intelligence

PUTTING IT ALL TOGETHER

Make an important decision. Put the decision making process to work on something that matters to you. You will apply your analytical, creative, and practical thinking skills. Use a separate sheet of paper for Steps 2 and 3.

Step 1. Analyze: *Define the decision.* Write an important long-term goal that you have, and define the decision that will help you fulfill it. Example: "My goal is to become a nurse. My decision: What to specialize in."

_____

_____

_____

Step 2. Analyze: *Examine needs and concerns.* What do you want? What are your needs, and how do your values come into play? What needs of others will you need to take into account? What roadblocks might be involved? List everything you come up with. For example, the prospective nurse might list needs like: "I need to feel that I'm helping people. I intend to help with the nursing shortage. I need to make a good living."

Step 3. Be creative: *Generate options.* Ask questions to imagine what's possible. Where might you work? What might be the schedule and pace? Who might work with you? What would you see, smell, and hear on your job? What would you do every day? List, too, all of the options you know of. The prospective nurse, for example, might list ER, pediatrics, surgery, oncology, geriatrics, and so on. Brainstorm other options that might not seem so obvious.

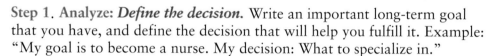

create your future

Step 4. Analyze: *Evaluate options.* Think about how well your options will fulfill your needs. For two of your options, write potential positive and negative effects (pros and cons) of each.

Option 1: _____

Potential pros: _____

_____

Potential cons: _____

_____

Option 2: _____

Potential pros: _____

_____

Potential cons: _____

_____

Step 5. Get practical: *Imagine acting on your decision.* Describe one practical course of action, based on your thinking so far, that you might follow. List the specific steps you would take. For example, the prospective nurse might list actions that help him determine what type of nursing suits him best, such as interning, summer jobs, academic goals, and talking to working nurses.

_____

_____

_____

Finally, over time, plan to put your decision into action. Eventually you will need to complete the two final steps of the process. Step 6 is to evaluate the decision: How did it work out? Analyze whether you and others got what you needed. Step 7 is to practically apply what you've learned from the decision to other decisions you make in the future.

Team Building

COLLABORATIVE SOLUTIONS

Powerful group problem solving. On an index card or a plain sheet of paper, each student in the class writes a school-related problem—this could be a fear, a challenge, a sticky situation, or a roadblock. Students hand these in without names. The instructor writes the list on the board.

Divide into groups of two to four. Each group chooses one problem to work on (try not to have two groups working on the same problem). Use the empty problem-solving flow chart (Key 4.14) on p. 122 to fill in your work.

Step 1. Analyze: *Define the problem.* As a group, look at the negative effects and state your problem specifically. Then, explore and write down the causes.

Step 2. Analyze: *Examine the problem.* Pick it apart to see what's happening. Gather information from all group members, verify facts, go beyond assumptions.

Step 3. Create: *Generate possible solutions.* From the most likely causes of the problem, derive possible solutions. Record all the ideas that group members offer. After ten minutes or so, each group member should choose one possible solution to evaluate independently.

Step 4. Analyze: *Evaluate each solution.* In thinking independently through the assigned solution, each group member should (a) weigh the positive and negative effects, (b) consider similar problems, and (c) describe how the solution affects the causes of the problem. Evaluate your assigned solution. Is it a good one? Will it work?

Step 5. Get practical: *Choose a solution.* Group members come together, share observations and recommendations, and then take a vote: Which solution is the best? You may have a tie or may want to combine two different solutions. Try to find the solution that works for most of the group. Then, together, come up with a plan for how you would put your solution to work.

Step 6. Analyze: *Evaluate your solution.* As a group, share and discuss what you had individually imagined the positive and negative effects of this solution would be. Try to come to an agreement on how you think the solution would work out.

Writing

DISCOVERY THROUGH JOURNALING

Record your thoughts on a separate piece of paper or in a journal.

Wiser choices. Think about a choice you made that, looking back, you wish you had handled differently. First, describe what the decision was, what option you chose, and what the consequences were. Then write about what you would do if you could make the decision again. What did you learn from your experience that you can apply to other decisions? How could being analytical, creative, and practical have helped you reach a more effective outcome?

Career Portfolio

PLAN FOR SUCCESS

Generating ideas for internships. People often put more time and effort into deciding what cell phone to buy than they do with life-altering decisions like how to prepare for career success. Pursuing internships is part of a

Work through a problem using this flow chart.

DEFINE PROBLEM HERE:	ANALYZE THE PROBLEM

Use boxes below to list possible solutions:

POTENTIAL POSITIVE EFFECTS	SOLUTION #1	POTENTIAL NEGATIVE EFFECTS
List for each solution:		*List for each solution:*

SOLUTION #2

SOLUTION #3

Now choose the solution you think is best—circle it and make it happen.

ACTUAL POSITIVE EFFECTS	PRACTICAL ACTION	ACTUAL NEGATIVE EFFECTS
List for chosen solution:		*List for chosen solution:*

FINAL EVALUATION: Was it a good or bad solution?

comprehensive career decision-making process. It's a practical way to get experience, learn what you like and don't like, and make valuable connections.

Fill in the following:

Career areas that I'm considering. Why?

1. _____ *Because:* _____

2. _____ *Because:* _____

3. _____ *Because:* _____

People whom I want to interview about their fields/professions. Why?

1. _____ *Because:* _____

2. _____ *Because:* _____

3. _____ *Because:* _____

Next, take practical steps to investigate internships. Talk to the people you listed. Contact companies you would like to work for and see what internship opportunities are available. Talk with someone in your school's career office. If a company doesn't offer internships, ask them if you might be the pioneer intern.

Finally, after you have gathered some useful information, use a separate sheet of paper to creatively envision your internship experience. Describe it: What would it look like? What would you do each day? Each week? Where would you go? With whom would you work? What would you contribute with your gifts and talents? Make it happen with your successful intelligence.

SUGGESTED READINGS

Cameron, Julia, with Mark Bryan. *The Artist's Way: A Spiritual Path to Higher Creativity*, 10th ed. New York: G.P. Putnam's Sons, 2002.

de Bono, Edward. *Lateral Thinking: Creativity Step by Step*. New York: Perennial Library, 1990.

Goleman, Daniel. *Emotional Intelligence: Why It Can Matter More Than IQ*. New York: Bantam, 1995.

Moscovich, Ivan. *1000 Playthinks*. New York: Workman Publishing, 2001.

Noone, Donald J., Ph.D. *Creative Problem Solving*. New York: Barron's, 1998.

Sark. *Make Your Creative Dreams Real: A Plan for Procrastinators, Perfectionists, Busy People, and People Who Would Rather Sleep All Day*. New York: Fireside Press, 2004.

von Oech, Roger. *A Kick in the Seat of the Pants*. New York: Harper & Row Publishers, 1986.

von Oech, Roger. *A Whack on the Side of the Head*. New York: Warner Books, 1998.

INTERNET RESOURCES

Creativity at Work (resources for workplace creativity): **www.creativityatwork.com**

Creativity for Life (tips and strategies for creativity): **www.creativityforlife.com**

Reasonably appreciate the importance of critical thinking at Reason!Able: **www.goreason.com**

Learn more about critical thinking from the University of Victoria's Counselling Services: **www.coun.uvic.ca/learn/crit.html**

Roger von Oech's Creative Think Web site: creativethink.com

1. Robert J. Sternberg, *Successful Intelligence*. New York: Plume, 1997, p. 12.

2. Ibid, p. 127.

3. Matt Thomas, "What Is Higher-Order Thinking and Critical/Creative/Constructive Thinking?" The Center for Studies in Higher-Order Literacy [on-line]. Available at: http://members.aol.com/MattT10574/HigherOrderLiteracy.htm#What (April 2004).

4. Sternberg, p. 128.

5. Vincent Ruggiero, *The Art of Thinking*, 2001, quoted in "Critical Thinking," Oregon State University [on-line]. Available at: http://success.oregonstate.edu/template/criticalthinking.html (April 2004).

6. Richard Paul, "The Role of Questions in Thinking, Teaching, and Learning," The Critical Thinking Community [on-line]. Available at: http://www.criticalthinking.org/resources/articles/the-role-of-questions.shtml (April 2004).

7. "The Best Innovations Are Those That Come from Smart Questions," *Wall Street Journal*, April 12, 2004, B1.

8. Lawrence F. Lowery, "The Biological Basis of Thinking and Learning," 1998, Full Option Science System at the University of California at Berkeley [on-line]. Available at: http://lhsfoss.org/newsletters/archive/pdfs/FOSS_BBTL.pdf (April 2004).

9. Ivan Moscovich, *1000 Playthinks*. New York: Workman Publishing, p. 7.

10. Colby Glass, "Strategies for Critical Thinking," March 1999 [on-line]. Available at: www.accd.edu/pac/philosop/phil1301/ctstrategies.htm (April 2004).

11. Sternberg, p. 49.

12. Charles Cave, "Definitions of Creativity," August 1999 [on-line]. Available at: http://members.ozemail.com.au/ྂcaveman/Creative/Basics/definitions.htm [subscription-based] (April 2003).

13. Elizabeth F. Farrell, "Engineering a Warmer Welcome for Female Students: The Discipline Tries to Stress its Social Relevance, an Important Factor for Many Women," *The Chronicle of Higher Education*, February 22, 2002 [on-line]. Available at: http://chronicle.com/weekly/v48/i24/24a03101.htm [subscription-based] (March 2004).

14. Roger von Oech, *A Kick in the Seat of the Pants*. New York: Harper & Row Publishers, 1986, pp. 5–21.

15. Dennis Coon, *Introduction to Psychology: Exploration and Application*, 6th ed. St. Paul: West Publishing Company, 1992, p. 295.

16. Roger von Oech, *A Whack on the Side of the Head*. New York: Warner Books, 1990, pp. 11–168.

17. J. R. Hayes, *Cognitive Psychology: Thinking and Creating*. Homewood, IL: Dorsey, 1978.

18. Sternberg, p. 219.

19. Adapted from T. Z. Tardif and R. J. Sternberg, "What Do We Know About Creativity?" in *The Nature of Creativity*, ed. R. J. Sternberg, 1988. London: Cambridge University Press.

20. Sternberg, p. 212.

21. Hayes.

22. Sternberg, p. 202.

23. "The Best Innovations Are Those That Come from Smart Questions," *Wall Street Journal*, April 12, 2004, B1.

24. Sternberg, pp. 229–230.

25. Sternberg, p. 236.

26. Robert J. Sternberg and Elena L. Grigorenko, "Practical Intelligence and the Principal," Yale University: Publication Series No. 2, 2001, p. 5.

27. Sternberg, p. 241.

28. Daniel Goleman, *Emotional Intelligence: Why It Can Matter More Than IQ*. New York: Bantam, 1995.

29. Sternberg, pp. 251–269.

30. Sternberg, p. 19.

31. Sternberg, p. 128.

STUDY BREAK: GET READY FOR EXAMS

Start with a Study Plan and Schedule

Because some instructors may schedule exams early and often in the semester, begin right away to develop strategies for test success. Starting off on the right foot will boost your confidence and motivate you to work even harder. The saying that "success breeds more success" couldn't be more true as you begin college.

The material in this Study Break is designed to help you organize yourself as you prepare for exams. As you learn to create a pre-test study plan and schedule, you will also build your ability to use your time efficiently.

When you reach Chapter 8, "Test Taking: Showing What You Know," you will study test taking in depth, including test preparation, test anxiety, general test-taking strategies, strategies for handling different types of test questions, and learning from test mistakes.

Decide on a study plan

Start your test preparation by deciding what you will study. Go through your notes, texts, related primary sources, and handouts, and set aside materials you don't need. Then prioritize the remaining materials. Your goal is to focus on information that is most likely to be on the exam. Use the test preparation tips in Chapter 8 and the material on studying your text in Chapter 5 to boost your effectiveness as you prepare.

Create a study schedule and checklist

Next, use the time-management and goal-setting skills from Chapter 2 to prepare a schedule. Consider all of the relevant factors—your study materials, the number of days until the test, and the time you can study each day. If you establish your schedule ahead of time and write it in a planner, you are more likely to follow it.

Let our advance worrying become advance thinking and planning.

WINSTON CHURCHILL

A checklist like the one on the following page will help you organize and stay on track as you prepare. Use a checklist to assign specific tasks to particular study times and sessions. That way, not only do you know when you have time to study, but you also have defined goals for each study session. Make extra copies of the checklist so that you can fill out a new one each time you have an exam.

Course: _____ Instructor: _____

Date, time, and place of test: _____

Type of test (is it a midterm or a minor quiz?): _____

What the instructor said about the test, including the types of test questions, test length, and how much the test counts toward your final grade:

_____

_____

Topics to be covered on the test, in order of importance (information should also come from your instructor):

1. _____

2. _____

3. _____

4. _____

5. _____

Study schedule, including materials you plan to study (texts, class notes, homework problems, and so forth) and dates you plan to complete each:

MATERIAL   DATE OF COMPLETION

1. _____   _____

2. _____   _____

3. _____   _____

4. _____   _____

5. _____   _____

Materials you are expected to bring to the test (textbook, sourcebook, calculator, etc.):

_____

_____

Special study arrangements (for example, plan study group meetings, ask the instructor for special help, get outside tutoring):

_____

_____

_____

Life-management issues (such as rearranging work hours):

_____

_____

_____

Source: Adapted from Ron Fry, "Ace" Any Test, 3rd ed. Franklin Lakes, NJ: Career Press, 1996. pp. 123–24.

Decide how well these techniques work for you

After you've used these studying and scheduling techniques to prepare for a few exams, answer the following questions:

- How did this approach help you organize your time before an exam?

_____

_____

_____

- How did this approach help you organize your study material so that you remembered to cover every topic?

_____

_____

_____

- Can you think of ways to change the checklist to improve your test-prep efficiency? If you can, list the ways here and incorporate them into the checklist.

_____

_____

_____

SELF STUDY QUIZ

MULTIPLE CHOICE

Circle or highlight the answer that seems to fit best.

1. A *motivator* is
   a. the ability to achieve a goal.
   b. progress toward a goal.
   c. a decision to take action.
   d. a want or need that moves a person to action.

2. The direct benefits of responsibility include
   a. earning the trust of others at school, work, and home.
   b. getting motivated to achieve study goals.
   c. improved ability to plan strategically.
   d. moving up at work.

3. A *learning style* is
   a. the best way to learn when attending classes.
   b. a particular way of being intelligent.
   c. an affinity for a particular job choice or career area.
   d. a way in which the mind receives and processes information.

4. The best way to use learning-style assessments is to see them as
   a. a reference point rather than a label; a tool with which to see yourself more clearly.
   b. a road map for your life; a message that shows the paths you must take in order to be successful.

   c. a lesson about group learning; a way to find the group of learners with whom you work best.
   d. a definitive label for your working style; a clear-cut category where you fit.

5. When choosing and evaluating your values, it is important to
   a. set goals according to what your friends and family value.
   b. keep your values steady over time.
   c. re-evaluate values periodically as you experience change.
   d. set aside values that no one else seems to think are good for you.

6. It is important to link daily and weekly goals with long-term goals because
   a. the process will help you focus on the things that are most important to you.
   b. short-term goals have no meaning if they are not placed in a longer time frame.
   c. the process will help you eliminate frivolous activities.
   c. others expect you to know how everything you do relates to what you want to accomplish in life.

FILL-IN-THE-BLANK

Complete the following sentences with the appropriate word(s) or phrase(s) that best reflect what you learned in the chapter. Choose from the items that follow each sentence.

1. When you make a _____, you do what you say you will do. (initiative, motivation, commitment)

2. Showing _____ helps you to take that first step toward a goal and respond to changes in your life. (motivation, initiative, integrity)

3. One way to look at learning style is to divide it into two equally important aspects: _____ and _____. (learning preferences/personality traits, verbal/visual, interests/abilities)

4. The best careers and majors/programs for you are ones that take into consideration your _____ and _____. (references/contacts, learning style/abilities, interests/abilities)

5. Your _____ is a philosophy outlining what you want to be, what you want to do, and the principles by which you live. (responsibility, mission, integrity)

6. Being _____ helps you cope with day-to-day changes and life changes. (organized, flexible, on time)

ESSAY QUESTIONS

The following essay questions will help you organize and communicate your ideas in writing, just as you must do on an essay test. Before you begin answering a question, spend a few minutes planning (brainstorm possible approaches, write a thesis statement, jot down main thoughts in outline or think link form). To prepare yourself for actual test conditions, limit writing time to no more than 30 minutes per question.

1. Discuss habits, both good and bad. What are the effects of each? Describe a useful plan for changing a habit that is having negative effects.

2. Define *values* and *value system*. How do values develop and what effect do they have on personal choices? How are values connected to goal setting? Give an example from your life of how values have influenced a personal goal.

UNDERSTAND

5

IN THIS CHAPTER

In this chapter you will explore answers to the following questions: • What will help you understand what you read? • How can you set the stage for reading? • How can SQ3R help you own what you read? • How can you respond critically to what you read? • How and why should you study with others?

Reading and studying

YOUR ability to read—and to understand, analyze, and use what you read—is the cornerstone of college learning. However, your background as a reader may not have prepared you for the amount and the complexity of the reading you will be assigned in college. It isn't just students with learning disabilities who face challenges. Almost all students need to adjust their habits in order to handle the increased demands of a college reading load.

Taking a step-by-step approach linked to analytical, creative, and practical thinking techniques will help you get what you need from the materials you read and study. This chapter introduces you to strategies to increase your speed, efficiency, and depth of understanding. When you use these strategies to learn more and retain more of what you learn, every hour you spend with your books will be more valuable.

focusing on content

What will *help you understand* what you read?

More than anything else, reading is a process that requires you, the reader, to *make meaning* from written words. When you make meaning, you connect yourself to the concepts being communicated. Your prior knowledge or familiarity with a subject, culture and home environment, life experiences, and even personal interpretation of words and phrases affect your understanding. Because these factors are different for every person, your reading experiences are uniquely your own.

Reading *comprehension* refers to your ability to understand what you read. True comprehension goes beyond just knowing facts and figures—a student can parrot back a pile of economics statistics on a test, for example, without understanding what they mean. Only when you thoroughly comprehend the information you read can you make the most effective use of that information.

All reading strategies help you to achieve a greater understanding of what you read. Therefore, every section in this chapter will in some way help you maximize your comprehension. Following are some general comprehension boosters to keep in mind as you work through the chapter and as you tackle individual reading assignments.

Build knowledge through reading and studying. More than any other factor, what you already know before you read a passage influences your ability to understand and remember important ideas. Previous knowledge gives you a **context** for what you read.

CONTEXT

Written or spoken knowledge that can help to illuminate the meaning of a word or passage.

Think positively. Instead of telling yourself that you cannot understand, think positively. Tell yourself: *I can learn this material. I am a good reader.*

Think critically. Ask yourself questions. Do you understand the sentence, paragraph, or chapter you just read? Are ideas and supporting examples clear? Could you explain the material to someone else? Later in this chapter, you will learn strategies for responding critically to what you read.

Build vocabulary. Lifelong learners consider their vocabulary a work in progress. They never stop learning new words. The more you know, the more material you can understand without stopping to wonder what new words mean.

Look for order and meaning in seemingly chaotic reading materials. The information in this chapter on the SQ3R reading technique (defined on p. 142) and on critical reading will help you discover patterns and achieve a depth of understanding. Finding order within chaos is an important skill, not just in the mastery of reading, but also in life. This skill gives you power by helping you "read" (think through) work dilemmas, personal problems, and educational situations.

get creative!

Think about a book that made a difference for you.

Henry David Thoreau, a nineteenth-century author, poet, and philosopher, made the following observation: "How many a man has dated a new era in his life from the reading of a book." What do you think Thoreau meant by this statement?

_____

_____

Think of a book that influenced your education—or life—and describe why it is important.

_____

_____

If you could write a book that would help others succeed in college, what would be the book's message? Why do you think your book would be important for others to read?

_____

_____

_____

How can you *set the stage* for reading?

On any given day during your college or university career, you may be faced with reading assignments like these:

- A textbook chapter on the contributions made by Native Canadians (Canadian history)
- An original research study on the relationship between sleep deprivation and the development of memory problems (psychology)
- Chapters 4–6 in Margaret Laurence's classic novel *The Stone Angel* (Canadian literature)
- A technical manual on the design of computer anti-spam programs (computer science—software design)

This material is rigorous by anyone's standards. To get through it—and master its contents—you need a systematic approach. The following strategies help you set the stage for reading success.

If you have a reading disability, if English is not your primary language, or if you have limited reading skills, you may need additional support. Most colleges and universities in Canada provide services for students through a reading centre or tutoring program. Take the initiative to seek help if you need it. Many accomplished learners benefit from help in specific areas. Remember: The ability to succeed is often linked to the ability to ask for help.

Take an Active Approach to Difficult Texts

Because texts are often written to challenge the intellect, even well-written, useful texts may be difficult to read. Some textbook authors may not explain information in the friendliest manner for non-experts. And, as every student knows, some textbooks are poorly written and organized.

Generally, the further you advance in your education, the more complex your required reading. You may encounter new concepts, words, and terms that seem like a foreign language. Assignments can also be difficult when the required reading is from *primary sources*—original documents rather than another writer's interpretation of these documents—or from academic journal articles and scientific studies that don't define basic terms or supply a wealth of examples. Primary sources include:

- historical documents
- works of literature (e.g., novels, poems, and plays)
- scientific studies, including lab reports and accounts of experiments
- journal articles

The following strategies may help you approach difficult material actively and positively:

Approach your reading assignments with an open mind. Be careful not to pre-judge them as impossible or boring before you even start.

Know that some texts may require extra work and concentration. Set a goal to make your way through the material and learn. Do whatever it takes.

Define concepts that your material does not explain. Consult resources—instructors, students, reference materials—for help.

To help with your make-meaning-of-textbooks mission, you may want to create your own mini-library at home. Collect reference materials that you use often, such as a dictionary, a thesaurus, a writer's style handbook, and maybe an atlas or computer manual (many of these are available as computer software or CD-ROMs). You may also benefit from owning reference materials in your particular areas of study. "If you find yourself going to the library to look up the same reference again and again, consider purchasing that book for your personal or office library," advises library expert Sherwood Harris.[1]

Choose the Right Setting

Finding a place and time that minimize distractions helps you achieve the focus and discipline that your reading requires. Here are some suggestions.

Select the right company (or lack thereof). If you prefer to read alone, establish a relatively interruption-proof place and time such as an out-of-the-way spot at the library or an after-class hour in an empty classroom. Even if you don't mind activity nearby, try to minimize distraction.

Select the right location. Many students study at a library desk. Others prefer an easy chair at the library or at home, or even the floor. Choose a spot that's comfortable but not so cushy that you fall asleep. Make sure that you have adequate lighting and aren't too hot or cold. You may also want to avoid the distraction of studying in a room where people are talking or a television is on.

No barrier of the senses shuts me out from the sweet, gracious discourse of my book friends. They talk to me without embarrassment or awkwardness.

HELEN KELLER

Select the right time. Choose a time when you feel alert and focused. Try reading just before or after the class for which the reading is assigned, if you can. Eventually, you will associate preferred places and times with focused reading.

Deal with internal distractions. Although a noisy environment can get in the way of your work, so can internal distractions—for example, personal worries, anticipation of an event, or even hunger. Different strategies may help. You may want to take a break and tend to one of the issues that worry you. Physical exercise may relax and refocus you. For some people, studying while listening to music quiets a busy mind. For others, silence may do the trick. If you're hungry, take a snack break and come back to your work.

Students with families have an additional factor involved when deciding when, where, and how to read. Key 5.1 explores some ways that parents or others caring for children may be able to maximize their study efforts. These techniques will also help after graduation if you choose to telecommute—work from home through an Internet-linked computer—while your children are still at home under your care.

Define Your Purpose for Reading

When you define your purpose, you ask yourself *why* you are reading a particular piece of material. One way to do this is by completing this sentence: "In reading this material, I intend to define/learn/ answer/ achieve..." With a clear purpose in mind, you can decide how much time and what kind of effort to expend on various reading assignments.

Achieving your reading purpose requires adapting to different types of reading materials. Being a flexible reader—adjusting your reading strategies and pace—helps you to adapt successfully.

Purpose Determines Reading Strategy

With purpose comes direction; with direction comes a strategy. Following are four reading purposes. You may have one or more for any "reading event."

Purpose 1: Read for understanding. In college and university, studying means reading to comprehend the material. The two main components of comprehension are *general ideas* and *specific facts or examples*. Facts and examples help to explain or support ideas, and ideas provide a framework that helps the reader remember facts and examples.

Keep them up to date on your schedule.

Let them know when you have a big test or project due and when you are under less pressure, and what they can expect of you in each case.

Explain what your education entails.

Tell them how it will improve your life and theirs. This applies, of course, to older children who can understand the situation and compare it with their own schooling.

Find help.

Ask a relative or friend to watch your children or arrange for a child to visit a friend. Consider trading babysitting hours with another parent, hiring a sitter to come to your home, or using a day-care centre.

Keep them active while you study.

Give them games, books, or toys. If there are special activities that you like to limit, such as watching videos or TV, save them for your study time.

Offset study time with family time and rewards.

Children may let you get your work done if they have something to look forward to, such as a movie night or a trip for ice cream.

Study on the phone.

You might be able to have a study session with a fellow student over the phone while your child is sleeping or playing quietly.

SPECIAL NOTES FOR INFANTS

Study at night if your baby goes to sleep early, or in the morning if your baby sleeps late.

Study during nap times if you aren't too tired yourself.

Lay your notes out and recite information to the baby. The baby will appreciate the attention, and you will get work done.

Put baby in a safe and fun place while you study, such as a playpen, motorized swing, or jumping seat.

- **General ideas.** Reading for a general idea is rapid reading that seeks an overview of the material. You search for general ideas by focusing on headings, subheadings, and summary statements.
- **Specific facts or examples.** At times, readers may focus on locating specific pieces of information—for example, the stages of intellectual development in children. Often, a reader may search for examples that support or explain general ideas—for example, the causes of economic recession.

Purpose 2: Read to evaluate critically. Critical evaluation involves understanding. It means approaching the material with an open mind, examining causes and effects, evaluating ideas, and asking questions that test the writer's argument and search for assumptions. Critical reading brings an understanding of the material that goes beyond basic information recall (see page 148 for more on critical reading).

Purpose 3: Read for practical application. A third purpose for reading is to gather usable information that you can apply toward a specific goal. When you read a computer manual or an instruction sheet for assembling a gas barbecue, your goal is to learn how to do something. Reading and action usually go hand in hand. Remembering the specifics requires a certain degree of general comprehension.

Purpose 4: Read for pleasure. Some materials you read for entertainment, such as *Sports Illustrated* magazine or the latest John Grisham courtroom thriller. Recreational reading may also go beyond materials that seem obviously designed to entertain. Whereas some people may read a Jane Austen novel for comprehension, as in a class assignment, others may read her books for pleasure.

Match Strategies to Different Areas of Study

Different subject matter presents different reading challenges. This is due in part to essential differences between the subjects (a calculus text and history of world religions text have very little in common) and in part to reader learning style and preferences (you are likely more comfortable with some subjects than you are with others).

When you have a good idea of the kind of reading that is tough for you, you can choose the strategies that seem to help you the most. Although the information in this chapter will help with any academic subject, math and science often present unique challenges. You may benefit from using some of these specific techniques when reading math or science.

Interact with the material critically as you go. Math and science texts tend to move sequentially (later chapters build on concepts and information introduced in previous chapters) and are often problem-and-solution-based. Keep a pad of paper nearby and take notes of examples. Work steps out on your pad. Draw sketches to help visualize the material. Try not to move on until you understand the example and how it relates to the central ideas. Write down questions to ask your instructor or fellow students.

Note formulas. Evaluate the importance of formulas and recall whether the instructor emphasized them. Make sure you understand the principle behind the **formula**—why it works—rather than just memorizing the formula itself. Read the assigned material to prepare for any homework.

Use memory techniques. Science textbooks are often packed with vocabulary specific to that particular science (e.g., a chapter in a psychobiology course may give medical names for the parts of the brain). Put your memory skills to use when reading science texts—use mnemonic devices, test yourself using flash cards, and rehearse aloud or silently (see Chapter 6). Selective highlighting and writing summaries of your readings, in table format for example, also helps.

FORMULA
A general fact, rule, or principle usually expressed in mathematical symbols.

MULTIPLE INTELLIGENCE STRATEGIES FOR
Reading

Use selected reading techniques in Multiple Intelligence areas to strengthen your ability to read for meaning and retention.

INTELLIGENCE	SUGGESTED STRATEGIES	WHAT WORKS FOR YOU? WRITE NEW IDEAS HERE
Verbal–Linguistic	• Mark up your text with marginal notes while you read. • When tackling a chapter, use every stage of SQ3R, taking advantage of each writing opportunity (writing Q-stage questions, writing summaries, and so on).	
Logical–Mathematical	• Read material in sequence. • Think about the logical connections between what you are reading and the world at large; consider similarities, differences, and cause-and-effect relationships.	
Bodily–Kinesthetic	• Take physical breaks during reading sessions—walk, stretch, exercise. • Pace while reciting important ideas.	
Visual–Spatial	• As you read, take particular note of photos, tables, figures, and other visual aids. • Make charts, diagrams, or think links illustrating difficult concepts you encounter in your reading.	
Interpersonal	• With a friend, have a joint reading session. One should read a section silently and then summarize aloud the important concepts for the other. Reverse the order of summarizer and listener for each section. • Discuss reading material and clarify important concepts in a study group.	
Intrapersonal	• Read in a solitary setting and allow time for reflection. • Think about how a particular reading assignment makes you feel, and evaluate your reaction by considering the material in light of what you already know.	
Musical	• Play music while you read. • Recite important concepts in your reading to rhythms or write a song to depict those concepts.	
Naturalistic	• Read and study in a natural environment. • Before reading indoors, imagine your favourite place in nature in order to create a relaxed frame of mind.	

In this chapter's exercise set, you will see excerpts from textbooks treating three different subject areas. As you read them, notice the differences—and notice which seem easier or harder to you. This will give you some clues as to how you might approach longer reading assignments.

Build Reading Speed

Many students balance heavy academic loads with other important responsibilities. It's difficult to make time to study at all, let alone handle all of your reading assignments. If you can increase your reading speed, you will save valuable time and effort—as long as you don't sacrifice comprehension. Greater comprehension is the primary goal and actually promotes faster reading.

The average adult reads between 150 and 350 words per minute, and faster readers can be capable of speeds up to 1000 words per minute.[2] However, the human eye can only move so fast; reading speeds in excess of 350 words per minute involve "skimming" and "scanning" (see page 142). The following suggestions will help increase your reading speed:

- Try to read groups of words rather than single words.
- Avoid pointing your finger to guide your reading; use an index card to move quickly down the page.
- When reading narrow columns, focus your eyes in the middle of the column. With practice, you'll be able to read the entire column width as you read down the page.
- Avoid *vocalization*—speaking the words or moving your lips—when reading.

The key to building reading speed is practice and more practice, says reading expert Steve Moidel. To achieve your goal of reading between 500 and 1000 words per minute, Moidel suggests that you start practising at three times the rate you want to achieve, a rate that is much faster than you can comprehend.[3] For example, if your goal is 500 words per minute, speed up to 1500 words per minute. Reading at such an accelerated rate pushes your eyes and mind to adjust to the faster pace. When you slow down to 500 words per minute—the pace at which you can read and comprehend—your reading rate will feel comfortable even though it is much faster than your original speed. You may even want to check into self-paced computer software that helps you improve reading speed.

Expand Your Vocabulary

As your reading materials at school and at work become more complex, how much you comprehend—and how readily you do it—depends on your vocabulary. A strong vocabulary increases reading speed and comprehension; when you understand the words in your reading material, you don't have to stop as often to think about what they mean.

The best way to build your vocabulary is to commit yourself to learning new and unfamiliar words as you encounter them. This involves certain steps.

Analyze Word Parts. Often, if you understand part of a word, you can figure out what the entire word means. This is true because many English words are made up of a combination of Greek and Latin prefixes, **roots**, and suffixes. *Prefixes* are word parts that are added to the beginning of a root. *Suffixes* are added to the end of the root. Key 5.2 contains just a few of the prefixes, roots, and suffixes you will encounter as you read. Knowing these verbal building blocks dramatically increases your vocabulary. Key 5.3 shows how one root can be the stem of many different words.

Using prefixes, roots, and suffixes, you can piece together the meaning of many new words you encounter. To use a simple example, the word *prologue* is made up of the prefix *pro* (before) and the root *logue* (to speak). Thus, *prologue* refers to words spoken or written before the main text.

Use Words in Context. Most people learn words best when they read and use them in written or spoken language. Although a definition tells you what a word means, it may not include a context. Using a word in context after defining it helps to anchor the information so that you can remember it and continue to build on it. Here are some strategies for using context to solidify new vocabulary words.

- Use new words in a sentence or two right away. Do this immediately after reading their definitions while everything is still fresh in your mind.
- Reread the sentence where you originally saw the word. Go over it a few times to make sure that you understand how the word is used.
- Use the word over the next few days whenever it may apply. Try it while talking with friends, writing letters or notes, or in your own thoughts.
- Consider where you may have seen or heard the word before. When you learn a word, going back to sentences you previously didn't "get" may solidify your understanding.
- Seek knowledgeable advice. If after looking up a word you still have trouble with its meaning, ask an instructor or friend to help you figure it out.

Use a Dictionary. Standard dictionaries provide broad information such as word origin, pronunciation, part of speech, and multiple meanings. Using a dictionary whenever you read increases your comprehension. Buy a standard dictionary, keep it nearby, and consult it for help in understanding passages that contain unfamiliar words. Some textbooks also have a text-specific "dictionary" called a *glossary* that defines terms found in the text. Such definitions are often limited to the meaning of the term as used in that particular textbook.

You may not always have time to use the following suggestions, but when you can use them, they will help you make the most of your dictionary.

- Read every meaning of a word, not just the first. Think critically about which meaning suits the context of the word in question, and choose the one that makes the most sense to you.

Common prefixes, roots, and suffixes.

PREFIX	PRIMARY MEANING	EXAMPLE
a-, ab-	from	abstain, avert
con-, cor-, com-	with, together	convene, correlate, compare
il-	not	illegal, illegible
sub-, sup-	under	subordinate, suppose

ROOT	PRIMARY MEANING	EXAMPLE
-chron-	time	synchronize
-ann-	year	biannual
-sper-	hope	desperate
-voc-	speak, talk	convocation

SUFFIX	PRIMARY MEANING	EXAMPLE
-able	able	recyclable
-meter	measure	thermometer
-ness	state of	carelessness
-y	inclined to	sleepy

Building words from a single root.

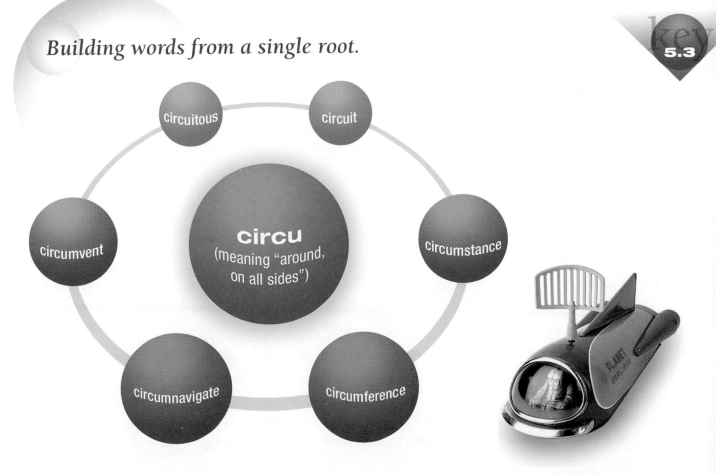

circuitous

circuit

circumvent

circu
(meaning "around, on all sides")

circumstance

circumnavigate

circumference

- **Substitute a word or phrase from the definition for the word.** Use the definition you have chosen. Imagine, for example, that you read the following sentence and do not know the word *indoctrinated*:

The cult indoctrinated its members to reject society's values.

In the dictionary, you find several definitions, including *brainwashed* and *instructed*. You decide that the one closest to the correct meaning is brainwashed. With this term, the sentence reads as follows:

The cult brainwashed its members to reject society's values.

So far, this chapter has focused on reading as a deliberate, purposeful process of meaning construction. Recognizing obstacles and defining reading purposes lay the groundwork for effective studying—the process of mastering the concepts and skills contained in your texts.

How can SQ3R *help you own* what you read?

When you study, you take ownership of the material you read, meaning that you learn it well enough to apply it to what you do. For example, by the time students studying to be computer hardware technicians complete their course work, they should be able to analyze hardware problems that lead to malfunctions. On-the-job computer technicians use the same study technique to keep up with changing technology. Studying to understand and learn also gives you mastery over concepts. For example, a dental hygiene student learns the causes of gum disease, and a business student learns about marketing.

SQ3R is a technique that will help you grasp ideas quickly, remember more, and review effectively for tests. SQ3R stands for *Survey, Question, Read, Recite,* and *Review*—all steps in the studying process. Developed more than 55 years ago by Francis Robinson, the technique is still used today because it works.[4]

Moving through the stages of SQ3R requires that you know how to skim and scan. **Skimming** involves the rapid reading of chapter elements, including introductions, conclusions, and summaries; the first and last lines of paragraphs; boldfaced or italicized terms; and pictures, charts, and diagrams. The goal of skimming is a quick construction of the main ideas. In contrast, **scanning** involves the careful search for specific facts and examples. You might use scanning during the review phase of SQ3R when you need to locate particular information (such a formula in a chemistry text).

Approach SQ3R as a framework on which you build your house, not as a tower of stone. In other words, instead of following each step by rote, bring your personal learning styles and study preferences to the system. For example, you and another classmate may focus on elements in a different order when you survey, write different types of questions, or favour different sets of review strategies. Explore the strategies, evaluate what works, and then make the system your own.

SKIMMING

Rapid, superficial reading of material that involves glancing through to determine central ideas and main elements.

SCANNING

Reading material in an investigative way, searching for specific information.

Survey

Surveying refers to the process of previewing, or pre-reading, a book before you actually study it. Compare it to looking at a map before you drive somewhere—those few minutes spent taking a look at your surroundings and where you intend to go will save you a lot of time and trouble once you are on the road.

Most textbooks include devices that give students an overview of the whole text as well as of the contents of individual chapters. When you survey, pay attention to the following elements.

The front matter. Before you even get to page 1, most textbooks have a table of contents, a preface, and other materials. The table of contents gives you an overview with clues about coverage, topic order, and features. The preface, in particular, can point out the book's unique approach.

The chapter elements. Generally, each chapter has devices that help you make meaning out of the material. Among these are:

- The chapter title, which establishes the topic and perhaps author perspective.
- The chapter introduction, outline, list of objectives, or list of key topics.
- Within the chapter, headings, tables and figures, quotes, marginal notes, and photographs that help you perceive structure and important concepts.
- Special chapter features, often presented in boxes set off from the main text, that point you to ideas connected to themes that run through the text.
- Particular styles or arrangements of type (**boldface**, *italics*, <u>underline</u>, larger fonts, bullet points, boxed text) that call your attention to new words or important concepts.

At the end of a chapter, a summary may help you tie concepts together. Review questions and exercises help you review and think critically about the material. Skimming these *before* reading the chapter gives you clues about what's important.

The back matter. Here some texts include a glossary. You may also find an *index* to help you locate individual topics and a *bibliography* that lists additional reading on particular topics covered in the text.

Key 5.4 shows the many devices that books employ. Think about how many of these devices you already use, and which you can start using now to boost your comprehension.

Question

Your next step is to examine the chapter headings and, on a separate piece of paper or in the margins, to write *questions* linked to them. If your reading material has no headings, develop questions as you read.

These questions focus your attention and increase your interest, helping you build comprehension and relate new ideas to what you already know. You can take questions from the textbook or from your lecture notes, or come up with them on your own when you survey, based on what ideas you think are most important.

Read

Your questions give you a starting point for *reading,* the first R in SQ3R. Learning from textbooks requires that you read *actively.* Active reading means engaging with the material through questioning, writing, note taking, and other activities. As you can see in Key 5.5, the activities of SQ3R promote active reading. Following are some specific strategies that will keep you active when you read.

Focus on your Q-stage questions. Read the material with the purpose of answering each question. As you come upon ideas and examples that relate to your question, write them down or note them in the text.

Look for important concepts. As you read, record key words, phrases, and concepts in your notebook. Some students divide the notebook into two columns, writing questions on the left and answers on the right. This method is called the Cornell note-taking system (see Chapter 6).

Text and chapter previewing devices.

key 5.4

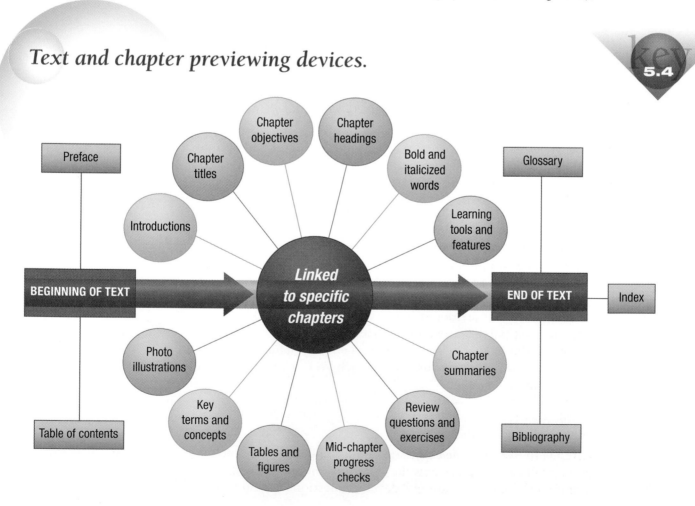

Use SQ3R to become an active reader.

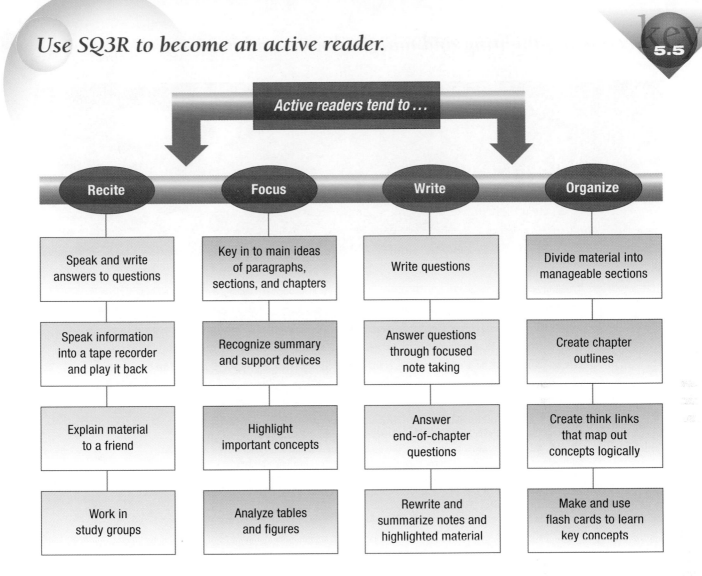

Active readers tend to ...

Recite
- Speak and write answers to questions
- Speak information into a tape recorder and play it back
- Explain material to a friend
- Work in study groups

Focus
- Key in to main ideas of paragraphs, sections, and chapters
- Recognize summary and support devices
- Highlight important concepts
- Analyze tables and figures

Write
- Write questions
- Answer questions through focused note taking
- Answer end-of-chapter questions
- Rewrite and summarize notes and highlighted material

Organize
- Divide material into manageable sections
- Create chapter outlines
- Create think links that map out concepts logically
- Make and use flash cards to learn key concepts

Mark up your textbook. Being able to make notations will help you to make sense of the material; for this reason, owning your textbooks is an enormous advantage. You may want to write notes in the margins, circle key ideas, or highlight key points. Key 5.6 shows effective highlighting and marginal notes on the page of a marketing text. Some people prefer to underline, although underlining adds more ink to the lines of text and may overwhelm your eyes. Bracketing an entire key passage is a good alternative to underlining.

Selective highlighting may help you pinpoint material to review before an exam, although excessive highlighting may actually interfere with comprehension. Here are some tips on how to strike a balance.

- Mark the text *after* you read the material once through. If you do it on the first reading, you may mark less important passages.
- Highlight key terms and concepts. Mark the examples that explain and support important ideas.
- Avoid over-marking. A phrase or two in any paragraph is usually enough. Set off long passages with brackets rather than marking every line.

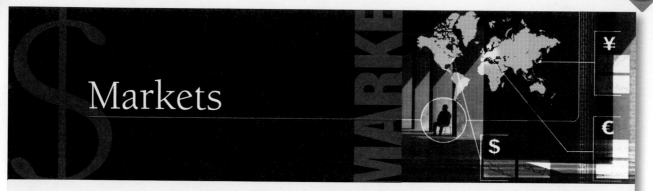

Markets

The term *market* has acquired many meanings over the years. In its original meaning, a market is a physical place where buyers and sellers gather to exchange goods and services. Medieval towns had market squares where sellers brought their goods and buyers shopped for goods. In today's cities, buying and selling occur in shopping areas rather than markets. To an economist, a market describes all the buyers and sellers who transact over some good or service. Thus, the soft-drink market consists of sellers such as Coca-Cola and PepsiCo, and of all the consumers who buy soft drinks. To a marketer, a market is the set of all actual and potential buyers of a product or service.

Definition of a market

Organizations that sell to consumer and business markets recognize that they cannot appeal to all buyers in those markets, or at least not to all buyers in the same way. Buyers are too numerous, too widely scattered, and too varied in their needs and buying practices. And different companies vary widely in their abilities to serve different segments of the market. Rather than trying to compete in an entire market, sometimes against superior competitors, each company must identify the parts of the market that it can serve best.

Companies can't appeal to everyone

Sellers have not always practiced this philosophy. Their thinking has passed through three stages:

One-size-fits-all approach

- *Mass marketing*. In mass marketing, the seller mass produces, mass distributes, and mass promotes one product to all buyers. At one time, Coca-Cola produced only one drink for the whole market, hoping it would appeal to everyone. The argument for mass marketing is that it should lead to the lowest costs and prices and create the largest potential market.

Offer variety to buyers

- *Product-variety marketing*. Here, the seller produces two or more products that have different features, styles, quality, sizes, and so on. Later, Coca-Cola produced several soft drinks packaged in different sizes and containers that were designed to offer variety to buyers rather than to appeal to different market segments. The argument for product-variety marketing is that consumers have different tastes that change over time. Consumers seek variety and change.

A tailored approach to specific market segments

- *Target marketing*. Here, the seller identifies market segments, selects one or more of them, and develops products and marketing mixes tailored to each. For example, Coca-Cola now produces soft drinks for the sugared-cola segment (Coca-Cola Classic and Cherry Coke), the diet segment (Diet Coke and Tab), the no-caffeine segment (Caffeine-Free Coke), and the noncola segment (Minute Maid sodas).

Current approach is usually TARGET MARKETING

Today's companies are moving away from mass marketing and product-variety marketing toward target marketing. Target marketing can better help sellers find their marketing opportunities. Sellers can develop the right product for each target market and adjust their prices, distribution channels, and advertising to reach the target market efficiently. Instead of scattering their marketing efforts (the "shotgun" approach), they can focus on the buyers who have greater purchase interest (the "rifle" approach).

87

Source: *Marketing: An Introduction,* 4th ed., by Kotler/Armstrong, © 1997. Reprinted with permission of Pearson Education, Inc., Upper Saddle River, NJ.

- Don't mistake highlighting for learning. You will not learn what you highlight unless you interact with it through careful review— questioning, writing, and reciting.

Be sure to divide your reading into digestible segments, pacing yourself so that you understand as you go. If you find you are losing the thread of the ideas, you may want to try smaller segments or take a break and come back to it later. Try to avoid reading in mere sets of time—such as, "I'll read for 30 minutes and then quit"—or you may short-circuit your understanding by stopping in the middle of a key explanation.

Finding the main idea

One crucial skill in textbook reading is finding the main, or central, idea of a piece of writing (e.g., a book, a chapter, an article, a paragraph). The *main idea* refers to the thoughts that are at the heart of the writing, the idea that creates its essential meaning. Comprehension depends on your ability to recognize main ideas and to link the author's other thoughts to them.

Where do you find the main idea? As an example, consider a paragraph. The main idea may be:

- In a *topic sentence* at the very beginning of the paragraph, stating the topic of the paragraph and what the author wants to communicate about that topic, and followed by sentences adding support.
- At the end of the paragraph, following supporting details that lead up to it.
- Buried in the middle of the paragraph, sandwiched between supporting details.
- In a compilation of ideas from various sentences, each of which contains a critical element. It is up to the reader to piece these elements together to create the essence of meaning.
- Never explicitly stated, but implied by the information presented in the paragraph.

How, then, do you decide just what the main idea is? Ophelia H. Hancock, a specialist in improving reading skills for post-secondary students, takes a three-step approach:[5]

1. *Search for the topic of the paragraph.* The topic of the paragraph is not the same thing as the main idea. Rather, it is the broad subject being discussed—for example, former prime minister Jean Chrétien, or downloading music from the Internet.

2. *Identify the aspect of the topic that is the paragraph's focus.* If the general topic is former prime minister Jean Chrétien, the writer may choose to focus on any of literally thousands of aspects of that topic. Here are just a few: his relationship with George W. Bush, the fallout from the Gomery Inquiry, key events in his early adult years, the people he chose as cabinet ministers, his effectiveness as prime minister, his relationship with family.

3. *Find what the author wants you to know about the specific aspect being discussed, which is the main idea.* The main idea of a paragraph dealing with former prime minister Jean Chrétien as a public speaker may be this: *Prime Minister Jean Chrétien was a gifted,*

charismatic speaker who used his humour, charm, and intelligence to help the federal Liberal Party win three consecutive terms in Ottawa.

Recite

Once you finish reading a topic, stop and answer the questions you raised in the Q-stage of SQ3R. You may decide to *recite* each answer aloud, silently speak the answers to yourself, tell or teach the answers to another person, or write your ideas and answers in brief notes. Writing is often the most effective way to solidify what you have read because writing from memory checks your understanding.

The best effect of any book is that it excites the reader to self-activity.

THOMAS CARLYLE

---

get analytical!   FIND THE MAIN IDEA

Develop your ability to analyze the parts of a paragraph.

Use the three-step approach described on page 147 to find the main idea of the following paragraph from the Fourth Canadian Edition of *The Simon and Schuster Handbook for Writers* by Troyka and Hesse:

> Tone is more than what you say; tone is how you say it. Your tone reveals your attitude toward your audience as well as the topic. Tone in writing operates like tone of voice, except in writing you can't rely on facial expressions and voice intonations to communicate your message. Your diction (choice of words), level of formality and writing style create your tone. While you can use slang and other highly informal language in a note to your roommate or a close friend, such a relaxed tone isn't appropriate for academic writing or business writing. In business and professions, if you write a memo to your supervisor about a safety hazard in your workplace, avoid writing a chatty message with a joke about an accident that could happen. Such a tone directed at your supervisor would be considered flippant or irresponsible.[6]

● What is the topic of this paragraph?

_____

_____

● What aspect of tone is being discussed?

_____

_____

● What main idea is being communicated?

_____

_____

Now choose a meaty paragraph from one of the texts you are currently studying, and use the same questions to find the paragraph's main idea. How do these questions help you focus on the paragraph's most important points?

Keep your learning styles (Chapter 3) in mind when you explore different strategies. For example, an intrapersonal learner may prefer writing, while an interpersonal learner might want to recite answers aloud to a classmate. A logical–mathematical learner may benefit from organizing material into detailed outlines, while a musical learner might want to chant information aloud to a rhythm.

After you finish one section, read the next. Repeat the question–read–recite cycle until you complete the entire chapter. If you find yourself fumbling for thoughts, you may not yet "own" the ideas. Reread the section that's giving you trouble until you master its contents. Understanding each section as you go is crucial because the material in one section often forms a foundation for the next.

Review

Review soon after you finish a chapter. Reviewing, both immediately and periodically in the days and weeks after you read, is the step that solidifies your understanding. Chances are good that if you close the book after you read, much of your focused reading work will slip away from memory. Here are some techniques for reviewing—try many and use what works best for you.

- Skim and reread your notes. Then try summarizing them from memory.
- Answer the text's end-of-chapter review, discussion, and application questions.
- Quiz yourself, using the questions you raised in the Q stage. If you can't answer one of your own or one of the text's questions, go back and scan the material for answers.
- Review and summarize in writing the material you have highlighted or bracketed.
- Create a chapter outline in standard outline form or think link form.
- Reread the preface, headings, tables, and **summary**.
- Recite important concepts to yourself, or record important information on a cassette tape and play it on your car's tape deck or your portable cassette player.
- Make flash cards that have an idea or word on one side and examples, a definition, or other related information on the other. Test yourself.
- Think critically: Break ideas down into examples, consider similar or different concepts, recall important terms, evaluate ideas, and explore causes and effects (see the next section for details).
- Discuss the concepts with a classmate or in a study group. Trying to teach study partners what you learned will pinpoint the material you know and what still needs work.
- Make think links that show how important concepts relate to one another.

If you need help clarifying your reading material, ask your instructor. Pinpoint the material you want to discuss, schedule a meeting during office hours, and bring a list of questions.

SUMMARY

A concise restatement of the material, in your own words, that covers the main points.

Refreshing your knowledge is easier and faster than learning it the first time. Set up regular review sessions; for example, once a week. Reviewing in as many different ways as possible increases the likelihood of retention. Critical reading may be the most important of these ways.

How can you *respond* critically to what you read?

The fundamental purpose of all college reading is understanding. Think of your reading process as an archaeological dig. The first step is to excavate a site and uncover the artifacts —that's your initial survey and reading of the material. As important as the excavation is, the process is incomplete if you stop there. The second step is to investigate each item, evaluate what they all mean, and derive knowledge

STRESSBUSTER

CLAIRE DOUGLAS York University, Toronto, Ontario

Do you sometimes find it difficult to find the time or proper setting to study? What sorts of distractions do you face? How do you cope with these distractions and reduce the stress associated with them?

We all occasionally have trouble finding the time to study. There always seems to be something else that needs to be done. I find the greatest distractions are assignments and readings from other courses I am taking. If I have many things due around the same time, I sometimes get overwhelmed with figuring out how I am going to get everything done on time.

I have learned over the years that I am most effective if I am calm and if I can focus on one task at a time. When I start to feel overwhelmed I take time to prioritize my assignments, my studying, and my reading and to come up with a general timeline for each project.

Once I have the time laid out, I choose a setting where I can study without external distractions. I know that I often get distracted by the television, email, and telephone. I am probably like most people in that I can get quite bored with the repetition of studying. It always seems like a great idea to pick up the phone so I can have a "quick study break," but it usually isn't very quick. Study breaks should be times that you can control. I find that a quick walk around the block to get some exercise is really refreshing and allows me to focus more on studying. When it is really cold out I drink a cup of peppermint tea to refresh my mind.

Finally, I try to remember that I can only do so much studying. Instead of worrying about the mark I might get on an exam, I focus on being prepared for the exam and on doing the best I can.

from what you discover. Critical reading allows you to complete that crucial second step.

Like critical thinking, critical reading is a part of analytical thinking (see Chapter 4). Instead of simply accepting what you read, seek understanding by questioning the material as you move from idea to idea. The best critical readers question every statement for accuracy, relevance, and logic. They also extend critical analysis to all media.

Use knowledge of fact and opinion to evaluate arguments

Critical readers evaluate arguments to determine whether they are accurate and logical. In this context, *argument* refers to a persuasive case—a set of connected ideas supported by examples—that a writer makes to prove or disprove a point.

It's easy—and common—to accept or reject an argument outright, according to whether it fits with your point of view. If you ask questions, however, you can determine the argument's validity and understand it in greater depth. Evaluating an argument involves

- evaluating the quality of the evidence.
- evaluating whether support fits the concept.
- evaluating the logical connections.

When quality evidence combines with appropriate support and tight logic, the argument is solid.

What is the quality of the evidence? Ask the following questions to evaluate the evidence:

- What is the source?
- Is the source reliable and free of bias?
- Who wrote this and with what intent?
- What assumptions underlie this material?
- Is the argument based on opinion?
- How does the evidence compare with evidence from other sources?

How well does the evidence support the idea? Ask these questions to determine whether the evidence fits the concept:

- Is there enough evidence to support the central idea?
- Do examples and ideas logically connect to one another?
- Is the evidence convincing? Do the examples build a strong case?
- What different and perhaps opposing arguments seem just as valid?

Approach every argument with healthy skepticism. Have an open mind in order to assess whether you are convinced or have serious questions. Use critical thinking to make an informed decision.

If, for example, you read an article with this premise: "The dissolution of the traditional family unit (working father, stay-at-home mother, dependent children) is contributing to society's problems," you might examine the facts and examples the writer uses to support this statement, looking carefully at the cause-and-effect structure of the argument. You might question the writer's sources. You might think of examples that support the statement. You might find examples that disprove this argument, such as statistics that show strong job numbers and college degree completion in areas where non-traditional family units are common. Finally, you might think of opposing arguments, including the ideas and examples to support those arguments.

Media literacy

The agencies of mass communication—radio, television, film, journalism (magazines and newspapers), books, and the Internet.

Use your analytical thinking skills to analyze the information you receive through the **media**, including television, radio, film, the Internet, newspapers, magazines, and books. By improving your *media literacy*, you will approach every media message with a healthy skepticism that leads you to ask questions, look for evidence, recognize perspectives, and challenge assumptions. This approach will help you decide which information you can trust and use.

The Center for Media Literacy explains "Five Core Concepts of Media Literacy":[7]

1. **All media are constructions.** All media are carefully constructed presentations designed for particular effect—to encourage you to feel certain emotions, to develop particular opinions, or to buy advertised products.

2. **Media use unique "languages."** Creators of media carefully choose wording, music, colours, timing, and other factors to produce a desired effect.

3. **Different audiences understand the same media message differently.** Individuals understand media in the context of their unique experiences. Someone who has climbed a mountain, for example, will experience a Mount Everest documentary differently than someone who has not.

4. **Media have commercial interests.** Creators of media are driven by the intent to sell products, services, or ideas. Advertising is chosen to appeal to the most likely audience (for example, beer and automobile ads directed at 20- to 30 year-old men, often appear during sporting events).

5. **Media have embedded values and points of view.** Any media product reflects the values and biases of the people who created it.

Critical reading of texts and the media takes time and focus. You can learn from others by working in pairs or groups whenever you can.

How and why should you *study with others*?

Much of what you know and will learn comes from your interaction with the outside world. Often this interaction takes place between you and one or more people. You listen to instructors and other students, you read materials that people have written, and you try out the behaviour and ideas of those whom you most trust and respect. You often work in a *team*—a group of fellow students, co-workers, family members, or others who strive together to reach an objective.

Learning takes place the same way in your career and personal life. Today's workplace puts the emphasis on work done through team effort. Companies value the ideas, energy, and co-operation that result from a well-coordinated team.

Leaders and Participants

Study groups and other teams rely on both leaders and participants to accomplish goals. Becoming aware of the roles each plays will increase your effectiveness.[8] Keep in mind that participants sometimes perform leadership tasks and vice versa. In addition, some teams shift leadership frequently during a project.

Being an Effective Participant. Some people are most comfortable when participating in a group that someone else leads. However, even when they are not leading, participants are "part owners" of the team process with a responsibility for, and a stake in, the outcome. The following strategies will help you become more effective in this role.

- *Get involved.* Let people know your views on decisions.
- *Be organized.* The more focused your ideas, the more other group members will take them seriously.
- *Be willing to discuss.* Be open to the opinions of others, even if they differ from your own.

FORM A STUDY GROUP

get practical!

Form a study group for one of your courses.

Get a group together and use this form to decide on and record the details.

- Course name: _____
- Study group members (names, phone numbers, e-mail addresses):

Member #1 _____

Member #2 _____

Member #3 _____

Member #4 _____

Member #5 _____

- Regular meeting time(s):
- Regular meeting place(s):
- Three strategies you plan to use to make the most of group time:

Strategy #1: _____

Strategy #2: _____

Strategy #3: _____

- *Keep your word.* Carry out whatever tasks you promise to do.
- *Play fairly.* Give everyone a chance to participate and always be respectful.

Being an Effective Leader. Some people prefer to initiate the action, make decisions, and control how things proceed. Leaders often have a "big-picture" perspective that allows them to envision how different aspects of a group project will come together. In any group, the following strategies help a leader succeed.

- **Define and limit projects.** The leader should define the group's purpose (e.g., brainstorming, decision making, or project collaboration) and limit tasks so that the effort remains focused.
- **Assign work and set a schedule.** A group functions best when everyone has a particular contribution to make and when deadlines are clear.
- **Set meeting and project agendas.** The leader should, with advice from other group members, establish and communicate goals and define how the work will proceed.
- **Focus progress.** It is the leader's job to keep everyone on target and headed in the right direction.
- **Set the tone.** If the leader is fair, respectful, encouraging, and hard working, group members are likely to follow the example.
- **Evaluate results.** The leader should determine whether the team is accomplishing its goals on schedule. If the team is not moving ahead, the leader should make changes.

Strategies for Study Group Success

Every study group is unique. The way a group operates may depend on the members' personalities, the subject you study, the location of the group, and the size of the group. No matter what your particular group's situation, though, certain general strategies will help.

- **Choose a leader for each meeting.** Rotating the leadership among members willing to lead helps all members take ownership of the group. If a leader has to miss class for any reason, choose another leader for that meeting.
- **Set long-term and short-term goals.** At your first meeting, determine what the group wants to accomplish over the semester. At the start of each meeting, have one person compile a list of questions to address.
- **Adjust to different personalities.** Respect and communicate with members. The art of getting along will serve you well in the workplace, where you don't often choose your co-workers.
- **Share the workload.** The most important factor is a willingness to work, not a particular level of knowledge.
- **Set a regular meeting schedule.** Try every week, every two weeks, or whatever the group can manage.

- **Create study materials for one another.** Give each group member the task of finding a piece of information to compile, photocopy, and review for the other group members.
- **Help each other learn.** One of the best ways to solidify knowledge is to teach it. Have group members teach pieces of information; make up quizzes for each other; go through flash cards together.
- **Pool your note-taking resources.** Compare notes with your group members and fill in any information you don't have. Try other note-taking styles: For example, if you generally use outlines, rewrite your notes in a think link. If you tend to map out ideas in a think link, try the Cornell System (see Chapter 6 for more on note taking).

Benefits of Working with Others

If you apply this information to your schoolwork, you will see that studying with a partner or in a group can enhance your learning in many ways. You benefit from shared knowledge, solidified knowledge, increased motivation, and increased teamwork ability.

The wise person learns from everyone.

ETHICS OF THE FATHERS

Shared knowledge. Each student has a unique body of knowledge and individual strengths. Students can learn from one another. To have individual students pass on their knowledge to each other in a study group requires less time and energy than for each of those students to learn all of the material alone.

Solidified knowledge. When you discuss concepts or teach them to others, you reinforce what you know and strengthen your critical thinking. Part of the benefit comes from simply repeating information aloud and rewriting it on paper, and part comes from how you think through information in your mind before you pass it on to someone else.

Increased motivation. When you study by yourself, you are accountable to yourself alone. In a study group, however, others see your level of work and preparation, which may increase your motivation.

Increased teamwork ability. The more you understand the dynamics of working with a group and the more experience you have at it, the more you build your ability to work well with others. This is an invaluable skill for the workplace, and it contributes to your personal marketability.

читать

This word may look completely unfamiliar to you, but anyone who can read the Russian language and knows the alphabet will know that it means "read." People who read languages that use different kinds of characters, such as Russian, Japanese, or Greek, learn to process those characters as easily as you process the letters of your native alphabet. Your mind learns to process individually each letter or character you see. This ability enables you to move to the next level of understanding—making sense of those letters or characters when they are grouped to form words, phrases, and sentences.

Think of this concept when you read. Remember that your mind processes immeasurable amounts of information so that you can understand the concepts on the page. Give yourself the opportunity to succeed by reading often and by focusing on the elements that help you read to the best of your ability.

BUILDING SKILLS

FOR ACADEMIC, CAREER, AND LIFE SUCCESS

Developing Successful Intelligence

Studying a text page. The following page is from the chapter "Groups and Organizations" in the Fourth Canadian Edition of *Sociology* by John J. Macionis and Linda Gerber. Apply SQ3R as you read the excerpt. Using what you learned in this chapter about study techniques, complete the questions that follow (some questions ask you to mark the page itself).

Step 1. Think it through: *Gather information and analyze it.* First gather: Skim the excerpt. Identify the headings on the page and the relationships among them. Mark primary-level headings with a #1, secondary headings with a #2, and tertiary (third-level) headings with a #3. Then analyze:

Which heading serves as an umbrella for the rest?

_____

What do the headings tell you about the content of the page?

_____

What are three concepts that seem important to remember?

*1.*_____

*2.*_____

*3.*_____

create your future

Volunteers and emergency personnel help injured vacationers from a tornado-ravaged campground at Pine Lake, Aberta, in July 2000. Extraordinary circumstances such as storms, floods, tornadoes, or accidents can turn a crowd into a group, and strangers into neighbours.

maintaining their individuality, the members of social groups also think of themselves as a special "we."

GROUPS, CATEGORIES, AND CROWDS

People often use the term *group* imprecisely. Below, we distinguish the group from the similar concepts of category and crowd.

Category

A *category* refers to people who have some status in common. Women, single fathers, homeowners, and Roman Catholics are all examples of categories.

Why are categories not considered groups? Simply because, while the individuals involved are aware that they are not the only ones to hold that particular status, the vast majority are strangers to one another.

Crowd

A *crowd* refers to a temporary cluster of individuals who may or may not interact. Students sitting together in a lecture hall engage one another and share a common identity as college classmates; thus, such a crowd might be called a loosely formed group. By contrast, riders on a subway train or bathers enjoying a summer day at the beach pay little attention to one another and amount to an anonymous aggregate of people. In effect, crowds are too transitory and too impersonal to qualify as social groups.

Circumstances, however, can turn a crowd into a group. As Torontonians learned so tragically in August 1995, people riding in a subway train that crashes under the city streets become keenly aware of their common plight and begin to help one another—often with heroic effort. Such extraordinary experiences may become the basis for lasting relationships.

PRIMARY AND SECONDARY GROUPS

Acquaintances commonly greet one another with a smile and the simple phrase "Hi! How are you?" The response is usually a well-scripted "Just fine, thanks. How about you?" This answer, of course, is often more formal than truthful. In most cases, providing a detailed account of how you are *really* doing would prompt the other person to beat a hasty and awkward exit.

Sociologists classify social groups by measuring them against two ideal types based on members' level of genuine personal concern. This variation is the key to distinguishing *primary* from *secondary* groups.

According to Charles Horton Cooley (1864–1929), who observed the effects of urbanization and industrialization on people's relationships over a century ago, a **primary group** is *a small social group whose members share personal and enduring relationships*. Bound together by *primary relationships*, individuals in these groups typically spend a great deal of time together, engage in a wide range of activities with one another, and feel that they know one another well. Although not without periodic conflict, members of primary groups display sincere concern for their mutual welfare. In every society, the family is the most important primary group.

Cooley characterized these personal and tightly integrated groups as *primary* because they are among the first groups we experience in life. In addition, the family and early play groups hold primary importance in the socialization process, shaping attitudes, behaviour, and social identity.

The strength of primary relationships gives people a comforting sense of security. In the familiar social circles of family or friends, people feel they can "be themselves" without constantly worrying about the impressions they are making.

162 Sociology

Source: *Sociology* Fourth Canadian Edition by John J. Macionis and Linda M. Gerber © 2002. Reprinted by permission of Pearson Education Canada, Inc., Toronto, ON.

Step 2. Think out of the box: *Create useful study questions.* Based on the three concepts you pulled out, write three study questions that you can review with an instructor, a teaching assistant, or a fellow student.

1. _____

2. _____

3. _____

Step 3. Make it happen: *Read and remember.* Read the excerpt, putting SQ3R to work. Using a marker pen, highlight key phrases and sentences. Write short marginal notes to help you review the material later. After reading this page thoroughly, write a short summary paragraph.

_____

_____

_____

Team Building

COLLABORATIVE SOLUTIONS

Organizing a study group. Organize a study group with three or four members of your class. At the group's first meeting:

- Set a specific goal for the group—to prepare for an upcoming test or project, for example—and create a weekly schedule. Write everything down and make sure everyone has a copy.
- Talk about the specific ways you will work together. Discuss which of the following methods you want to try in the group: pooling your notes, teaching each other difficult concepts; making up, administering, and grading quizzes for each other; creating study flash cards; using SQ3R to review required readings. Set specific guidelines for how group members will be held accountable.

As an initial group exercise, try the following:

- Review the study questions that you wrote for the *Sociology* excerpt. Each person should select one question to focus on while reading (no two people should have the same question). Group members should then reread the excerpt individually, thinking about their questions as they read and answering them in writing.
- When you finish reading critically, gather as a group. Each person should take a turn presenting the question, the response or answer that was derived through critical reading, and any other ideas that came up while reading. The other members of the group may then present any other ideas to add to the discussion. Continue until all group members have had a chance to present their concepts.

Over several weeks, try the group study methods you have chosen. Then evaluate the methods as a group, singling out the methods that most effectively helped group members master the course material. Finally, revise the group's methods if necessary, to focus on those most useful methods.

Writing

Record your thoughts on a separate piece of paper or in a journal.

Reading challenges. What course this semester presents your most difficult reading challenge? What makes it tough—the type of material you have to read, the amount, the level of difficulty? Thinking about the strategies in this chapter, create and describe a plan that addresses this challenge. What techniques might help, and how will you use them? What positive effects do you think they'll have?

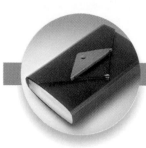

Career Portfolio

PLAN FOR SUCCESS

Complete the following in your electronic portfolio or on separate sheets of paper.

Reading skills on the job. Today's society revolves around the written word. The focus on word processing and computerized documents has increased the need for literate employees. As a recent *Condition of Education* report states, literacy is "viewed as one of the fundamental tools necessary for successful economic performance in industrialized societies. Literacy is no longer defined merely as a basic threshold of reading ability, but rather as the ability to understand and use printed information in daily activities, at home, at work, and in the community."[9] This is echoed by the Conference Board of Canada, which says that the power to "read and understand information presented in a variety of forms" is a fundamental employability skill.

For each of the following skill areas listed, indicate all of the ways in which you use that skill on the job or know you will need to use it in your future career. Then, also for each skill, rate your ability on a scale from 1 to 10, with 10 being highest. Finally, on the same document or sheet of paper, highlight or circle the two skills that you think will be most important for your career as well as for your success as a learner in college.

- ability to define your reading purpose
- reading speed
- reading comprehension
- vocabulary building
- identification and use of text-surveying devices
- using analytical thinking skills when reading
- evaluating reading material with others
- ability to understand and use visual aids

For the two skill areas in which you rated yourself lowest, think about how you can improve your abilities. Make a problem-solving plan for each (you may want to use a flow chart like the one on page 122 in Chapter 4). Check your progress in one month and at the end of the semester.

SUGGESTED READINGS

Armstrong, William H., and M. Willard Lampe II. *Barron's Pocket Guide to Study Tips: How to Study Effectively and Get Better Grades*. New York: Barron's Educational Series, 2004.

Chesla, Elizabeth. *Reading Comprehension Success: In 20 Minutes a Day*, 2nd ed. Florence, KY: Thomson Delmar Learning, 2002.

Frank, Steven. *The Everything Study Book*. Holbrook, MA: Adams Media, 1997.

Labunski, Richard E. *The Educated Student: Getting the Most Out of Your College Years*. Versailles, KY: Marley and Beck, 2003.

Luckie, William R., Wood Smethurst, and Sarah Beth Huntley. *Study Power Workbook: Exercises in Study Skills to Improve Your Learning and Your Grades*. Cambridge, MA: Brookline Books, 1999.

Silver, Theodore. *The Princeton Review Study Smart: Hands-on, Nuts and Bolts Techniques for Earning Higher Grades*. New York: Villard Books, 1996.

INTERNET RESOURCES

Academictips.org (study tips and links): www.academictips.org

How to Study (study advice with valuable links): www.howtostudy.com

Prentice Hall Student Success Supersite Study Skills: www.prenhall.com/success/

ENDNOTES

1. Sherwood Harris, *The New York Public Library Book of How and Where to Look It Up*. Englewood Cliffs, NJ: Prentice Hall, 1991, p. 12.

2. Steve Moidel, *Speed Reading*. Hauppauge, NY: Barron's Educational Series, 1994, p. 18.

3. Ibid.

4. Francis P. Robinson, *Effective Behaviour*. New York: Harper & Row, 1941.

5. Ophelia H. Hancock, *Reading Skills for College Students*, 5th ed. Upper Saddle River, NJ: Prentice Hall, 2001, pp. 54–59.

6. Excerpted from Lynn Quitman Troyka and Douglas Hesse, *Simon & Schuster Handbook for Writers, Fourth Canadian Edition*. Pearson Education Canada, Inc., 2006, pp. 13-14.

7. Center for Media Literacy, 1998.

8. Louis E. Boone, David L. Kurtz, and Judy R. Block, *Contemporary Business Communication*. Englewood Cliffs, NJ: Prentice Hall, 1994, pp. 489–499.

9. U.S. Department of Education, National Center for Education Statistics, *The Condition of Education, 1996*, NCES 96–304, by Thomas M. Smith. Washington, DC: U.S. Government Printing Office, 1996, p. 84.

FOCUS

IN THIS CHAPTER

In this chapter you will explore answers to the following questions: • **How can you become a better listener?** • **How can you make the most of note taking? Which note-taking system should you use?** • **How can you write faster when taking notes?** • **How does memory work?** • **What memory strategies can improve recall?**

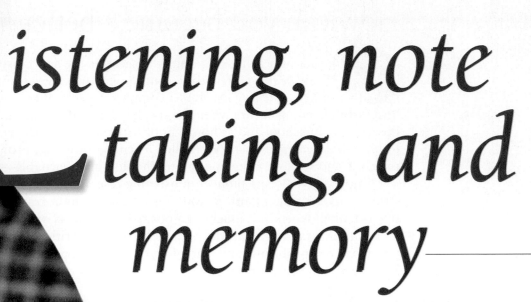

Listening, note taking, and memory

POST-SECONDARY education exposes you daily to facts, opinions, and ideas—and, as the Conference Board of Canada points out, the ability to "listen and ask questions to understand" is a key employability skill. This chapter shows you how to do just that through listening (taking in information), note taking (recording what's important), and memory skills (remembering information). Compare your skills to using a camera: You start by locating an image through the viewfinder, then you carefully focus the lens (listening), record the image on film (note taking), and produce a print (remembering). This chapter also shows you how better retention leads to the ability to apply your new knowledge to new situations.

taking in, recording, and retaining information

How can you become a better *listener*?

The act of hearing isn't quite the same as the act of **listening**. While *hearing* refers to sensing spoken messages from their source, *listening* involves a complex process of communication. Successful listening occurs when the speaker's intended message reaches the listener. In school and at home, poor listening may cause communication breakdowns and mistakes. Skilled listening, however, promotes progress and success. Listening is a teachable—and learnable—skill.

Ralph G. Nichols, a pioneer in listening research, studied 200 students over a nine-month period. His findings demonstrate that effective listening depends as much on a positive attitude as on specific skills.[1] Just as understanding the mind actions involved in critical thinking helps you work out problems, understanding the listening process helps you become a better listener.

Know the stages of listening

Listening is made up of four stages that build on one another: sensing, interpreting, evaluating, and reacting. These stages take the message from the speaker to the listener and back to the speaker (see Key 6.1).

- During the *sensation* stage (also known as hearing), your ears pick up sound waves and transmit them to the brain. For example, you are sitting in class and hear your instructor say, "The only opportunity to make up last week's test is Tuesday at 5:00 p.m."

Stages of listening.

key 6.1

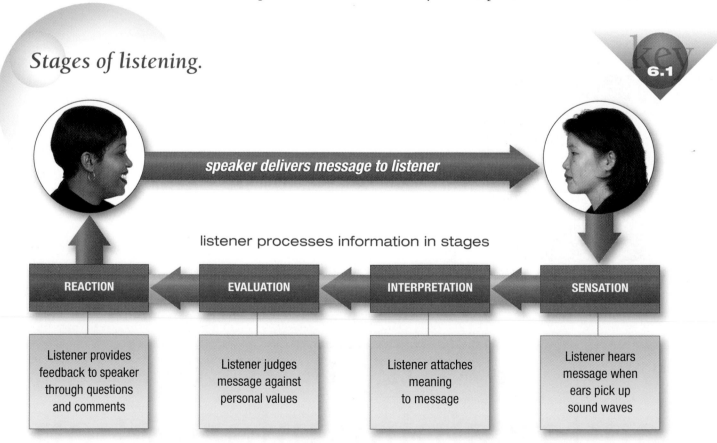

speaker delivers message to listener

listener processes information in stages

REACTION	EVALUATION	INTERPRETATION	SENSATION
Listener provides feedback to speaker through questions and comments	Listener judges message against personal values	Listener attaches meaning to message	Listener hears message when ears pick up sound waves

- In the *interpretation* stage, listeners attach meaning to a message. This involves understanding what is being said and relating it to what you already know. For example, you relate this message to your knowledge of the test, whether you need to make it up, and what you are doing on Tuesday at 5:00 p.m.

- In the *evaluation* stage of listening, you decide what you think or how you feel about the message—whether, for example, you like it or agree with it. This involves considering the message as it relates to your needs and values. In this example, if you do need to make up the test but have to work Tuesday at 5:00 p.m., you may evaluate the message as less than satisfactory.

- The final stage of listening involves a *reaction* to the message in the form of direct feedback. Your reaction, in this example, may be to ask the instructor for an alternative to the scheduled makeup test time.

Improving your listening skills involves two primary actions: managing listening challenges and becoming an active listener. Although becoming a better listener will help in every class, it is especially important in subjects that are challenging for you.

Manage listening challenges

Communication barriers can interfere with listening at every stage. In fact, classic studies have shown that immediately after listening, students are likely to recall only half of what was said. This is partly due to particular listening challenges such as divided attention and distractions, the tendency to shut out the message, the inclination to rush to judgment, and partial hearing loss or learning disabilities.[2]

To help create a positive listening environment in both your mind and your surroundings, explore how to manage these challenges.

Divided attention and distractions. Imagine you are talking with a co-worker in the company cafeteria when you hear your name mentioned across the room. You strain to hear what someone might be saying about you and, in the process, hear neither your friend nor the person across the room very well. This situation illustrates the consequences of divided attention. Although you are capable of listening to more than one message at the same time, you may not completely hear or understand any of them.

Internal and external distractions often divide your attention. *Internal distractions* include anything from hunger to headache to personal worries. Something the speaker says may also trigger a recollection that causes your mind to drift. In contrast, *external distractions* include noises (e.g., whispering or sirens) and excessive heat or cold. It can be hard to listen in an overheated room in which you are falling asleep.

Your goal is to reduce distractions so that you can focus on what you're hearing. Sitting near the front where you can clearly see and hear helps you to listen. To avoid distracting activity, you may want to sit away from people who might chat or make noise. Dress comfortably, paying attention to the temperature of the classroom, and try not to go to class hungry or thirsty. Work to concentrate on class when you're in class and worry about personal problems later.

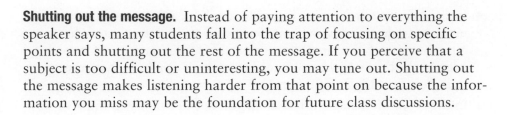

Shutting out the message. Instead of paying attention to everything the speaker says, many students fall into the trap of focusing on specific points and shutting out the rest of the message. If you perceive that a subject is too difficult or uninteresting, you may tune out. Shutting out the message makes listening harder from that point on because the information you miss may be the foundation for future class discussions.

> No one cares to speak to an unwilling listener. An arrow never lodges in a stone; often it recoils upon the sender of it.

ST. JEROME

Creating a positive listening environment includes accepting responsibility for listening. Although the instructor is responsible for communicating information to you, he or she cannot force you to listen. You are responsible for taking in that information. Instructors often cover material from outside the textbook during class and then test on that material. If you work to take in the whole message in class, you can read over your notes later and think critically about what is most important.

The rush to judgment. People tend to stop listening when they hear something they don't like. If you rush to judge what you've heard, making a quick uncritical assumption about it, your focus turns to your personal reaction rather than the content of the message. Judgments also involve reactions to the speakers themselves. If you do not like your instructors or if you have preconceived notions about their ideas or background, you may assume that their words have little value.

Work to recognize and control your judgments by listening first without jumping to conclusions. Ask critical-thinking questions about assumptions. Stay aware of what you tend to judge so that you can avoid rejecting messages that clash with your opinions. Consider education as a continuing search for evidence, regardless of whether that evidence supports or negates your perspective.

Partial hearing loss and learning disabilities. Good listening techniques don't solve every listening problem. If you have some level of hearing loss, seek out special services that can help you listen in class. For example, you may be able to tape record the lecture and play it back at a louder-than-normal volume after class, have special tutoring, or arrange for a classmate to take notes for you. In addition, you may be able to arrange to meet with your instructor outside of class to clarify your notes.

Other disabilities, such as attention deficit disorder (ADD) or a problem with processing spoken language, can make it hard to focus on and understand oral messages. If you have one of these disabilities, don't blame yourself for your difficulty. Visit your school's counselling or student health centre, or talk with your advisor or instructors about getting the help you need to meet your challenges.

Become an active listener

On the surface, listening seems like a passive activity; you sit back and listen as someone else speaks. Effective listening, however, is really an active process that involves setting a purpose for listening, paying attention to **verbal signposts**, and asking questions.

Set purposes for listening. Active listening is possible only if you know (and care) why you are listening. In any situation, establish what you want to achieve through listening, such as greater understanding of the material or better note taking. Having a purpose gives you a goal that motivates you to listen.

Pay attention to verbal signposts. You can identify important facts and ideas and predict test questions by paying attention to the speaker's specific choice of words. Verbal signposts often involve transition words and phrases that help organize information, connect ideas, and indicate what is and is not important. Let phrases like those in Key 6.2 direct your attention to the material that follows them.

Ask questions. Successful listening is closely linked to asking questions. A willingness to ask questions shows a desire to learn and is the mark of a critical thinker. Asking questions has two benefits. First of all, it helps you to deepen your understanding of what you hear. This happens when you ask either informational or clarifying questions. *Informational* questions, such as any questions beginning with "Can you explain…" seek information that you haven't yet heard or acquired. *Clarifying* questions ask if your understanding of something you just heard is correct, such as "So some learning disabilities can be improved with treatment?" Second of all, questions help to solidify your memory of what you are hearing. As you think of the question, raise your hand, speak, and listen to the answer, brain activity and physical activity combine to reinforce the information you are taking in.

Effective listening skills prepare you to take effective notes—a necessary and powerful study tool.

VERBAL SIGNPOSTS

Spoken words or phrases that call your attention to the information that follows.

Verbal signposts point out important information.

Key 6.2

SIGNALS POINTING TO KEY CONCEPTS	SIGNALS OF SUPPORT
There are two reasons for this…	For example,…
A critical point in the process involves…	Specifically,…
Most importantly,…	For instance,…
The result is…	Similarly,…

SIGNALS POINTING TO DIFFERENCES	SIGNALS THAT SUMMARIZE
On the contrary,…	Finally,…
On the other hand,…	Recapping this idea,…
In contrast,…	In conclusion,…
However,…	As a result,…

get analytical! **DISCOVER YOURSELF AS A LISTENER**

Take a look at your personal listening habits.

Complete the following:

● Analyze how present you are as a listener. Are you easily distracted, or can you focus well? Do you prefer to listen, or do you tend to talk?

_____

_____

● When you are listening, what tends to distract you?

_____

_____

● What happens to your listening skills when you become confused?

_____

_____

● How do you react when you strongly disagree with something your instructor says—when you are convinced that you are "right" and your instructor is "wrong"?

_____

_____

● Thinking about your answers and about your listening challenges, list two strategies from the chapter that can help you focus and improve your listening skills.

1. _____

2. _____

How can you make the most of *note taking?*

Notes help you learn when you are in class, doing research, or studying. Because it is virtually impossible to take notes on everything you hear or read, the act of note taking encourages you to decide what is worth remembering, and involves you in the learning process in many important ways:

● Your notes provide material that helps you study and prepare for tests.
● When you take notes, you listen better and become more involved in class.
● Notes help you think critically and organize ideas.
● The information you learn in class may not appear in any text; you will have no way to study it without writing it down.

- If it is difficult for you to process information while in class, having notes to read can help you process and learn the information.
- Note taking is a skill that you will use on the job, in community activities, and in your personal life.

Good note taking demands good listening. The listening skills you just explored are what allow you to hear what you will be evaluating and writing down. Listening and note taking depend on one another.

Recording information in class

Your notes have two purposes: First, they should reflect what you heard in class, and second, they should be a resource for studying, writing, or comparing with your text material. If lectures include material that is not in your text or if your instructor talks about specific test questions, your class notes become even more important as a study tool.

Preparing to take class notes. Taking good class notes depends on good preparation.

Preview your reading material. Survey the text (or any other assigned reading material) to become familiar with the topic and any new concepts that it introduces. Visual familiarity helps note taking during lectures.

Gather your supplies. Use separate pieces of notebook paper for each class. If you use a three-ring binder, punch holes in handouts and insert them immediately following your notes for that day. Make sure your pencils are sharp and your pens aren't about to run out.

Location, location, location. Find a comfortable seat where you can easily see and hear. Sitting near the front, where you minimize distraction and maximize access to the lecture or discussion, might be your best bet. Be ready to write as soon as the instructor begins speaking.

Choose the best note-taking system. Select a system that is most appropriate for the situation. Later in the chapter, you will learn about different note-taking systems. Take the following factors into account when choosing one to use in any class:

- **The instructor's style** (you'll be able to determine this style after a few classes). Whereas one instructor may deliver organized lectures at a normal speaking rate, another may jump from topic to topic or talk very quickly.
- **The course material.** After experimenting for a few class meetings, you may decide that an informal outline works best for your philosophy course, but that a think link works for your sociology course.
- **Your learning style.** Choose strategies that make the most of your strong points and help boost weaker areas. A visual–spatial learner might prefer think links or the Cornell system (see page 175), for example, while a thinker type might stick to outlines; an interpersonal learner might use the Cornell system and fill in the cue column in a study group setting (see Chapter 3 for a complete discussion of learning styles).

get practical! FACE A NOTE-TAKING CHALLENGE

Prepare to take notes in your toughest class.

In the spaces below, record the specific steps you will take to prepare to take notes in what you consider to be your most challenging course.

- Course name and date of class:

  _____

- List all the reading you must complete before your next class (include pages from text and supplemental sources):

  _____

  _____

- Where will you sit in class to focus your attention and minimize distractions?

  _____

- Which note-taking system is best suited for the class, and why?

  _____

- Write the names and e-mail addresses of two classmates whose notes you can borrow if you miss a class:

  _____

  _____

Gather support. For each class, set up a support system with two students. That way, when you are absent, you can get the notes you missed from one or the other.

What to do during class

Because no one has time to write down everything he or she hears, the following strategies will help you choose and record what you feel is important in a format that you can read and understand later. This is not a list of "musts." Rather, it is a list of ideas to try as you work to find the note-taking strategies that work best for you. Experiment until you feel that you have found a successful combination.

Remember that the first step in note taking is to listen actively; you can't write down something that you don't hear. Use the listening strategies you read earlier in the chapter to make sure you are prepared to take in the information that comes your way.

- Date and identify each page. When you take several pages of notes during a lecture, add an identifying letter or number to the date on each page; for example, 27/11 A, 27/11 B, or 27/11—1 of 3, 27/11—2 of 3. This helps you keep track of the order of your pages. Add the specific topic of the lecture at the top of the page. For example: 27/11—Canadian Immigration Policy After World War II.

- If your instructor jumps from topic to topic during class, try starting a new page for each new topic.

- Ask yourself critical-thinking questions: Do I need this information? Is the information important or just a digression? Is the information

Note Taking ◀

Note taking is a critical learning tool. The tips below will help you retain information for both the short and long term.

INTELLIGENCE	SUGGESTED STRATEGIES	WHAT WORKS FOR YOU? WRITE NEW IDEAS HERE
Verbal–Linguistic	• Rewrite important ideas and concepts in class notes from memory. • Write summaries of your notes in your own words.	
Logical–Mathematical	• Organize the main points of a lecture or reading using outline form. • Make charts and diagrams to clarify ideas and examples.	
Bodily–Kinesthetic	• Make note taking as physical as possible—use large pieces of paper and different coloured pens. • When in class, choose a comfortable spot where you have room to spread out your materials and shift body position when you need to.	
Visual–Spatial	• Take notes using coloured markers. • Rewrite lecture notes in think link format, focusing on the most important and difficult points from the lecture.	
Interpersonal	• Whenever possible, schedule a study group right after a lecture to discuss class notes. • Review class notes with a study buddy. See what you wrote that he or she missed and vice versa.	
Intrapersonal	• Schedule some quiet time as soon as possible after a lecture to reread and think about your notes. If no class is meeting in the same room after yours and you have free time, stay in the room and review there.	
Musical	• Play music while you read your notes. • Write a song that incorporates material from one class period's notes or one particular topic. Use the refrain to emphasize the most important concepts.	
Naturalistic	• Read or rewrite your notes outside. • Review notes while listening to a nature CD—running water, rain, forest sounds.	

How to pick up on instructors' cues.

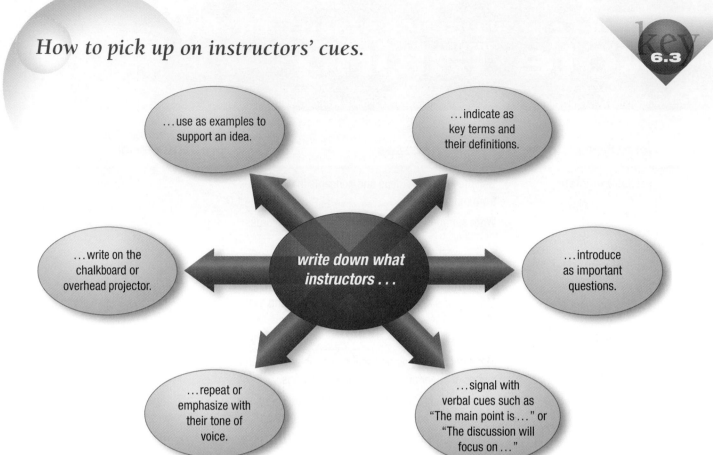

...use as examples to support an idea.

...indicate as key terms and their definitions.

...write on the chalkboard or overhead projector.

write down what instructors . . .

...introduce as important questions.

...repeat or emphasize with their tone of voice.

...signal with verbal cues such as "The main point is . . ." or "The discussion will focus on . . ."

fact or opinion? If it is opinion, is it worth remembering? (Chapter 4 discusses how to distinguish between fact and opinion.)

- Record whatever an instructor emphasizes—key terms, definitions, ideas, and examples (see Key 6.2 for specifics on how an instructor might call attention to particular information).

- Continue to take notes during class discussions and question-and-answer periods. What your fellow students ask about may help you as well.

- Leave one or more blank spaces between points. This white space helps you review your notes because information appears in self-contained sections.

- Draw pictures and diagrams that help illustrate ideas.

- Indicate material that is especially important with a star, with underlining, with a highlighter, or by writing words in capital letters.

- If you don't understand something, leave space and place a question mark in the margin. Then, take advantage of your resources—ask the instructor to explain it after class, discuss it with a classmate, or consult your textbook—and fill in the blank when the idea is clear.

- Take notes until the instructor stops speaking. If you stop writing a few minutes before the class is over, you might miss critical information.

- Make your notes as legible and organized as possible—you can't learn from notes that you can't read or understand. But don't be too fussy; you can always rewrite and improve your notes.

- Consider that your notes are part, but not all, of what you need to learn. Using your text to add to your notes after class makes a superior, "deeper and wider" set of information to study.

Reviewing and Revising Your Notes

Even the most comprehensive notes in the world won't do you any good unless you review them. The crucial act of reviewing helps you solidify the information in your memory so that you can recall it and use it. It also helps you link new information to information you already know, which is a key step in building new ideas. The review and revision stage of note taking should include time for planning, critical thinking, adding information from other sources, summarizing, and working with a study group.

Plan a review schedule

When you review your notes affects how much you are likely to remember. Reviewing right after the lecture but not again until the test, reviewing here and there without a plan, or cramming it all into one crazy night does not allow you to make the most of your abilities. Do yourself a favour by planning your time strategically.

Review within a day of the lecture. Reviewing while the material is still fresh in your mind helps you to remember it. You don't have to sit down for two hours and focus on every word. Just set some time aside to reread your notes, if you can, and perhaps write questions and comments on them. If you know you have an hour between classes, for example, that is an ideal time to work in a quick review.

Review regularly. Try to schedule times during the week for reviewing notes from that week's class meetings. For example, if you know you always have from 2:00 p.m. to 5:00 p.m. free every Tuesday and Thursday afternoon, you can plan to review notes from two courses on Tuesday and from two others on Thursday. Having a routine helps ensure that you look at material regularly.

Review with an eye toward tests. When you have a test coming up, step up your efforts. Schedule longer review sessions, call a study group meeting, and review more frequently. Shorter sessions of intense review work interspersed with breaks may be more effective than long hours of continuous studying. Some students find that recopying their notes before an exam or at an earlier stage helps cement key concepts in memory.

Revise using other sources and critical thinking

Revising and adding to your notes using material from your texts, other required course readings, and the Internet is one of the best ways to build your understanding and link new information to information you already know. Try using the following critical-thinking actions when you add to your notes:

- Brainstorm and write down examples from other sources that illustrate central ideas in your notes.
- Pay attention to similarities between your text materials and class notes (ideas that appear in both are probably important to remember).
- Think of facts or ideas from the reading that can support and clarify ideas from your notes.
- Consider what in your class notes differs from your reading, and why.

- Write down any new ideas that come up when reviewing your notes.
- Look at cause-and-effect relationships between material from your notes and reading material. Note how ideas, facts, and examples relate to one another.

Summarize

Writing a summary of your notes is another important review technique. Summarizing involves critically evaluating which ideas and examples are most important and then rewriting the material in a shortened form, focusing on those important ideas and examples.

You may prefer to summarize as you review, with the notes in front of you. If you are using the Cornell system (see page 175), you summarize in the space saved at the bottom of the page. Other ideas include summarizing on a separate page that you insert in your loose-leaf binder or summarizing on the back of the previous page (this is possible if you only take notes on one side of the paper).

Another helpful review technique is to summarize your notes from memory after you review them. This gives you an idea of how well you have retained the information. You may even want to summarize as you read, then summarize from memory, and compare the two summaries.

Work with study groups

When you work with a study group, you have the opportunity to review both your personal notes and those of other members of the class. This can be an enormous help if, for example, you lost concentration during part of a lecture and your notes don't make much sense. You and another student may even have notes that contradict each other or have radically different information. When this happens, try to reconstruct what the instructor said and, if necessary, bring in a third group member to clear up the confusion. See Chapter 5 for more on effective studying in groups.

You can take notes in many ways. Different note-taking systems suit different people and situations. Explore each system and choose what works for you.

Which *note-taking system* should you use?

There is more than one way to take good notes. You benefit most from the system that feels most comfortable to you and makes the most sense for the course content. For example, you might take notes in a different style for a history class than for a foreign language class. The most common note-taking systems include outlines, the Cornell system, and think links.

As you consider each system, remember your learning styles from Chapter 3. In each class, choose a system that takes both your learning styles and the class material into account. For example, a visual learner may take notes in think link style most of the time, but may find that only the Cornell style works well for a particular chemistry course. Experiment to discover what works best in any situation.

Taking notes in outline form

When a reading assignment or lecture seems well organized, you may choose to take notes in outline form. When you use an outline, you construct a line-by-line representation, with certain phrases set off by varying indentations, showing how ideas relate to one another and are supported by facts and examples.

Formal outlines indicate ideas and examples using Roman numerals, capital and lowercase letters, and numbers. When you are pressed for time, such as during class, you can use an informal system of consistent indenting and dashes instead. Formal outlines also require at least two headings on the same level—that is, if you have a IIA you must also have a IIB. Key 6.4 shows an outline on early Canadian history prior to 1500.

From time to time, an instructor may give you a guide, usually in the form of an outline, to help you take notes in the class. This outline may be on a page that you receive at the beginning of the class, on the board, on an overhead projector, or even posted online prior to the class. Because these are guided notes are usually general and sketchy, they require that you fill in the details.

Using the Cornell note-taking system

The Cornell note-taking system, also known as the T-note system, was developed more than 45 years ago by Walter Pauk at Cornell University.[3] The system is successful because it is simple—and because it works. It consists of three sections on ordinary notepaper:

- Section 1, the largest section, is on the right. Record your notes here in informal outline form.

- Section 2, to the left of your notes, is the *cue column*. Leave it blank while you read or listen; then fill it in later as you review. You might fill it with comments that highlight main ideas, clarify meaning, suggest examples, or link ideas and examples. You can even draw diagrams.

- Section 3, at the bottom of the page, is the *summary area*. Here you use a sentence or two to summarize the notes on the page. When you review, use this section to reinforce concepts and provide an overview.

When you use the Cornell system, create the note-taking structure before class begins. Picture an upside-down letter T and use Key 6.5 as your guide.

- Start with a sheet of standard loose-leaf paper. Label it with the date and title of the lecture.

- To create the cue column, draw a vertical line about 6 centimetres from the left side of the paper. End the line about 5 centimetres from the bottom of the sheet.

- To create the summary area, start at the point where the vertical line ends (about 5 centimetres from the bottom of the page) and draw a horizontal line that spans the entire paper.

Key 6.5 shows how a student used the Cornell system to take notes in an introductory business course.

EARLY CANADIAN HISTORY PRIOR TO 1500

I.   Early Canadian History

   A.   It is a myth that Canadian "history" began with the Europeans in the 1400s

      1.   Norsemen arrived in Newfoundland in 1000

      2.   Irish Monks arrived 200–300 years earlier

   B.   Aboriginal peoples mark the real start of Canadian history as they lived in what is now Canada 40 000 years before the Europeans arrived

II. Arrival of the First Peoples

   A.   Aboriginal oral histories say that it was a matter of creation

   B.   Anthropologists claim it was due to the last ice age about 40 000 to 1 000 000 years ago

      1.   A land bridge formed between North America and Asia

      2.   Animals began to cross the bridge; humans soon followed

      3.   Genetics shows that various groups migrated during this time

      4.   These groups, like many immigrants, lost contact with their homelands

      5.   As a result, Aboriginal culture began to develop in Canada

Creating a think link

VISUALIZATION

The interpretation of verbal ideas through the use of mental visual images.

A *think link*, also known as a mind map, is a visual form of note taking. When you draw a think link, you diagram ideas by using shapes and lines that link ideas and supporting details and examples. The visual design makes the connections easy to see, and the use of shapes and pictures extends the material beyond just words. Many learners respond well to the power of **visualization**. You can use think links to brainstorm ideas for paper topics as well.

Sample Cornell system notes.

October 3, 200X, p. 1

UNDERSTANDING EMPLOYEE MOTIVATION

Why do some workers have a better attitude toward their work than others?	Purpose of motivational theories — To explain role of human relations in motivating employee performance — Theories translate into how managers actually treat workers
Some managers view workers as lazy; others view them as motivated and productive.	2 specific theories — Human resources model, developed by Douglas McGregor, shows that managers have radically different beliefs about motivation. — Theory X holds that people are naturally irresponsible and uncooperative — Theory Y holds that people are naturally responsible and self-motivated
Maslow's Hierarchy self-actualization needs (challenging job) esteem needs (job title) social needs (friends at work) security needs (health plan) physiological needs (pay)	— Maslow's Hierarchy of Needs says that people have needs in 5 different areas, which they attempt to satisfy in their work. — Physiological need: need for survival, including food and shelter — Security need: need for stability and protection — Social need: need for friendship and companionship — Esteem need: need for status and recognition — Self-actualization need: need for self-fulfillment Needs at lower levels must be met before a person tries to satisfy needs at higher levels. — Developed by psychologist Abraham Maslow

Two motivational theories try to explain worker motivation. The human resources model includes Theory X and Theory Y. Maslow's Hierarchy of Needs suggests that people have needs in 5 different areas: physiological, security, social, esteem, and self-actualization.

One way to create a think link is to start by writing your topic in the middle of a sheet of paper and putting a circle around it. Next, draw a line from the circled topic and write the name of one major idea at the end of the line. Circle that idea also. Then, jot down specific facts related to the idea, linking them to the idea with lines. Continue the process, connecting thoughts to one another by using circles, lines, and words. Key 6.6 shows a think link on a sociology concept called social stratification.

This is only one of many think link styles; other examples include stair steps (showing connecting ideas that build to a conclusion) and a tree shape (roots as causes and branches as effects). Look back to Key 5.4 on page 145 for a type of think link sometimes referred to as a "jellyfish." You can design any think link that makes sense to you.

A think link may be tough to construct in class, especially if your instructor talks quickly. In this case, use another note-taking system during class. Then, make a think link as you review your notes.

Sample think link.

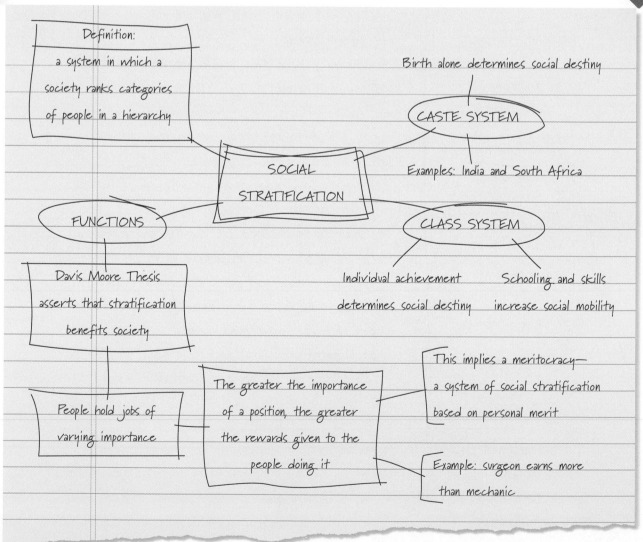

Definition:
a system in which a society ranks categories of people in a hierarchy

SOCIAL STRATIFICATION

Birth alone determines social destiny

CASTE SYSTEM

Examples: India and South Africa

CLASS SYSTEM

Individual achievement determines social destiny

Schooling and skills increase social mobility

FUNCTIONS

Davis Moore Thesis asserts that stratification benefits society

People hold jobs of varying importance

The greater the importance of a position, the greater the rewards given to the people doing it

This implies a meritocracy— a system of social stratification based on personal merit

Example: surgeon earns more than mechanic

Using other visual note-taking strategies

Several other note-taking strategies help you organize your information and are especially useful to visual learners. These strategies may be too involved to complete quickly during class, so you may want to use them when taking notes on a text chapter or when rewriting your notes for review.

Time lines. A time line can help you organize information—such as the dates Canadian prime ministers took office or eras of different psychology practices—into chronological order. Draw a vertical or horizontal line on the page and connect each item to the line, in order, noting the dates.

Tables. There are tables throughout this text that show information through vertical or horizontal columns. Use tables to arrange information according to particular categories.

Hierarchy charts. These charts can help you understand information in terms of how each piece fits into the **hierarchy**. A hierarchy chart could show levels of government, for example, or levels of the scientific classification of animals and plants. One version of a hierarchy is called a *matrix*—a table that has categories listed across the top and along the left side. Each box inside shows information that relates to the categories above and beside it. Key 10.4 on page 311 is an example of a matrix.

HIERARCHY
A graded or ranked series.

Once you choose a note-taking system, your success depends on how well you use it. Personal shorthand will help you make the most of whatever system you choose.

How can you *write faster* when taking notes?

When taking notes, many students feel that they can't keep up with the instructor. Using some personal **shorthand** (not standard secretarial shorthand) can help you push your pen faster. Shorthand is writing that shortens words or replaces them with symbols. Because you are the only intended reader, you can misspell and abbreviate words in ways that only you understand.

The only danger with shorthand is that you might forget what your writing means. To avoid this problem, review your shorthand notes while your abbreviations and symbols are fresh in your mind. If there is any confusion, spell out words as you review.

Here are some suggestions that will help you master this important skill:

SHORTHAND
A system of rapid handwriting that employs symbols, abbreviations, and shortened words to represent words, phrases, and letters.

1. Use the following standard abbreviations in place of complete words:

w/	with	cf	compare, in comparison to
w/o	without	ff	following
→	means; resulting in	Q	question
←	as a result of	p.	page

↑	increasing	*	most importantly
↓	decreasing	<	less than
∴	therefore	>	more than
∵ or b/c	because	=	equals
≈	approximately	%	percent
+ or &	and	△	change symbol
—	minus; negative	2	to; two; too
no. or #	number	vs.	versus; against
i.e.,	that is	e.g.	for example
etc.	and so forth	c/o	care of
ng	no good	lb	pound

2. Shorten words by removing vowels from the middle of words:

   prps = purpose

   Crvtte = Corvette (as on a vanity licence plate for a car)

3. Substitute word beginnings for entire words:

   assoc = associate; association

   info = information

4. Form plurals by adding *s*:

   prblms = problems

   prntrs = printers

5. Make up your own symbols and use them consistently:

   b/4 = before

   2thake = toothache

6. Use key phrases instead of complete sentences ("German—nouns capped" instead of "In German, all nouns are capitalized").

Finally, throughout your note taking, remember that the primary goal is for you to generate materials that help you learn and remember information. No matter how sensible any note-taking strategy, abbreviation, or system might be, it won't do you any good if it doesn't help you reach that goal. Keep a close eye on what works for you and stick to it.

If you find that your notes aren't comprehensive, legible, or focused enough, think critically about how you might improve them. Can't read your notes? You might have been too sleepy, or you might have a handwriting issue. Confusing gaps in the information? You might be distracted in class, have an instructor who skips around, or have a lack of understanding of the course material. Put your problem-solving skills to work and brainstorm solutions from the variety of strategies in this chapter. With a little time and effort, your notes will truly become a helpful learning tool in school and beyond.

Once you have figured out how to effectively record what you hear, your next task is to remember it so that you can use it. The following information about memory will help you remember what you learn so that you can put it to use.

How does *memory* work?

Your accounting instructor is giving a test tomorrow on the double-entry accounting system. You feel confident because you spent hours last week memorizing your notes. Unfortunately, by the time you take the test, you remember very little. This is not surprising, since most forgetting occurs within minutes after memorization.

In a classic study conducted in 1885, researcher Herman Ebbinghaus memorized a list of meaningless three-letter words such as CEF and LAZ. He then examined how quickly he forgot them. Within one hour he forgot more than 50 percent of what he had learned; after two days, he knew fewer than 30 percent of the material. Although Ebbinghaus's recall of the nonsense syllables remained fairly stable after that, his experiment shows how fragile memory can be—even when you take the time and expend the energy to memorize information.[4]

How your brain remembers: Short-term and long-term memory

Memories are stored in three different "storage banks" in your brain. The first, called sensory memory, is an exact copy of what you see and hear and lasts for a second or less. Certain information is then selected from sensory memory and moved into short-term memory, a temporary information storehouse that lasts no more than 10 to 20 seconds. You are consciously aware of material in short-term memory. Unimportant information is quickly dumped. Important information is transferred to long-term memory—the mind's more permanent storehouse.

Although all three stages are important, targeting long-term memory will solidify learning the most. "Short-term—or working—memory is useful when we want to remember a phone number until we can dial," says biologist James Zull. "We use short-term memory for these momentary challenges, all the time, every day, but it is limited in capacity, tenacity, and time."[5] Zull explains that short-term memory can hold only small amounts of information for brief periods. In addition, it is unstable—a distraction can easily dislodge information.

Retaining information in long-term memory

In order to retain information in long-term memory, your brain moves through a four-stage process, which relates directly to the stages of the listening process described on page 164. Key 6.7 illustrates the process.

1. **Experiencing the material** (concrete experience). Your brain takes in the information through one or more of your senses.

2. **Relating the material to what you already know** (reflexive observation). You reflect on the new information and connect it to previous knowledge.

3. **Forming new ideas** (abstract hypothesis). You come up with new insights from the combination of what you knew before and what you are learning now.

4. **Trying out and communicating new ideas** (active testing). You explore your ideas to see if they make sense and work.

Here's an example to illustrate the process.

1. In your Introduction to Business course, you hear the following information during the lecture: "During the economic bubble of the 1990s, ethical lapses were frequent at the highest levels of business. Among the corporations involved in ethical abuses were Enron and Tyco. Corporate executives at these companies bent the rules and ignored the law to maximize personal gain."

STRESSBUSTER

ANNA GRIFFIN   Algonquin College, Ottawa, ON

Do you ever have trouble following a lecture? Do you find it difficult to keep track of everything you are supposed to remember? What have you done to overcome these challenges?

Starting a new day can be extremely overwhelming. Knowing that school will take up all of a normal working day and knowing that you have to go to a job right afterwards is enough to make you want to quit. School is a full-time job, and it feels like the rest of the world has no idea what you're going through. When you do get to class, you can't take good notes or concentrate on what the professor is saying because all you can think about is the long day ahead.

The way that I've come to terms with this is to wake up in the morning and meet the day ahead of me straight on. You've got a challenge for me... bring it on! I start by doing something as simple as listening to my favourite music on the way to school, which always brightens my day. If I don't understand a question when I'm sitting in class, I ask. If **you** don't get it, you can almost guarantee that at least 50% of the people around you are lost too. That might sound obvious, but you will only take good notes and remember things that you understand. Asking questions takes a huge weight off your shoulders, and with it goes a lot of the stress you were carrying.

Also, be sure to have something that you enjoy outside of school and work. It could be music, photography, or friends—as long as it isn't school-related. Tension just melts away when you don't make school your entire world. When you have other hobbies, you will see the change in your attitude towards school... you will begin to enjoy it even more.

Long-term memory involves four stages.

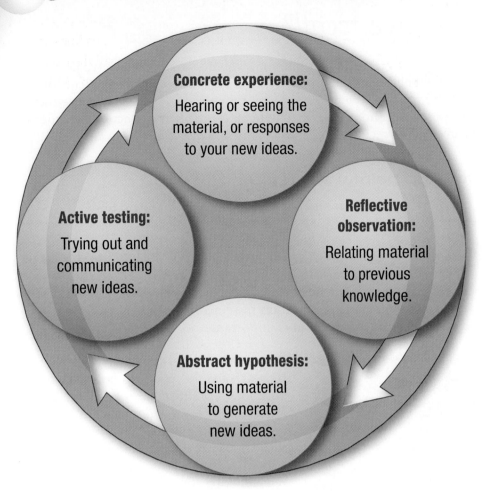

2. You think about the material in relation to what you know. First, you remember reading about the unethical practices of the billionaires of the 1930s, including J. P. Morgan and Andrew Carnegie, who built corporate empires—and amassed personal fortunes—through unethical business practices. Second, you begin to think about the findings of Canada's Gomery Inquiry and the implications for both business and government. Finally, you think about ethical and unethical behaviour you have seen in people you know personally.

3. You form a new idea: Government regulations are necessary to curb the all-too-human tendency to bend rules for personal gain.

4. You try out your idea by talking to classmates and thinking further.

Result: Information about business ethics is solidly anchored in long-term memory.

We rarely forget that which has made a deep impression on our minds.

TRYON EDWARDS

What memory strategies can improve *recall*?

I f forgetting is so common, why do some people have better memories than others? Some may have an inborn talent for remembering. More often, though, they succeed because they have practised and mastered analytical, creative, and practical techniques for improving recall.

Develop helpful strategies

The following practical and analytical strategies will help improve your recall.

Have purpose and intention. Why can you remember the lyrics to dozens of popular songs but not the functions of the pancreas? Perhaps this is because you want to remember the lyrics or you have an emotional tie to them. To strengthen your intention to remember academic information, focus on why the information is important and how you can use it.

Understand what you memorize. The best way to guarantee that concepts become part of your long-term memory is to use your analytical ability to understand them inside and out. With a depth of learning comes the framework on which to place related concepts. Thus, if you are having trouble remembering something new, think about how the idea fits into what you already know. A simple example: If a new vocabulary word puzzles you, try to identify the word's root, prefix, or suffix. Knowing that the root *bellum* means "war" and the prefix *ante* means "before" will help you recognize and remember that *antebellum* means "before the war."

Attending class with a clear, focused mind can help you retain what you hear. This professor begins and ends each class with a short meditation, with the goal of improving how he and his students perform.

Recite, rehearse, and write. When you *recite* material, you repeat key concepts aloud, in your own words, to help you memorize them. *Rehearsing* is similar to reciting but is done silently. It is the process of mentally repeating, summarizing, and associating information with other information. *Writing* is reciting on paper. Organizational tools, such as an outline or a think link, will help you record material in ways that show the logical connections within its structure.

Study during short, frequent sessions. Research has shown that you can improve your chances of remembering material if you learn it more than once. To get the most out of study sessions, spread them over time and rest in between. You may feel as though you accomplish a lot by studying for an hour without a break; however, you'll probably remember more from three 20-minute sessions.

Sleep can actually aid memory because it reduces interference from new information. Since you can't always go to sleep immediately after studying for an exam, try postponing the study of other subjects until your exam is over. When studying for several tests at once, avoid studying two similar subjects back to back. Your memory is likely to be more accurate when you study History right after Biology rather than, for example, Chemistry after Biology.

Limit and organize material. This involves two key activities:

- **Separate main points from unimportant details.** Ask yourself: What is the most important information? Highlight only the key points in your texts, and write notes in the margins about central ideas. See the example in Key 5.6 on page 146.

- **Divide material into manageable sections.** Generally, when material is short and easy to understand, studying it from start to finish improves recall. With longer material, however, you may benefit from dividing it into logical sections, mastering each section, putting all the sections together, and then testing your memory of all the material. Actors take this approach when learning the lines of a play, and it can work just as well for students trying to learn new concepts.

Practise the middle. When you are trying to learn something, you usually study some material first, attack other material in the middle of the session, and approach still other topics at the end. The weak link in your recall is likely to be the material you study midway. It pays to give this material special attention.

Create groupings. When items do not have to be remembered in any particular order, the act of grouping can help you recall them better. Say, for example, that you have to memorize these four 10-digit numbers:

9806875087   9876535703   7636983561   6724472879

It may look impossible. If you group the numbers to look like telephone numbers, however, the job may become more manageable:

(980) 687–5087   (987) 653–5703   (763) 698–3561   (672) 447–2879

In general, try to limit groups to 10 items or fewer. It's hard to memorize more at one time.

Use flash cards. Flash cards are a great visual memory tool. They give you short, repeated review sessions that provide immediate feedback, and they are portable, which gives you the flexibility to use them wherever you go. Use the front of an index card to write a word, idea, or phrase you want to remember. Use the back for a definition, an explanation, and other key facts. Key 6.8 shows two flash cards used to study for a Psychology exam.

Here are some suggestions for making the most of your flash cards:

- Carry the cards with you and review them frequently.
- Shuffle the cards and learn the information in various orders.

THEORY
- Definition: Explanation for a phenomenon based on careful and precise observations
- Part of the scientific method
- Leads to hypotheses

HYPOTHESIS
- Prediction about future behaviour that is derived from observations and theories
- Methods for testing hypotheses: case studies, naturalistic observations, and experiments

● Test yourself in both directions. First, look at the terms and provide the definitions or explanations. Then turn the cards over and reverse the process.

Use a tape recorder. Use a tape recorder as an immediate feedback "audio flash card." Record short-answer study questions on tape, leave 10 to 15 seconds between questions to answer out loud, then record the correct answer after each pause. For example, a question for a writing class might be, "What are the three elements of effective writing?... (10–15 second pause)... topic, audience, and purpose."

Use mnemonic devices

MNEMONIC DEVICES

Memory techniques that involve associating new information with information you already know.

Certain performers entertain their audiences by remembering the names of 100 strangers or flawlessly repeating 30 ten-digit phone numbers. Although these performers probably have superior memories, they also rely on memory techniques, known as **mnemonic devices** (pronounced neh-MAHN-ick), for assistance.

Mnemonic devices depend on vivid associations (relating new information to other information). Instead of learning new facts by rote (repetitive practice), associations give you a "hook" on which to hang these facts and retrieve them later. Mnemonic devices make information familiar and meaningful through unusual, unforgettable mental associations and visual pictures. Forming mnemonics depends on activating your creative ability.

There are different kinds of mnemonic devices, including visual images and associations, acronyms, and songs and rhymes. Study how these devices work, then use your creative thinking skills to apply them to your own memory challenges.

Create visual images and associations. You are more likely to remember a piece of information if you link it to a visual image. The best mental images often involve bright colours, three dimensions, action scenes, inanimate objects with human traits, ridiculousness, and humour.

Turning information into mental pictures helps improve memory, especially for visual learners. To remember that the Spanish artist Picasso painted *The Three Women*, you might imagine the women in a circle dancing to a Spanish song with a pig and a donkey (pig-asso). The more outlandish the image the better, since these images are the most memorable.

Memory is the stepping-stone to thinking, because without remembering facts, you cannot think, conceptualize, reason, make decisions, create, or contribute.

HARRY LORAYNE

Use the mental walk strategy to remember items in a list. Using the mental walk strategy, you imagine that you store new ideas in familiar locations. Say, for example, that for biology you have to remember the major endocrine glands. To do this, you can think of the route you take to the library. You pass the college theatre, the science centre, the bookstore, the cafeteria, the athletic centre, and the social science building before reaching the library. At each spot along the route, you "place" the idea or concept you wish to learn. You then link the concept with a similar-sounding word that brings to mind a vivid image:

- At the campus theatre, you imagine bumping into the actor Brad Pitt, who is holding two terriers (pituitary gland).
- At the science centre, you visualize Mr. Universe with bulging thighs. When you are introduced, you learn that his name is Roy (thyroid gland).
- At the campus bookstore, you envision a second Mr. Universe with his thighs covered in mustard (thymus gland).
- In the cafeteria, you see an ad for Dean Al for president (adrenal gland).
- At the athletic centre, you visualize a student throwing a ball into a pan and creatures applauding from the bleachers (pancreas).
- At the social science building, you imagine receiving a standing ovation (ovaries).
- And at the library, you visualize sitting at a table taking a test that is easy (testes).

Create acronyms. Another helpful association method involves the use of **acronyms.** For example, suppose you want to remember the names of the first six prime ministers of Canada. The first letters of their last names—Macdonald, Mackenzie, Abbott, Thompson, Bowell, and Tupper—together read MMATBT. To remember them, you might add a "y" to the end and create a short nonsense word—"mmatbty"—and remember it as the word "mmat-bity." Since there are two "t's" in your nonsense word, just remember that alphabetically, and historically, Thompson comes before Tupper. To remember their first names—John, Alexander, John, John, Mackenzie, and Charles—you might set the names to the tune of "Happy Birthday," or any other musical tune you know.

ACRONYM

A word formed from the first letters of a series of words, created in order to help you remember the series.

An acronym will help you recall the colours of the spectrum.

red

orange

yellow

green

blue

indigo

violet

R O Y G. B I V

Other acronyms take the form of an entire sentence in which the first letter of each word in each sentence stands for the first letter of the memorized term. This is called a *list order acronym*. For example, when science students want to remember the list of planets in order of their distance from the sun (Mercury, Venus, Earth, Mars, Jupiter, Saturn, Uranus, Neptune, and Pluto), they can learn the sentence:

My very elegant mother just served us nine pickles.

Use songs or rhymes. Some of the classic mnemonic devices are rhyming poems that tend to stick in your mind. One you may have heard is the rule about the order of "i" and "e" in spelling:

I before E, except after C, or when sounded like "A" as in "neighbour" and "weigh." Four exceptions if you please: either, neither, seizure, seize.

get creative!

CRAFT YOUR OWN MNEMONIC

Make a mnemonic device to help you remember something important to you.

- As you study your texts in the next few weeks, identify a group of connected facts that you have to memorize—for example, for a political science course, the names of every presidential candidate after World War II; for an English Literature course, the names of all the characters in Shakespeare's *Romeo and Juliet.* Indicate your choice here:

_____

_____

- Now create a mnemonic that will help you memorize the group. Use any of the mnemonic devices presented in this chapter including visual images and associations, acronyms, and songs and rhymes. Write the mnemonic here (use additional paper if necessary).

_____

_____

_____

Make up your own poems or songs, linking tunes or rhymes that are familiar to you with information you want to remember. Improving your memory requires energy, time, and work. In school, it also helps to master SQ3R, the textbook study technique that was introduced in Chapter 5. By going through the steps in SQ3R and using the specific memory techniques described in this chapter, you will be able to learn more in less time—and remember what you learn long after exams are over.

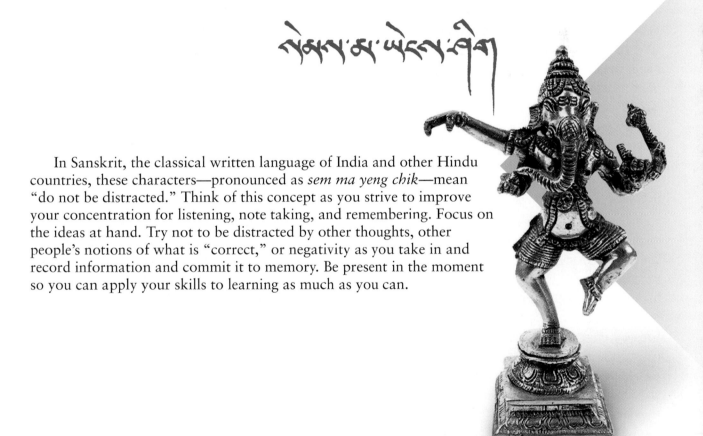

In Sanskrit, the classical written language of India and other Hindu countries, these characters—pronounced as *sem ma yeng chik*—mean "do not be distracted." Think of this concept as you strive to improve your concentration for listening, note taking, and remembering. Focus on the ideas at hand. Try not to be distracted by other thoughts, other people's notions of what is "correct," or negativity as you take in and record information and commit it to memory. Be present in the moment so you can apply your skills to learning as much as you can.

PERSONAL TRIUMPH

DANIEL IGALI   Olympic Gold Medal wrestler

Personal success isn't just about setting and achieving your goals. For some, it's also about remembering where you came from and trying to make life better for others. For Canada's Olympic Gold Medal–winning wrestler Daniel Igali, life has been about sacrifices and making the life changes it takes to realize your dreams.

Baraladei Daniel Igali grew up poor in Eniwari, Bayelsa State, Nigeria. While he may not have had many material things, he did have one thing—wrestling—which was as important a part of his culture as hockey is to Canadians. That, combined with the fact he was one of 21 children in the family, meant there was always someone to wrestle with. Sometimes there were battles over basic necessities, like having a chair and desk to work at while in school. According to Igali, "I did not have a shortage of wrestling partners and was notorious for having a different school uniform every month as I was always wrestling around and getting my uniforms torn."

Daniel didn't actually wrestle professionally until he was 16. Not only was he fortunate enough to win his first tournament; he was also beginning his studies in Mass Communication at university. Between competing in wrestling tournaments and his academic studies, life was becoming busy. So busy that he needed to take control of his life and make a difficult choice. He needed to choose between school and wrestling, "I wanted to pursue my wrestling dreams and solidify myself as one of the best wrestlers in Nigeria. As you can imagine, my decision caused a few problems with my parents, but we were able to work out the difference so that I could continue to wrestle."

He began to wrestle throughout Africa and would eventually win the African championship in 1993, at the age of 19. While being the African champion was certainly gratifying, he set his sights on other championships, including the 1994 Commonwealth Games here in Canada. The Games were a bittersweet experience for Daniel. While he finished a disappointing 11th place, he also made the decision to stay in Canada. According to Igali, "the political situation in Nigeria was very volatile and my aims of studying alongside sports were becoming impossible. So after the Games, I decided to stay in Canada," says Igali.

The one event that changed Igali's life came in 1996 at the Clansman International Tournament. Leading on points 7–1 with just one minute left in the match, Daniel lost the match in overtime and was humbled, not only for himself, but also for his coach. "After this match, I vowed never to be embarrassed that way again. With the help of my coaches, I immediately changed my training regimen and went on to place fourth at the 1998 World Championships in Iran. "Since then, Igali's accomplishments include being named Canada's Athlete of the Year (1999 and 2000), winning an Olympic Gold Medal at the 2000 Sydney Olympics, and earning another Gold at the 2002 Commonwealth Games.

Success also means "coming full circle" and recognizing the values you were raised with. Sometimes, that means not forgetting where you came from. Says Igali, "One of the questions I had difficulty answering in Nigeria was: What am I doing to help people in Nigeria? Most of the people back home are happy that I won the Olympic Gold Medal for Canada. What they want is something for Nigeria." In 2001, Igali worked with students from Heritage Park School in British Columbia to help build schools in his hometown of Eniwari. He's also helping build wells for clean drinking water in Nigeria. In 2005, he did a different kind of "fighting." He ran for the Liberal Party during in the Spring 2005 election in the BC riding of Surrey-Newton. Although he was defeated, he looks forward to perhaps entering politics in the future.

If you'd like more information about Daniel's charity work, go to www.igali.com or contact the "Daniel Igali School Project" at CUSO, Revenue Generation Department, 2255 Carling Avenue, Suite 500, Ottawa, ON, K2B 1A6.

Compiled with files from www.igali.com and "Superman, SuperKid—Well Suited to Help—Wrestler Igali, 10-Year-Old Aids Nigerian Village," by Randy Starkman, *Toronto Sun*, October 13, 2001.

BUILDING SKILLS

FOR ACADEMIC, CAREER, AND LIFE SUCCESS

SUCCESSFUL INTELLIGENCE

PRACTICAL CREATIVE

ANALYTICAL

SUCCESSFUL INTELLIGENCE

Developing Successful Intelligence

PUTTING IT ALL TOGETHER

Learn from the experiences of others. Look back to Daniel Igali's Personal Triumph on page 190. After you've read his story, relate his experience to your own life by completing the following:

Think it through: *Analyze your experience and compare it to Daniel's.* What goal (academic or personal) are you trying to reach now that will take you a long time, and how does this relate to Daniel's experience? Why is this goal important to you? From your memory of reaching other important goals, what strategies will help you achieve it? Sometimes we don't achieve our goals. Daniel ran for MPP in British Columbia in 2005 but did not win. How can we learn from our losses as well as our victories?

Think out of the box: *Let others inspire ideas.* Choose two people whom you respect. Put your listening skills to work: Spend a few minutes talking with each of them about your goal. Ask them about similar experiences they have had, and listen to the ideas that they used. From what you've heard, begin brainstorming ideas about how you will achieve your goal.

Make it happen: *Put a practical plan together.* Map out how you will achieve your goal. Create a mnemonic device that will help you remember your plan. Envision your success as you put your plan into action.

Team Building

COLLABORATIVE SOLUTIONS

Create a note-taking team. Although students often focus much more on taking notes in class than on taking notes while reading, reading notes are just as important to your understanding of the course material. In your

create your future

most demanding course, form a study group with two other people and choose a reading assignment—a text chapter, an article, or any other assigned reading—to work on together. Agree to read it and take notes independently before your next meeting. Each student should make photocopies of his or her notes for the other group members.

When you meet again, compare your notes, focusing on the following characteristics:

- legibility (Can everyone read what is written?)
- completeness (Did you all record the same information? If not, why not?)
- organizational effectiveness (Does everyone get an idea of how ideas flow?)
- value of the notes as a study aid (Will this help everyone remember the material?)

Based on what you've discussed with your group, come up with specific ways to improve your personal note-taking skills. You can also work with your study group to compare notes taken in a particular class period and work on improving in-class note-taking techniques.

Writing

DISCOVERY THROUGH JOURNALING

Record your thoughts on a separate piece of paper or in a journal.

How people retain information. How do you react to the following statement? "We retain 10 percent of what we read, 20 percent of what we hear, 30 percent of what we see, 50 percent of what we hear and see, 70 percent of what we say, 90 percent of what we say and do." How can you use this insight to improve your ability to retain information? What will you do differently as a result of this insight?

Career Portfolio

PLAN FOR SUCCESS

Matching career to curriculum. Your success in most career areas depends in part on your academic preparation. Some careers, such as medicine, require very specific curriculum choices (for example, specific biology and chemistry courses are required for medical school). Some careers require certain courses that teach basic competencies; for example, to be an accountant, you have to take accounting and bookkeeping. Other career areas, such as many business careers, don't have specific requirements, but employers often look for certain curriculum choices that indicate the mastery of particular skills and knowledge.

Put your listening and note-taking skills to work as you investigate your options. Choose a career area that interests you. Interview two people in that area—one from an academic setting (such as an instructor in a related subject area or an academic advisor) and one from the working world (such as a person working in that career or a career planning and placement office counsellor). Choose a setting where you can listen well and take effective notes.

Ask your interviewees two questions: First, ask them about curriculum—what courses are required for this area, and what courses are beneficial but not required. Then ask them how you can stretch yourself outside of class in ways that will help you stand out—extracurricular activities, internships, leadership roles, part-time work, and any other helpful pursuits.

When you have completed your interviews, create two lists—one of recommended courses, marking the required ones with a star, and one of activities, internships, and any other recommendations.

SUGGESTED READINGS

Burley-Allen, Madelyn. *Listening: The Forgotten Skill: A Self-Teaching Guide.* New York: John Wiley & Sons, 1995.

DePorter, Bobbi, and Mike Hernacki. *Quantum Notes: Whole-Brain Approaches to Note-Taking.* Chicago: Learning Forum, 2000.

Dunkel, Patricia A., Frank Pialorsi, and Joane Kozyrez. *Advanced Listening Comprehension: Developing Aural & Note-Taking Skills,* 3rd ed. Boston: Heinle & Heinle, 2004.

Higbee, Kenneth L. *Your Memory: How It Works and How to Improve It.* New York: Marlowe & Co., 2001.

Lebauer, R. Susan. *Learn to Listen, Listen to Learn: Academic Listening and Note-Taking.* Upper Saddle River, NJ: Prentice Hall, 2000.

Levin, Leonard. *Easy Script Express: Unique Speed Writing Methods to Take Fast Notes and Dictation.* Chicago: Legend Publishing, 2000.

Lorayne, Harry. *Super Memory—Super Student: How to Raise Your Grades in 30 Days.* Boston: Little, Brown & Company, 1990.

Lorayne, Harry. *The Memory Book: The Classic Guide to Improving Your Memory at Work, at School, and at Play.* New York: Ballantine Books, 1996.

Robbins, Harvey A. *How to Speak and Listen Effectively.* New York: AMACOM, 1992.

Roberts, Billy. *Working Memory: Improving Your Memory for the Workplace.* London: Bridge Trade, 1999.

Roberts, Billy. *Educate Your Memory: Improvement Techniques for Students of All Ages.* London: Allison & Busby, 2000.

INTERNET RESOURCES

York University offers note-taking advice for its students: http://www.yorku.ca/cdc/lsp/notesonline/note1.htm

ForgetKnot: A Source for Mnemonic Devices: http://members.tripod.com/~ForgetKnot/

Prentice Hall Student Success Supersite—Study Skills: www.prenhall.com/success/StudySkl/index.html

Helpful advice on listening from the Kishwaukee College Learning Skills Center: kish.cc.il.us/lsc/ssh/listening.shtml

ENDNOTES

1. Ralph G. Nichols, "Do We Know How to Listen? Practical Helps in a Modern Age," *Speech Teacher* (March 1961), pp. 118–124.

2. Ibid.

3. Walter Pauk, *How to Study in College,* 5th ed. Boston, MA: Houghton Mifflin Company, 1993, pp. 110–114.

4. Herman Ebbinghaus, *Memory: A Contribution to Experimental Psychology,* trans. H. A. Ruger and C. E. Bussenius. New York: New York Teacher's College, Columbia University, 1885.

5. James Zull, *The Art of Changing the Brain: Enriching Teaching by Exploring the Biology of Learning.* Sterling, VA: Stylus Publishing, 2002

EMPOWER

IN THIS CHAPTER

In this chapter you will explore answers to the following questions: • How can you make the most of your library? • How can you do research on the Internet? • What are the elements of effective writing? • What is the writing process? • How can you deliver an effective oral presentation?

Researching and writing

RESEARCH and writing, powerful tools that engage your successful intelligence, are at the heart of your education. Through library and Internet research, you gather and analyze information from sources all over the world. Through writing, you analyze ideas, think creatively about what they mean, and communicate information and perspectives to others. Whether you write an essay in English or a summary of a scientific study for biology, the writing process helps sharpen your thinking and your practical communication skills.

This chapter has two goals: To help you improve your skill in finding information at your college library and on the Internet, and to reinforce some of the writing basics that most students study in an English composition course. In school and in your career, researching and writing are essential to success. The Conference Board of Canada lists being able to manage information as a key employability skill. This skill includes the capacity to "locate, gather and organize information using appropriate technology." Employees must also be able to "access, analyze and apply knowledge from various disciplines."

This chapter also helps you achieve two goals: To improve your skill in finding information at your college or university library and on the Internet, and to use words to communicate your thoughts and research findings. You also learn how good writing is linked to clear thinking and effective research. In class or at work, knowing how to find information and writing well are essential to learning and success.

gathering and communicating ideas

How can you *make the most* of your library?

A library is a home for information; consider it the "brain" of your college or university. Your job is to find what you need as quickly and efficiently as you can.

Start with a road map

Most college and university libraries are bigger than high school and community libraries, so you may feel lost on your first few visits. Make your life easier by learning how your library is organized.

Circulation desk. All publications are checked out at the circulation desk, which is usually near the library entrance.

Reference area. Here you'll find reference books, including encyclopedias, directories, dictionaries, almanacs, and atlases. You'll also find librarians and other library employees who can direct you to information. Computer terminals, containing the library's catalogue of holdings, as well as on-line bibliographic and full-text databases, are usually part of the reference area.

Book area. Books—and, in many libraries, magazines and journals in bound or boxed volumes—are stored in the *stacks*. A library with "open stacks" allows you to search for materials on your own. In a "closed-stack" system, a staff member retrieves materials for you.

Periodicals area. Here you'll find recent issues of popular and scholarly magazines, journals, and newspapers. Most libraries collect periodicals ranging from *Maclean's* to the *Canadian Journal of Communication* and *New England Journal of Medicine*. Because unbound **periodicals** are generally not circulated, you may find photocopy machines nearby where you can copy pages.

PERIODICALS

Magazines, journals, and newspapers that are published on a regular basis throughout the year.

Audio/visual materials areas. Many libraries have special areas for video, art and photography, and recorded music collections.

Computer areas. Computer terminals, linked to databases and the Internet, may be scattered throughout the building or set off in particular areas. You may be able to access these databases and the Internet from computer labs and writing centres. Many college and university residence rooms are also wired for computer access, enabling students to connect via their personal computers.

Microform areas. Most libraries have microform reading areas. Microforms are materials printed in reduced size on film,

While the library is still a major resource centre, on-line research has become a significant source of information for many students.

either *microfilm* (a reel of film) or *microfiche* (a sheet or card of film), that is viewed through special machines. Many microform reading machines can print hard copies of images.

To learn about your school's library, take a tour or training session. Almost all college and university libraries offer orientation sessions on how to locate books, periodicals, and databases and use the Internet. If your school has more than one library, explore each one you intend to use.

Learn how to conduct an information search

The most successful and time-saving library research involves following a specific *search strategy*—a step-by-step method for finding information that takes you from general to specific sources. Starting with general sources usually works best because they provide an overview of your research topic and can lead you to more specific information and sources. For example, an encyclopedia article on the archaeological discovery of the Dead Sea Scrolls—manuscripts written between 250 BC and AD 68 that trace the roots of Judaism and Christianity—may mention that one of the most important books on the subject is *Understanding the Dead Sea Scrolls,* edited by Hershel Shanks (New York: Random House, 1992). This book, in turn, leads you to 13 experts who wrote specialized text chapters.

DISCOVER YOUR SCHOOL'S LIBRARY

get practical!

Learn the nuts and bolts of your school's library system.

Identify the following:

- Name and location of the library. (If your college or university has more than one library, identify the branch you are most likely to use.)

  _____

  _____

- Hours of operation: _____
- Library Web site address: _____
- Important e-mail addresses and phone numbers, including those of the reference and circulation desks:

  _____

  _____

- Stack locations of the books and other publications you may need in this semester's courses:
- Names and URLs of computer databases you are likely to use:

  _____

  _____

- Location of a library nook or chair that is ideal for studying:

  _____

Narrowing your topic is critical to research success because broad topics yield too much data. Here, instead of using "Dead Sea Scrolls" in your search, consider narrowing your topic. For example:

- How the Dead Sea Scrolls were discovered by Bedouin shepherds in 1947
- The historical origins of the scrolls
- The process archaeologists used to reconstruct scroll fragments

Conducting a keyword search. To narrow your topic, conduct a *keyword search* of the library database—a method for locating sources through the use of topic-related words and phrases. For example, instead of searching through the broad category *Art,* use a keyword search to focus on *French Art* or, more specifically, *19th-century French Art.*

Keyword searches use natural language, rather than specialized classification vocabulary. Key 7.1 includes tips that will help you use the keyword system. The last three entries describe how to use "or," "and," and "not" to narrow searches with what is called Boolean logic.

As you search, keep in mind that:

- double quotation marks around a word or phrase will locate the exact term you entered ("financial aid").
- using upper or lower case does not affect the search (*Scholarships* will find *scholarships*).
- singular terms will find the plural (*scholarship* will find *scholarships*).

Conducting research using a search strategy

Knowing where to look during each phase of your search helps you find information quickly and efficiently. A successful search strategy often starts with general references and moves to more specific references (see Key 7.2). Your search may also involve electronic sources from the Internet.

How to perform an effective keyword search.

IF YOU ARE SEARCHING FOR...	DO THIS	EXAMPLE
A word	Type the word normally	aid
A phrase	Type the phrase in its normal word order (use regular word spacing) or surround the phrase with double quotation marks	financial aid or "financial aid"
Two or more keywords without regard to word order	Type the words in any order, surrounding the words with quotation marks (use "and" to separate the words)	"financial aid" and "scholarships"
Topic A or topic B	Type the words in any order, surrounding the words with quotation marks (use "or" to separate the words)	"financial aid" or "scholarships"
Topic A but not topic B	Type topic A first within quotation marks, and then topic B within quotation marks (use "not" to separate the words)	"financial aid" not "scholarships"

Use general reference works

Begin your research with *general reference works*. These works cover many different topics in a broad, non-detailed way. General reference guides are often available on-line or on **CD-ROM**.

Among the works that fall into the general reference category are these:

- encyclopedias such as the multi-volume *Canadian Encyclopedia Plus*
- almanacs such as the *Canadian Global Almanac,* and the *Canadian Almanac and Directory*
- yearbooks such as the *Canadian Parliamentary Guide* and the *Canada Yearbook*
- dictionaries such as the *Canadian Oxford Dictionary* and the *Gage Canadian Dictionary*
- biographical reference works such as the *Webster's Biographical Dictionary* and *Canadian Who's Who*
- bibliographies such as *Books in Print* (especially the *Subject Guide to Books in Print*)
- material from Statistics Canada published in *Canadian Social Trends*
- *Canadian Newsdisk* features information from Canadian news broadcasts and newspapers from 1996 onward

Scan these sources for an overview of your topic. Bibliographies at the end of encyclopedia articles may also lead to important sources.

CD-ROM

A compact disk containing words and images in electronic form that can be read by a computer (CD-ROM stands for "compact disk read only memory").

Browse through books on your subject

Use the computerized *library catalogue* to find books and other materials on your topic. The catalogue tells you which publications the library owns and where they can be found and is searchable by author, title, and subject. For example, a library that has *The Apprenticeship of Duddy Kravitz* by Mordecai Richler may list the book in the author catalogue

Library search strategy.

key 7.2

Check general and specific reference works	→	Read appropriate sections
Check the book catalogue for authors and book titles	→	Read books
Check periodical indices for author and article titles	→	Read articles
Check the Internet, on-line services, and CD-ROM databases for complete articles and other data	→	Read computer screen and print information

under Richler, Mordecai (last name first); in the title catalogue under *Apprenticeship of Duddy Kravitz* (articles such as *the, a,* and *an* are dropped from the beginnings of titles and subjects); and in the subject catalogue under "Canadian Literature."

Each catalogue listing refers to the library's classification system, which tells you exactly where the publication can be found. The Dewey Decimal and Library of Congress systems are among the most common classification systems. Getting to know your library's system will help save time and trouble.

Use periodical indices to search for periodicals

Periodicals are a valuable source of current information and include journals, magazines, and newspapers. *Journals* are written for readers with specialized knowledge. Whereas *Maclean's* magazine may run a general-interest article on AIDS research, the *Journal of the American Medical Association* may print the original scientific study for an audience of doctors and scientists. Many libraries display periodicals that are up to a year or two old and convert older copies to microfilm or microfiche. Many full-text articles are also available on computer databases.

Periodical indices lead you to specific articles. The *Reader's Guide to Periodical Literature,* available in print and on CD-ROM, indexes general information sources including articles in hundreds of general-interest publications. The Canadian Periodical Index is an excellent tool for searching Canadian publications. You might also want to look in the *BiblioCentre* family of databases (a Canadian company that makes on-line databases available to libraries) that your school might subscribe to. Some common on-line databases available in colleges and universities include *Ebsco Host, ProQuest,* and the *Financial Post Corporate Reports.*

Indexing information is listed in the *Standard Periodical Directory, Ulrich's International Periodicals Directory,* and *Magazines for Libraries.* Each database also lists the magazines and periodicals it indexes. Because there is no all-inclusive index for technical, medical, and scholarly journal articles, you'll have to search indices that specialize in narrow subject areas. Such indices also include *abstracts* (article summaries). Among the available indices are *ERIC (Educational Resources Information Center),* the *Humanities Index, Index Medicus,* and *Psychological Abstracts.* You'll also find separate newspaper indices in print, in microform, on CD-ROM, or on-line.

Almost no library owns all of the publications listed in these and other specialized indices. However, journals that are not part of your library's collection or that are not available in full-text form on-line may be available through an interlibrary loan, which requests materials from other libraries. The librarian will help you arrange the loan.

Ask the librarian

Librarians can assist you in solving research problems. They can help you locate unfamiliar or hard-to-find sources, navigate catalogues and databases, and uncover research shortcuts. Librarians are not the only helpful people in the library. For simplicity's sake, this book uses the term *librarian* to refer to both librarians and other staff members who are trained to help. Here are some tips that will help you get the advice you are seeking from the librarian.

Be prepared and be specific. Instead of asking for information on Canadian prime ministers, focus on the topic you expect to write about in your Canadian politics paper—for example, how Brian Mulroney's passion for free trade with the United States and Mexico may have led to the political demise of the federal Progressive Conservative party in the 1990s.

Ask for help when you can't find a specific source. For example, when a specific book is not on the shelf, the librarian may direct you to another source that works as well.

Ask for help with computer and other equipment. Librarians are experts in using the library's computers and other equipment, so turn to them if you encounter a technical problem you can't solve.

The library is one of your school's most valuable resources, so take advantage of it. Your library research and critical-thinking skills give you the ability to collect information, weigh alternatives, and make decisions. These skills last a lifetime and may serve you well if you choose one of the many careers that require research ability. The library is not your only research resource, however. The Internet is becoming a primary research tool for both school and work.

How can you do *research* on the Internet?

The *Internet* is a computer network that links organizations and people around the world. A miracle of technology, it can connect you to billions of information sources instantaneously. According to recent Statistics Canada research, over 90 per cent of college and university aged students use the Internet on a regular basis and over 75 per cent of Canadians regularly use the Internet for information.[1]

Because of its widespread reach, the Internet is an essential research tool—if used wisely. This section helps you make the most of the time you spend on-line now and in the future. As the Internet becomes more important, it opens up a world of opportunities: For example, it may be the medium through which you continue your studies via on-line courses, do your work at a home-based office, purchase products and services, find medical information, book airline tickets and hotel rooms, investigate potential employers, file your taxes, make investments, and more.

Internet research depends on your critical judgment. Erindale College, at the University of Toronto at Mississauga, claims that "more and more students are turning to the Internet when doing research for their assignments, and more and more instructors are requiring such research when setting topics. However, research on the Net is very different from traditional library research, and the differences can cause problems. The Net is a tremendous resource, but it must be used carefully and critically." Erindale College advises students to double check what they uncover on the Internet with some other library sources.[2]

The basics

With a basic knowledge of the Internet, you can access facts and figures, read articles and reports, purchase products, download files, send messages electronically via email, and even "talk" to people in real time. Following is some basic information.

Access. Users access the Internet through Internet Service Providers (ISPs). Some ISPs are commercial, such as Sympatico, or AOL Canada. Others are linked to companies, colleges, and other organizations. When you sign up with an ISP, you choose a *screen name*, which is your on-line address.

Information locations. Most information is displayed on *Web sites*, cyber-space locations developed by companies, government agencies, organizations, and individuals. Together, these sites make up the *World Wide Web*.

Finding locations. The string of text and numbers that identifies an Internet site is called a *URL* (Universal Resource Locator). Look at the Internet Resources at the end of this chapter or any other for some examples of URLs. You can type in a URL to access a specific site. Many Web sites include *hyperlinks*—URLs that are underlined and highlighted in colour—that take you directly to another location when you click on them.

Now that you have some basic knowledge, explore how to search for information.

Search directories and search engines

You need a *search directory* or *search engine* to find and select Web sites and other information locations. Following are some details about these essential search tools.

Commercial search engines and directories are your portal to the World Wide Web. Among the most powerful and popular Canadian search sites are Google (www.google.ca), Yahoo! (ca.yahoo.com), Homer (www.homer.ca), MSN Search (http://sympatico.msn.ca), Excite (www.excite.com), Alta Vista (http://altavista.com), HotBot (www.hotbot.com), Ask (www.ask.com), and Lycos (www.lycos.com). Information is accessible through simple or advanced keyword searches.

Seeing research as a quest for an answer makes clear that you cannot know whether you have found something unless you know what it is you are looking for.

LYNN QUITMAN TROYKA

Internet search strategy. Start with this basic search strategy when researching on-line:

1. *Think carefully about what you want to locate.* University of Michigan Prof. Eliot Soloway recommends phrasing your search in the form of a question—for example, *What vaccines are given to children before age 5?* Then, he advises identifying the important

GOOGLE (YES, IT'S A VERB)

get creative!

Explore ways to use Google and other search engines effectively.

Google accesses 6 billion documents and has the capacity to return 750,000 Internet links in a third of a second. Despite this, Leon Botstein, president of Bard College, warns of Google's pitfalls: "In general, Google overwhelms you with too much information, much of which is hopelessly unreliable or beside the point. It's like looking for a lost ring in a vacuum bag. What you end up with mostly are bagel crumbs and dirt."[4]

With this warning in mind, use your creativity and analysis to complete the following:

- Choose a common topic—for example, apples, hockey, snowflakes. Google the topic to see how many Web sites you access. Write that number here. _____ Now spend ten minutes scanning the Web listings. How many different topics did your search uncover other than the topic you intended?

_____

_____

- Pick three of the off-the-topic links you found and write a thesis statement to a paper that would require you to use these leads in your research. Be creative.

_____

_____

_____

- In all likelihood, your thesis statement makes little sense. What does this tell you about the need for critical thinking when using Google and other search directories and engines in your research?

_____

_____

_____

- Finally, open your mind to the creative possibilities your research uncovered. Did any of the Web sites spark ideas about your topic that you had never considered? Write down two ideas you never thought of before.

1. _____

2. _____

words in the question (*vaccines, children, before age 5*) as well as other related words (*chicken pox, tetanus, polio, shot, pediatrics,* and so on). This gives you a collection of terms to use in different combinations as you search.[3]

2. *Use a search directory to isolate sites under your desired topic or category.* Save the sites that look useful. (Most browsers have a "bookmark" feature for sites you want to find again.)

3. *Explore these sites to get a general idea of what's out there.* If the directory takes you where you need to go, you're in luck. More often in academic research, you need to dig deeper. Notice useful keywords and information locations in the search directory.

4. *Move on to a search engine to narrow your search.* Use your keywords in a variety of ways to uncover as many possibilities as you can.

   - Vary their order if you are using more than one keyword (e.g., search under *education, college, statistics,* and *statistics, education, college*).
   - Use *Boolean operators*—the words "and," "not," and "or"—in ways that limit your search (see Key 7.1 for techniques for using keywords for library searches).

5. *Evaluate the list of links that appear.* If there are too many, narrow your search by using more keywords or more specific keywords (*Broadway* could become *Broadway* AND *"fall season"* AND *2007*). If there are too few, broaden your search by using fewer or different keywords.

6. *When you think you are done, start over.* Choose another search directory or search engine and perform your search again. Why do this? Because different systems access different sites.

Use analytical thinking to evaluate every source

It is up to you to evaluate the truth and usefulness of Internet information. Since the Internet is largely uncensored and unmonitored—a kind of "information free-for-all"—you must decide which sources to value and which to ignore. Use the following strategies to analyze the validity and usefulness of each source.[5]

- **Ask questions about the source.**

  Is the author a recognized expert? Does he or she write from a particular perspective that may bias the presentation? Is the source recent enough for your purposes? Where did the author get the information?

  Note also the Web site's name and the organization that creates and maintains the site. Is the organization reputable? Is it known as an authority on the topic you are researching? If you are not sure of the source, the URL may give you a clue. For example, URLs ending in.edu originate at an educational institution, and.gov sites originate at government agencies.

- **Evaluate the material.** Evaluate Internet sources the way you would other material. Is the source a published document (newspaper article, professional journal article, etc.), or is it simply one person's views? Can you verify the data by comparing it to other material? Pay attention also to writing quality. Texts with grammatical and spelling errors, poor organization, or factual errors are likely to be unreliable.

Take advantage of the wealth of material the Internet offers—but be picky. Always remember that your research will only be as strong as your thinking. If you work hard to ensure that your research is solid and comprehensive, the product of your efforts will speak for itself.

Library and Internet research is often done as a step in writing a research paper. The success of your paper depends on the quality of your research and on your ability to write.

What are the elements of *effective writing?*

Over the years to come you may write papers, essays, answers to essay test questions, job application letters, résumés, business proposals and reports, emails to co-workers, and letters to customers and suppliers. Good writing skills help you achieve the goals you set with each writing task.

Good writing depends on and reflects clear thinking and is influenced greatly by reading. Exposing yourself to the works of other writers introduces you to new concepts and perspectives as it helps you discover different ways to express ideas.

Every writing situation is unique, depending on your purpose, topic, and **audience**. Your goal is to understand each element before you begin.

Writing purpose

Writing without a clear purpose is like driving without a destination. You'll get somewhere, but chances are it won't be the right place. Therefore, when you write, always decide what you want to accomplish before you start. The two most common writing purposes are to inform and to persuade.

Informative writing presents and explains ideas in an unbiased way. A research paper on how hospitals process blood donations informs readers without trying to mould opinions. Most newspaper articles, except on the opinion and editorial pages, are examples of informative writing.

Persuasive writing attempts to convince readers to adopt a point of view. For example, as the health editor of a magazine, you write a column to persuade readers to give blood. Examples of persuasive writing include newspaper editorials, business proposals, and books with a point of view.

Knowing your audience

In almost every case, a writer creates written material so that others can read it. The writer and audience are partners in this process. Knowing who your audience is helps you communicate successfully.

Key questions about your audience. In school, your primary audience is your instructors. For many assignments, instructors want you to assume that they are *typical readers* who know little about your topic and need full explanations. In contrast, *informed readers* know your subject and require less information. Ask yourself some or all of the following questions to help you define how much information your readers need:

- What are my readers' roles? Are they instructors, students, employers, customers?

- How much do they know about my topic? Are they experts or beginners?

- Are they interested, or do I have to convince them to read my material?

- Can I expect readers to have open or closed minds about my topic?

AUDIENCE
The reader or readers of any piece of written material.

Use your answers as a guide to help you shape what you write. Remember, communication is successful only when readers understand your message as you intended it. Effective and successful writing involves following the steps in the writing process.

What is the *writing process*?

The writing process for research papers gives you the opportunity to state and rework your thoughts until you have expressed yourself clearly. The four main parts of the process are planning, drafting, revising, and editing. Critical thinking plays an important role throughout.

Planning

PREWRITING STRATEGIES

Techniques for generating ideas about a topic and finding out how much you already know before you start your research and writing.

Planning gives you a chance to think about what to write and how to write it. Planning involves brainstorming for topic ideas, using **prewriting strategies** to define and narrow your topic, conducting research, writing a thesis statement, and writing a working outline. Although these steps are listed in sequence, in real life they overlap one another as you plan your document.

Open your mind through brainstorming

Whether your instructor assigns a specific topic (language and identity in Rita Wong's *monkeypuzzle*), a partially defined topic (poet Rita Wong), or a general category within which you make your own choice (Asian-Canadian authors), you should brainstorm to develop topic ideas. Brainstorming is a creative technique that involves generating ideas about a subject without making judgments (see page 207).

First, let your mind wander. Write down anything on the assigned subject that comes to mind, in no particular order. Then, organize that list into an outline or think link that helps you see the possibilities more clearly. To make the outline or think link, separate the items you've listed into general ideas or categories and sub-ideas or examples. Then, associate the sub-ideas or examples with the ideas they support or fit. Key 7.3 shows a portion of an outline that student Sam Gordon constructed from his brainstorming list. The assignment is a five-paragraph essay on a life-changing event. Here Sam chose to brainstorm the topic of "pro-wrestling camp" as he organized his ideas into categories.

Narrow your topic through prewriting strategies

Next, narrow your topic, focusing on the specific sub-ideas and examples from your brainstorming session. Explore one or more of these with prewriting strategies such as brainstorming, freewriting, and asking journalists' questions.[6] Prewriting strategies help you decide which of your possible topics you would most like to pursue.

Brainstorming. The same process you used to generate ideas also helps you narrow your topic. Write down your thoughts about the possibility you have chosen, and then organize them into categories, noticing any patterns that appear. See if any of the sub-ideas or examples might make good topics.

Part of a brainstorming outline.

A LIFE CHANGING EVENT
—family
—childhood
→ watching wrestling with my father
— high-school sports
→ football, hockey, and amateur wrestling
— wrestling camp in Alberta
· a dream come true
· Hart Brothers
— physical conditioning
· nightly training
· 3—5 hour sessions
· painful exercises
— dream turned into a nightmare
· drastic weight loss
· a matter of survival
· still have respect for wrestling

Freewriting. When you freewrite, you write whatever comes to mind without censoring ideas or worrying about grammar, spelling, punctuation, or organization. Freewriting helps you think creatively and gives you an opportunity to begin integrating the information you know. Freewrite on the sub-ideas or examples you created to see if you want to pursue them. Here is a sample of freewriting:

Asking journalists' questions. When journalists start working on a story, they ask themselves: Who? What? Where? When? Why? and How? You can use these *journalists' questions* to focus your thinking. Ask these questions about any sub-idea or example to discover what you may want to discuss.

As you prewrite, keep an eye on paper length, due date, and other requirements (such as topic area or purpose). These requirements influence your choice of a final topic. For example, if you have a month to write an informative 20-page paper on a learning disability, you might discuss the symptoms, effects, and treatment of attention deficit disorder. If you have a week to write a five-page persuasive essay, you might write about how elementary school students with ADD need special training.

My chance to train at the Hart Brothers Wrestling Camp was an influence on my life. I used to watch wrestling with my dad when I was a kid. I was told that to be successful in wrestling, you had to be in really good shape. I figured my years of high school football, hockey, and amateur wrestling had me in shape. Boy, was I wrong! We trained on our own during the day. We met every night for several hours to jog, ride bikes and lift weights. Ed and Keith were in charge of training me. We had to practise doing knee bends: about 200 each night. We also had a chance to practise taking falls in a ring that they had set up at the gym. Being flexible was an important point for wrestlers at the camp. All these things made you tough. By the end of the first week of camp, I had lost a ton of weight and a lot of my enthusiasm for wrestling. Although I had been a fan of wrestling for a lot of years and had been planning to go to wrestling camp since I started high school, I had come to the conclusion that it wasn't for me. At least I can say that while I didn't finish the course, I did survive it.

Who?   Who was at wrestling camp? Who influenced me the most?
What?   What about wrestling changed my life? What did we do?
When?   When in my life did I go to wrestling camp, and for how long?
Where?   Where was camp located? Where did we spend our day-to-day time?
Why?   Why did I decide to go there? Why was it such an important experience?
How?   How did we train in the camp? How were we treated? How do I feel about not achieving my goal?

Prewriting helps you develop a topic broad enough to give you something with which to work but narrow enough to be manageable. Prewriting also helps you see what you know and what you don't know. If your assignment requires more than you already know, you may need to do research.

Conduct research

In some cases, prewriting strategies may generate all the ideas and information you need. In other writing situations, research is needed to find outside sources. Try doing your research in stages. In the first stage, look for a basic overview that can lead to a thesis statement. In the second stage, go into more depth, tracking down information that helps you fill in gaps and complete your thoughts.

As you research, create source notes and content notes on index cards. These help you organize your work, keep track of your sources, and avoid plagiarism.

Source notes are the preliminary notes you take as you review research. They include vital bibliographic information, as well as a short summary and critical evaluation of the work. Each source note should include the author's full name; the title of the work; the edition, if any; the publisher, year, and city of publication; issue and/or volume number when applicable (such as for a magazine); and the page numbers you consulted. Key 7.4 shows an example of how you can write source notes on index cards.

Content notes provide an in-depth look at the source, taken during a thorough reading. They are longer and more detailed than source notes. Use them to record the information you need to write your draft.

Write a thesis statement

Your work has prepared you to write a thesis statement, the central message you want to communicate to readers. The thesis statement states your subject and point of view, reflects your writing purpose and audience, and acts as the organizing principle of your paper. Here is an example from Sam's paper:

Topic: Hart Brothers Pro Wrestling Camp

Purpose: To inform

Audience: Instructor who probably knows little about the topic

Thesis statement: It may look easy on television, but it's not. Although I was a high school football and hockey player and a fan of wrestling for many years, nothing I had experienced prepared me for the longest week of my life: my week at the Hart Brothers Wrestling Camp.

Sample source note.

TUCKWELL, KEITH J. *Canadian Advertising in Action,* Fifth Edition.

Scarborough: Prentice Hall, 2000, pp. 107–108.

Summary: Descriptions of how to identify a target market for your product or service in Canada.

Evaluation: Detailed analysis of how to market your product. Added pluses: Many examples and Web links.

A thesis statement is just as important in a short document, such as a letter, as it is in a long paper. For example, when you write a job application letter, a clear thesis statement helps you tell the recruiter why you should be hired.

Write a working outline

The final step in the preparation process is writing a working outline. Use this outline as a loose guide instead of a final structure. As you draft your paper, your ideas and structure may change. Only by allowing changes to occur do you get closer to what you really want to say. Some students prefer a formal outline structure, while others like to use a think link.

Create a checklist

Use the checklist in Key 7.5 to make sure your preparation is complete. Under Date Due, create your own writing schedule, giving each task an intended completion date. Work backward from the date the assignment is due and estimate how long it will take to complete each step. Refer to Chapter 2 for time-management skills that will help you schedule your writing process.

You'll probably move back and forth among the tasks on the schedule. You might find yourself doing two and even three things on the same day. Stick to the schedule as best you can, while balancing the other demands of your life, and check off your accomplishments as you complete them.

Drafting

A *first draft* involves putting ideas down on paper for the first time—but not the last. You may write many versions of the assignment until you are satisfied. Each version moves you closer to saying exactly what you want in the way you want to say it.

Preparation checklist.

DATE DUE	TASK	IS IT COMPLETE?
	Brainstorm	
	Define and narrow	
	Use prewriting strategies	
	Conduct research if necessary	
	Write thesis statement	
	Write working outline	
	Complete research	

The process of writing a first draft includes freewriting, crafting an introduction, organizing the ideas in the body of the paper, formulating a conclusion, citing sources, and soliciting feedback. When you think of drafting, it might help to imagine that you are creating a kind of "writing sandwich." The bottom slice of bread is the introduction, the top slice is the conclusion, and the sandwich stuffing is made of central ideas and supporting examples (see Key 7.6).

Freewriting your draft. Take everything that you have developed in the planning stages and freewrite a rough draft. For now, don't consciously think about your introduction, conclusion, or the structure within the paper's body. Simply focus on getting your ideas out onto paper. When you have the beginnings of a paper, you can start to shape it into something with a more definite form. First, work on how you want to begin.

Writing an introduction. The introduction tells readers what the rest of the paper contains, and includes a thesis statement. On page 212, for example, is a draft of an introduction for Sam's paper about wrestling camp. The thesis statement is underlined at the end of the paragraph.

When you write an introduction, use one or more *hooks* to catch the reader's attention and encourage him or her to want to read further. Useful hooks include relevant anecdotes, quotations, dramatic statistics, or questions that encourage thinking. Always link your strategy to your thesis statement. After you craft an introduction that establishes the purpose of your paper, make sure the body fulfills that purpose.

Creating the body of a paper. The body of the paper contains your central ideas and supporting evidence. *Evidence*—proof that informs or persuades—consists of the facts, statistics, examples, and expert opinions.

Look at the array of ideas and evidence in your draft in its current state. Think about how you might group evidence with the particular ideas it supports. Then, try to find a structure that helps you organize your ideas and evidence into a clear pattern. Here are some strategies to consider:

Think of the parts of your draft as a "writing sandwich."

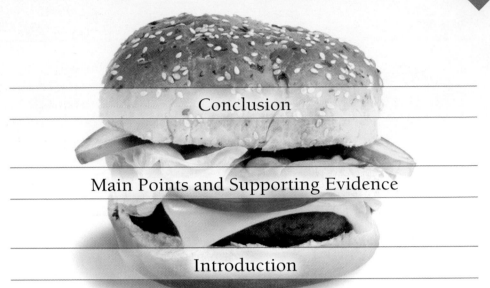

Conclusion

Main Points and Supporting Evidence

Introduction

INTRODUCTION

As a boy, I watched some greats of the sport with my father—wrestlers like Whipper Billy Watson and Stu Hart would grace our television set Saturday afternoons. The kids in my class would often pretend to be wrestlers; we would act like our heroes during recess and after school. However, unlike most people, I had the chance to train at a professional wrestling school when I graduated from high school. Though this had been a lifelong goal of mine, nothing I had done could have prepared me for what I experienced during my week at the Hart Brothers Wrestling Camp in Alberta.

- **Arrange ideas by time.** Describe events in order or in reverse order.
- **Arrange ideas according to importance.** Start with the idea that carries the most weight and move to less important ideas. Or move from the least important to the most important idea.
- **Arrange ideas by problem and solution.** Start with a specific problem and then discuss solutions.

You might want to use "chain-link support"—a set of reasons that build on one another. Be sure to consider arguments that oppose yours, and consider presenting evidence that counteracts such arguments.

Writing the Conclusion. Your conclusion is a statement or paragraph that summarizes the information that is in the body of your paper and critically evaluates what is important about it. Try one of the following strategies:

- Summarize main points (if material is longer than three pages).
- Relate a story, statistic, quotation, or question that makes the reader think.
- Call the reader to action.
- Look to the future.

Try not to introduce new facts or restate what has already been proven ("I have shown that violent cartoons are linked to violence in children"). Let your ideas in the body of the paper speak for themselves. Readers should feel that they have reached a natural point of completion.

Omit needless words.... This requires not that the writer make all his sentences short, or that he avoid all detail and treat his subjects only in outline, but that every word tell.

WILLIAM STRUNK, JR.

Avoiding plagiarism: Crediting authors and sources. When you incorporate ideas from other sources into your work, you are using other writers' *intellectual property.* Using another writer's words, content, unique approach, or illustrations without crediting the author is called **plagiarism** and is illegal and unethical. The following techniques will help you properly credit sources and avoid plagiarism:

- **Make source notes as you go.** Plagiarism often begins accidentally during research. You may forget to include quotation marks around a quotation, or you may intend to cite or paraphrase a source but never do. To avoid forgetting, write detailed source and content notes as you research. Try writing something like "Quotation from original, rewrite later" next to quoted material you copy into notes, and add bibliographic information (title, author, source, page number, etc.) so you don't spend hours trying to locate it later.

- **Learn the difference between a quotation and a paraphrase.** A *quotation* repeats a source's exact words, which are set off from the rest of the text by quotation marks. A *paraphrase* is a restatement of the quotation in your own words. A restatement requires that you completely rewrite the idea, not just remove or replace a few words. As Key 7.7 illustrates, a paraphrase may not be acceptable if it is too close to the original.

- **Use a citation even for an acceptable paraphrase.** Take care to credit any source that you quote, paraphrase, or use as evidence. To credit a source, write a footnote or endnote that describes it, using the format preferred by your instructor. Writing handbooks, such as the *Simon & Schuster Handbook for Writers, Fourth Canadian Edition* by Lynn Quitman Troyka, explain the two standard documentation styles

<u>PLAGIARISM</u>
The act of using someone else's exact words, figures, unique approach, or specific reasoning without giving appropriate credit.

Avoid plagiarism by learning how to paraphrase.

7.7

QUOTATION

From Searle, John R. "I Married a Computer." Rev. of *The Age of Spiritual Machines*, by Ray Kurzweil. *New York Review of Books* 8 Apr. 1999: 34+.

"We are now in the midst of a technological revolution that is full of surprises. No one thirty years ago was aware that one day household computers would become as common as dishwashers. And those of us who used the old Arpanet of twenty years ago had no idea that it would evolve into the Internet."

UNACCEPTABLE PARAPHRASE

The current <u>technological revolution</u> is <u>surprising</u>. <u>Thirty years ago, no one</u> expected computers to be <u>as common</u> today as air conditioners. What once was the Arpanet has <u>evolved into the Internet</u>, and no one expected that.

ACCEPTABLE PARAPHRASE

John Searle states that we live in a technologically amazing time of change in which computers have "become as common as dishwashers" (37). Twenty years ago, no one could have predicted the Arpanet would become the Internet (37).

Source: Lynn Quitman Troyka and Douglas Hesse, *Simon & Schuster Handbook for Writers*, Fourth Canadian Edition (Toronto, ON: Pearson Education Canada, 2006) 519–520.

from the American Psychological Association (APA) and the Modern Language Association (MLA). A good writing handbook tells you how to cite various types of sources in the body of a paper and compile a list of works cited at the end of your paper.

- **Understand that lifting material off the Internet is plagiarism.** Words in electronic form belong to the writer just as words in print form do. If you cut and paste sections from a source document onto your draft, you are committing plagiarism.

Instructors consider work to be plagiarized when a student

- submits a paper from a Web site that sells or gives away research papers.
- buys a paper from a non-Internet service.
- hands in a paper written by a fellow student or a family member.
- copies material in a paper directly from a source without proper quotation marks or source citation.
- paraphrases material in a paper from a source without proper source citation.

Students who choose to plagiarize are placing their academic careers at risk because of instructors' increasing use of anti-plagiarism computer software. These programs find strings of words that are identical to those in a database and alert the instructor to suspicious patterns. When a physics professor at the University of Virginia in the United States suspected that his students were copying term papers, he ran their papers through a program

AVOID PLAGIARISM

Think about plagiarism and explore your views on this growing problem.

Complete the following:

- Why is plagiarism considered an offence that involves both stealing and lying? Describe how you look at it.

  _____

  _____

- Citing sources indicates that you respect the ideas of others. List two additional ways that accurate source citation strengthens your writing and makes you a better student.

  1. _____

  2. _____

- What specific penalties for plagiarism are described in your college handbook? Explain whether you feel that these penalties are reasonable or excessive and whether they will keep students from plagiarizing.

  _____

  _____

  _____

- Many experts believe that researching on the Internet is behind many acts of plagiarism. Do you agree? Why or why not?

  _____

  _____

that looked for similarities of six or more consecutive words. He found 122 cases of abuse. These students are facing possible expulsion.[7]

Continue your checklist. Create a checklist for your first draft (see Key 7.8). The elements of a first draft do not have to be written in order. In fact, many writers prefer to write the introduction after the body of the paper, so the introduction reflects the paper's content and tone. Whatever order you choose, make sure your schedule allows you to get everything done—with enough time left over for revisions.

Revising

When you revise, you critically evaluate the word choice, paragraph structure, and style of your first draft. Be thorough as you add, delete, replace, and reorganize words, sentences, and paragraphs. You may want to print your draft and correct the hard copy before you make changes on the computer. Some classes include a peer review process in which students read one another's work and offer suggestions. Having a

First draft checklist.

DATE DUE	TASK	IS IT COMPLETE?
	Freewrite a draft	
	Plan and write the introduction	
	Organize the body of the paper	
	Include research evidence in the body	
	Plan and write the conclusion	
	Check for plagiarism and rewrite passages to avoid it	
	Credit your sources	
	Solicit feedback	

different perspective on your writing is extremely valuable. The elements of revision include being a critical writer, evaluating paragraph structure, and checking for clarity and conciseness.

During the revision process, you assess what you have done and revisit any part of your work that is off the mark. The best time to critically evaluate your writing is after you let it sit for a while, says Dr. Mel Levine, author of *The Myth of Laziness*. "The writing experience needs time to incubate. It is preferable to check something several days later or the night after it came to be. With time, it is much easier to evaluate your own work, to detect and correct its flaws with some objectivity, and to deftly surmount the impasses that felt insurmountable while you were immersed in the act of writing."[8]

Being an analytical writer. Critical thinking helps you move beyond restating what you learned from other sources to creating your own perspective. One key to critical writing is asking the question "So what?" For example, if you were writing a piece on nutrition, you might discuss a variety of good eating habits. Asking "So what?" could lead into a discussion of *why* these habits are helpful.

If your paper contains arguments, use critical thinking to make sure they are well constructed and convincing. Using what you know from the discussion in Chapter 4, think through your arguments and provide solid support with facts and examples.

Use the mind actions to guide your revision. Ask yourself questions that can help you evaluate ideas, develop original insights, and be complete and clear. Here are some examples of questions you may ask:

- Are these examples clearly connected to the idea?
- Am I aware of similar concepts or facts that can act as support?
- What else can I recall that can help to support this idea?
- In evaluating a situation, have I clearly indicated causes and effects?

MULTIPLE INTELLIGENCE STRATEGIES FOR
Writing

The techniques below allow you to access your power as a writer by uncovering valuable research sources and clearly communicating what you really want to say.

INTELLIGENCE	SUGGESTED STRATEGIES	WHAT WORKS FOR YOU? WRITE NEW IDEAS HERE
Verbal–Linguistic	• Read many resources and take comprehensive notes on them. Summarize the main points from your resources. • Interview someone about the topic and take notes.	
Logical–Mathematical	• Take notes on index cards and organize them according to topics and subtopics. • Create a detailed, sequential outline of your writing project, making sure that your argument is logical if your assignment requires persuasive writing.	
Bodily–Kinesthetic	• Pay a visit to numerous sites that hold resources you need or that are related to your topic—businesses, libraries, etc. • After brainstorming ideas for an assignment, take a break involving physical activity. During the break, think about your top three ideas and see what insight occurs to you.	
Visual–Spatial	• Create full-colour charts as you read each resource or interview someone. • Use think link format or another visual organizer to map out your main topic, subtopics, and related ideas and examples. Use different colours for different subtopics.	
Interpersonal	• Discuss material with a fellow student as you gather it. • Pair up with a classmate and become each other's peer editors. Read each other's first drafts and next-to-final drafts, offering constructive feedback.	
Intrapersonal	• Take time to mull over any assigned paper topic. Think about what emotions it raises in you, and why. Let your inner instincts guide you as you begin to write. • Schedule as much research time as possible.	
Musical	• Play your favourite relaxing music while you brainstorm topics for a writing assignment.	
Naturalistic	• Pick a research topic that relates to nature. • Build confidence by envisioning your writing process as a successful climb to the top of a mountain.	

- What new idea comes to mind when I think about these facts?
- How do I evaluate any effect, fact, or situation?
- Are there different arguments that I should address here?

Finally, critical thinking can help you evaluate the content and form of your paper. As you start your revision, ask yourself these questions:

- Will my audience understand my thesis and how I've supported it?
- Does the introduction prepare the reader and capture attention?
- Is the body of the paper organized effectively?
- Is each idea fully developed, explained, and supported by examples?
- Are my ideas connected to one another through logical transitions?
- Do I have a clear, concise, simple writing style?
- Does the paper fulfill the requirements of the assignment?
- Does the conclusion provide a natural ending to the paper?

Evaluating paragraph structure. Make sure that each paragraph has a *topic sentence* that states the paragraph's main idea (a topic sentence does for a paragraph what a thesis statement does for an entire paper). The rest of the paragraph should support the idea with evidence. Most topic sentences are at the start of the paragraph, although sometimes topic sentences appear elsewhere. The topic sentence in the following paragraph is underlined:

Examine how paragraphs flow into one another by evaluating your transitions, which connect ideas. Transitions take the form of connecting sentences, phrases, and words. Among the words and phrases that are helpful are *also*, *in addition*, and *next*. Similarly, *finally*, *as a result*, and *in conclusion* tell readers that a summary is on its way.

Checking for clarity and conciseness. Aim to say what you want to say clearly and concisely. Try to eliminate extra words and phrases. Rewrite wordy phrases in a more straightforward, conversational way. For example, write "if" instead of "in the event that," or "now" instead of "at this point in time."

When I arrived at camp, I had little idea of what to expect. <u>While I used to weight train, jog, and ride my bike for conditioning, nothing prepared me for the reality of the Hart camp.</u> From the first day, they meant business. Each session began with a 2 km run through the Alberta foothills. Then the real fun began. The stretching and agility exercises were designed to improve stamina and improve balance while in the wrestling ring.

See revision as 'envisioning again.' If there are areas in your work where there is a blur or vagueness, you can simply see the picture again and add the details that will bring your work closer to your mind's picture.

NATALIE GOLDBERG

Editing

Editing involves correcting technical mistakes in spelling, grammar, and punctuation, as well as checking style consistency for such elements as abbreviations and capitalization. Editing comes last, after you are satisfied with your ideas, organization, and writing style. If you use a computer, start with the grammar check and spell check to find mistakes,

STRESSBUSTER

ALICIA BRETT St. Francis Xavier University, Antigonish, Nova Scotia

What part of the writing process (researching, planning, drafting, revising, editing) causes you the most stress, and why? What techniques do you use to minimize stress when writing longer papers? If you had to give an oral presentation in front of your class, would you be stressed? How would you overcome this challenge?

Drafting is the most difficult part of the writing process for me. Planning is not a problem, but when I have all my thought maps and summaries prepared, I still don't know where to begin. I often find myself staring at a blank page. When there is nothing left to do but write, I sit down and remind myself that I have to start with something—anything—so that I can edit and revise. Then the words start coming, and by following my framework, things start to fall into place. If I've thought about the assignment and how I want the concepts to be organized, then I know where to add information, citations, and examples so that the essay flows. It's hard to take ideas and find the right words with which to

convey them; however, mediocre words will do for the time being. Tweaking the paper comes later.

To keep stress at a minimum when writing long papers, I break down the assignment into chunks of work, and when I complete each, I reward myself by doing something fun, like watching TV with friends. When I sit down to work and I'm having an especially rough time, I go for a quick walk and think of everything but the paper. Then I'm ready to think when I return.

Oral presentations stress me out. If I were to give a presentation to my class, I would make sure that I knew the material well beforehand. I'd practise, to myself and to others, and ask my practice audience to think of questions for me. That way, I could adjust the parts that may be unclear in my presentation. Also, if my professor or classmates had questions, I'd be less likely to be caught off guard by them. I would also think about hand gestures and body positioning; the words are important, but so is the delivery.

Sam Gordon   March 19, 2004

The Pain Isn't Fake

Bitten by the wrestling bug at an early age, I was determined to become a professional wrestler. As a child, I used to watch wrestling with my father Saturday afternoons. At school, my friends and I used to act out the role of "good guys" and "bad guys" during recess. As a teenager, I participated in a variety of contact sports. When I graduated from high school and the opportunity arose to attend a professional wrestling camp, I jumped at the chance. What I discovered was that, while it might look easy on television, in reality it's hard.

Located in the foothills of Alberta is the small town of Okotoks, home of the Hart Brothers Wrestling Camp. The Harts are recognized as some of the best trainers. They have built a strong reputation for running one of the most physically demanding schools in the world. Their philosophy comes from the patriarch of the family, Stu Hart. The wrestling world affectionately knows his training basement as the "dungeon." Many a spirit (and bone) has been broken here. His sons have continued his reputation for toughness, and, once a year, take in a new set of trainees. Any notion of wrestling camp as an acting school for "fakers" is quickly dismissed during the first training session. Let me explain.

When I arrived at camp, I, like most others, had little idea of what to expect. The camp itself is regimented in its methods. One of Stu Hart's sons, Keith, was in charge of my sessions, which were held five nights a week and lasted between three and five hours. Each session began with a 2 km run up and down the Alberta foothills. Once we returned to the camp, we had to do stretching exercises. Part of the workout was designed to improve our flexibility, and we would sit on the ground with the bottoms of our feet touching and our knees pointed out. Then, a 120-kg man would stand on our inner thighs, putting incredible pressure on the muscles and ligaments in our upper legs. As you can imagine, this stretching exercise brought tears to many eyes, mine included.

The session did not end there. From the stretching exercises, we began to learn how to take "bumps." The term "bump" refers to a wrestler falling down during a match. At the Hart camp, they teach many different ways of taking bumps. While it may sound simple to get into the ring and start falling down, there is a right way and a wrong way to take a bump without causing serious harm to yourself. When we first started taking bumps, many of my colleagues began to vomit. This is the body's natural reaction to the stress it takes when a person takes a bump. Adjusting to bumps, combined with the rigours of training, take their toll on the weight of the students. They told us that most students could expect to lose approximately 10 kg during the first week of camp. I lost 15 kg in my first four days alone.

Survival is a key word when describing the Hart wrestling camp. The Harts not only run a tough camp, they also run a professional and legitimate business. Most trainees, myself included, cannot get used to the punishment and decide to leave. The intensity of the training is physically taxing. The Harts were gracious enough to reimburse most of my money because I couldn't last a full week at their camp. I left Okotoks a little poorer, but a lot wiser. I had a new-found respect for those who wrestled professionally. I still watch wrestling with my father Saturday afternoons, but with a more critical eye and admiration for its participants, especially any wrestler with the last name "Hart."

realizing that you still need to check your work. Although a spell checker won't pick up the mistake in the sentence, "They are not hear on Tuesdays," someone who is reading for sense will.

Look also for *sexist language,* which characterizes people according to gender. Sexist language often involves the male pronouns *he, him,* or *his.* For example, "An executive often spends hours a day going through his email" implies that executives are always men. A simple change to a plural subject eliminates the problem: "Executives often spend hours each day going through their email." Try to be sensitive to words that slight women. *Mail carrier* is preferable to *mailman, chair* to *chairman.*

Revising and editing checklist.

DATE DUE	TASK	IS IT COMPLETE?
	Check the body of the paper for clear thinking and adequate support of ideas	
	Finalize introduction and conclusion	
	Check word spelling, usage, and grammar	
	Check paragraph structure	
	Make sure language is familiar and concise	
	Check punctuation and capitalization	
	Check transitions	
	Eliminate sexist language	
	Get feedback from peers and/or instructor	

Proofreading is the last editing stage and happens after your paper is in its final form. Proofreading means reading every word and sentence for accuracy. Look for technical mistakes, run-on sentences, and sentence fragments. Look for incorrect word usage and unclear references.

A Final Checklist You are now ready to complete your revising and editing checklist. All the tasks listed in Key 7.5 should be done before you submit your paper. Key 7.9 shows the final version of Sam's paper.

Your final paper reflects your hard work. Ideally, you have a piece of work that shows your writing ability and that communicates interesting and important ideas. Because of how closely writing and speaking skills are related, solid writing skills also help you craft a speech or oral presentation.

How can you deliver an *effective* oral presentation?

In school, you may be asked to deliver a speech, take an oral exam, or present a team project. When you ask a question or make a comment in class, you are using public speaking skills. On the job, you will need these skills to deliver presentations to clients, run meetings, and give speeches.

The public speaking skills that you learn for *formal* presentations help you make a favourable impression in *informal* settings, such as when you meet with an instructor, summarize a reading for your study group, or have a planning session at work. When you are articulate, others take notice.

Prepare as for a writing assignment

Speaking in front of others involves preparation, strategy, and confidence. Planning a speech is similar to planning a piece of writing; you must know your topic and audience and think about presentation strategy, organization, and word choice. Specifically, you should:

- **Think through what you want to say and why.** What is your purpose—to make or refute an argument, present information, entertain? Have a goal for your speech.

- **Plan.** Take time to think about who your listeners are and how they are likely to respond. Then, get organized. Brainstorm your topic—narrow it with prewriting strategies, determine your thesis, write an outline, and do research.

- **Draft your thoughts.** Draft your speech. Illustrate ideas with examples, and show how examples lead to ideas. As in writing, have a clear beginning and end. Start with an attention-getter and conclude with a wrap-up that summarizes your thoughts and leaves your audience with something to remember.

- **Integrate visual aids.** Think about building your speech around visual aids including charts, maps, slides and photographs, and props. Learn software programs to create presentation graphics.

Practise your performance

The element of performance distinguishes speaking from writing. Here are tips to keep in mind:

- **Know the parameters.** How long do you have? Where are you speaking? Be aware of the setting—where your audience will be and available props (e.g., a podium, table, a blackboard).

- **Use index cards or notes.** Reduce your final draft to "trigger" words or phrases that remind you of what you want to say and refer to the cards and to your visual aids during your speech.

- **Pay attention to the physical.** Your body position, voice, and clothing contribute to the impression you make. Your goal is to look and sound good and to appear relaxed. Try to make eye contact with your audience, and walk around if you are comfortable presenting in that way.

- **Practise ahead of time.** Do a test run with friends or alone. If possible, practise in the room where you will speak. Audiotape or videotape your practice sessions and evaluate your performance.

- **Be yourself.** When you speak, you express your personality through your words and presence. Don't be afraid to add your own style to the presentation. Take deep breaths. Smile. Know that you can speak well and that your audience wants to see you succeed. Finally, envision your own success.

Suà

Suà is a Shoshone Indian word, derived from the Uto-Aztecna language, meaning "think." By focusing on *suà,* you are able to evaluate research sources as the basis for your positions and communicate your conclusions effectively in your writing and speaking. Through the power of thought, you can choose sources that support your thesis and express your insights.

BUILDING SKILLS

FOR ACADEMIC, CAREER, AND LIFE SUCCESS

Developing Successful Intelligence

PUTTING IT ALL TOGETHER

Be a planner. Engage analytical, creative, and practical skills as you work through the planning stage of writing.

Step 1. Think it through: *Analyze your writing goal.* Imagine that you have been asked to write an essay on a time when you turned a difficulty into an opportunity. First, write a brief description of your topic:

_____

_____

Next, think about your purpose and audience. How might you frame your purpose if you were writing to a person who is going through a tough time and needs inspiration? How would your purpose change if you were writing to an instructor who wanted to know what you learned from a difficult experience? Write your purpose and intended audience here.

_____

_____

_____

_____

Step 2. Think out of the box: *Prewrite to create ideas.* On a separate sheet of paper, use prewriting strategies to start the flow of ideas.

- Brainstorm your ideas.
- Freewrite.
- Ask journalists' questions.

create your future

Step 3. *Make it happen: Write a thesis statement.* With the thesis statement, you make your topic as specific as possible and you clearly define your purpose. Write your thesis statement here:

_____

_____

_____

Team Building

COLLABORATIVE SOLUTIONS

Team research. Join with three other classmates and decide on two relatively narrow research topics that interest all of you and that you can investigate by spending no more than an hour in the library. The first topic should be current and in the news—for example, safety problems in sport utility vehicles (SUVs), body piercing, or the changing nature of the Canadian family. The second topic should be more academic and historical—for example, the polio epidemic in the 1950s, the Irish potato famine, or multiculturalism in Canada.

Working alone, team members will use your school's library and the Internet to research both topics. Set a research time limit of no more than one hour per topic. The goal should be to collect a list of sources for later investigation. When everyone is through, the group should come together to discuss the research process. Ask each other questions such as:

- How did you "attack" and organize your research for each topic?
- What research tools did you use to investigate each topic?
- How did your research differ from topic to topic? Why do you think this was the case?
- How did your use of library and Internet resources differ from topic to topic?
- Which research techniques yielded the best results? Which techniques led to dead ends?

Next, compare the specific results of everyone's research. Analyze each source for what it is likely to yield in the form of useful information. Finally, come together as a group and discuss what you learned that might improve your approach to library and Internet research.

Writing

DISCOVERY THROUGH JOURNALING

Record your thoughts on a separate piece of paper or in a journal.

Learning from other writers. Identify a piece of powerful writing that you have recently read. (It could be a work of literature, a biography, a magazine or newspaper article, or even a section from one of your college texts.) Describe, in detail, why it was powerful. Did it make you feel something, think something, or take action? Why? What can you learn about writing from this piece that you can apply to your own writing?

Career Portfolio

Writing sample: A job interview cover letter. To secure a job interview, you will, at some point, have to write a letter describing your background and explaining your value to the company. For your portfolio, write a one-page, three-paragraph cover letter to a prospective employer. (The letter will accompany your résumé.) Be creative—you may use fictitious names, but select a career and industry that interest you. Use the format shown in the sample letter in Key 7.11 on p. 227.

- **Introductory paragraph:** Start with an attention getter—a statement that convinces the employer to read on. For example, name a person the employer knows who told you to write, or refer to something positive about the company that you read in the paper. Identify the position for which you are applying, and tell the employer that you are interested in working for the company.

- **Middle paragraph:** Sell your value. Try to convince the employer that hiring you will help the company in some way. Centre your "sales effort" on your experience in school and the workplace. If possible, tie your qualifications to the needs of the company. Refer indirectly to your enclosed résumé.

- **Final paragraph:** Close with a call to action. Ask the employer to call you, or tell the employer to expect your call to arrange an interview.

Exchange your first draft with a classmate. Read each other's letter and make notes in the margins that try to improve the letter's impact and persuasiveness, as well as its writing style, grammar, punctuation, and spelling. Discuss each letter and make whatever corrections are necessary to produce a well-written, persuasive letter. Create a final draft for your portfolio.

A cover letter should express your job interest and summarize why you are a strong candidate.

First name Last name
1234 Your Street
City, Province Postal Code

November 1, 200X

Ms. Prospective Employer
Prospective Company
5432 Their Street
City, Province Postal Code

Dear Ms. Employer:

On the advice of Mr. X, career centre advisor at Y College, I am writing to inquire about the position of production assistant at C101.5 Radio. I read the description of the job and your company on the career centre's employment-opportunity bulletin board, and I would like to apply for the position.

I will graduate this spring with a degree in communications. Since my second year when I declared my major, I have wanted to pursue a career in radio. For the last year I have worked as a production intern at CCOL Radio, the campus's station, and have occasionally filled in as a disc jockey on the evening news show. I enjoy being on the air, but my primary interest is production and programming. My enclosed résumé will tell you more about my background and experience.

I would be pleased to talk with you in person about the position. You can reach me anytime at (555) 555-5555 or by email at xxxx@xx.com. Thank you for your consideration, and I look forward to meeting you.

Sincerely,

Sign Your Name Here

First name Last name
Enclosure(s) *(use this notation if you have included a résumé or other item with your letter)*

SUGGESTED READINGS

Becker, Howard S. *Tricks of the Trade: How to Think About Your Research While You're Doing It.* Chicago: University of Chicago Press, 1998.

Booth, Wayne C., Gregory G. Columb, and Joseph M. Williams. *The Craft of Research,* 2nd ed. Chicago: University of Chicago Press, 2003.

Cameron, Julia. *The Right to Write: An Invitation into the Writing Life.* New York: Putnam, 2000.

Gibaldi, Joseph, and Phyllis Franklin. *MLA Handbook for Writers of Research Papers,* 6th ed. New York: Modern Language Association of America, 2003.

LaRocque, Paula. *Championship Writing: 50 Ways to Improve Your Writing.* Oak Park, IL: Marion Street Press, 2000.

Markman, Peter T., and Roberta H. Markman. *10 Steps in Writing the Research Paper,* 6th ed. New York: Barron's Educational Series, 2001.

Strunk, William, Jr., and E. B. White. *The Elements of Style,* 4th ed. New York: Allyn and Bacon, 2000.

Troyka, Lynn Quitman, and Douglas Hess. *Simon & Schuster Handbook for Writers,* Fourth Canadian Edition. Toronto: Pearson Education Canada, 2006.

Walsch, Bill. *Lapsing into a Comma: A Curmudgeon's Guide to the Many Things That Can Go Wrong in Print—and How to Avoid Them.* New York: Contemporary Books, 2000.

Williams, Joseph M. *Style: Ten Lessons in Clarity and Grace.* Chicago: University of Chicago Press, 2003.

INTERNET RESOURCES

Diana Hacker from Prince George Community College offers this link to help students with all their documentation questions: http://www.dianahacker.com/resdoc/index.html

The University of Toronto offers their students these practical tips on writing essays at their web site: http://www.utoronto.ca/writing/

English Professor John Lye at Brock University has a great Web page devoted to helping students become better writers: www.brocku.ca/english/jlye/index.html#style

Jack Lynch from Rutgers University offers great advice and many useful links for disorganized writers: http://andromeda.rutgers.edu/~jlynch/Writing/links.html

Need more information about the issue of plagiarism? Check out this handy site: http://www.plagiarism.org/

Turnitin is a Web site that many post-secondary schools are using in their fight to maintain academic integrity: www.turnitin.com

1. Statistics Canada, *The Daily*, March 26, 2001. "Changing Our Ways: Why and How Canadians Use the Internet."

2. Robert Harris, "Research Using the Internet" [on-line]. *VirtualSalt*, November 17, 1997. Available at: www.virtualsalt.com/evalu8it.htm.

3. Lori Leibovich, "Choosing Quick Hits Over the Card Catalog," *The New York Times,* August 10, 2000, p. 1.

4. David Hochman, "In Searching We Trust," *New York Times,* March 14, 2004, Section 9, p. 1.

5. Floyd H. Johnson (May 1996), "The Internet and Research: Proceed With Caution" [on-line]. Available at: **http://showcase.netins.net/web/nwc-iowa/ InternetResearch.html** (August 2000).

6. Analysis based on Lynn Quitman Troyka, *Simon & Schuster Handbook for Writers*. Upper Saddle River, NJ: Prentice Hall, 1996, pp. 22–23.

7. *The Elements of Style,* Strunk and White, © 2000. Reprinted by permission of Pearson Education, Inc.

8. Mel Levine, *The Myth of Laziness*. New York: Simon & Schuster, 2003, p. 183

ANALYZE

8

IN THIS CHAPTER

In this chapter you will explore answers to the following questions: • How can preparation improve test performance? • How can you work through test anxiety? • What general strategies can help you succeed on tests? • How can you master different types of test questions? • How can you learn from test mistakes?

Test taking

FOR A RUNNER, a race is the equivalent of a test because it measures ability at a given moment. Doing well in a race requires training similar to the studying you do for exams. The best runners—and test takers—understand that they train not just for the race or test, but also to achieve a level of competence that will stay with them. Knowing that you will continue to use the skills on which you are being tested gives you the perspective that *owning* these skills is more important than achieving a perfect score. Test taking in school prepares you to solve problems and think, two skills listed by the Conference Board of Canada as being fundamental employability skills. It's also about conquering fears, paying attention to details, and learning from mistakes.

showing what you know

How can preparation improve *test performance*?

Like a runner who prepares for a marathon by exercising, eating right, taking practice runs, and getting enough sleep, you can take steps to master your exams. The primary step, occupying much of your preparation time, is to listen when material is presented, read carefully, and study until you know the material that will be on the test (Chapter 5 examines the art of effective studying). In this sense, staying on top of your class meetings, readings, and assignments over the course of the semester is one of the best ways to prepare for tests. Other important steps are the preparation strategies that follow.

Identify test type and material covered

Before you begin studying, find out as much as you can about the type of test you will be taking and what it will cover. Try to identify:

- What topics the test will cover (Will it cover everything since the semester began or will it be limited to a narrow topic?).
- The type of questions on the test—objective (multiple choice, true–false, sentence completion), subjective (essay), or a combination.
- What material you will be tested on (Will the test cover only what you learned in class and in the text or will it also cover outside readings?).

Your instructors may answer these questions for you. Even though they may not reveal specific test questions, they might let you know the question format or information covered. Some instructors may even drop hints about possible test questions, either directly ("I might ask a question on this subject on your next exam") or more subtly ("One of my favourite theories is...").

Here are a few other strategies for predicting what may be on a test.

Use SQ3R to identify what's important. Often, the questions you write and ask yourself when you read assigned materials may be part of the test. Textbook study questions are also good candidates.

Talk to people who already took the course. Try to find out how difficult the instructor's tests are, whether they focus primarily on assigned readings or on class notes, what materials are usually covered, and what types of questions are asked. Also ask about instructors' preferences. If you learn that the instructor pays close attention to specific facts, for example, use flash cards to drill yourself on major and minor details.

Examine old tests, if they are available. You may find them in class, on-line, or on reserve in the library. Old tests help to answer the following questions:

- Does the instructor focus on examples and details, general ideas and themes, or a combination?
- Can you do well through straight memorization or should you take a critical-thinking approach?
- Are the questions straightforward or confusing and sometimes tricky?
- Do the tests require that you integrate facts from different areas in order to draw conclusions?

> A little knowledge that acts is worth infinitely more than much knowledge that is idle.

KAHLIL GIBRAN

If you can't get copies of old tests and your instructor doesn't give too many details, use clues from the class to predict test questions. After taking the first exam in the course, you will have more information about what to expect.

Create a study plan and schedule

Once you have identified as much as you can about what will be covered on the test, choose your study materials. Go through your notes, texts, related primary sources, and handouts, and then set aside materials you don't need.

Then use your time-management skills to prepare a schedule. Consider all of the relevant factors—your study materials, the number of days until the test, and the time you can study each day. If you establish your schedule ahead of time and write it in a date book, you are more likely to follow it.

WRITE YOUR OWN TEST

get creative!

Prepare for an upcoming exam using a pretest you create yourself.

Use the tips in this chapter to predict the material that will be covered, the types of questions that will be asked (multiple choice, essay, etc.), and the nature of the questions (a broad overview of the material or specific details).

Then be creative. Your goal is to write questions that your instructor is likely to ask—interesting questions that tap what you have learned and make you think about the material in different ways. Go through the following steps:

1. Write the questions you come up with on a separate sheet of paper.

2. Use what you created as a pretest. Set up test-like conditions—a quiet, timed environment—and see how well you do. Avoid looking at your text or notes unless the test is open book.

3. Evaluate your pretest answers against your notes and the text. How did you do?

4. Finally, after you take your instructor's exam, evaluate whether you think this exercise improved your performance on the actual exam. Would you use this technique again when you study for another exam? Why or why not?

Schedules vary widely according to the situation. For example, if you have three days before the test and no other obligations during that time, you might set two 2-hour study sessions during each day. On the other hand, if you have two weeks before a test, classes during the day, and work three nights a week, you might spread out your study sessions over the nights you have off during those two weeks.

A checklist like the one in Key 8.1 helps you get organized and stay on track as you prepare. Use a checklist to assign specific tasks to particular study times and sessions. That way, not only do you know when you have time to study, but you also have defined goals for each study session.

Prepare through careful review

By thoroughly reviewing your materials, you will have the best shot at remembering their contents. Use the following strategies when you study.

Use SQ3R. The reading method you studied in Chapter 5 provides an excellent structure for reviewing your reading materials.

- Surveying gives you an overview of topics.
- Questioning helps you focus on important ideas and determine what the material is trying to communicate.
- Reading (or, in this case, rereading) reminds you of the ideas and supporting information.
- Reciting helps to anchor the concepts in your head.
- Review tasks, such as quizzing yourself on the Q-stage questions, summarizing sections you have highlighted, making flash cards for important concepts, and constructing a chapter outline, help you solidify your learning so that you are able to use it at test time and beyond.

Review your notes. Recall the section in Chapter 6 for making your notes a valuable after-class reference. Use the following techniques to effectively review notes:

- **Time your reviews carefully.** Review notes for the first time within a day of the lecture, if you can, and then review again closer to the test day.
- **Mark up your notes.** Reread them, filling in missing information, clarifying points, writing out abbreviations, and highlighting key ideas.
- **Organize your notes.** Consider adding headings and subheadings to your notes to clarify the structure of the information. Rewrite them using a different organizing structure—for example, an outline if you originally used a think link.
- **Summarize your notes.** Evaluate which ideas and examples are most crucial, and then rewrite your notes in shortened form, focusing on those ideas and examples. Summarize your notes in writing or with a summary think link. Try summarizing from memory as a self-test.

Think critically. Using the techniques from Chapter 4, approach test preparation as a critical thinker, working to understand the material rather than

Pretest checklist.

Course: _____   Instructor: _____

Date, time, and place of test: _____

Type of test *(e.g., is it a mid-term or a minor quiz?)*: _____

What the instructor has told you about the test, including the types of test questions, the length of the test, and how much the test counts toward your final grade:

_____

_____

Topics to be covered on the test in order of importance:

1. _____

2. _____

3. _____

4. _____

5. _____

Study schedule, including materials you plan to study *(e.g., texts and class notes)* and dates you plan to complete each:

MATERIAL	DATE OF COMPLETION
1. _____	_____
2. _____	_____
3. _____	_____
4. _____	_____
5. _____	_____

Materials you are expected to bring to the test *(e.g., your textbook, a sourcebook, a calculator)*:

_____

_____

Special study arrangements *(e.g., plan study group meetings, ask the instructor for special help, get outside tutoring)*:

_____

_____

Life-management issues *(e.g., rearrange work hours)*:

_____

_____

_____

Source: Adapted from Ron Fry, "Ace" Any Test, 3rd ed. (Franklin Lakes, NJ: Career Press, 1996), 123–124.

just repeat facts. As you study, try to analyze causes and effects, look at issues from different perspectives, and connect concepts that, on the surface, appear unrelated. This work will increase your understanding and probably result in a higher exam mark. Critical thinking is especially important for essay tests that ask you to develop and support a thesis.

Take a pretest

Use questions from your textbook to create your own pretest. Most textbooks include end-of-chapter questions. If your course doesn't have an assigned text, develop questions from your notes and assigned outside readings. Choose questions that are likely to be covered on the test, then answer them under test-like conditions—in quiet, with no books or notes to help you (unless your exam is open book), and with a clock telling you when to quit.

Prepare physically

Most tests ask you to work efficiently under time pressure. If your body is tired or under stress, your performance may suffer. If you can, avoid staying up all night. Get some sleep so that you can wake up rested and alert. Remember that adequate sleep can help cement memories by reducing interference from new memories (see Chapter 6).

Eating right is also important. Sugar-laden snacks bring up your energy, only to send you crashing down much too soon. Also, too much caffeine can add to your tension and make it difficult to focus. Eating nothing leaves you drained, but too much food can make you sleepy. The best advice is to eat a light, well-balanced meal before a test. When time is short, grab a quick-energy snack such as a banana, orange juice, or a granola bar.

Make the most of last-minute studying

Cramming—studying intensively, and often round the clock, right before an exam—often results in information going into your head and popping right back out shortly after the exam is over. Because study conditions aren't always ideal, nearly every student crams during their college or university career, especially when a busy schedule leaves only a few hours to prepare. Use these hints to make the most of your study time:

- Go through your flash cards, if you have them, one last time.
- Focus on crucial concepts; don't worry about the rest. Resist reviewing notes or texts page by page.
- Create a last-minute study sheet. On a single sheet of paper, write down key facts, definitions, formulas, and so on. Try to keep the material short and simple. If you prefer visual notes, use think links to map out ideas and supporting examples.
- Arrive early. Study the sheet or your flash cards until you are asked to clear your desk.
- While it is still fresh, record any helpful information on scrap paper. Do this before looking at the test. Review this information as needed during the test.

Test Preparation

If the topic or format of a test challenges your stronger or weaker intelligences, these tips will help you make the most of your time and abilities.

INTELLIGENCE	SUGGESTED STRATEGIES	WHAT WORKS FOR YOU? WRITE NEW IDEAS HERE
Verbal–Linguistic	• Think of and write out questions your instructor may ask on a test. Answer the questions and then try rewriting them in a different format (essay, true–false, and so on). • Underline important words in review questions or practice questions.	
Logical–Mathematical	• Make diagrams of review or practice questions. • Outline the key steps involved in topics on which you may be tested.	
Bodily–Kinesthetic	• Use your voice to review out loud. Recite concepts, terms and definitions, important lists, dates, and so on. • Create a sculpture, model, or skit to depict a tough concept that will be on your test.	
Visual–Spatial	• Create a think link to map out an important topic and its connections to other topics in the material. Study it and redraw it from memory a day before the test. • Make drawings related to possible test topics.	
Interpersonal	• Develop a study group and encourage each other. • In your group, come up with as many possible test questions as you can. Ask each other these questions in an oral exam-type format.	
Intrapersonal	• Brainstorm test questions. Then, come back to them after a break or even a day's time. On your own, take the sample "test" you developed. • Make time to review in a solitary setting.	
Musical	• Play music while you read if it does not distract you. • Study concepts by reciting them to rhythms you create or to music.	
Naturalistic	• Bring your text, lecture notes, and other pertinent information to an outdoor spot that inspires you and helps you to feel confident, and review your material there.	

After your exam, evaluate the effects cramming had on your learning. Even if you passed, you might remember very little. This low level of retention won't do you much good in the real world where you have to make use of information instead of just recalling it for a test. Think about how you can plan strategically to start earlier and improve the situation next time.

Whether you have to cram or not, you may experience anxiety on test day. Following are some ideas for how to handle test anxiety when it strikes.

How can you work through *test anxiety*?

A certain amount of stress can be a good thing. Your body is alert, and your energy motivates you to do your best (for more on stress and stress management, see Chapter 10 and the Stressbuster boxes throughout the text). Some students, however, experience incapacitating stress levels before and during exams, especially midterms or finals.

Test anxiety can cause physical symptoms, such as sweating, nausea, dizziness, headaches, and fatigue, as well as psychological symptoms such as the inability to concentrate and feeling overwhelmed. You can minimize your anxiety by working on your preparation and attitude.

— TEST ANXIETY —

A bad case of nerves that can make it hard to think or to remember.

Preparation

Preparation is the basic defence against anxiety. The more confident you feel about the material, the better you will perform on test day. In this sense, consider all the preparation and study information in this chapter as test anxiety assistance. Also, finding out what to expect on the exam will help you feel more in control. Seek out information about what material will be covered, the question format, the length of the exam, and the points assigned to each question.

Creating a detailed study plan builds knowledge as it combats anxiety. Divide the plan into small tasks. As you finish each, you will increase your sense of accomplishment, confidence, and control. Instead of worrying about the test, take active steps that will help you succeed.

Attitude

Although good preparation is a confidence builder, maintaining a positive *attitude* is equally important. Here are some key ways to maintain an attitude that will help you succeed.

See the test as an opportunity to learn. A test is an opportunity to show what you have learned. All too often, students view tests as contests. If you pass, or "win" a contest, you might feel no need to retain what you've learned. If you fail, or "lose" the contest, you might feel no need to try again.

However, if you see the test as a signpost along the way to a greater goal, mastering the material will be more important than "winning."

Understand that tests measure performance, not personal value. Your grade does not reflect your ability to succeed. Whether you get an A or an F, you are still the same person.

Appreciate your instructor's purpose. Instructors don't intend to make you miserable. They test you to give you an opportunity to grow and demonstrate what you have accomplished. They test you so that, in rising to the challenge, you become better prepared for challenges outside of school. Don't hesitate to engage your instructors in your quest to learn and succeed. Visit them during office hours; send them email questions to clarify material and issues before tests.

Seek study partners who challenge you. Your anxiety may get worse if you study with someone who is also anxious. Find someone who can inspire you to do your best. For more on how to study effectively with others in study groups, see Chapter 5.

Set yourself up for success. Expect progress and success—not failure. Take responsibility for creating success through your work and attitude. Know that, ultimately, you are responsible for the outcome.

Practise relaxation. When you feel test anxiety mounting, breathe deeply, close your eyes, and visualize positive mental images such as getting a good mark and finishing with time to spare. Do whatever you have to do to ease muscle tension—stretch your neck, tighten and then release your muscles.

These strategies will help in most test anxiety situations. However, many students have issues surrounding math tests that require special attention.

Test anxiety and the returning student

If you're returning to school after years away, you may wonder if you can compete with younger students or if your mind is still able to learn. To counteract these feelings of inadequacy, focus on the useful skills you have learned in life. For example, managing work and a family requires strong time-management, planning, and communication skills that can help you plan your study time, juggle school responsibilities, and interact with students and instructors.

In addition, life experiences give you contexts through which you can understand ideas. For example, your relationship experiences may help you understand social psychology concepts, and managing your finances may help you understand accounting. If you permit yourself to feel positive about the knowledge and skills you have acquired, you may improve your ability to achieve your goals.

Parents who have to juggle child-care with study time can find the challenge especially difficult before a test. Here are some suggestions that might help:

- **Tell your children why the test is important.** Discuss the situation in concrete terms. For example, doing well in school might mean a high-paying job after graduation, which, in turn, can mean more money for family vacations, summer camps, and less stress over paying bills.
- **Explain the time frame.** Tell them your study schedule and when the test will occur. Plan a reward after your test—going for ice cream, seeing a movie, or having a picnic.
- **Plan activities.** Stock up on games, books, and videos.
- **Find help.** Ask a relative or friend to watch the children during study time, or arrange for your child to visit a friend. Consider trading babysitting hours with another parent, hiring a babysitter who will come to your home, or enrolling your child in daycare.

Fear is nature's warning sign to get busy.

HENRY C. LINK

What *general strategies* can help you succeed on tests?

 ven though every test is different, there are general strategies that will help you handle almost all tests, including short-answer and essay exams.

Write down key facts

Before you even look at the test, write down key information—including formulas, rules, and definitions—that you studied recently. Use the back of the question sheet or a piece of scrap paper for your notes (be sure your instructor knows that this paper didn't come into the test room already filled in). Recording this information at the start makes forgetting less likely.

Begin with an overview of the exam

Although exam time is precious, spend a few minutes at the start of the test getting a sense of the kinds of questions you'll be answering, what type of thinking they require, the number of questions in each section, and their point values. Use this information to schedule your time. For example, if a two-hour test is divided into two sections of equal point value—an essay section with four questions and a short-answer section with 60 questions—you can spend an hour on the essays (15 minutes per question) and an hour on the short-answer section (one minute per question). As you calculate, think about the level of difficulty of each section. If you think you can handle the short-answer questions in less than an hour and that you'll need more time for the essays, re-budget your time.

Read test directions

Reading test directions carefully can save you trouble. For example, although a history test of 100 true-or-false questions and one essay may look straightforward, the directions may tell you to answer 80 of the 100 questions or that the essay is an optional bonus. If the directions indicate that you are penalized for incorrect answers—meaning that you lose points instead of simply not gaining points—avoid guessing unless you're fairly certain. These questions may do damage, for example, if you earn two points for every correct answer and lose one point for every incorrect answer.

When you read directions, you may learn that some questions or sections are weighted more heavily than others. For example, the short-answer questions may be worth 30 points, whereas the essays are worth 70. In this case, it's smart to spend more time on the essays than on the short answers.

Work from easy to hard

Begin with the questions that seem easiest to you. You can answer these questions quickly, leaving more time for questions that require greater effort. If you like to work through questions in order, mark difficult questions as you reach them and return to them after you answer the questions you know. Answering easier questions first also boosts your confidence.

Watch the clock

Keep track of how much time is left and how you are progressing. You may

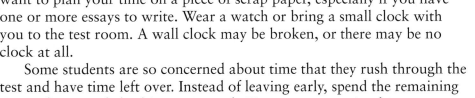

While it's tempting to rush through a test to get it over with, taking your time to think when you need to will help you be more sure of your answers and may even help you stay calm.

want to plan your time on a piece of scrap paper, especially if you have one or more essays to write. Wear a watch or bring a small clock with you to the test room. A wall clock may be broken, or there may be no clock at all.

Some students are so concerned about time that they rush through the test and have time left over. Instead of leaving early, spend the remaining time refining and checking your work. You may correct inadvertent errors, change answers, or add more information to an essay.

Master the art of intelligent guessing

When you are unsure of an answer on a short-answer test, you can leave it blank or you can guess. As long as you are not penalized for incorrect answers, guessing helps you. "Intelligent guessing," writes Steven Frank, an authority on student studying and test taking, "means taking advantage of what you do know in order to try to figure out what you don't. If you guess intelligently, you have a decent shot at getting the answer right."[1]

First, eliminate all the answers you know—or believe—are wrong. Try to narrow your choices to two possible answers; then choose the one you think is more likely to be correct. Strategies for guessing the correct answer on a multiple-choice test are discussed later in the chapter.

Follow directions on machine-scored tests

Machine-scored tests require that you use a special pencil to fill in a small box on a computerized answer sheet. When the computer scans the sheet, it can tell whether you answered the questions correctly.

Taking these tests requires special care. Use the right pencil (usually a number 2) and mark your answer in the correct space, filling the space completely. Periodically, check the answer number against the question number to make sure they match. If you mark the answer to question 4 in the space for question 5, not only do you get question 4 wrong, but your responses for all subsequent questions are off by a line. To avoid this problem, put a small dot next to any number you skip and plan to return to later.

Use Critical Thinking to Avoid Errors

Critical thinking can help you work through each question thoroughly and avoid errors. Following are some critical-thinking strategies to use during a test.

Recall facts, procedures, rules, and formulas. Base your answers on the information you recall. Think carefully to make sure your recall is accurate.

Think about similarities. If you don't know how to attack a question or problem, consider similar questions or problems that you have worked on in class or while studying.

Note differences. Especially with objective questions, items that seem different from the material you studied may lead to answers you can eliminate.

Think through causes and effects. For a numerical problem, think about how you plan to solve it and see if the answer—the effect of your plan—makes sense. For an essay question that asks you to analyze a condition or situation, consider both what caused it and what effects it has.

Find the best idea to match the example(s) given. For a numerical problem, decide what formula (idea) best applies to the example or examples (the data of the problem). For an essay question, decide what idea applies to or links the examples given.

Support ideas with examples. When you present an idea in an answer to an essay question, be sure to back it up with supporting examples.

Evaluate each test question. In your initial approach to a question, decide what kinds of thinking will best help you solve it. For example, essay questions often require cause-and-effect and idea-to-example thinking, whereas objective questions often benefit from thinking about similarities and differences.

Maintain academic integrity

When you take a test honestly, following all the rules of the test, you strengthen the principle of trust between students and instructors, which is at the heart of academic integrity (see Chapter 2). You also receive an accurate reading on your performance, from which you can determine what you know and what you still have to learn. Finally, you reinforce the habit of honesty.

Cheating as a strategy to pass a test or get a better grade robs you of the opportunity to learn the material on which you are being tested, which, ultimately, is your loss. It also makes fair play between students impossible. When one student studies hard for an exam and another cheats and both get the same high grade, the efforts of the hard-working student are diminished. It is important to realize that cheating jeopardizes your future post-secondary education if you are caught. You may be seriously reprimanded—or even expelled—if you violate your school's code of academic integrity.

How can you master *different types* of test questions?

Every type of test question has a different way of finding out how much you know about a subject. Answering different types of questions is part science and part art. The strategy changes according to whether the question is objective or subjective.

For **objective questions**, you choose or write a short answer you believe is correct, often making a selection from a limited number of choices. Multiple-choice, fill-in-the-blank, matching, and true-or-false questions fall into this category. **Subjective questions** demand the same information recall as objective questions, but they also require you to plan, organize, draft, and refine a written response. They may also require more extensive critical thinking and evaluation. All essay questions are subjective. Although some guidelines will help you choose the right answers to both types of questions, part of the skill is learning to "feel" your way to an answer that works.

Multiple-choice questions

Multiple-choice questions are the most popular type of question on standardized tests. The following strategies can help you answer them.

Carefully read the directions. Directions can be tricky. For example, whereas most test items ask for a single correct answer, some give you the option of marking several choices that are correct. For some tests, you might be required to answer only a certain number of questions.

Read each question thoroughly. Then, look at the choices and try to answer the question. This strategy reduces the possibility that the choices will confuse you.

OBJECTIVE QUESTIONS

Short-answer questions that test your ability to recall, compare, and contrast information and to choose the right answer from a limited number of choices.

SUBJECTIVE QUESTIONS

Essay questions that require you to express your answer in terms of your own personal knowledge and perspective.

Underline key words and phrases. If the question is complicated, try to break it down into small sections that are easy to understand.

Pay attention to words that could throw you off. For example, it is easy to overlook negatives in a question ("Which of the following is not...").

If you don't know the answer, eliminate those answers you know or suspect are wrong. Your goal is to leave yourself with two possible answers, which would give you a 50–50 chance of making the right choice. The following questions will help you eliminate choices:

- Is the choice accurate on its own terms? If there's an error in the choice—for example, a term that is incorrectly defined—the answer is wrong.

- Is the choice relevant? An answer may be accurate, but it may not relate to the essence of the question.

- Are there any qualifiers? Absolute qualifiers, like *always, never, all, none,* or *every,* often signal an exception that makes a choice incorrect. For example, the statement "Children always begin talking before the age of two" is untrue (most children begin talking before age two, but some start later). Analysis has shown that choices containing conservative qualifiers (e.g., *often, most, rarely,* or *may sometimes be*) are often correct.

- Do the choices give clues? Does a puzzling word remind you of a word you know? If you don't know a word, does any part of the word—its prefix, suffix, or root—seem familiar? (See Chapter 5 for information on the meanings of common prefixes, suffixes, and roots.)

Make an educated guess by following helpful patterns. The ideal is to know the material so well that you don't have to guess, but that isn't always possible. Test-taking experts have found patterns in multiple-choice questions that may help you. Here is their advice:

- Consider the possibility that a choice that is *more general* than the others is the right answer.

- Consider the possibility that a choice that is *longer* than the others is the right answer.

- Look for a choice that has a middle value in a range (the range can be from small to large or from old to recent). It is likely to be the right answer.

- Look for two choices that have similar meanings. One of these answers is probably correct.

- Look for answers that agree grammatically with the question. For example, a fill-in-the-blank question that has an *a* or *an* before the blank gives you a clue to the correct answer.

Make sure you read every word of every answer. Instructors have been known to include answers that are almost right, except for a single word. Focus especially on qualifying words such as *always, never, tend to, most, often,* and *frequently.*

When questions are keyed to a reading passage, read the questions first. This will help you focus on the information you need to answer the questions.

Here are some examples of the kinds of multiple-choice questions you might encounter in an Introduction to Psychology course[2] (the correct answer follows each question):

1. Arnold is at the company party and has had too much to drink. He releases all of his pent-up aggression by yelling at his boss, who promptly fires him. Arnold normally would not have yelled at his boss, but after drinking heavily he yelled because
    A. parties are places where employees are supposed to be able to "loosen up"
    B. alcohol is a stimulant
    C. alcohol makes people less concerned with the negative consequences of their behaviour
    D. alcohol inhibits brain centres that control the perception of loudness

(The correct answer is C)

2. Which of the following has not been shown to be a probable cause of or influence on the development of alcoholism in our society?
    A. intelligence   C. personality
    B. culture   D. genetic vulnerability

(The correct answer is A)

3. Blanche is a heavy coffee drinker who has become addicted to caffeine. If she completely ceases her intake of caffeine over the next few days, she is likely to experience each of the following except
    A. depression   C. insomnia
    B. lethargy   D. headaches

(The correct answer is C)

True-or-false questions

True-or-false questions test your knowledge of facts and concepts. Read them carefully to evaluate what they truly say. If you're stumped, guess (unless you're penalized for wrong answers).

Look for qualifiers in true-or-false questions—such as *all*, *only*, and *always* (the absolutes that often make a statement false) and *generally*, *often*, *usually*, and *sometimes* (the conservatives that often make a statement

Here are some examples of the kinds of true-or-false questions you might encounter in an Introduction to Psychology course (the correct answer follows each question).

Are the following questions true or false?

1. Alcohol use is clearly related to increases in hostility, aggression, violence, and abusive behaviour. (True)

2. Marijuana is harmless. (False)

3. Simply expecting a drug to produce an effect is often enough to produce the effect. (True)

4. Alcohol is a stimulant. (False)

true)—that can turn a statement that would otherwise be true into one that is false or vice versa. For example, "The grammar rule 'I before E except after C' is always true" is false, whereas "The grammar rule 'I before E except after C' is usually true" is true. The qualifier makes the difference.

Matching questions

Matching questions ask you to match the terms in one list with the terms in another list, according to the directions. For example, the directions may tell you to match a communicable disease with the pathogen that usually causes it. The following strategies will help you handle these questions.

Make sure you understand the directions. The directions tell you whether each answer can be used once or more than once.

Work from the column with the longest entries. This saves time because you are looking at each long phrase only once as you scan the column with the shorter phrases for the match.

Start with the matches you know. On your first run-through, mark these matches immediately with a pencilled line, waiting to finalize your choices after you've completed all the items. Keep in mind that if you can use an answer only once, you may have to change answers if you reconsider any of your original choices.

Finally, tackle the matches you're not sure of. On your next run-through, focus on the more difficult matches. Look for clues and relationships you might not have thought of at first. Think back to class lectures, notes, and study sessions and try to visualize the correct response.

Fill-in-the-blank questions

Fill-in-the-blank questions, also known as sentence completion questions, ask you to supply one or more words or phrases with missing information that completes the sentence. These strategies will help you make the right choices.

Be logical. Insert your answer; then reread the sentence from beginning to end to be sure it is factually and grammatically correct and makes sense.

Note the length and number of the blanks. Use these as important clues, but not as absolute guideposts. If two blanks appear right after one another, the instructor is probably looking for a two-word answer. If a blank is longer than usual, the correct response may require additional space. However, if you are certain of an answer that doesn't fit the blanks, trust your knowledge and instincts.

Pay attention to how blanks are separated. If there is more than one blank in a sentence and the blanks are widely separated, treat each one separately. Answering each as if it were a separate sentence-completion question increases the likelihood that you will get at least one answer correct. Here is an example:

After Preston Manning left _____ politics, he joined _____ as a lecturer.

(Answer: After Preston Manning left federal politics, he joined the University of Toronto as a lecturer.)

In this case, and in many other cases, your knowledge of one answer has little impact on your knowledge of the other answer.

Think out of the box. If you can think of more than one correct answer, put them both down. Your instructor may be impressed by your assertiveness and creativity.

Make a guess. If you are uncertain of an answer, make an educated guess. Use qualifiers like *may, sometimes*, and *often* to increase the chance that your answer is at least partially correct. Have faith that, after hours of studying, the correct answer is somewhere in your subconscious mind and that your guess is not completely random.

Here are examples of fill-in-the-blank questions you might encounter in an Introduction to Astronomy course3 (correct answers follow questions):

1. A _____ is a collection of hundreds of billions of stars. (galaxy)

2. Rotation is the term used to describe the motion of a body around some _____. (axis)

3. The solar day is measured relative to the sun; the sidereal day is measured relative to the _____. (stars)

4. On December 21, known as the _____ _____, the sun is at its _____ _____. (winter solstice; southernmost point)

Essay questions

An essay question allows you to express your knowledge and views more extensively than a short-answer question. With the freedom to express your views, though, comes the challenge to exhibit knowledge and demonstrate your ability to organize and express that knowledge clearly.

Strategies for answering essay questions. The following steps will help improve your responses to essay questions. Many of these guidelines reflect methods for approaching any writing assignment. That is, you undertake an abbreviated version of the writing process as you plan, draft, revise, and edit your response (see Chapter 7). The primary differences here are that you are writing under time pressure and that you are working from memory.

1. *Start by reading the questions.* Decide which to tackle (if there's a choice). Then, focus on what each question is asking and the mind actions you need to use. Read the directions carefully and do everything that you are asked to do. Some essay questions may contain more than one part. Knowing what you have to accomplish, budget your time accordingly. For example, if you have one hour to answer 3

STRESSBUSTER

STEPHANIE JACK   Kwantlen University College, Surrey, British Columbia

Test anxiety can have an enormous effect on your ability to succeed on mid-terms and exams. How do you avoid test anxiety? If you can't avoid it, what do you do to reduce its effect on your studying? Do you feel other stress associated with tests, e.g., finding enough time to study? How do you deal with this stress?

Writing an exam in college or university is very stressful. Often it is the only mark you have to see how you are really doing in your course, so you want to do well. Most of my instructors have not given chapter tests or quizzes like they did in high school, so I have no way of knowing how well I am prepared for a mid-term exam.

I have found that the more I study right before an exam, the more nervous I get and the less I remember.

The most important thing I can do is make sure I have some time right before to relax a little bit. The best exams I have written were first thing in the morning after I have had a good night's sleep. I know that isn't always possible so I try to give myself at least half an hour before the exam in which I have nothing to do. Even if you don't have that long, take a 5- to 10-minute walk to clear your head. Try not to think about the exam. Maybe sit and watch the clouds or the sunset. Anything that relaxes me and clears my head is a good bet right before an exam.

When I get into the exam and have been told to start, I reduce my stress by looking over every question in the exam and start with the questions I know. This reduces my stress level because it gives me the confidence I often need to answer every question on the exam.

questions, you might budget 20 minutes for each question and break that down into stages (3 minutes for planning, 15 minutes for drafting, 2 minutes for revising and editing).

2. *Watch for action verbs.* Certain verbs can help you figure out how to think. Table 8.2 explains some words commonly used in essay questions. Underline these words as you read the question, clarify what they mean, and use them to guide your writing.

3. *Plan your essay.* Brainstorm ideas and examples. Create an informal outline or think link to map your ideas and indicate the examples you plan to cite in support. (See Chapter 7 for a discussion of these organizational devices.)

4. *Draft your essay.* Start with a thesis statement that states clearly what your essay will say. Then devote one or more paragraphs to the main points in your outline. Back up the general statement that starts each paragraph with evidence in the form of examples, statistics, and so on. Use simple, clear language, and look back at your outline to make sure you cover everything. Wrap it up with a short, pointed conclusion.

Focus on action verbs on essay tests.

Analyze—Break into parts and discuss each part separately.

Compare—Explain similarities and differences.

Contrast—Distinguish between items being compared by focusing on differences.

Criticize—Evaluate the positive and negative effects of what is being discussed.

Define—State the essential quality or meaning. Give the common idea.

Describe—Visualize and give information that paints a complete picture.

Discuss—Examine in a complete and detailed way, usually by connecting ideas to examples.

Enumerate/List/Identify—Recall and specify items in the form of a list.

Evaluate—Give your opinion about the value or worth of something, usually by weighing positive and negative effects, and justify your conclusion.

Explain—Make the meaning of something clear, often by making analogies or giving examples.

Illustrate—Supply examples.

Interpret—Explain your personal view of facts and ideas and how they relate to one another.

Outline—Organize and present the main examples of an idea or sub-ideas.

Prove—Use evidence and argument to show that something is true, usually by showing cause and effect or giving examples that fit the idea to be proven.

Review—Provide an overview of ideas and establish their merits and features.

State—Explain clearly, simply, and concisely, being sure that each word gives the image you want.

Summarize—Give the important ideas in brief.

Trace—Present a history of the way something developed, often by showing cause and effect.

5. *Revise your essay.* Make sure you have answered the question completely and have included all of your points. Look for ideas you left out, ideas you didn't support with examples, paragraphs with faulty structure, and confusing sentences. Make cuts or changes or add sentences in the margins, indicating with an arrow where they fit. Try to be as neat as possible when making last-minute changes.

6. *Edit your essay.* Check for mistakes in grammar, spelling, punctuation, and usage. No matter your topic, being technically correct in your writing makes your work more impressive. Keep in mind that neatness is a crucial factor in essay writing. If your instructor can't read your ideas, it doesn't matter how good they are.

Key 8.3 on page 251 shows an essay that responds effectively to question 3 in the box above.

get analytical!

WRITE TO THE VERB

Hone your ability to read and follow essay instructions accurately.

Focusing on the action verbs in essay test instructions can mean the difference between giving instructors what they want and answering off the mark.

- Start by choosing a topic you learned about in this text—for example, the concept of successful intelligence or internal and external barriers to listening. Write your topic here:

  _____

  _____

- Put yourself in the role of instructor. Write an essay question on this topic, using one of the action verbs in Key 8.2 to frame the question. For example, "List the three aspects of successful intelligence," or "Analyze the classroom-based challenges associated with internal barriers to listening."

  _____

  _____

- Now choose three other action verbs from Key 8.2. Use each one to rewrite your original question.

  1. _____

  2. _____

  3. _____

- Finally, analyze how each new verb changes the focus of the essay.

  1. _____

     _____

  2. _____

     _____

  3. _____

     _____

Here are some examples of essay questions you might encounter in an Interpersonal Communication course. In each case, notice the action verbs from Key 8.2.

1. Summarize the role of the self-concept as a key to interpersonal relationships and communication.

2. Explain how internal and external noise affects the ability to listen effectively.

3. Describe three ways that body language affects interpersonal communication.

Response to an essay question.

Question: Describe three ways that body language affects interpersonal
             communication.

Body language plays an important role in interpersonal communication and helps
shape the impression you make, especially when you meet someone for the
first time. Two of the most important functions of body language are to
contradict and reinforce verbal statements. When body language contradicts
verbal language, the message conveyed by the body is dominant. For example,
if a friend tells you that she is feeling "fine," but her posture is slumped,
her eye contact minimal, and her facial expression troubled, you have every
reason to wonder whether she is telling the truth. If the same friend tells
you that she is feeling fine and is smiling, walking with a bounce in her
step, and has direct eye contact, her body language is accurately reflecting
and reinforcing her words.

   The non-verbal cues that make up body language also have the power to
add shades of meaning. Consider this statement: "This is the best idea I've
heard all day." If you were to say this three different ways—in a loud voice
while standing up; quietly while sitting with arms and legs crossed and looking away; and while maintaining eye contact and taking the receiver's
hand—you might send three different messages.

   Finally, the impact of non-verbal cues can be greatest when you meet
someone for the first time. Although first impressions emerge from a combination of non-verbal cues, tone of voice, and choice of words, non-verbal
elements (cues and tone) usually come across first and strongest. When you
meet someone, you tend to make assumptions based on non-verbal behaviour
such as posture, eye contact, gestures, and speed and style of movement.

   In summary, non-verbal communication plays a crucial role in interpersonal
relationships. It has the power to send an accurate message that may
belie the speaker's words, offer shades of meaning, and set the tone of
a first meeting.

How can you learn from *test mistakes*?

The purpose of a test is to see how much you know, not merely to achieve a grade. Making mistakes, or even failing a test, is human. Rather than ignoring mistakes, examine them and learn from them as you learn from mistakes on the job and in relationships. Working through your mistakes helps you avoid repeating them on another test. The following strategies will help.

Try to identify patterns in your mistakes. Look for the following:

- Careless errors. In your rush to complete the exam, did you misread the question or directions, blacken the wrong box on the answer sheet, inadvertently skip a question, or write illegibly?
- Conceptual or factual errors. Did you misunderstand a concept or never learn it? Did you fail to master certain facts? Did you skip part of the text or miss classes in which ideas were covered?

If you have time, rework the questions you got wrong. Based on instructor feedback, try to rewrite an essay, recalculate a math problem from the original question, or redo questions following a reading selection. If you see patterns of careless errors, promise yourself that you'll be more careful in the future and that you'll save time to double-check your work.

After reviewing your mistakes, fill in your knowledge gaps. If you made mistakes on questions because you didn't know or understand them, develop a plan to comprehensively learn the material. Solidifying your knowledge can help you on future exams and in life situations that involve the subject you're studying. You might even consider asking to retake the exam. The score might not count, but you may find that focusing on learning, rather than on grades, can improve your knowledge.

The secret of a leader lies in the tests he has faced over the whole course of his life and the habit of action he develops in meeting those tests.

GAIL SHEEHY

Talk to your instructors. You can learn a lot from consulting an instructor about specific mistakes you made or about subjective essays on which you were marked down. Respectfully ask the instructor for an explanation of marks or comments. In the case of a subjective test where the answers are often not clearly right or wrong, ask for specifics about what you could have done to earn a better mark. Take advantage of this opportunity to find out solid details about how you can do better next time.

If you fail a test, don't throw it away. Keep it as a reminder that many students have been in your shoes and that you have room to improve if you supply the will to succeed.

LEARN FROM YOUR MISTAKES

Examine what went wrong on a recent exam to build knowledge for next time.

Look at an exam on which your performance fell short of expectations. If possible, choose one that contains different types of objective and subjective questions. With the test and answer sheet in hand, use your analytical and practical thinking skills to answer the following questions:

- Identify the types of questions on which you got the most correct answers (for example, matching, essay, or multiple choice).

  _____

- Identify the types of questions on which you made the greatest number of errors.

  _____

- Analyze your errors to identify patterns—for example, did you misread test instructions, or did you ignore qualifiers that changed the questions' meanings? What did you find?

  _____

  _____

- Finally, what are two practical actions you are committed to take during your next exam to avoid the same problems?

  Action 1: _____

  Action 2: _____

sine qua non

Although Latin is no longer spoken and is considered a "dead" language, it plays an important role in modern English because many English words and phrases have Latin roots. The Latin phrase *sine qua non* (pronounced sihn-ay kwa nahn) means, literally, "without which not." In other words, a *sine qua non* is "an absolutely indispensable or essential thing."

Think of mastery as the *sine qua non* of test taking. When you have worked hard to learn, review, and retain information, you are well prepared for tests, no matter what form they take. Focus on knowledge to transform test taking from an intimidating challenge into an opportunity to demonstrate your mastery.

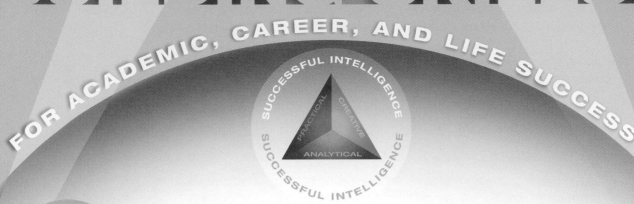

Developing Successful Intelligence

PUTTING IT ALL TOGETHER

Prepare effectively for tests. Take a detailed look at your performance on and preparation for a recent test.

Step 1. Think it through: *Analyze how you did.* Were you pleased or disappointed with your performance and grade? Why?

_____

_____

Thinking about your performance, look at the potential problems listed below. Circle any that you feel were a factor in this exam. Fill in the empty spaces with any key problems not listed.

- Incomplete preparation
- Fatigue
- Feeling rushed during the test
- Shaky understanding of concepts
- Poor guessing techniques

- Feeling confused about directions
- Test anxiety
- _____
- _____
- _____

If you circled any problems, think about why you made mistakes (if it was an objective exam) or why you didn't score well (if it was an essay exam).

Step 2. Think out of the box: *Be creative about test-preparation strategies.* If you had absolutely no restrictions on time or on access to materials, how would you have prepared for this test?

Describe briefly what your plan would be and how it would minimize any problems you encountered.

_____

_____

Now think back to your actual preparation for this test. Describe techniques you used and note time spent. _____

_____

_____

How does what you would like to do differ from what you actually did? _____

_____

_____

Step 3. Make it happen: *Improve preparation for the future.* Think about the practical actions you will take the next time you face a similar test.

Actions I took this time, but do not intend to take next time: _____

_____

_____

Actions I did not take this time, but intend to take next time: _____

_____

_____

Team Building

COLLABORATIVE SOLUTIONS

Test study group. Form a study group with two or three other students. When your instructor announces the next exam, ask each study group member to record everything he or she does to prepare for the exam, including:

- learning what to expect on the test (topics and material that will be covered, types of questions that will be asked)
- examining old tests
- creating and following a study schedule and checklist
- using SQ3R to review material
- taking a pretest
- getting a good night's sleep before the exam
- doing last-minute cramming
- mastering general test-taking strategies
- mastering test-taking strategies for specific types of test questions (multiple-choice, true/false, matching, fill-in-the-blank, essay)

After the exam, come together to compare preparation regimens. What important differences can you identify in the routines followed by group members? How do you suspect that different routines affected test performance and outcome? On a separate piece of paper, for your own reference, write down what you learned from the test preparation habits of your study mates that may help you as you prepare for upcoming exams.

Writing

DISCOVERY THROUGH JOURNALING

To record your thoughts, use a separate journal or the lined page at the end of the chapter.

Test anxiety. Do you experience test anxiety? Describe how tests generally make you feel (you might include an example of a specific test situation and what happened). Identify your specific test-taking fears, and write out your plan to overcome fears and self-defeating behaviours.

Career Portfolio

PLAN FOR SUCCESS

On-the-job testing. Depending on what careers you are considering, you may encounter one or more tests. Some are for entry into the field (e.g., Bar exams for lawyers); some test your proficiency on particular equipment (e.g., a proficiency test on Microsoft Word); and some move you to the next level of employment (e.g., Chartered Financial Analyst exam). Choose one career you are thinking about and investigate what tests are involved as you advance through different stages of the field. Be sure to look for tests in any of the areas described above. On a separate piece of paper, write down everything you find out about each test involved. For example:

- what it tests you on
- when you would need to take the test in the course of pursuing this career
- what preparation is necessary for the test (including course work)
- whether the test needs to be retaken at any time (e.g., airline pilots usually need to be recertified every few years)

Finally, see if you can review any of the tests you will face if you pursue this career. For example, if your career choice requires proficiency on a specific computer program, your school's career or computer centre may have the test available.

SUGGESTED READINGS

Browning, William G., Ph.D. *Cliffs Memory Power for Exams*. Lincoln, NE: CliffsNotes Inc., 1990.

Frank, Steven. *Test Taking Secrets: Study Better, Test Smarter, and Get Great Grades*. Holbrook, MA: Adams Media Corporation, 1998.

Fry, Ron. *"Ace" Any Test*, 3rd ed. Franklin Lakes, NJ: Career Press, 1996.

Hamilton, Dawn. *Passing Exams: A Guide for Maximum Success and Minimum Stress*. Herndon, VA: Cassell Academic, 1999.

Kesselman, Judy, and Franklynn Peterson. *Test Taking Strategies*. New York: NTC/Contemporary Publishing, 1981.

Luckie, William R., and Wood Smethurst. *Study Power: Study Skills to Improve Your Learning and Your Grades*. Cambridge, MA: Brookline Books, 1997.

INTERNET RESOURCES

Prentice Hall Student Success Supersite (testing tips in study skills section): **www.prenhall.com/success**

Concordia University offers these test-taking tips for its students: **http://cdev.concordia.ca/CnD/studentlearn/Help/Ten_Tips.html#Test**

Florida State University (list of sites offering information on test-taking skills): **http://osi.fsu.edu/hot/testtaking/skills.htm**

NetStudyAids.com—(study aids, skills, guides, and techniques): **www.netstudyaids.com**

The Ontario Ministry of Training, Education and Colleges offers this page of web links for students who want to improve their test taking skills: **http://www.edu.gov.on.ca/eng/career/study-t.html**

ENDNOTES

1. Steven Frank, *The Everything Study Book*. Holbrook, MA: Adams Media Corporation, 1996, p. 208.

2. Many of the examples of objective questions used in this chapter are from Gary W. Piggrem, Test Item File for Charles G. Morris, *Understanding Psychology*, 3rd ed. Upper Saddle River, NJ: Prentice Hall, 1996.

3. Questions from Eric Chaisson and Steve McMillan, *Astronomy Today*, 2nd ed. Upper Saddle River, NJ: Prentice Hall, 1996, p. 27.

Slay the Math Anxiety Dragon

A special form of test anxiety, math anxiety is based on common misconceptions about math, such as the notion that people are born with or without an ability to think quantitatively or that men are better at math than women. Students who feel they can't do math may give up without asking for help. On exams, these students may experience a range of physical symptoms—including sweating, nausea, dizziness, headaches, and fatigue—that reduce their ability to concentrate and leave them feeling defeated.

The material in this Study Break is designed to help you deal with the kind of math-related anxiety that affects your grades on exams. As you learn concrete ways to calm your nerves and discover special techniques for math tests, you will feel more confident in your ability to succeed.

Use special techniques for math tests

Use the general test-taking strategies presented in this chapter as well as the techniques below to achieve better results on math exams.

- **Read through the exam first.** When you first get an exam, read through every problem quickly and make notes on how you might attempt to solve the problems.

> Do not worry about your difficulties in mathematics; I assure you that mine are greater.

ALBERT EINSTEIN

- **Analyze problems carefully.** Categorize problems according to type. Take the "givens" into account, and write down any formulas, theorems, or definitions that apply before you begin. Focus on what you want to find or prove.
- **Estimate before you begin to come up with a "ballpark" solution.** Work the problem and check the solution against your estimate. The two answers should be close. If they're not, recheck your calculations. You may have made a calculation error.

Gauge your level of math anxiety

Use the questionnaire on the next page to get an idea of your math anxiety level.

Are you Anxious about Math?

Rate each of the following statements on a scale of 1 (Strongly Disagree) to 5 (Strongly Agree).

1. _____ I cringe when I have to go to math class.

2. _____ I am uneasy when asked to go to the board in a math class.

3. _____ I am afraid to ask questions in math class.

4. _____ I am always worried about being called on in math class.

5. _____ I understand math now, but I worry that it's going to get really difficult soon.

6. _____ I tend to zone out in math class.

7. _____ I fear math tests more than any other kind.

8. _____ I don't know how to study for math tests.

9. _____ Math is clear to me in math class, but when I go home it's like I was never there.

10. _____ I'm afraid I won't be able to keep up with the rest of the class.

SCORING KEY

40–50   Sure thing, you have math anxiety.

30–39   No doubt! You're still fearful about math.

20–29   On the fence.

10–19   Wow! Loose as a goose!

Source: Freedman, Ellen. (March 1997). *Test Your Math Anxiety* [on-line]. Available: www.mathpower.com/anxtest.htm (May 2004).

The best way to overcome math-related anxiety is through practice. Keeping up with your homework, attending class, preparing well for tests, and doing extra problems will help you learn the material and boost your confidence.

Following are ten additional ways to reduce math anxiety and do well on tests.

1. Overcome your negative self-image about math by remembering that even Albert Einstein wasn't perfect.

2. Ask questions of your teachers and your friends, and seek outside assistance when needed.

3. Math is a foreign language—practise it often.

4. Don't study mathematics by trying to memorize information and formulas.

5. READ your math textbook.

6. Study math according to your personal learning style.

7. Get help the same day you don't understand something.

8. Be relaxed and comfortable while studying math.

9. "TALK" mathematics. Discuss it with people in your class. Form a study group.

10. Develop a sense of responsibility for your own successes and failures.

Source: Adapted from Freedman, Ellen. *Ten Ways to Reduce Math Anxiety* [on-line]. Available: www.mathpower.com/reduce.htm (May 2004).

Improve your math performance with these techniques.

- Break the calculation into the smallest possible pieces. Go step-by-step and don't move on to the next step until you are clear about what you've done so far.
- Recall how you solved similar problems. Past experience can provide valuable clues.
- Draw a picture to help you see the problem. Visual images such as a diagram, chart, probability tree, or geometric figure may help clarify your thinking.
- Be neat. Sloppy numbers can mean the difference between a right and a wrong answer. A 4 that looks like a 9 will be marked wrong.
- Use the opposite operation to check your work. Work backward from your answer to see if you are right.
- Look back at the question to be sure you did everything. Did you answer every part of the question? Did you show all required work?

Decide how well these techniques work for you. Use what you just learned about yourself and math to answer the following questions:

- What did you learn from the math anxiety questionnaire? Describe your current level of math anxiety.

_____

_____

_____

- What effect do you think your attitude toward math will have on your future?

_____

_____

_____

- Which suggestions for reducing math anxiety are you likely to use? How do you think they will help you feel more comfortable with math?

_____

_____

_____

- Which suggestions for improving your performance on math tests are you likely to use?

_____

_____

_____

- What other ways can you think of to improve your math performance?

_____

_____

_____

SELF STUDY QUIZ

MULTIPLE CHOICE

Circle or highlight the answer that seems to fit best.

1. The activity that lies at the heart of critical thinking is
   A. solving problems.
   B. taking in information.
   C. reasoning.
   D. asking questions.

2. *Primary sources* are defined as
   A. periodicals.
   B. original documents.
   C. expert opinions on experimental results.
   D. resource materials.

3. When in class, you should choose a note-taking system that
   A. suits the instructor's style, the course material, and your learning style.
   B. you've used in other classes successfully.
   C. matches what you use when you study outside of class.
   D. is recommended by your instructor.

4. *Association* means
   A. considering how information is updated.
   B. finding the differences between two sets of information.
   C. considering new information on its own terms.
   D. considering new information in relation to information you already know.

5. A library search strategy takes you from
   A. specific reference works to general reference works.
   B. general reference works to specific reference works.
   C. encyclopedias to almanacs.
   D. encyclopedias to the Internet.

6. When answering an essay question on a test
   A. spend most of your time on the introduction because the grader sees it first.
   B. skip the planning steps if your time runs short.
   C. use the four steps of the writing process but take less time for each step.
   D. write your essay and then rewrite it on another sheet or booklet.

FILL-IN-THE-BLANK

Complete the following sentences with the appropriate word(s) or phrase(s) that best reflect what you learned in the chapter. Choose from the items that follow each sentence.

1. The three parts of the path of critical thinking are
   _____, _____, and _____.
   (recall/idea to example/example to idea; taking in information/asking questions about information/using information; taking in information/using information/communicating information)

2. A broad range of interests and a willingness to take risks are two common characteristics of _____. (creativity, critical thinking, cause and effect)

3. When you begin to read new material, what you already know gives you _____ that helps you understand and remember new ideas. (ideas, context, headers)

4. In the Cornell note-taking system, Section 2 is called the _____ and is used for filling in comments and diagrams as you review. (cue column, summary area, main body)

5. A _____ is a memory technique that works by connecting information you are trying to learn with simpler or familiar information. (mnemonic device, acronym, idea chain)

6. _____ encourages you to put your _____ ideas on paper and is an important part of the _____ process. (Freewriting/uncensored/planning, Editing/polished/planning, Researching/censored/editing)

ESSAY QUESTIONS

The following essay questions will help you organize and communicate your ideas in writing, just as you must do on an essay test. Before you begin answering a question, spend a few minutes planning (brainstorm possible approaches, write a thesis statement, jot down main thoughts in outline or think link form). To prepare yourself for actual test conditions, limit writing time to no more than 30 minutes per question.

1. Describe the steps of the reading strategy SQ3R. What is involved in each step? How does each step contribute to your understanding of your reading material?

2. Write an essay that supports or rejects all or part of the following statement: *"The tests you take in college not only help ensure that you acquire important skills and knowledge, but also help prepare you for the day-to-day learning demands that are associated with 21st-century careers."* If possible, support your position with references to career areas that interest you.

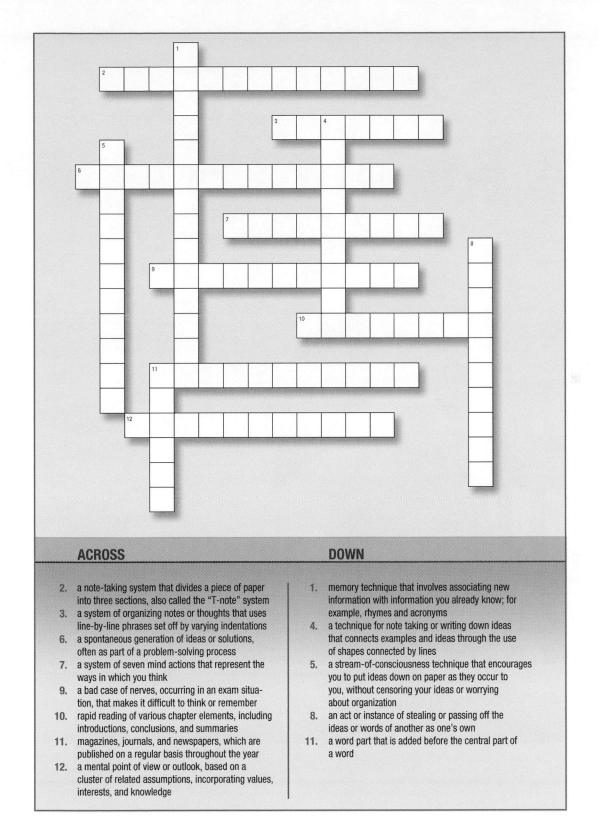

ACROSS

2. a note-taking system that divides a piece of paper into three sections, also called the "T-note" system
3. a system of organizing notes or thoughts that uses line-by-line phrases set off by varying indentations
6. a spontaneous generation of ideas or solutions, often as part of a problem-solving process
7. a system of seven mind actions that represent the ways in which you think
9. a bad case of nerves, occurring in an exam situation, that makes it difficult to think or remember
10. rapid reading of various chapter elements, including introductions, conclusions, and summaries
11. magazines, journals, and newspapers, which are published on a regular basis throughout the year
12. a mental point of view or outlook, based on a cluster of related assumptions, incorporating values, interests, and knowledge

DOWN

1. memory technique that involves associating new information with information you already know; for example, rhymes and acronyms
4. a technique for note taking or writing down ideas that connects examples and ideas through the use of shapes connected by lines
5. a stream-of-consciousness technique that encourages you to put ideas down on paper as they occur to you, without censoring your ideas or worrying about organization
8. an act or instance of stealing or passing off the ideas or words of another as one's own
11. a word part that is added before the central part of a word

IN THIS CHAPTER

In this chapter you will explore answers to the following questions: • **How do you experience diversity?** • **How can you develop cultural competence?** • **How can minority students make the most of college or university?** • **How can you communicate effectively?** • **How do you make the most of personal relationships?**

Relating to others

Among your most meaningful, life-changing experiences at college will be those that take you out of your "comfort zone" and force you to question your thinking and even your basic beliefs. Encountering the diversity of the people around you can inspire this kind of questioning. As you read this chapter, you will explore how accepting differences and rejecting prejudice can lead to respect for others and strong teamwork skills, both of which are key ingredients for success in school and beyond.

In this chapter, you will investigate how analytical, creative, and practical abilities can help you build the cultural competence that will allow you to relate successfully to others. You will explore how to communicate effectively, investigating different communication styles and methods for handling conflict. Finally, you will look at how your personal relationships can inspire you and enhance your college and life experience.

Being able to "recognize and respect people's diversity, individual experiences and perspectives" is highlighted by the Conference Board of Canada's Employability Skills 2000+ report. Furthermore, the Canadian Charter of Rights and Freedoms offers everyone in Canada "freedom of thought, belief and expression." Diversity isn't just part of your academic experience, it's part of every Canadian's life.

communicating in a diverse world

How do you experience *diversity*?

A Whether you grew up in a small town, a suburb, or a large city, inevitably you will encounter people who are nothing like anyone you've ever met. They may be of a different race or mix of races, have different religious beliefs, or express their sexuality in non-traditional ways. With society becoming more diverse, the likelihood of these encounters is increasing.

Canada has always been a nation of immigrants, and immigration levels are on the rise again. As Monica Boyd and Michael Vickers point out in their article "100 Years of Immigration in Canada," "Record numbers of immigrants came to Canada in the early 1900s. During World War I and the Depression years, numbers declined, but by the close of the 20th Century, they had again approached those recorded almost 100 years earlier."[1] According to Statistics Canada's *The Daily,* immigrants make up roughly 18 percent of Canada's population. While early immigrants to Canada tended to come from Europe, recent immigrants tend to come from Asia and the Middle East. Seventy-three per cent of new immigrants to Canada live in three general areas: Vancouver, Montreal, and Toronto.[2]

The diversity within you

To think about the concept of diversity, look first within yourself. You are a complex jumble of internal and external characteristics that makes you markedly different than everyone else. Just as no two snowflakes are alike, no two people are alike—not even identical twins.

Everything about you—your gender, race, ethnicity, sexual orientation, age, unique personality, talents, and skills—adds up to who you are. Accepting your strengths and weaknesses, your background and group identity is a sign of psychological health. You have every reason to feel proud and to make no apologies for your choices, as long as they do not intentionally hurt anyone.

Diversity on campus

College and university campuses reflect society, so diversity on campus is on the upswing. You are likely to meet classmates or instructors who reflect Canada's growing diversity, including:

- bi- or multiracial individuals or individuals who come from families with more than one religious tradition.
- non-native people who speak English as a second language and who may be immigrants.
- people who are older than "traditional" 18- to 22-year-old students.
- classmates and instructors in wheelchairs or who have other disabilities.
- people practising different lifestyles—often expressed in the way they dress, their interests, their sexual orientation, and leisure activities.

Every time you meet someone new, you have a *choice* about how to relate—or whether to relate at all. No one can force you to interact or to adopt a particular attitude because it is "right." Considering two important responsibilities may help you analyze your options:

Your responsibility to yourself is to carefully consider your feelings. Observe your reactions to others. Then, use critical thinking to make decisions that are fair to others and right for you.

Your responsibility to others lies in treating people with tolerance and respect. You won't like everyone, but acknowledging that others have a right to their opinions builds understanding. Being open-minded rather than closed-minded about others is necessary for relationships to thrive.

Minds are like parachutes. They only function when they are open.

SIR JAMES DEWAR

Key 9.1 demonstrates the dramatic difference between an open-minded and a closed-minded approach to diversity.

Accepting others depends on being able to answer the following question with a firm yes: *Do I always give people a chance no matter who they are?* Prejudice, stereotyping, and discrimination often get in the way of fairness to others. Your problem-solving skills will help you overcome these barriers.

The value of an open-minded approach to diversity in Canada.

key 9.1

YOUR ROLE	SITUATION	CLOSED-MINDED ACTIONS	OPEN-MINDED ACTIONS
Fellow student	For an assignment, you are paired with a student old enough to be your mother.	You assume the student will be clueless about the modern world. You think she might preach to you about how to do the assignment.	You get to know the student as an individual. You stay open to what you can learn from her experiences and knowledge.
Friend	You are invited to dinner at a friend's house. When he introduces you to his partner, you realize that he is gay.	You are turned off by the idea of two men in a relationship. You make an excuse to leave early. You avoid your friend after that.	You have dinner with the two men and make an effort to get to know more about them, individually and as a couple.
Employee	Your new boss is of a different racial and cultural background than yours.	You assume that you and your new boss don't have much in common. You think he will be distant and uninterested in you.	You rein in your stereotypes. You pay close attention to how your new boss communicates and leads. You adapt to his style and make an effort to get to know him better.

How can you develop *cultural competence*?

As you learned in Chapter 2, *cultural competence* refers to the ability to understand and appreciate differences among people and change your behaviour in a way that enhances, rather than detracts from, relationships and communication. According to the National Center for Cultural Competence, to develop cultural competence you must act upon the following five steps:[3]

1. Value diversity.
2. Identify and evaluate personal perceptions and attitudes.
3. Be aware of what happens when different cultures interact.
4. Build knowledge about other cultures.
5. Use what you learn to adapt to diverse cultures as you encounter them.

As you develop cultural competence, you heighten your ability to analyze how people relate to one another. Most important, you develop practical skills that enable you to connect to others by bridging the gap between who you are and who they are.[4]

Identify and evaluate personal perceptions and attitudes

Whereas people may value the *concept* of diversity, attitudes and emotional responses may influence how they act when they confront the *reality* of diversity in their own lives. As a result, many people have prejudices that lead to damaging stereotypes.

Prejudice. Almost everyone has some level of **prejudice**, meaning that they prejudge others, usually on the basis of characteristics such as gender, race, sexual orientation, and religion. People judge others without knowing anything about them because of

- **influence of family and culture.** Children learn attitudes, including intolerance, superiority, and hate, from their parents, peers, and community.
- **fear of differences.** It is human to fear, and to make assumptions about, the unfamiliar.
- **experience.** One bad experience with a person of a particular race or religion may lead someone to condemn all people with the same background.

Stereotypes. Prejudice is usually based on **stereotypes**—assumptions made without proof or critical thinking about the characteristics of a person or group of people. Stereotyping emerges from

- **a desire for patterns and logic.** People often try to make sense of the world by using the labels, categories, and generalizations that stereotypes provide.

PREJUDICE

A preconceived judgment or opinion, formed without just grounds or sufficient knowledge.

STEREOTYPE

A standardized mental picture that represents an oversimplified opinion or uncritical judgment.

- **media influences.** The more people see stereotypical images—the airhead beautiful blonde, the jolly fat man—the easier it is to believe that stereotypes are universal.
- **laziness.** Labelling group members according to a characteristic they seem to have in common takes less energy than exploring the qualities of individuals.

Stereotypes stall the growth of relationships because pasting a label on a person makes it hard for you to see the real person underneath. Even stereotypes that seem "positive" may not be true and may get in the way of perceiving people as individuals. Key 9.2 shows some "positive" and "negative" stereotypes.

Use your analytical abilities to question your own ideas and beliefs and to weed out the narrowing influence of prejudice and stereotyping. Giving honest answers to questions like the following is an essential step in the development of cultural competence:

- How do I react to differences?
- What prejudices or stereotypes come to mind when I see people in real life or the media who are a different colour than I am? From a different culture? Making different choices?
- Where did my prejudices and stereotypes come from?
- Are these prejudices fair? Are these stereotypes accurate?
- What harm can having these prejudices and believing these stereo-types cause?

With the knowledge you build as you answer these questions, move on to the next stage: Looking carefully at what happens when people from different cultures interact.

Stereotypes involve generalizations that may not be accurate.

POSITIVE STEREOTYPE	NEGATIVE STEREOTYPE
Women are nurturing.	Women are too emotional for business.
White people are successful in business.	White people are cold and power hungry.
Gay men have a great sense of style.	Gay men are sissies.
People with disabilities have strength of will.	People with disabilities are bitter.
Older people are wise.	Older people are set in their ways.
Asians are good at math and science.	Asians are poor leaders.

EXPAND YOUR PERCEPTION OF DIVERSITY

Heighten your awareness of diversity by examining your own uniqueness.

Being able to respond to people as individuals requires that you become more aware of the diversity that is not always on the surface. Brainstorm ten words or phrases that describe you. The challenge: Keep references to your ethnicity or appearance (brunette, gay, Aboriginal, wheelchair dependent, and so on) to a minimum, and fill the rest of the list with characteristics others can't see at a glance (laid-back, only child, 24 years old, drummer, marathoner, inter-personal learner, and so on).

1. _____
2. _____
3. _____
4. _____
5. _____

6. _____
7. _____
8. _____
9. _____
10. _____

Use a separate piece of paper to make a similar list for someone you know well—a friend or family member. Again, stay away from the most obvious visible characteristics. See if anything surprises you about the different image you create of this familiar person.

Be aware of what happens when cultures interact

As history has shown, when people from different cultures interact, they often experience problems caused by lack of understanding, by prejudice, and by stereotypic thinking. At their mildest, these problems create road-blocks that obstruct relationships and communication. At their worst, they set the stage for acts of discrimination and hate crimes.

Discrimination. Discrimination refers to actions that deny people equal employment, education, and housing opportunities, or that treat people as second-class citizens. If you are the victim of discrimination, it is impor-tant to know that the Canadian Charter of Rights and Freedoms is on your side: You cannot be denied basic opportunities and rights because of your race, creed, colour, age, gender, national or ethnic origin, religion, marital status, potential or actual pregnancy, or potential or actual illness or disability (unless the illness or disability prevents you from performing required tasks and unless accommodations are not possible).

Despite these legal protections, discrimination is common and often appears on campuses. Students may not want to work with students of other races. Members of campus clubs may reject prospective members because of religious differences. Outsiders may harass students attending gay and lesbian alliance meetings. Instructors may judge students accord-ing to their weight, accent, or body piercings.

Hate crimes. When prejudice turns violent, it often manifests itself in **hate crimes** directed at racial, ethnic, and religious minorities, and at homo-sexuals. The Canadian Criminal Code defines hate crimes as crimes "motivated by bias, prejudice or hate based on race, national or ethnic origin, language, colour, religion, sex, age, mental or physical disability,

(HATE CRIME)

A crime motivated by a hatred of a specific characteristic thought to be possessed by the victim.

sexual orientation, or any other similar factor." According to Statistics Canada's 2004 Pilot Survey of Hate Crime:[5]

- 57% of hate crimes are motivated by the victim's race or ethnicity.
- The most likely targets of hate crimes in Canada are Jews, Blacks, and Muslims.
- The most common incidents categorized as hate crimes include vandalism (the most common hate crime in Canada), assault, uttering threats, arson and hate propaganda. These statistics include only reported incidents, so they tell only a part of the story—many more crimes likely go unreported by victims fearful of what might happen if they contact authorities.

Build cultural knowledge

The successfully intelligent response to discrimination and hate, and the next step in your path toward cultural competence, is to gather knowledge. You have a personal responsibility to learn about people who are different from you, including those you are likely to meet on campus.

What are some practical ways to begin?

- *Read* newspapers, books, magazines, and Web sites.
- *Ask questions* of all kinds of people, about themselves and their traditions.
- *Observe* how people behave, what they eat and wear, how they interact with others.
- *Travel internationally* to unfamiliar places where you can experience firsthand different ways of living.
- *Travel locally* to equally unfamiliar places where you will encounter a variety of people.
- *Build friendships* with fellow students or co-workers you would not ordinarily approach.

Building knowledge also means exploring yourself. Talk with family, read, seek experiences that educate you about your own cultural heritage. Then share what you know with others.

Adapt to diverse cultures

Here's where you take everything you have gathered—your value of diversity, your self-knowledge, your understanding of how cultures interact, your information about different cultures—and put it to work with practical actions. With these actions you can improve how you relate to others and perhaps even change how people relate to one another on a larger scale. Think carefully and creatively about what kinds of actions feel right to you. Make choices that you feel comfortable with, that cause no harm, and that may make a difference, however small.

Dr. Martin Luther King Jr. believed that careful thinking could change attitudes. He said:

> The tough-minded person always examines the facts before he reaches conclusions: in short, he postjudges. The tender-minded person reaches

conclusions before he has examined the first fact; in short, he prejudges and is prejudiced.... There is little hope for us until we become tough minded enough to break loose from the shackles of prejudice, half-truths, and down-right ignorance.[6]

Try the following suggestions. In addition, let them inspire your own creative ideas about what else you can do in your daily life to improve how you relate to others.

Look past external characteristics. If you meet a woman with a disability, get to know her. She may be an accounting major, a daughter, and a mother. She may love baseball, politics, and science fiction novels. These characteristics—not just her physical person—describe who she is.

Put yourself in other people's shoes. Shift your perspective and try to understand what other people feel, especially if there's a conflict. If you make a comment that someone interprets as offensive, for example, think about why what you said was hurtful. If you can talk about it with the person, you may learn even more about how he or she heard what you said and why.

Adjust to cultural differences. When you understand someone's way of being and put it into practice, you show respect and encourage communication. If a friend's family is formal at home, dress appropriately and behave formally when you visit. If an instructor maintains a lot of personal space, keep a respectful distance when you visit during office hours. If a study group member takes offence at a particular kind of language, avoid it when you meet.

When you meet different people, you discover many ways of being and learning. After having a stroke, this student learned how to write with her feet using a special device.

Help others in need. Newspaper columnist Sheryl McCarthy wrote about an African American who, in the midst of the 1992 Los Angeles riots, saw an Asian American man being beaten and helped him to safety: "When asked why he risked grievous harm to save an Asian man he didn't even know, the African-American man said, 'Because if I'm not there to help someone else, when the mob comes for me, will there be someone there to save me?'"[7]

Stand up against prejudice, discrimination, and hate. When you hear a prejudiced remark or notice discrimination taking place, think about what you can do to encourage a move in the right direction. You may choose to make a comment, or to get help by approaching an authority such as an instructor or dean. Sound the alarm on hate crimes—let authorities know if you suspect that a crime is about to occur, join campus protests, support organizations that encourage tolerance.

Recognize that people everywhere have the same basic needs. Everyone loves, thinks, hurts, hopes, fears, and plans. When you are trying to find common ground with diverse people, remember that you are united first through your essential humanity.

How can *minority students* make the most of college or university?

Who fits into the category of "minority student" at your school? The term *minority* includes students of colour; students who are not part of the majority Christian religions; and gay, lesbian, and bisexual students. Most colleges and universities have special organizations and support services that centre on minority groups. Among these are specialized student associations, cultural centres, arts groups with a minority focus, residence halls for minority students, minority fraternities and sororities, and political-action groups. Your level of involvement with these groups depends on whether you are comfortable within a community of students who share your background or whether you want to extend your social connections.

Define your experience

When you start school and know no one, it's natural to gravitate to people with whom you share common ground. You may choose to live with a roommate from the same background, sit next to other minority students in class, and attend minority-related social events and parties. However, if you define your *entire* post-secondary experience by these ties, you may be making a choice that limits your understanding of others, thereby limiting your opportunities for growth. Many minority students adopt a balanced approach, involving themselves in activities with members of their group, as well as with the college mainstream. To make choices as a minority student on campus, ask yourself these questions:

- Do I want to limit my social interactions as much as possible to people who share my background? How much time do I want to spend pursuing minority-related activities?

- Do I want to minimize my ties with my minority group and be "just another student"? Will I care if other minority students criticize my choices?

- Do I want to achieve a balance in which I spend part of my time among people who share my background and part with students from other groups?

You may feel pressured to make certain choices based on what your peers do—but if these decisions go against your gut feelings, they are almost always a mistake. Your choice should be right for you, especially because it will determine your college experiences. Plus, the attitudes and habits you develop now may have implications for the rest of your life—in your choice of friends, where you decide to live, your work, and even your family. Think long and hard about the path you take, and always follow your head and heart.

get practical!

MAKE A DIFFERENCE

Find personal ways to connect with other cultures.

Rewrite three strategies in the "Adapt to Diverse Cultures" section on pages 271–72 as specific actions to which you commit. For example, "Help others in need" might become "Sign up to tutor in the Writing Centre." Circle or check the number when you have completed each task or, if it is ongoing, when you have begun the change.

1. _____

   _____

2. _____

   _____

   _____

3. _____

   _____

   _____

> I have a dream that one day on the red hills of Georgia the sons of former slaves and the sons of former slave owners will be able to sit down together at the table of brotherhood.

MARTIN LUTHER KING, JR.

So far, this chapter has focused on the need to accept and adapt to diversity and the realities of Canadian multiculturalism in many forms. However, some forms of diversity are subtler, including differences in the way people communicate. While one person may be direct and disorganized, another may be analytical and organized, and a third may hardly say a word. Just as there is diversity in skin colour and ethnicity, there is also diversity in the way people communicate.

How can you *communicate effectively?*

Clear spoken communication promotes success at school, at work, and in your personal relationships. Clarity comes from understanding communication styles, learning to give and receive criticism, becoming knowledgeable about body language, and developing techniques to solve specific communication problems.

Adjust to communication styles

When you speak, your goal is for listeners to receive the message as you intended. Problems arise when one person has trouble "translating" a message that comes from someone with a different style of communication.

Your knowledge of the Personality Spectrum (see Chapter 3) will help you understand different styles of communication. Particular communication styles tend to accompany dominance in particular dimensions. Recognizing specific styles in yourself and others will help you communicate more effectively.

Identifying your styles

Following are some communication styles that tend to be associated with the four dimensions in the Personality Spectrum. No one style is better than another. Successful communication depends on understanding your personal style and becoming attuned to the styles of others.

Thinker-dominant communicators focus on facts and logic. As speakers, they tend to rely on logic to communicate ideas and prefer quantitative concepts to those that are conceptual or emotional. As listeners, they often do best with logical messages. They may also need time to process what they have heard before responding. Written messages—on paper or via email—are often useful because writing can allow for time to put ideas together logically.

Organizer-dominant communicators focus on structure and completeness. As speakers, they tend to deliver well-thought-out, structured messages that fit into an organized plan. As listeners, they often appreciate a well-organized message that has tasks defined in clear, concrete terms. As with Thinkers, a written format is often an effective form of communication to or from an Organizer.

Giver-dominant communicators focus on concern for others. As speakers, they tend to cultivate harmony and work toward closeness in their relationships. As listeners, they often appreciate messages that emphasize personal connection and address the emotional side of the issue. Whether speaking or listening, they often favour direct, in-person interaction over written messages.

Adventurer-dominant communicators focus on the present. As speakers, they tend to convey a message as soon as the idea arises and then move on to the next activity. As listeners, they appreciate up-front, short, direct messages that don't get sidetracked. Like Givers, they tend to communicate and listen more effectively in person.

Use this information not as a label but as a jumping-off point for your self-exploration. Just as people tend to demonstrate characteristics from more than one Personality Spectrum dimension, communicators may demonstrate different styles. Think about the communication styles associated with your dominant Personality Spectrum dimensions. Consider, too, how you tend to communicate and how others generally respond to you. Are you convinced only in the face of logical arguments? Are you attuned most to feelings? Use what you discover to get a better idea of what works best for you.

Speakers adjust to listeners

Listeners may interpret messages in ways you never intended. Think about how you can address this problem as you read the following example involving a Giver-dominant instructor and a Thinker-dominant student (the listener):

> Instructor: "Your essay didn't communicate any sense of your personal voice."
>
> Student: "What do you mean? I spent hours writing it. I thought it was on the mark."

- Without adjustment: The instructor ignores the student's need for detail and continues to generalize. Comments like, "You need to elaborate. Try writing from the heart. You're not considering your audience," will probably confuse and discourage the student.

- With adjustment: Greater logic and detail will help. For example, the instructor might say: "You've supported your central idea clearly, but you didn't move beyond the facts into your interpretation of what they mean. Your essay reads like a research paper. The language doesn't sound like it is coming directly from you."

Listeners adjust to speakers

As a listener, you can improve understanding by being aware of stylistic differences and translating the message into one that makes sense to you. The following example of an Adventurer-dominant employee speaking to an Organizer-dominant supervisor shows how adjusting can pay off.

> Employee: "I'm upset about the email you sent me. You never talked to me and just let the problem build into a crisis. I don't feel I've had a chance to defend myself."

- Without adjustment: If the supervisor is annoyed by the employee's insistence on direct personal contact, he or she may become defensive: "I told you clearly what needs to be done, and my language wasn't a problem. I don't know what else there is to discuss."

- With adjustment: In an effort to improve communication, the supervisor responds by encouraging the in-person, real-time exchange that is best for the employee. "Let's meet after lunch so you can explain to me how we can improve the situation."

Although adjusting to communication styles helps you speak and listen more effectively, you also need to understand the nature of criticism and learn to handle criticism as a speaker and listener.

Constructive and non-constructive criticism

CONSTRUCTIVE
Promoting improvement
or development.

Criticism can be either **constructive** or non-constructive. *Constructive criticism* involves goodwill suggestions for improvement, promoting the hope that things will be better. In contrast, *non-constructive criticism* focuses on what went wrong, doesn't offer alternatives or help, and is often delivered negatively, creating bad feelings and defensiveness.

Consider a case in which someone has continually been late to study group sessions. The group leader can comment in either of these ways:

- **Constructive.** The group leader talks privately with the student: "I've noticed that you've been late a lot. Because our success depends on what

Communication ◀

Using techniques corresponding to your stronger intelligences boosts your communication skills both as a speaker and as a listener.

INTELLIGENCE	SUGGESTED STRATEGIES	WHAT WORKS FOR YOU? WRITE NEW IDEAS HERE
Verbal–Linguistic	• Find opportunities to express your thoughts and feelings to others—either in writing or in person. • Remind yourself that you have two ears and only one mouth. Listening is more important than talking.	
Logical–Mathematical	• Allow yourself time to think through solutions before discussing them—try writing out a logical argument on paper and then rehearsing it orally. • Accept the fact that others may have communication styles that vary from yours and that may not seem logical.	
Bodily–Kinesthetic	• Have an important talk while walking or performing a task that does not involve concentration. • Work out physically to burn off excess energy before having an important discussion.	
Visual–Spatial	• Make a drawing or diagram of points you want to communicate during an important discussion. • If your communication is in a formal classroom or work setting, use visual aids to explain your main points.	
Interpersonal	• Observe how you communicate with friends. If you tend to dominate the conversation, brainstorm ideas about how to communicate more effectively. • Remember to balance speaking with listening.	
Intrapersonal	• When you have a difficult encounter, take time alone to evaluate what happened and to decide how you can communicate more effectively next time. • Remember that in order for others to understand clearly, you may need to communicate more than you expect to.	
Musical	• Play soft music during an important discussion if it helps you, making sure it isn't distracting to the others involved.	
Naturalistic	• Communicate outdoors if that is agreeable to all parties. • If you have a difficult exchange, imagine how you might have responded differently had it taken place outdoors.	

each of us contributes, we are all depending on your contribution. Is there a problem that is keeping you from being on time? Can we help?"

- **Non-constructive.** The leader watches the student arrive late and says, in front of everyone, "Nice to see you could make it. If you can't start getting here on time, we might look for someone else who can."

Which comment would encourage you to change your behaviour? When offered constructively and carefully, criticism can help bring about important changes.

While at school, your instructors will constructively criticize your class work, papers, and exams. On the job, constructive criticism comes primarily from supervisors and co-workers. No matter the source, positive comments can help you grow as a person. Be open to what you hear, and always remember that most people want to help you succeed.

Offering constructive criticism. When offering constructive criticism, use the following strategies to be effective:

- **Criticize the behaviour rather than the person.** Avoid personal attacks—they inevitably result in defensive behaviour. In addition, make sure that a behaviour is within a person's power to change. Chronic lateness can be changed if the person has poor time-management skills; it can't be changed if a physical disability slows the person down.
- **Define specifically the behaviour that bothers you.** Focus on the facts. Substantiate with specific examples and avoid emotions. Avoid dragging in other complaints. People can hear criticisms better if they are discussed one at a time.
- **Suggest new approaches.** Talk about different ways of handling the situation. Help the person see options he or she may have never considered.
- **Use a positive approach and hopeful language.** Express the conviction that changes will occur and that the person can turn the situation around.
- **Stay calm and be brief.** Avoid threats, ultimatums, or accusations. Use "I" messages that help the person see how his or her actions are affecting you.
- **Offer help in changing the behaviour.** Do what you can to make the person feel supported.

Receiving criticism. When you find yourself on criticism's receiving end, use the following techniques:

- **Use critical thinking to analyze the comments.** Listen carefully and then carefully evaluate what you heard. Does it come from a desire to help or from jealousy or frustration? Try to let non-constructive comments go without responding.
- **If the feedback is constructive, ask for suggestions on how to change your behaviour.** Ask, "How would you like me to handle this in the future?"
- **Summarize the criticism and your response to it.** Make sure everyone understands the situation in the same way.
- **Plan a specific strategy.** Decide how to change and then take concrete steps to make it happen.

GIVE CONSTRUCTIVE CRITICISM

Imagine how you would offer constructive criticism.

Briefly describe a situation in your life that could be improved if you were able to offer constructive criticism to a friend or family member. Describe the improvement you want:

_____

_____

Imagine that you have a chance to speak to this person. First describe the setting—time, place, atmosphere—where you think you would be most successful:

_____

_____

Now develop your "script." Keeping in mind what you know about constructive criticism, analyze the situation and decide on what you think would be the best approach. Freewrite what you would say. Keep in mind the goal you want your communication to achieve.

_____

_____

_____

_____

_____

Finally, if you can, make your plan a reality. Will you do it?   Yes   No

If you do have the conversation, note here: Was it worth it?   Yes   No

---

Criticism, as well as other thoughts and feelings, may be communicated through non-verbal communication. You will become a more effective communicator if you understand what body language may be saying.

Understand body language

Body language has an extraordinary capacity to express people's real feelings through gestures, eye movements, facial expressions, body positioning and posture, touching behaviours, vocal tone, and use of personal space. Why is it important to know how to analyze body language?

Nonverbal cues shade meaning. What you say can mean different things depending on body positioning or vocal tone. The statement "That's a great idea" sounds positive. However, said while sitting with your arms and legs crossed and looking away, it may communicate that you dislike the idea. Said sarcastically, the tone may reveal that you consider the idea a joke.

Culture influences how body language is interpreted. For example, in North America, looking away from someone may be a sign of anger or distress; in Japan, the same behaviour is usually a sign of respect.

Nonverbal communication strongly influences first impressions. First impressions emerge from a combination of verbal and nonverbal cues. Nonverbal elements, including tone of voice, posture, eye contact, and speed and style of movement, usually come across first and strongest.

Although reading body language is not an exact science, the following practical strategies will help you use it to improve communication.

- **Pay attention to what is said through nonverbal cues.** Focus on your tone, your body position, and whether your cues reinforce or contradict your words. Then do the same for those with whom you are speaking. Look for the level of meaning in the physical.
- **Note cultural differences.** Cultural factors influence how an individual interprets nonverbal cues. In cross-cultural conversation, discover what seems appropriate by paying attention to what the other person does on a consistent basis, and by noting how others react to what you do.
- **Adjust body language to the person or situation.** What body language might you use when making a presentation in class? Meeting with your advisor? Confronting an angry co-worker? Think through how to use your physicality to communicate successfully.

Communicate across cultures

As you meet people from other countries and try to form relationships with them, you may encounter communication issues that are linked to cultural differences.[8] As you recall from Chapter 2, these problems often stem from the different communication styles that are found in high-context and low-context cultures.

You cannot shake hands with a clenched fist.

INDIRA GANDHI

In North American and other low-context cultures, communication is linked primarily to words and to the explicit messages sent through these words. In contrast, in high-context cultures, such as those in the Middle and Far East, words are often considered less important than such factors as context, situation, time, formality, personal relationships, and nonverbal behaviour.

Key 9.3 will help you see how 12 world cultures fit on the continuum of high- to low-context communication styles. Key 9.3 summarizes some major communication differences you should be aware of when talking with someone from a different culture. Being attuned to culture-based communication differences will help you interact comfortably with people who come from different parts of the world.

Language barriers may also arise when communicating cross-culturally. When speaking with someone who is struggling with your language, make the conversation easier by choosing words the person is likely to know, avoiding slang expressions, being patient, and using body language to fill in what words can't say. Also, invite questions—and ask them yourself—so that you both can be as clear as possible.

The continuum of high- and low-context cultures.

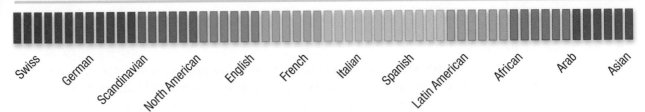

LOW-CONTEXT CULTURES   HIGH-CONTEXT CULTURES

Swiss German Scandinavian North American English French Italian Spanish Latin American African Arab Asian

One of the biggest barriers to successful communication is conflict, which can result in anger and even violence. With effort, you can successfully manage conflict and stay away from those who cannot.

Manage conflict

Conflicts, both large and small, arise when there is a clash of ideas or interests. You may have small conflicts with a housemate over a door left unlocked. You may have major conflicts with your partner about finances or with an instructor about a failing grade. Conflict, as unpleasant as it can be, is a natural element in the dynamic of getting along with others.

Some ways communication differs in high- and low-context cultures.

FACTORS AFFECTING COMMUNICATION	LOW-CONTEXT CULTURES	HIGH-CONTEXT CULTURES
Personal Relationships	The specific details of the conversation are more important than what people know about each other.	Personal trust is the basis for communication, so sharing personal information forms a basis for strong, long-lasting relationships.
Time	People expect others to be punctual and to meet schedules.	Time is seen as a force beyond the person's control. Therefore lateness is common, and not considered rude.
Formality	A certain degree of civility is expected when people meet, including handshakes and introductions.	People often require formal introductions that emphasize status differences. As a result, a student will speak with great respect to an instructor.
Eye Contact	Expect little direct eye contact.	• Arab natives may use prolonged, direct eye contact. • Students from Japan and other Far Eastern countries are likely to turn their eyes away from instructors as a sign of respect.
Personal Space	In North America, people converse while remaining between 4 and 12 feet apart.	People from Latin America and the Middle East may sit or stand between 18 inches and 4 feet away from you.

Source: Adapted from Louis E. Boone, David L. Kurtz, and Judy R. Block. *Contemporary Business Communication,* 2nd ed. Upper Saddle River, NJ: Prentice Hall, 1997, p. 72.

Prevent it when you can—and when you can't, use problem-solving strategies to resolve it.

Conflict prevention strategies

These two strategies can help you to prevent conflict from starting in the first place.

Being assertive. No matter what your dominant learning styles, you tend to express yourself in one of three ways—aggressively, assertively, or passively. Aggressive communicators focus primarily on their own needs and can become impatient when needs are not satisfied. **Assertive** communicators are likely both to get their message across and to give listeners the opportunity to speak, without attacking others or sacrificing their own needs. Passive communicators focus primarily on the needs of others and often deny themselves power, causing frustration.

Key 9.5 contrasts the characteristics of these three. Assertive behaviour strikes a balance between aggression and passivity and promotes the most productive communication. Aggressive and passive communicators can use practical strategies to move toward a more assertive style of communication.

- Aggressive communicators might take time before speaking, use "I" statements, listen to others, and avoid giving orders.
- Passive communicators might acknowledge anger, express opinions, exercise the right to make requests, and know that their ideas and feelings are important.

Send "I" messages. "I" messages help you communicate your needs rather than attacking someone else. Creating these messages involves some simple rephrasing: "You didn't lock the door!" becomes "I felt uneasy when I came to work and the door was unlocked." Similarly, "You never called last night" becomes "I was worried when I didn't hear from you last night."

"I" statements soften the conflict by highlighting the effects that the other person's actions have on you, rather than focusing on the person or the actions themselves. These statements help the receiver feel freer to respond, perhaps offering help and even acknowledging mistakes.

Conflict resolution

All too often, people deal with conflict through avoidance (a passive tactic that shuts down communication) or escalation (an aggressive tactic that often leads to fighting). Conflict resolution demands calm communication, motivation, and careful thinking. Use your analytical, creative, and practical thinking skills to apply the problem-solving plan (see Chapter 4):

- Define and analyze the problem.
- Brainstorm possible solutions.
- Analyze potential solutions.
- Choose a solution and make it happen with practical action.

Trying to calm anger is an important part of resolving conflict. All people get angry at times—at people, events, and themselves. However,

ASSERTIVE

Able to declare and affirm one's own opinions while respecting the rights of others to do the same.

Assertiveness fosters successful communication.

AGGRESSIVE	ASSERTIVE	PASSIVE
Loud, heated arguing	Expressing feelings without being nasty or overbearing	Concealing one's own feelings
Blaming, name-calling, and verbal insults	Expressing oneself and giving others the chance to express themselves	Feeling that one has no right to express anger
Walking out of arguments before they are resolved	Using "I" statements to defuse arguments	Avoiding arguments
Being demanding: "Do this"	Asking and giving reasons: "I would appreciate it if you would do this, and here's why . . ."	Being noncommittal: "You don't have to do this unless you really want to . . ."

excessive anger can contaminate relationships, stifle communication, and turn friends and family away.

Manage anger

Strong emotions can get in the way of happiness and success. It is hard to concentrate on American History when you are raging over being cut off in traffic or can't let go of your anger with a friend. Psychologists report that angry outbursts may actually make things worse. When you feel yourself losing control, try some of these practical anger-management techniques.

- **Relax.** Breathe deeply. Slowly repeat a calming phrase or word like "Take it easy" or "Relax."

- **Change your environment.** Take a break from what's upsetting you. Go for a walk, go to the gym, see a movie. Come up with some creative ideas about what might calm you down.

- **Think before you speak.** When angry, most people tend to say the first thing that comes to mind, even if it's hurtful. Inevitably, this escalates the hard feelings and the intensity of the argument. Instead, wait to say something until you are in control.

- **Do your best to solve a problem, but remember that not all problems can be solved.** Instead of blowing up, think about how you can handle what's happening. Analyze a challenging situation, make a plan, resolve to do your best, and begin. If you fall short, you will know you made an effort and be less likely to turn your frustration into anger.

- **Get help if you can't keep your anger in check.** If you consistently lash out, you may need the help of a counsellor. Many schools have mental health professionals available to students.

Your ability to communicate and manage conflict has a major impact on your relationships with friends and family. Successful relationships are built on self-knowledge, good communication, and hard work.

How do you make the most of *personal relationships?*

Personal relationships with friends, classmates, spouses and partners, and parents can be sources of great satisfaction and inner peace. Relationships have the power to motivate you to do your best in school, on the job, and in life.

When things go wrong with relationships, however, nothing in your world may seem right. You may be unable to eat, sleep, or concentrate. Because of this, relationship strategies can be viewed as all-around survival strategies that add to your mental health. Sigmund Freud, the father of modern psychiatry, defined mental health as the ability to love and to work.

Use positive relationship strategies

Here are some strategies for improving your personal relationships.

Make personal relationships a high priority. Life is meant to be shared. In some marriage ceremonies, the bride and groom share a cup of wine, symbolizing that the sweetness of life is doubled by tasting it together and the bitterness is cut in half when shared by two.

Invest time. You devote time to education, work, and sports. Relationships benefit from the same investment. In addition, spending time with people you like can relieve stress.

Spend time with people you respect and admire. Life is too short to hang out with people who bring you down or encourage you to do things that go against your values. Develop relationships with people whose choices you admire and who inspire you to fulfill your potential.

If you want a friend, be a friend. If you treat others with the kind of loyalty and support that you appreciate yourself, you are likely to receive the same in return.

Work through tensions. Negative feelings can fester when left unspoken. Instead of facing a problem, you may become angry about something else or irritable in general. Get to the root of a problem by discussing it, compromising, forgiving, and moving on.

Take risks. It can be frightening to reveal your deepest dreams and frustrations, to devote yourself to a friend, or to fall in love. However, if you open yourself up, you stand to gain the incredible benefits of companionship, which for most people outweigh the risks.

Don't force yourself into a pattern that doesn't suit you. Some students date exclusively and commit early. Some students prefer to socialize in groups. Some students date casually. Be honest with yourself—and others—about what you want in a relationship, and don't let peer pressure change your mind.

Keep personal problems in their place. Try to separate your problems from your schoolwork. Mixing the two may hurt your performance, while doing nothing to solve your problem.

If a relationship fails, find ways to cope. When an important relationship becomes strained or breaks up, use coping strategies to help you move on. Some people need time alone; others need to be with friends and family. Some seek counselling. Some throw their energy into school or exercise. Some cry. Whatever you do, believe that in time you will emerge from the experience stronger.

Avoid destructive relationships

On the far end of the spectrum are relationships that turn destructive. University and college campuses see their share of violent incidents. The more informed you are, the less likely you are to add to these sobering statistics.

Sexual harassment

The facts. Sexual harassment covers a wide range of behaviour, divided into the following types:

- **Quid pro quo harassment** refers to a request for some kind of sexual favour or activity in exchange for something else. It is a kind of bribe or threat. ("If you don't do X for me, I will fail you/fire you/make your life miserable.")
- **Hostile environment harassment** indicates any situation where sexually charged remarks, behaviour, or displayed items cause discomfort. Harassment of this type ranges from lewd conversation or jokes to the display of pornography.

Both men and women can be victims of sexual harassment, although the most common targets are women. Sexist attitudes can create an environment in which men feel they have the right to make statements that degrade women. Even though physical violence is not involved, the fear and mental trauma associated with harassment are harmful.

How to cope. If you feel degraded by anything that goes on at school or work, address the person who you believe is harassing you. If you are uncomfortable doing that, speak to an authority. Try to avoid assumptions—perhaps the person is unaware that the behaviour is offensive. On the other hand, the person may know exactly what is going on and even enjoy your discomfort. Either way, you are entitled to ask the person to stop.

Violence in relationships

The facts. Violent relationships among students are increasing. Here are some chilling statistics from the Canadian Federation of Students:[9]

- The most common form of violence in Canada is male against female. It accounts for almost half of all violent crime in Canada.
- Eighty-seven per cent of female victims know their attacker.

Women in their teens and twenties, who make up the majority of women in university and college, are more likely to be victims of domestic violence than older women. Here's why: First, when trouble occurs, students are likely to turn to friends rather than counsellors or the law. Second, peer pressure makes them uneasy about leaving the relationship. And finally, some inexperienced women may believe that the violence is normal.

How to cope. Start by recognizing the warning signs of impending violence, including possessive, jealous, and controlling behaviour; unpredictable mood swings; personality changes associated with alcohol and drugs; and outbursts of anger. If you see a sign, think about ending the relationship.

If you are being abused, your safety and sanity depend on seeking help. Call a shelter or abuse hotline and talk to someone who understands. Seek counselling at your school or at a community centre. If you need medical attention, go to a clinic or hospital emergency room. If you believe that your life is in danger, get out. Then, get a restraining order that requires your abuser to stay away from you.

Rape and date rape

The facts. Any intercourse or anal or oral penetration perpetrated by a person against another person's will is defined as rape. Rape is primarily a controlling, violent act of rage, not a sexual act.

Rape, especially acquaintance rape or **date rape**, is a problem on many campuses. Any sexual activity during a date that is against one partner's will constitutes date rape, including situations where one partner is too drunk or drugged to give consent. Currently appearing on campuses is a drug called Rohypnol, also known as "Roofies," that is sometimes used by date rapists to sedate victims. Rohypnol is difficult to detect in a drink. The Canadian Federation of Students offers more sobering numbers on this issue:

DATE RAPE
Sexual assault perpetrated by the victim's escort during an arranged social encounter.

- One in five Canadian women is the victim of a sexual assault.
- One in four women of college/university age (18–24) has been sexually assaulted by a date or boyfriend.
- One in five college/university aged women admitted being coerced into intercourse with their date/boyfriend.

This last statistic is particularly disturbing because, in 1999, the Supreme Court of Canada ruled that under Canadian law, "no means no":

A belief that silence, passivity or ambiguous conduct constitutes consent is a mistake in law and provides no defence. An accused cannot say he thought "no" meant "yes." The complainant either consented or not.[10]

How to cope. Beware of questionable situations or drinks when on a date with someone you don't know well or who you suspect is unstable or angry. If you are raped, get medical attention immediately. Don't shower or change clothes; doing so destroys evidence. Next, talk to a close friend or counsellor. Consider reporting the incident to the police or to campus officials, if it occurred on campus. Finally, consider pressing charges, especially if you can identify your assailant. Whether or not you take legal action, continue to get help through counselling, a rape survivor group, or a hotline.

Choose communities that enhance your life

Personal relationships often take place in the context of communities, or groups, that include people who share your interests—for example, martial arts groups, bridge clubs, sororities, fraternities, athletic teams, political groups, etc. It is common to have ties to several communities, often with one holding your greatest interest.

Try to affiliate with communities that are involved in life-affirming activities. You will surround yourself with people who are responsible and character-rich and who may be your friends and professional colleagues for the rest of your life. You may find among them your future husband, wife, or partner; best friend; the person who helps you land

STRESSBUSTER

NANCY E. SHAW   St. Lawrence College, Kingston, Ontario

Have you ever felt that you were stereotyped or prejudged in some way? How did that make you feel? Did it cause you stress? How did you deal with the situation?

I try hard to be true to myself all the time, whether I'm choosing what courses to take next semester or what toppings I want on my sub. Unfortunately, it's not always that easy. When it come to my choice of clothes, sometimes I like to wear skirts, heels, and makeup, but more often I just want to wear jeans and my coziest sweater.

Since I've been at college, I've noticed that on the days I dress up that guys hold doors for me, let me off the bus first, and ask me for the time even though they're wearing watches. Why don't I get that kind of attention on a dress-down day? Aren't I the same person no matter what I'm wearing? Why do guys assume that a girl in heels is going to want their company more than a girl in skateboarding shoes?

It stresses me out to think that I have to get out of bed an hour earlier in the morning and put on $10 worth of makeup if I want a cute classmate to talk to me. I feel that I'm the victim of a stereotype: that girls who don't dress to impress don't want attention.

My way of dealing with this is by reminding myself that a guy who talks to me because I'm dressed nicely probably won't be as good a friend as someone who talks to me because he likes the same class I do. No matter what the magazines say that Britney and Buffy wore last week, it's my personality that's going to attract good people. Those guys who only talk to the girls with the good hair, good nails and belly-button rings are missing out on a good thing.

your first job; your doctor, accountant, real estate agent, and so on. So much of what you accomplish in life is linked to your network of personal contacts, so start now to make positive connections.

If you find yourself drawn toward communities that are negative and even harmful, such as gangs or groups that haze new members, stop and think before you get in too deep. Be aware of cliques that bring out negative qualities including aggression, hate, and superiority. Use critical thinking to analyze why you are drawn to these groups. In many people, fears and insecurities spur these relationships. Look into yourself to understand the attraction and to resist the temptation to join. If you are already involved and want out, believe in yourself and be determined. Never consider yourself a "victim."

Kente

The African word *kente* means "that which will not tear under any condition." *Kente* cloth is worn by men and women in African countries such as Ghana, Ivory Coast, and Togo. There are many brightly coloured patterns of *kente*, each beautiful, unique, and special.

Think of how this concept applies to people. Like the cloth, all people are unique, with brilliant and subdued aspects. Despite mistreatment or misunderstanding by others, you need to remain strong so that you don't tear, allowing the weaker fibres of your character to show through. The *kente* of your character can help you endure, stand up against injustice, and fight peacefully but relentlessly for the rights of all people.

PERSONAL TRIUMPH

TOOKA SHAHRIARI   graduate of the University of British Columbia, Vancouver, BC

Connecting with others can be difficult, especially if you start out with a different cultural background. Tooka Shahriari spoke no English when she came to Canada as a teenager. Through hard work and getting involved in activities, she found her niche. Read the account, then use a separate piece of paper to answer the questions on p. 290.

Our first attempt to leave Iran not only failed, but it cost our family a lot of hard earned money. We were cheated by the people we paid to get us out. A year later, when I was 13, my mother, aunt and I went to Turkey where we waited for another 12 months for our Canadian immigration papers. Our destination was Vancouver where my brother and sister were living. My father, who had been taken political prisoner during the Iran–Iraq war, was not permitted to leave Iran. In Turkey, the three of us lived in one room in a boarding house—no kitchen or bathroom. A few months after arriving, I broke my leg. I thought life would never get better for me.

Our flight to Vancouver had a stopover in Calgary and because we didn't speak any English we thought Calgary was Vancouver! Luckily, attentive immigration officials put us back on the plane. I clearly remember spending hours in the shower those first few days making up for a year of cold sponge baths.

I arrived at junior high school in March and immediately began ESL classes. I was so sad because my English progress was slow and I wanted to go to high school in September. A poster in the hall advertising a three-month program of building trails around a northern lake caught my eye. But I didn't know enough English to write the application essay. Instead I wrote, "I want to learn English and make friends." I was one of 12 students chosen and what a lucky break that was. I was totally immersed in English while learning trail building skills in the beautiful outdoors. I credit that experience for giving me the head start I needed for success in high school.

University was a far greater challenge for me than high school. Every student feels nervous leaving the support of nurturing teachers and familiar friends but the immigrant student experiences much stress learning difficult new concepts in a second language. As well we must plan career goals that fit in with family expectations. Getting involved in campus politics was a positive way for me to enrich my university life. When I told my brother I was thinking of running for secretary of the student society, he said, "why secretary?" So I ran for president and won! I made lasting friendships with students as we worked together in common goals.

I think success at college or university is easier to achieve if you have clear goals. I knew from a young age that I wanted to work in health care. So when my studies in the first two years seemed overwhelmingly difficult I focused on my goal and wasn't afraid to ask for help. Seeking out the support of one or two of your professors or TAs is a wise thing to do. Teachers want hard-working students to succeed but you have to make the first move! Also, it gets easier. I found third and fourth year easier in many ways because I had already learned the "ins and outs" in my first two years.

Today, working in my chosen profession, I am very grateful to my family, friends, and teachers for helping me realize my dreams.

Developing Successful Intelligence

PUTTING IT ALL TOGETHER

Learn from the experiences of others. Look back to Tooka Shahriari's Personal Triumph on page 289. After you've read her story, relate her experience to your own life by completing the following:

Step 1. Think it through: *Analyze your experience and compare it to Tooka's.* When in your life have you felt like an outsider, and how does this feeling relate to Tooka's experience? What was the key to finding her place in his new world? What was yours?

Step 2. Think out of the box: *Create a challenge.* Think about the activities and organizations at your school with which you would most feel "at home." Then imagine that none of those are available—and that you are required to get involved with three organizations or activities that you would never naturally choose. How would you challenge yourself? Name the three choices and describe what you think you could gain from your experiences. Consider trying one—for real!

Step 3. Make it happen: *Use practical strategies to connect with others.* Choose one of those organizations or activities that feel natural to you. Then choose one from your list of those that would be a challenge. Now try them both. Contact a person involved with each organization or activity and ask them for details—when the group meets, what the group does, what the time commitment would likely be, what the benefit would be. Then join both in the coming semester, making an effort to get to know others who are involved.

create your future

Writing

Record your thoughts on a separate piece of paper or in a journal.

Opening your mind. On what topic is it most difficult for you to be accepting? Describe your difficulty with race, culture, ethnic origin, weight, gender, sexual orientation, or any other human characteristic. What do you think is the source of your uneasiness—parents, peers, experience, or any other source? Describe what you can do now to think more openly, and think about why doing it may help you to combat your prejudices.

Team Building

COLLABORATIVE SOLUTIONS

Problem solving close to home. Divide into groups of two to five students. Assign one group member to take notes. Discuss the following questions, one at a time:

1. What are the three greatest problems Canada faces with regard to how people get along with and accept others?
2. What could we do to deal with these three problems?
3. What can each individual student do to make improvements? (Talk about what you specifically feel that you can do.)

When all groups have finished, gather as a class and hear each group's responses. Observe the variety of problems and solutions. Notice whether more than one group came up with one or more of the same problems. If there is time, one person in the class, together with your instructor, could gather the responses to Question 3 into an organized document that you can send to your school or local paper.

Career Portfolio

PLAN FOR SUCCESS

Complete the following in your electronic portfolio or on separate sheets of paper.

Compiling a résumé. What you have accomplished in various work and school situations will be important for you to emphasize as you strive to land a job that is right for you. Your roles—on the job, in school, at home, or in the community—help you gain knowledge and experience.

On one electronic page or on a sheet of paper, list your education and skills information. On another, list job experience. For each job, record job title, the dates of employment, and the tasks that the job entailed (if the job had no particular title, come up with one yourself). Be as detailed as possible—it's best to write down everything you remember. When you compile your résumé, you can make this material more concise. Keep this list current by adding experiences and accomplishments as you go along.

Using the information you have gathered, draft a résumé for yourself. Remember that there are many ways to construct a résumé; consult other resources, such as those listed in the bibliography, for different styles. You may want to reformat your résumé according to a style that your career counsellor or instructor recommends, that best suits the career area you plan to enter, or that you like best.

Keep your résumé draft on hand—and on a computer disk. When you need to submit a résumé with a job application, update the draft and print it out on high-quality paper.

Here are some general tips for writing a résumé:

- Always put your name and contact information at the top. Make it stand out.

- State an objective if it is appropriate—if your focus is specific or you are designing this résumé for a particular interview or career area.

- List your post-secondary education, starting from the latest and working backward, including summer school, night school, seminars, and accreditations.

- List jobs in reverse chronological order (most recent job first). Include all types of work experience (full-time, part-time, volunteer, internship, and so on).

- When you describe your work experience, use action verbs and focus on what you have accomplished, rather than on the description of assigned tasks.

- Include keywords that are linked to the description of the jobs for which you will be applying (see page 198 for more on keywords).

- List references on a separate sheet. You may want to put "References available upon request" at the bottom of your résumé.

- Use formatting (larger font sizes, different fonts, italics, bold, and so on) and indents selectively to help the important information stand out.

- Get several people to look at your résumé before you send it out. Other readers will have ideas that you haven't thought of and may find errors that you have missed.

SUGGESTED READINGS

Dublin, Thomas, ed. *Becoming American, Becoming Ethnic: College Students Explore Their Roots.* Philadelphia: Temple University Press, 1996.

Feagin, Joe R., Hernan Vera, and Nikitah O. Imani. *The Agony of Education: Black Students at White Colleges and Universities.* New York: Routledge, 1996.

Gonzales, Juan L., Jr. *The Lives of Ethnic Americans,* 2nd ed. Dubuque, IA: Kendall/Hunt, 1994.

Hockenberry, John. *Moving Violations.* New York: Hyperion, 1996.

Levey, Marc, Michael Blanco, and W. Terrell Jones. *How to Succeed on a Majority Campus: A Guide for Minority Students.* Belmont, CA: Wadsworth Publishing Co., 1997.

Qubein, Nido R. *How to Be a Great Communicator: In Person, on Paper, and at the Podium.* New York: John Wiley & Sons, 1996.

Schuman, David. *Diversity on Campus.* Dubuque, IA: Kendall/Hunt, 2001.

Suskind, Ron. *A Hope in the Unseen: An American Odyssey from the Inner City to the Ivy League.* New York: Broadway Books, 1999.

Takaki, Ronald. *A Different Mirror: A History of Multicultural America.* Boston: Little, Brown & Company, 1994.

Tannen, Deborah. *You Just Don't Understand: Women and Men in Conversation.* New York: Perennial Currents, 2001.

Tatum, Beverly Daniel. *"Why Are All the Black Kids Sitting Together in the Cafeteria?" and Other Conversations About Race: A Psychologist Explains the Development of Racial Identity.* Philadelphia: Basic Books, 2003.

Terkel, Studs. *Race: How Blacks and Whites Think and Feel About the American Obsession.* New York: Free Press, 1995.

Trotter, Tamera, and Joycelyn Allen. *Talking Justice: 602 Ways to Build and Promote Racial Harmony.* Saratoga, CA: R & E Publishers, 1993.

INTERNET RESOURCES

Prentice Hall Student Success Supersite (see success stories from students from a diversity of backgrounds) at www.prenhall.com/success.

Canadian Charter of Rights and Freedoms is available online at http://laws.justice.gc.ca/en/charter.

Learn about how diversity makes Canada a better place at Canada's Cultural Gateway: www.culture.ca.

The history of multiculturalism in Canada and the importance of respecting our differences is available online at www.pch.gc.ca/progs/multi/respect_e.cfm.

More information about student issues such as date rape is available through the Canadian Federation of Students Web site at www.cfs-fcee.ca/html/english/home/index.php

1. Monica Boyd and Michael Vickers, "100 Years of Immigration in Canada," *Canadian Social Trends*. Autumn 2000, p. 2.

2. Statistics Canada, *The Daily*. Tuesday, January 21, 2003.

3. "Conceptual Frameworks/Models, Guiding Values and Principles," National Center for Cultural Competence, 2002 [on-line]. Available at: http://gucchd.georgetown.edu//nccc/framework.html (May 2004).

4. Information in the sections on the five stages of building competency is based on Mark A. King, Anthony Sims, and David Osher, "How Is Cultural Competence Integrated in Education?" Cultural Competence [on-line]. Available at: www.air.org/cecp/cultural/Q_integrated.htm#def (May 2004).

5. Statistics Canada, *The Daily*. June 1, 2004.

6. Martin Luther King, Jr., from his sermon, "A Tough Mind and a Tender Heart," *Strength in Love*. Philadelphia: Fortress Press. 1986, p. 14.

7. Sheryl McCarthy, *Why Are the Heroes Always White?* p. 137.

8. Information for this section from Philip R. Harris and Robert T. Moran, *Managing Cultural Differences*, 3rd ed. Houston, TX: Gulf Publishing Company, 1991; and Lennie Copeland and Lewis Griggs, *Going International: How to Make Friends and Deal Effectively in the Global Marketplace*. New York: Random House, 1985.

9. Canadian Federation of Students Fact Sheet, *No Means No: Violence Against Women, Date Rape and Drugs*. 1999.

10. Ibid.

BALANCE

10

IN THIS CHAPTER

In this chapter you will explore answers to the following questions: • How can you maintain a healthy body and mind? • How are alcohol, tobacco, and drugs used and abused? • How can you make smart decisions about sex?

Personal wellness

FOCUSING on personal wellness means targeting preventive actions you can take to stay healthy. Most likely, you have learned from personal experience that how well you do in school is directly related to your physical and mental health. Among the most important wellness strategies are those that deal with stress management. This chapter expands on the coverage of stress in Chapter 2 as it examines ways to manage stress through health maintenance and presents ideas for how to handle stress-related health issues.

Your personal wellness also depends on your decisions about drugs, alcohol, tobacco, and sex. Nearly every college student faces important choices on these issues. Your goal is to make decisions that are in your best interest and that keep you healthy. Taking care of your personal health and well-being is another key to success as outlined by the Conference Board of Canada's Employability Skills 2000+ report.

Approach all the topics in this chapter with successful intelligence. Analyze your situations and choices, brainstorm creative options, and take practical actions that work for you.

taking care of yourself!

How can you maintain a *healthy* body and mind?

Make your health a priority. The healthier you are, the more energy you'll have. Eating right, exercising, getting enough sleep, being up to date on your vaccinations, and taking steps to stay safe will help keep you well. Start by knowing yourself, and then apply critical thinking to your health and wellness choices.

Eat right

Making healthier choices about what you eat can lead to more energy, better general health, and an improved quality of life. Ironically, an Ipsos Reid poll exposed an interesting dichotomy. While eight in ten Canadians knew that nutrition was important, only three in ten said they were actually doing something about it.[1] Medical and nutritional experts list seven important rules of healthy eating:

1. Eat a variety of foods.
2. Maintain a healthy weight.
3. Choose a diet low in fat and cholesterol.
4. Choose a diet with plenty of vegetables, fruits, and grain products.
5. Use sugars in moderation.
6. Use salt only in moderation.
7. If you drink alcoholic beverages, do so in moderation.

You can sum up this list with two words: *balance* and *moderation*. Try to vary your diet by targeting different food groups—meats and meat substitutes, dairy, breads and grains, and fruits and vegetables. Key 10.1 shows the servings recommended by Health and Welfare Canada.

Taking steps to avoid obesity

Obesity is a problem of epidemic proportion in Canada. A common measure to determine obesity is the body mass index, which is based on weight and height. If you have an index of 25, you are considered *overweight*. If your index is 30 or greater, you are probably carrying 14 or more extra kilograms, and are considered *obese*. Government statistics indicate how widespread—and serious—obesity is:[2]

- Between one-third and one-half of Canadians are overweight.
- You decide if there is a gender "double standard": 50 per cent of women are on diets, compared with 23 per cent of men.
- Sixty-three per cent of college/university aged Canadians are concerned about their intake of fat.
- Canadians are eating more fast food. Only 27 per cent of Canadians eat a "homemade" meal each day, compared to half of Canadians a decade ago.

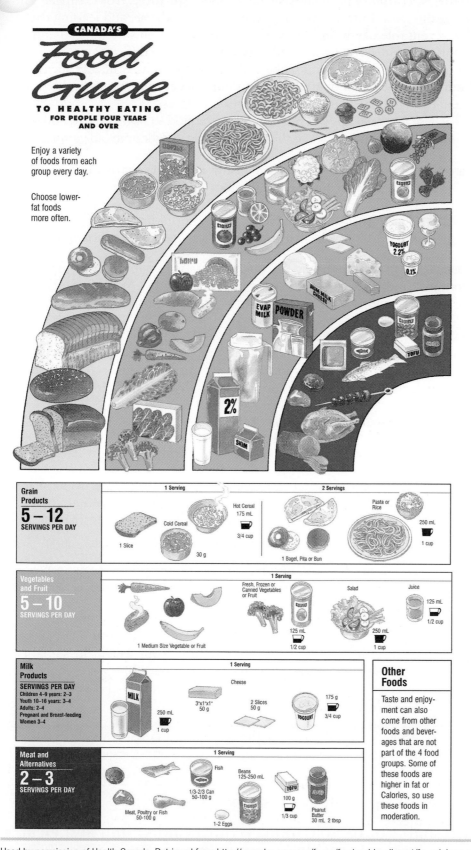

CANADA'S

Food Guide

TO HEALTHY EATING
FOR PEOPLE FOUR YEARS
AND OVER

Enjoy a variety
of foods from each
group every day.

Choose lower-
fat foods
more often.

Grain Products

5 – 12
SERVINGS PER DAY

1 Serving — Cold Cereal — Hot Cereal 175 mL, 3/4 cup — 1 Slice — 30 g

2 Servings — 1 Bagel, Pita or Bun — Pasta or Rice — 250 mL, 1 cup

Vegetables and Fruit

5 – 10
SERVINGS PER DAY

1 Serving — 1 Medium Size Vegetable or Fruit — Fresh, Frozen or Canned Vegetables or Fruit 125 mL, 1/2 cup — Salad 250 mL, 1 cup — Juice 125 mL, 1/2 cup

Milk Products

SERVINGS PER DAY
Children 4–9 years: 2–3
Youth 10–16 years: 3–4
Adults: 2–4
Pregnant and Breast-feeding
Women 3–4

1 Serving — MILK 250 mL, 1 cup — Cheese 3"x1"x1" 50 g — 2 Slices 50 g — YOGOURT 175 g, 3/4 cup

Other Foods

Taste and enjoyment can also come from other foods and beverages that are not part of the 4 food groups. Some of these foods are higher in fat or Calories, so use these foods in moderation.

Meat and Alternatives

2 – 3
SERVINGS PER DAY

1 Serving — Meat, Poultry or Fish 50-100 g — Fish 1/3-2/3 Can 50-100 g — 1-2 Eggs — Beans 125-250 mL, 1/3 cup — Tofu 100 g — Peanut Butter 30 mL, 2 tbsp

Obesity is a major risk factor in the development of adult-onset diabetes, coronary heart disease, high blood pressure, stroke, cancer, and other illnesses. In fact, after smoking, obesity is the second leading cause of preventable death. In addition, obese people often suffer social and employment discrimination and may find daily life difficult.

Post-secondary life can make it tough to eat right. Students spend hours sitting in class or studying, and tend to eat on the run, build social events around food, and eat as a reaction to stress.

These practical tips will help you pay attention to how you eat, and make changes when you need to, so that you can lose weight or avoid gaining.

Target your ideal weight. Your college health clinic has charts of ideal weight ranges for men and women with different body builds and heights.

Make small but effective changes. Pledge to stop drinking sugar-filled soda and to give up fried foods. Record your goals on paper so they become real.

Reduce portion size. A serving of cooked pasta is about one-half cup, for example, and a serving of cheese is about 50 grams. At restaurants, ask for a half portion or take home what you don't finish.

Make smart choices. Avoid high-fat, high-sugar foods. If you eat out, order a low-fat and balanced meal and limit your portions. Choose snacks with fewer than 200 calories, such as a frozen fruit juice bar or a container of low-fat fruit yogourt.

Plan your meals. Try to eat at regular times and in a regular location. Attempt to minimize late-night eating sprees during study sessions. Avoid skipping meals since it may make you more likely to overeat later.

Identify "emotional triggers" for your eating. If you eat to relieve stress or handle disappointment, try substituting a positive activity. If you are upset about a course, spend more time studying, talk with your instructor, or write in your journal.

Get help. If you need to lose weight, find a support group, such as Weight Watchers or an on-campus organization that can help you stay on target.

Set reasonable goals. Losing weight and keeping it off takes time and patience. Start by aiming to lose five to ten per cent of your current weight; for example, if you weigh 200 pounds, your weight-loss goal is ten to 20 pounds. Work toward your goal at a pace of approximately 1 to 2 pounds a week. When you reach it, set a new goal if you need to lose more, or begin a maintenance program.

Don't expect perfection. If you sometimes indulge a craving for chocolate, for example, don't stress about it. Just refocus your energies on your goal.

To keep the body in good health is a duty.... Otherwise we shall not be able to keep our mind strong and clear.

BUDDHA

Exercise

Being physically fit makes you healthier, adds energy for things that matter, and helps you handle stress. During physical activity, the brain releases endorphins, chemical compounds that have a positive and calming effect on the body. For maximum benefit, make regular exercise a way of life.

Types of exercise. There are three general categories of exercises. The type you choose depends on your exercise goals, available equipment, your time and fitness level, and other factors.

- Cardiovascular training strengthens your heart and lung capacity. Examples include running, swimming, in-line skating, aerobic dancing, and biking.

- Strength training strengthens different muscle groups. Examples include using weight machines and free weights, and doing push-ups and abdominal crunches.

- Flexibility training increases muscle flexibility. Examples include stretching and yoga.

Some exercises such as lifting weights or biking fall primarily into one category. Others combine elements of two or all three. For maximum benefit and a comprehensive workout, try alternating exercise methods through **cross-training**. For example, if you lift weights, also use a stationary bike for cardiovascular work. If possible, work with a fitness consultant to design an effective program.

CROSS-TRAINING

Alternating types of exercise and combining elements from different types of exercise.

Making exercise a priority. Student life, both in school and out, is crammed with responsibilities. You can't always spend two hours a day at the gym, and you may not have the money to join a health club. The following suggestions will help you make exercise a priority:

- Walk to classes and meetings on campus. When you reach your building, use the stairs.
- Find out about using your school's fitness centre.
- Do strenuous chores such as shovelling snow, raking, or mowing.
- Play team recreational sports at school or at a local YMCA.
- Use home exercise equipment such as weights, a treadmill, or a stair machine.
- Work out with a friend or family member to combine socializing and exercise.

Get enough sleep

During sleep, your body repairs itself while your mind sorts through problems and questions. A lack of sleep, or poor sleep, causes poor concentration and irritability, which can mean a less-than-ideal performance at school and at work. Irritability can also put a strain on personal relationships. Making up for lost sleep with caffeine may raise your stress level and leave you more tired than before.

On average, adults need about seven hours of sleep a night, but people in their late teens and early twenties may need eight to nine hours.

Gauge your needs by how you feel. If you are groggy in the morning or doze off during the day, you may be sleep-deprived.

Barriers to a good night's sleep

University and college students often get inadequate sleep. Long study sessions may keep you up late, and early classes get you up early. Socializing, eating, and drinking may make it hard to settle down. Some barriers to sleep are within your control, and some are not.

What is out of your control? Barriers such as outside noise may keep you up. Earplugs, playing relaxing music, or moving away from the noise (if you can) may help.

What is within your control? Late nights out, your eating and drinking choices, and your study schedule are often (although not always) within your power to change. Schedule your studying so that it doesn't pile up at the last minute.

Tips for quality sleep

Sleep expert Gregg D. Jacobs recommends the following steps to better sleep:[3]

- Reduce consumption of alcohol and caffeine. Caffeine may keep you awake. Alcohol causes you to sleep lightly, making you feel less rested when you awaken.
- Exercise regularly. Regular exercise, especially in the afternoon or early evening, promotes sleep.
- Complete tasks an hour or more before you sleep. Getting things done well before you turn in gives you a chance to wind down.
- Establish a comfortable sleeping environment. Take a shower, change into comfortable sleepwear, turn down the lights and noise, find a comfortable blanket and pillow.

Adequate sleep also helps fight illnesses. Another way to prevent illness is to make sure your immunizations are up to date.

Stay safe

Staying safe is another part of staying well. Take steps to prevent incidents that jeopardize your well-being.

Avoid situations that present clear dangers. Don't walk or exercise alone at night or in neglected areas—travel with one person or more. Don't work or study alone in a building. If a person looks suspicious, contact someone who can help.

Avoid drugs or overuse of alcohol. Anything that impairs judgment makes you more vulnerable to assault. Do not drive while impaired or be a passenger with someone who has taken drugs or alcohol.

Avoid people who make you uneasy. If a fellow student or co-worker gives you bad vibes,

IMPROVE YOUR PHYSICAL HEALTH

get practical!

Make a change in how you eat, exercise, or sleep.

First, decide what you most need to change. What's most important to your health right now—to eat better, exercise more, or get more sleep? Name it:

Now, considering your individual situation and looking at the strategies in this chapter, list five practical actions you can take right away to improve in this area. Word them as action statements. Examples: "I will leave earlier so that I can walk to my first class." "I will stop keeping candy bars in my room." "I will take a nap whenever I'm dragging in the afternoon."

1. _____
2. _____
3. _____
4. _____
5. _____

The final step: Just do it!

avoid situations that place you alone together. Speak to an instructor or supervisor if you feel threatened.

Communicate. Be clear about what you want from friends and acquaintances. Don't assume that others want what you want or even know what you want.

Recognize mental health problems

Emotional disorders limit your ability to enjoy life and to cope with its ups and downs. They affect people in all walks of life.

Depression

Almost everyone has experienced sadness or melancholy after the death of a friend or relative, the end of a relationship, or a setback such as a job loss. However, as many as ten per cent of us will experience a major depression at some point in our lives, and our reaction is more than temporary blues. A depressive disorder is an illness; it is not a sign of weakness or a mental state that can be escaped by just trying to "snap out of it." This illness requires a medical evaluation and is treatable.

A depressive disorder is "a 'whole-body' illness, involving your body, mood, and thoughts."[4] Among the symptoms of depression are the following:

- Feeling constantly sad, worried, or anxious
- Difficulty with decisions or concentration
- No interest in classes, people, or activities
- Frequent crying
- Hopeless feelings and thoughts of suicide
- Constant fatigue

- Sleeping too much or too little
- Low self-esteem
- Eating too much or too little
- Physical aches and pains
- Low motivation

Depression can have a genetic, psychological, physiological, or environmental cause, or a combination of causes. Key 10.3 describes these causes along with strategies for fighting depression.

If you recognize any of these feelings in yourself, seek help. Start with your school's counselling office or student health program. You may be referred to a specialist who will help you sort through your symptoms and determine treatment. For some people, adequate sleep, a regular exercise program, a healthy diet, and stress decompression are the solution. For others, medication is important. If you are diagnosed with depression, know that your condition is common, even among college students. Be proud that you have taken a step toward recovery.

Suicide prevention. At its worst, depression can lead to suicide. SAVE (Suicide Awareness Voices of Education), an organization dedicated to suicide prevention education, lists these suicide warning signs[5]:

Techniques to avoid burnout.

key 10.2

IF YOU ARE IN THIS SITUATION...	AND ENCOUNTER THESE STRESSES...	TRY THESE STRESS RELIEVERS.
You share a room with two first-year students.	Your roommates stay up late every night. Their music keeps you awake and sets your nerves on edge.	Talk with your roommates right away and brainstorm solutions. Offer to wear a sleeping blindfold if they will use stereo headphones when you go to bed.
During your first semester, you join the tennis team, write for the school paper, and carry a full course load.	You miss deadlines, fall asleep in class, and fail a test. Your stress level is high, but you are not sure what to do.	Use the prioritizing skills you learned in Chapter 2 to decide how much you can handle. Then, write a schedule that focuses on your academics and also allows time for activities and relaxation.
You live with your parents and commute to school.	Your parents make it hard to be independent. They question your schedule and even your friends. Your insides feel tight as a drum.	If you explain your feelings and your parents still treat you like a kid, re-evaluate your plan. Consider working part- or full-time and renting an apartment with a friend near school.
You carry a full course load and work part time to pay your bills.	There's no balance in your life. All you do is work—at your studies and your job. You feel overwhelmed so you drink every night.	Consider dropping a course or cutting back your work hours. Ask the financial aid office about loans that will help you meet expenses. Finally, cut back on your drinking.

Important information about depression.

10.3

POSSIBLE CAUSES OF DEPRESSION	HELPFUL STRATEGIES IF YOU FEEL DEPRESSED
A genetic trait that makes depression more likely	Do the best you can and don't have unreasonable expectations of yourself.
A chemical imbalance in the brain	Try to be with others rather than alone.
Seasonal Affective Disorder, which occurs when a person becomes depressed in reaction to reduced daylight during autumn and winter	Don't expect your mood to change right away; feeling better takes time.
Highly stressful situations such as financial trouble, school failure, a death in the family	Try to avoid making major life decisions until your condition improves.
Illnesses, injuries, lack of exercise, poor diet, reaction to medication	Remember not to blame yourself for your condition.

Source: U.S. National Institutes of Health Publication No. 94-3561, National Institutes of Health, 1994.

- Statements about hopelessness or worthlessness: "The world would be better off without me"
- Loss of interest in people, things, or activities
- Preoccupation with suicide or death
- Making final arrangements such as visiting or calling family and friends and giving things away
- Sudden sense of happiness or calm (A decision to commit suicide often brings a sense of relief, making others believe that the person "seemed to be on an upswing.")

If you recognize these symptoms in someone you know, do everything you can to get the person to a doctor. Be understanding and patient as you urge action. If you recognize these symptoms in yourself, be your own best friend by reaching out for help.

Eating disorders

Millions of people develop serious and sometimes life-threatening eating disorders every year. The most common disorders are anorexia nervosa, bulimia, and binge eating.

Anorexia nervosa. This condition, occurring mainly in young women, creates an intense desire to be thin, which leads to self-starvation. People with anorexia become dangerously thin through restricting food intake, constant exercise, and use of laxatives, all the time believing they are overweight.

Bulimia. People who binge on excessive amounts of food, usually sweets and fattening foods, and then purge through self-induced vomiting, have bulimia. They may also use laxatives or exercise obsessively. Bulimia can be hard to notice because bulimics are often able to maintain a normal appearance. The causes of bulimia, like those of anorexia, can be rooted in a desire to fulfill a body-type ideal or can come from a chemical imbalance.

Binge eating. Like bulimics, people with a binge-eating disorder eat large amounts of food and have a hard time stopping. However, they do not purge afterwards. Binge eaters are often overweight and feel that they cannot control their eating. As with bulimia, depression and other psychiatric illnesses may contribute to the problem.

Because eating disorders are a common problem on college campuses, most student health clinics and campus counselling centres can provide both medical and psychological help.

Mental health issues, stress, and other pressures may lead to substance abuse. Following is an exploration of the use and abuse of potentially addictive substances.

How are alcohol, tobacco, and drugs used and *abused*?

Alcohol, tobacco, and drug users are from all educational levels, racial and cultural groups, and areas of the country. Substance abuse can cause financial struggles, emotional traumas, health problems, and even death. Think critically as you read the following sections. Carefully consider the potential positive and negative effects of your actions, and take the time to make decisions that are best for you.

Alcohol

Alcohol is a drug as much as it is a beverage. People receive mixed messages about it as they grow up: "Alcohol is fun." "Alcohol is dangerous." "Alcohol is for adults only." These conflicting ideas can make drinking appear more glamorous, secretive, and exciting than it really is.

When used in moderation, alcohol may not cause a problem for many people. Many people drink only occasionally, and many others choose not to drink at all. The key is to be in control and to ask yourself why you drink. If you drink once in a while at a social gathering or because you like the taste, you are more likely to drink moderately than someone who drinks to escape problems or to fit in with the crowd.

Two Canadian reports offer these statistics about alcohol use in Canada:[6]

- The average Canadian drinks 7.6 litres of absolute alcohol per year. Young adults drink more than the average.

- Peer pressure is the key factor in whether or not a young person drinks. If more than half a young person's friends drink, 80 per cent also report drinking.

MULTIPLE INTELLIGENCE STRATEGIES FOR
Stress Management

Everyone handles stress differently—the strategies linked to your stronger intelligences help you improve your coping skills.

WHAT WORKS FOR YOU?

INTELLIGENCE	SUGGESTED STRATEGIES	WRITE NEW IDEAS HERE
Verbal–Linguistic	• Keep a journal of what makes you stressed. • Make time to write letters or email friends or talk with them.	
Logical–Mathematical	• Think through problems critically using a problem-solving process and devise a plan. • Analyze possible positive effects that may result from the stress.	
Bodily–Kinesthetic	• Choose a physical activity that helps you release tension—running, yoga, team sports—and do it regularly. • Plan fun physical activities for your free time—go for a hike, take a bike ride, go dancing with friends.	
Visual–Spatial	• Take as much time as you can to enjoy beautiful things—art, nature, etc. Visit an exhibit, see an art film, shoot a roll of film with your camera. • Use a visual organizer to plan out a solution to a stressful problem.	
Interpersonal	• Spend time with people who care about you and are very supportive. • Practise being a good listener to others who are stressed.	
Intrapersonal	• Schedule down time when you can think through what is stressing you. • Allow yourself five minutes a day for visualizing a positive way in which you want a stressful situation to evolve.	
Musical	• Play music that "feeds your soul." • Write a song about what stresses you out—or about anything that transports your mind.	
Naturalistic	• Spend as much time as possible in your most soothing places in nature. • Listen to tapes of outdoor sounds to help you relax.	

- First-year students and those living in residence may be the heaviest drinkers.
- Drinking and sex seem to mix. Unplanned sex was reported by most students who drank. Unwanted sexual advances also increase with alcohol consumption.

Of all alcohol consumption, binge drinking is associated with the greatest problems. The Canadian Centre for Addiction and Mental Health defines binge drinking as "having five or more drinks on one occasion."[7] In another study on post-secondary drinking, 43 per cent of the students surveyed labelled themselves as binge drinkers, and 21 per cent said that they binge drink frequently.[8]

The bottom line is that heavy drinking causes severe problems. It can damage the liver, digestive system, and brain cells, and impair the central nervous system. Prolonged use also can cause **addiction**, making it seem impossibly painful for the user to stop drinking. The Get Analytical exercise on page 309, a self-test, will help you analyze your drinking habits. If you think you have a problem, use your creative and practical thinking skills to come up with a viable solution. The information on addiction introduces possible options.

ADDICTION

Compulsive physiological need for a habit-forming substance.

Tobacco

Post-secondary students do more than their share of smoking when compared with national smoking rates. A report issued by the Addiction Research Foundation and the Canadian Centre on Substance Abuse claims that while the national smoking rate is 27 per cent, 35 per cent of young people aged 20 to 24 smoke.[9]

When people smoke they inhale nicotine, a highly addictive drug found in all tobacco products. Nicotine's immediate effects may include an increase in blood pressure and heart rate, sweating, and throat irritation. Long-term effects may include high blood pressure, bronchitis, emphysema, stomach ulcers, and heart conditions. Pregnant women who smoke run an increased risk of having low-birth–weight babies, premature births, or stillbirths.

Inhaling tobacco smoke damages the cells that line the air sacs of the lungs. Smoking has long been thought to cause lung cancer, and in late 1996 researchers found a definitive link. They exposed lung cells to tobacco smoke and saw that the damage done to the genes of the cells mirrors the damage they've seen in lung tumours.

Quitting smoking is extremely difficult and should be attempted gradually. Withdrawal symptoms include insomnia, irritability, depression, difficulty concentrating, and tobacco cravings. Suggestions for quitting include the following:

- Try the nicotine patch or nicotine gum, and be sure to use it consistently.
- Get support and encouragement from a health-care provider, a "quit smoking" program, a support group, and friends and family.
- Avoid situations that cause you to want to smoke, such as being around other smokers, drinking alcohol, and highly stressful encounters or events.

EVALUATE YOUR SUBSTANCE ABUSE

get analytical!

Even one "yes" answer may indicate a need to look carefully at your habits. Three or more "yes" answers indicates that you may benefit from discussing your use with a counselor.

WITHIN THE LAST YEAR:

(Y) (N) 1. Have you tried to stop drinking or taking drugs but found that you couldn't do so for long?

(Y) (N) 2. Do you get tired of people telling you they're concerned about your drinking or drug use?

(Y) (N) 3. Have you felt guilty about your drinking or drug use?

(Y) (N) 4. Have you felt that you needed a drink or drugs in the morning—as an "eye-opener"—in order to cope with a hangover?

(Y) (N) 5. Do you drink or use drugs alone?

(Y) (N) 6. Do you drink or use drugs every day?

(Y) (N) 7. Have you found yourself regularly thinking or saying, "I need" a drink or any type of drug?

(Y) (N) 8. Have you lied about or concealed your drinking or drug use?

(Y) (N) 9. Do you drink or use drugs to escape worries, problems, mistakes, or shyness?

(Y) (N) 10. Do you find you need increasingly larger amounts of drugs or alcohol in order to achieve a desired effect?

(Y) (N) 11. Have you forgotten what happened while drinking or using drugs because you had a blackout?

(Y) (N) 12. Have you been surprised by how much you were using alcohol or drugs?

(Y) (N) 13. Have you spent a lot of time, energy, and/or money getting alcohol or drugs?

(Y) (N) 14. Has your drinking or drug use caused you to neglect friends, your partner, your children, or other family members, or caused other problems at home?

(Y) (N) 15. Have you gotten into an argument or a fight that was alcohol- or drug-related?

(Y) (N) 16. Has your drinking or drug use caused you to miss class, fail a test, or ignore schoolwork?

(Y) (N) 17. Have you rejected planned social events in favor of drinking or using drugs?

(Y) (N) 18. Have you been choosing to drink or use drugs instead of performing other activities or hobbies you used to enjoy?

(Y) (N) 19. Has your drinking or drug use affected your efficiency on the job or caused you to fail to show up at work?

(Y) (N) 20. Have you continued to drink or use drugs despite any physical problems or health risks that your use has caused or made worse?

(Y) (N) 21. Have you driven a car or performed any other potentially dangerous tasks while under the influence of alcohol or drugs?

(Y) (N) 22. Have you had a drug- or alcohol-related legal problem or arrest (possession, use, disorderly conduct, driving while intoxicated, etc.)?

Source: Compiled and adapted from the *Criteria for Substance Dependence and Criteria for Substance Abuse* in the *Diagnostic and Statistical Manual of Mental Disorders, Fourth Edition*, published by the American Psychiatric Association, Washington, D.C.; and from materials entitled "Are You An Alcoholic?" developed by Johns Hopkins University.

- Find other ways of lowering your stress level, such as exercise or other activities you enjoy.
- Set goals. Set a quitting date and tell friends and family. Make and keep medical appointments.

The positive effects of quitting—increased life expectancy, greater lung capacity, and more energy—may inspire any smoker to consider making a lifestyle change. Quitting provides financial benefits as well. If you're a pack-a-day smoker, think about this: If you put $7 in the bank each day instead of buying a pack of cigarettes, you would have over $2500 in your account after a year. If you smoke two packs a day, you would have $5000 to spend on a new computer or stereo. In order to evaluate the level of your potential addiction, you may want to take the self-test in get analytical! Evaluate your Substance Abuse, replacing the words "alcohol" or "drugs" with "cigarettes" or "smoking."

Illegal drugs

Although alcohol remains the most abused drug by young people in Canada, use of illicit drugs can also be a problem. Drug users rarely think through the possible effects when choosing to take a drug. However, many of the so-called "rewards" of drug abuse are empty. Drug-using peers may accept you for your drug use and not for who you are. Problems and responsibilities may multiply when you emerge from a high. The pain of withdrawal may not compare to the pain of the damage that long-term drug use can do to your body. Key 10.4 shows the most commonly used drugs and their potential effects.

A habit is no damn private hell.... A habit is hell for those you love.

BILLIE HOLIDAY

One drug that doesn't fit cleanly into a particular category is MDMA, better known as Ecstasy. The use of this drug, a combination stimulant and hallucinogen, is increasingly common at parties, raves, and concerts. Its immediate effects include diminished anxiety and relaxation. When the drug wears off, nausea, hallucinations, shaking, vision problems, anxiety, and depression replace these highs. Long-term users risk permanent brain damage in the form of memory loss, chronic depression, and other disorders.[10]

You are responsible for thinking critically about what to introduce into your body. Ask questions like the following: Why do I want to do this? What positive and negative effects might my behaviour have? Why do others want me to take drugs? What do I really think of these people? How would my drug use affect the people in my life? The more critical analysis you do, the more likely you will make choices that are in your own best interest.

Identifying and overcoming addiction

If you need to make some changes, there are many resources that can help you along the way.

How drugs affect you.

DRUG CATEGORY	DRUG TYPES	HOW THEY MAKE YOU FEEL	PHYSICAL EFFECTS	DANGER OF PHYSICAL DEPENDENCE	DANGER OF PSYCHOLOGICAL DEPENDENCE
Stimulants	Cocaine, amphetamines	Alert, stimulated, excited	Nervousness, mood swings, stroke or convulsions, psychoses, paranoia, coma at large doses	Relatively strong	Strong
Depressants	Alcohol, Valium-type drugs	Sedated, tired	Cirrhosis; impaired blood production; greater risk of cancer, heart attack, and stroke; impaired brain function	Strong	Strong
Opiates	Heroin, codeine, other pain pills	Drowsy, floating, without pain	Infection of organs, inflammation of the heart, hepatitis	Yes, with high dosage	Yes, with high dosage
Cannabinols	Marijuana, hashish	Euphoric, mellow, little sensation of time	Impairment of judgment and coordination, bronchitis and asthma, lung and throat cancers, anxiety, lack of energy and motivation, reduced ability to produce hormones	Moderate	Relatively strong
Hallucinogens	LSD, mushrooms	Heightened sensual perception, hallucinatory, confused	Impairment of brain function, circulatory problems, agitation and confusion, flashbacks	Insubstantial	Insubstantial
Inhalants	Glue, aerosols	Giddy, lightheaded	Damage to brain, heart, liver, and kidneys	Insubstantial	Insubstantial

Source: Compiled and adapted from *Educating Yourself about Alcohol and Drugs: A People's Primer*, by Marc Alan Schuckit, M.D., Plenum Press, 1995.

Counselling and medical care. You can find help from school-based, private, government-sponsored, or workplace-sponsored resources. Ask your school's counselling or health centre, your personal physician, or a local hospital for a referral.

Detoxification ("detox") centres. If you have a severe addiction, you may need a controlled environment in which to separate yourself completely from drugs or alcohol. Some are outpatient facilities. Other programs provide a 24-hour environment to help you get through the withdrawal period.

Support groups. Alcoholics Anonymous (AA) is the premier support group for alcoholics. Based on a 12-step recovery program, AA membership costs little or nothing. AA has led to other support groups for addicts

SOUMIK KANUNGO   Champlain St. Lambert CEGEP, St. Lambert, Quebec

Healthy habits help people deal with the general stresses associated with student life. What do you think are healthy stress management habits and effective stress management techniques?

In order to deal with stress, we must look at what causes it. It can range from problems in the family, moving into a new school environment, having too much work to do in too short a time, or even from a minor change in one's life.

The ways in which I would suggest to reduce and manage stress are creating a timetable of daily activities and following it, talking to friends about your problems, and taking a break from stressful activities and relaxing.

Creating a timetable and following it is probably the best way to deal with stress. It allows a person to be better organized, and to be able to accomplish everything that they want to on any given day.

Talking to friends is also a great way to deal with the general stresses of student life. It gives you the chance to get advice from a friend who might have faced the same problem before, and your friends will be there to support you and to help you manage your stress.

Sometimes people need to take some free time and relax, and you should definitely do that from time to time. It will help you to relieve some stress and to enjoy life more. You can set aside an amount of time where you can do anything you want. You can have fun, watch television, call a friend, go on the Internet, walk outside, exercise, or do anything else that you enjoy.

Stress is definitely a big part of life. In order to overcome it we can't ignore it, but have to deal with it using one of these effective techniques.

such as Overeaters Anonymous and Narcotics Anonymous. Many Canadian schools have AA, NA, or other group sessions on campus.

When people address their problems directly instead of avoiding them through substance abuse, they can begin to grow and improve. Working through substance-abuse problems can lead to a restoration of health and self-respect.

How can you make smart decisions *about sex*?

Sexual relationships involve body and mind on many levels. Being informed about sexual decision making, birth control options, and sexually transmitted diseases will help you make decisions that are right for you.

Sex and critical thinking

What sexuality means to you and the role it plays in your life are your own business. However, the physical act of sex goes beyond the private realm. Individual sexual conduct can have consequences such as unexpected pregnancy and the transmission of sexually transmitted diseases (STDs). These consequences affect everyone involved in the sexual act and, often, their families.

Your self-respect depends on making choices that maintain your health and safety, as well as those of the person with whom you are involved. Think critically about sexual issues, weighing the positive and negative effects of your choices. Among the questions to ask are the following:

- Is this what I really want? Does it fit with my values?
- Do I feel ready?
- Is this the right person/moment/situation? Does my partner truly care for me and not just for what we might be doing? Will this enhance our emotional relationship or cause problems later?
- Do I have what I need to prevent pregnancy and exposure to STDs? If not, what may be the consequences (pregnancy or disease)? Are they worth it?

Birth control

Using birth control is a choice, and it is not for everyone. For some, using any kind of birth control is against their religious beliefs. Others may want to have children. Many sexually active people, however, choose one or more methods of birth control.

In addition to preventing pregnancy, some birth control methods also protect against sexually transmitted diseases. Key 10.5 describes the most

get creative!

FIND MORE FUN

Broaden your repertoire of fun things to do.

Sometimes, college and university students get involved in potentially unsafe activities because it seems like there isn't anything else to do. Use your creativity to make sure you have a variety of enjoyable activities to choose from when you hang out with friends. Check out your resources: What possibilities can you find at your student union, student activities centre, local arts organizations, athletic organizations, various clubs, or nature groups? Could you go hiking? Paint pottery? Check out a baseball game? Run a 5K? Try a new kind of cuisine? Volunteer at a children's hospital ward? See a play?

Expand your horizons. List here 10 specific activities available to you.

1. _____
2. _____
3. _____
4. _____
5. _____

6. _____
7. _____
8. _____
9. _____
10. _____

established methods of birth control, with effectiveness percentages and STD prevention based on proper and regular use.

Evaluate the pros and cons of each method for yourself as well as for your partner. Consider cost, ease of use, reliability, comfort, and protection against STDs. Communicate with your partner and together make a choice that is comfortable for both of you. For more information, check your library, the Internet, or a bookstore; talk to your doctor; or ask a counsellor at the student health centre.

Sexually transmitted diseases

Sexually transmitted diseases spread through sexual contact (intercourse or other sexual activity that involves contact with the genitals). All are highly contagious. The only birth control methods that offer protection are the male and female condoms (latex or polyurethane only)that prevent skin-to-skin contact. Most STDs can also spread to infants of infected mothers during birth. Have a doctor examine any irregularity or discomfort as soon as you detect it. Key 10.6 describes common STDs.

AIDS and HIV

The most serious of the STDs is AIDS (acquired immune deficiency syndrome), which is caused by the human immunodeficiency virus (HIV). Not everyone who tests positive for HIV will develop AIDS, but AIDS has no cure and results in eventual death. HIV can lie undetected in the body for up to ten years before surfacing, and a carrier can spread it during that time. Medical science continues to develop drugs to combat AIDS and its related illnesses. However, the drugs can cause severe side effects, many have not been thoroughly tested, and none offer a cure.

HIV is transmitted through two types of bodily fluids: fluids associated with sex (semen and vaginal fluids) and blood. People have acquired HIV through sexual relations, by sharing hypodermic needles for drug use, and by receiving infected blood transfusions. You cannot become infected unless one of those fluids is involved. Therefore, it is unlikely you can contract HIV from toilet seats, hugging, kissing, or sharing a glass.

Always use a latex condom, because natural skin condoms may let the virus pass through. If a lubricant is used, use K-Y Jelly or a spermicide because petroleum jelly can destroy the latex in condoms and diaphragms. Although some people dislike using condoms, it's a small price for preserving your life.

Methods of birth control.

METHOD	APPROXIMATE EFFECTIVENESS	PREVENTS STDS?	DESCRIPTION
Abstinence	100%	Only if no sexual activity occurs	Just saying no. No intercourse means no risk of pregnancy. However, alternative modes of sexual activity can still spread STDs.
Condom (male)	94%	Yes, if made of latex	A sheath that fits over the penis and prevents sperm from entering the vagina.
Condom (female)	90%	Yes	A sheath that fits inside the vagina, held in place by two rings, one of which hangs outside. Can be awkward. It is relatively new and may not be widely available.
Diaphragm or cervical cap	85%	No	A bendable rubber cap that fits over the cervix and pelvic bone inside the vagina (the cervical cap is smaller and fits over the cervix only). Both must be fitted initially by a gynecologist and used with a spermicide.
Oral contraceptives (the pill)	97%	No	A dosage of hormones taken daily by a woman, preventing the ovaries from releasing eggs. Side effects can include headaches, weight gain, and increased chances of blood clotting. Various brands and dosages; must be prescribed by a gynecologist.
Spermicidal foams, jellies, inserts	84% if used alone	No	Usually used with diaphragms or condoms to enhance effectiveness, they have an ingredient that kills sperm cells (but not STDs). They stay effective for a limited period of time after insertion.
Intrauterine device (IUD)	94%	No	A small coil of wire inserted into the uterus by a gynecologist (who must also remove it). Prevents fertilized eggs from implanting in the uterine wall. Possible side effects include bleeding.
Norplant	Nearly 100%	No	A series of up to five small tubes implanted by a gynecologist into a woman's upper arm, preventing pregnancy for up to five years. Can be tough to remove. Possible side effects may resemble those of oral contraceptives. Must be removed by a doctor.
Depo-Provera (the shot)	Nearly 100%	No	An injection that a woman must receive from a doctor every few months. Possible side effects may resemble those of oral contraceptives.
Tubal ligation	Nearly 100%	No	Surgery for women that cuts and ties the fallopian tubes, preventing eggs from travelling to the uterus. Difficult and expensive to reverse. Recommended for those who do not want any more children.
Vasectomy	Nearly 100%	No	Surgery for men that blocks the tube that delivers sperm to the penis. Like tubal ligation, difficult to reverse and only recommended for those who don't want children.
Rhythm method	Variable	No	Abstaining from intercourse during the ovulation segment of the woman's menstrual cycle. Can be difficult to time and may not account for cycle irregularities.
Withdrawal	Variable	No	Pulling the penis out of the vagina before ejaculation. Unreliable, because some sperm can escape in the fluid released prior to ejaculation. Dependent on a controlled partner.

DISEASE	SYMPTOMS	HEALTH PROBLEMS IF UNTREATED	TREATMENTS
Chlamydia	Discharge, painful urination, swollen or painful joints, change in menstrual periods for women	Can cause pelvic inflammatory disease (PID) in women, which can lead to sterility or ectopic pregnancies; infection; miscarriage or premature birth.	Curable with full course of antibiotics; avoid sex until treatment is complete.
Gonorrhea	Discharge, burning while urinating	Can cause PID, swelling of testicles and penis, arthritis, skin problems, infections.	Usually curable with antibiotics; however, certain strains are becoming resistant to medication.
Genital herpes	Blister-like itchy sores in the genital area, headache, fever, chills	Symptoms may subside and then reoccur, often in response to high stress levels; carriers can transmit the virus even when it is dormant.	No cure; some medications such as Acyclovir reduce and help heal the sores and may shorten recurring outbreaks.
Syphilis	A genital sore lasting one to five weeks, followed by a rash, fatigue, fever, sore throat, headaches, swollen glands	If it lasts over four years, it can cause blindness, destruction of bone, insanity, or heart failure; can cause death or deformity of a child born to an infected woman.	Curable with full course of antibiotics.
Human Papilloma Virus (HPV, or genital warts)	Genital itching and irritation, small clusters of warts	Can increase risk of cervical cancer in women; virus may remain in body and cause recurrences, even when warts are removed.	Treatable with drugs applied to warts or various kinds of wart removal surgery.
Hepatitis B	Fatigue, poor appetite, vomiting, jaundice, hives	Some carriers will have few symptoms; others may develop chronic liver disease that may lead to other diseases of the liver.	No cure; some will recover, some will not. Bed rest may help ease symptoms. Vaccine is available.

Joie de vivre

The French have a phrase that is commonly used in the English language as well: *joie de vivre*, which literally means "joy of living." A person with *joie de vivre* finds joy and optimism in all parts of life, is able to enjoy life's pleasures, and can find something positive in its struggles. Without experiencing challenges, people might have a hard time recognizing and experiencing happiness and satisfaction. Think of this concept as you examine your personal wellness. If you focus on the positive, your attitude can affect all areas of your life.

BUILDING SKILLS

FOR ACADEMIC, CAREER, AND LIFE SUCCESS

SUCCESSFUL INTELLIGENCE
PRACTICAL CREATIVE
ANALYTICAL
SUCCESSFUL INTELLIGENCE

Developing Successful Intelligence

PUTTING IT ALL TOGETHER

Take steps toward better health. Put your successful intelligence to work in improving your physical health.

Step 1. Think it through: *Analyze your habits.* Pick a topic—eating, drinking, sleeping, sexual activity—that is an issue for you. To examine why it is a problem, identify behaviours and attitudes and note their positive and negative effects.

Example:　*Issue:* binge drinking

Behaviour: I binge drink probably three times a week.

Attitude: I don't think it's any big deal. I like using it to escape.

Positive effects: I have fun with my friends. I feel confident, accepted, social.

Negative effects: I feel hung over and foggy the next day. I miss class. I'm irritable.

Your turn:　*Issue:*

Behaviour:

Attitude:

Positive effects:

Negative effects:

Question to think about: Is it worth it?

create your future

Step 2. Think out of the box: *Brainstorm ways to change.* First think about what you want to be different, and why. Then come up with changes you could make. Be creative!

How you might change your behaviour:

_____

How you might change your attitude:

_____

_____

Positive effects you think these changes would have:

_____

_____

Step 3. Make it happen: *Put a practical health improvement plan into action.* Choose two actions to take—one that would improve your attitude and one that would improve your behaviour—that you think would have the most positive effect for you. Commit to these actions with specific plans and watch the positive change happen.

Attitude improvement plan:

_____

_____

Behaviour improvement plan:

_____

_____

Team Building
COLLABORATIVE SOLUTIONS

Actively dealing with stress. By yourself, make a list of stressors—whatever events or factors cause you stress. As a class, discuss the stressors you have listed. Choose the five most common. Divide into five groups according to who would choose what stressor as his or her most important (redistribute some people if the group sizes are unbalanced). Each group should discuss its assigned stressor, brainstorming solutions and strategies. List your best coping strategies and present them to the class. Groups may want to make extra copies of the lists so that every member of the class has five, one for each stressor.

Writing
DISCOVERY THROUGH JOURNALING

Record your thoughts on a separate piece of paper or in a journal.

Addiction. At one time or another, many people have had to cope with some kind of addiction. Describe how you feel about addiction in any form—to alcohol, drugs, food, sex, the Internet, or gambling. How has addiction ensnared you, if at all? How did you deal with it? If you have never faced an addiction nor been close to someone who did, describe how you think you would work through the problem it if it ever happened to you.

Career Portfolio

Complete the following in your electronic portfolio or on separate sheets of paper.

Setting effective boundaries at work. In the current working world, many companies are putting pressure on their employees to do more in less time. The result is an environment that places workers under a great deal of stress. If you work in this kind of environment, you may be asked to step up your efforts in different ways—do more work, add tasks to your job description, work late nights, keep your cell phone on for work calls on weekends, and so on.

However, there is a boundary—a limit—to what you can do success-fully. If you hit that limit and don't overstep it, you may indeed keep your job and earn promotions. If you cross that boundary, your health and the quality of your work can suffer. If you don't work hard enough to approach it, you may lose your job or not advance.

Your challenge is to determine your limit and then monitor yourself to make sure that you work up to potential but don't overdo it. Answer the following questions in an effort to identify the most effective bound-ary for yourself as an employee:

- Are you willing to take on any job-related task, or do you get upset when people pile work on your desk that is not part of your job description?
- Are you willing to work late to meet a deadline, or do you get upset if you don't leave on time?
- Do you try to do your best work on everything or to get by with doing as little as possible?
- Are you likely to initiate different ideas that will improve your work product and then find ways to make them happen?
- Do you take a leadership position in your work team or try to stay in the background?
- When given a work request, do you tend to say "yes" right away, "no" right away, or take time to think about it thoroughly?
- Do you bring work into your personal life—socialize with co-workers, take work calls on personal time—or do you leave your job behind when you leave the workplace?

Analyze your answers as honestly as possible. Then, answer these questions: How do you think your attitudes will help or hurt you as a team member in your relationships with peers, managers, and others, and how do you think they will affect your career advancement? Check your personal attitude assessment against someone in a field you are interested in to see if you are on target or off base.

If you realize that your attitudes may stand in the way of success in a particular job or career area, consider what specific steps you are willing to take to change them. You might also consider whether you want to rethink your career or company choice to find a position or area that suits you better. Finally, think about how your ability to set effective boundaries may affect your success in school. Working up to your limits, but not too far beyond, will help you become the person you want to be both at school and in the world of work.

SUGGESTED READINGS

Grayson, Paul A., Phil Meilman, and Philip W. Meilman. *Beating the College Blues.* New York: Checkmark Books, 1999.

Johanson, Sue. *Sex, Sex and More Sex.* Reganbooks, 2004.

Kadison, Richard D., and Theresa Foy DiGeronimo. *College of the Overwhelmed: The Campus Mental Health Crisis and What to Do About It.*

San Francisco: Jossey-Bass, 2004.

Kuhn, Cynthia, et al. *Buzzed: The Straight Facts About the Most Used and Abused Drugs from Alcohol to Ecstasy,* 2nd ed. New York: W. W. Norton, 2003.

Mayo Clinic Family Health Book: The Ultimate Home Medical Reference, 3rd ed. New York: HarperResource, 2003.

The Physician's Desk Reference. *The Physician's Desk Reference Family Guide Encyclopedia of Medical Care.* New York: Ballantine Books, 1999.

Schuckit, Marc Alan. *Educating Yourself About Alcohol and Drugs: A People's Primer.* New York: HarperCollins, 1998.

Selkowitz, Ann. *The College Student's Guide to Eating Well on Campus.* Bethesda, MD: Tulip Hill Press, 2000.

Ward, Darrell. *The Amfar AIDS Handbook: The Complete Guide to Understanding HIV and AIDS.* New York: W. W. Norton, 1998.

INTERNET RESOURCES

Prentice Hall Student Success Supersite (fitness and well-being information): www.prenhall.com/success

Canadian Cancer Society (general information, prevention, and early detection tips): www.cancer.ca

Learn more about AIDS Awareness from the Canadian Foundation for AIDS Research: www.canfar.ca

Think you might be addicted? Check out the Canadian Centre for Substance Abuse Web site: www.ccsa.ca

Get more information about sex and issues regarding sexuality at Sue Johanson's FAQ. This Web site maintained by the W Network: http://www.wnetwork.com/topics/relationships/sue_faq/index.asp

1. Ipsos Reid, "Canadians and Nutrition." Released May 24, 2002.

2. The sources used in this section include Health Canada, *Canadians and Healthy Eating*, March 1997; and Ipsos Reid, *Canadians and Obesity, Measuring Awareness; Weighing Options.* June 2003.

3. Herbert Benson, M.D., and Eileen M. Stuart, R.N. C. M.S., et al., *The Wellness Book*. New York: Simon & Schuster, 1992, p. 292.

4. National Institutes of Health Publication No. 94-3561, National Institutes of Health, 1994.

5. www.save.org/depressed/symptoms.html (SAVE Web site, accessed 5/9/04).

6. Diane McKenzie, Eric Single, Minh Van Truong, and Gary Timoshenko, "Canadian Profile 1997: Tobacco." From the Canadian Centre for Substance Abuse Web site at www.ccsa.ca.

7. CAMH Population Studies Bulletin, July/August 2002.

8. H. Wechsler et al., "Changes in Binge Drinking and Related Problems Among American College Students Between 1993 and 1997," *Journal of American College Health* 47, September 1998, p. 57.

9. Diane McKenzie, Eric Single, Minh Van Truong, and Gary Timoshenko, "Canadian Profile 1997: Tobacco." From the Canadian Centre for Substance Abuse Web site at www.ccsa.ca.

10. Drug Enforcement Administration, U.S Department of Justice [on-line]. Available at: www.usdoj.gov/dea/concern/mdma/mdmaindex.htm (February 2003).

11

IN THIS CHAPTER

In this chapter you will explore answers to the following questions: ● **How can you prepare for workplace success?** ● **What does your learning style mean for your career?** ● **How can you find a career that's right for you?** ● **What will help you juggle work and school?** ● **How can you create a budget that works?** ● **How can you manage your credit cards?**

Managing career and money

ALL OF THE ways that you grow and learn in college will help you in your future career. Beginning to explore careers now, while you are a student, will help you find a career that suits you, whether it is being a teacher in Vancouver, an attorney in Sydney, an archaeologist in Egypt, or anything else you dream of. Money issues are another important concern— now, as you figure out how to finance school costs and manage credit cards, and later, when you are earning money in the working world. This chapter will show you how your successful intelligence can help you explore careers, hunt for jobs effectively, balance work and school, and manage your money so that you can make the most of what you earn.

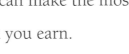

reality resources

How can you prepare for *workplace success?*

Students are in different stages when it comes to thinking about careers. Like many people, you may not have thought too much about it yet. You may have had a career for years and be looking for a change. Maybe you've decided on a particular career but are now having second thoughts. Regardless of your starting point, now is the time to make progress.

Everything in this book, particularly the guidelines provided by the Conference Board of Canada, is geared toward workplace success. Skills such as critical thinking, teamwork, writing skills, and long-term planning all prepare you to thrive in any career. Use the following strategies to start getting more specific in your preparation for career success.

Investigate career paths

Change happens in the working world all the time. You can get a good idea of what's out there—and what you think of it all—by exploring potential careers and building knowledge and experience.

Explore potential careers

Career possibilities extend far beyond what you can imagine. Brainstorm about career areas. Ask instructors, relatives, mentors, and fellow students about careers they are familiar with. Check your library for books on careers or biographies of people who worked in fields that interest you. Explore careers you discover through movies, newspapers, novels, or non-fiction.

Use your critical-thinking skills to broaden your investigation. Look at Key 11.1 for some of the questions you might ask as you talk to people or investigate materials. You may discover that:

A wide array of job possibilities exists for most career fields. For example, the medical world consists of more than doctors and nurses. Emergency medical technicians respond to emergencies, administrators run hospitals, researchers test new drugs, pharmacists prepare prescriptions, and so on.

> Whatever you think you can do or believe you can do, begin it. Action has magic, grace, and power in it.
>
> JOHANN WOLFGANG VON GOETHE

Within each job, there is a variety of tasks and skills. You may know that an instructor teaches, but you may not see that instructors also often write, research, study, design courses, give presentations, and counsel. Push past your first impression of any career and explore what else it entails.

Common assumptions about salaries don't always hold. Finance, medicine, law, and computer science aren't the only high-paying careers.

Critical-thinking questions for career exploration.

What can I do in this area that I like and do well?	Do I respect the company or the industry? The product or service?
What are the educational requirements (certificates or degrees, courses)?	Does this company or industry accommodate special needs (child care, sick days, flex-time)?
What skills are necessary?	Do I have to belong to a union?
What wage or salary and benefits can I expect?	Are there opportunities near where I live (or want to live)?
What kinds of personalities are best suited to this kind of work?	What other expectations exist (travel, overtime, etc.)?
What are the prospects for moving up to higher-level positions?	Do I prefer the service or production end of this industry?

Don't jump to conclusions until you have investigated. And remember to place earnings in perspective: Even if you earn an extraordinary salary, you may not be happy unless you truly enjoy and learn from what you are doing.

Your school's career centre may offer job listings, occupation lists, assessments of skills and personality types, questionnaires to help you pinpoint areas that may suit you, and information about different careers and companies. Visit the centre early in your post-secondary career and work with a counsellor there to develop a solid career game plan.

Build knowledge and experience

Having knowledge and experience specific to the career you want to pursue is valuable on the job hunt. Courses, internships, jobs, and volunteering are four great ways to build both.

Courses. When you narrow your career exploration to a couple of areas of interest, try to take a course or two in those areas. How you react to the material gives you clues as to how you feel about the area in general. Find out what courses you have to take to major in the field, what jobs are available in the field, what credentials (degrees or training) you need for particular jobs, and so on.

Internships. Companies that offer internships are looking for people who will work hard in exchange for experience they can't get in the classroom. An internship may or may not offer pay. Your career centre may be able to help you explore summer internship opportunities or those during the school year. Stick to areas that interest you, and look for an internship that you can handle while still being able to fulfill your financial obligations. An **internship** is a great way to gain real-world experience and show initiative.

Jobs. No matter what you do to earn money while you are in college or university, whether it is in your area of interest or not, you may discover

INTERNSHIP
A temporary work program in which a student can gain supervised practical experience in a particular professional field.

career opportunities that appeal to you. Someone who takes a third-shift legal proofreading job to make extra cash might discover an interest in law. Someone who answers phones for a newspaper company might be drawn into journalism. Be open to the possibilities around you.

Volunteering. Offering your services to others in need can introduce you to careers and increase your experience. Some schools have programs to help you find volunteering opportunities. Include volunteer activities on your résumé. Many employers look favourably on volunteering.

Even after you've completed a college or university degree, training program, course, book, or job, the key is to continually build on what you know. With the world's fast-paced changes in mind, today's employers value those who seek continual improvement in their skills and knowledge.

Know what employers want

When you look for a job in a particular career area, any technical skills, work experience, and academic credentials you have that apply to that career are important. Beyond those basics, though, other skills and qualities make you an excellent job candidate in any career.

Important skills

Particular skills and qualities tell an employer that you are likely to be an efficient and effective employee. Key 11.2 describes these skills.

These skills appear throughout this book, and they are as much a part of your school success as they are of your work success. The more you develop them now, the more employable and promotable you will be. You may already use them on the job if you are a student who works.

Emotional intelligence

Another quality employers seek is emotional intelligence. In his book *Working with Emotional Intelligence,* psychologist Daniel Goleman states that emotional intelligence can be even more important than IQ and knowledge. He defines emotional intelligence as a combination of these factors:[1]

- Personal competence. This includes self-awareness (knowing your internal states, preferences, resources, intuitions), self-regulation (being able to manage your internal states, impulses, and resources), and motivation (the factors that help you reach your goals).
- Social competence. This includes empathy (being aware of the feelings, needs, and concerns of others) and social skills (your ability to create desirable responses in those with whom you interact).

The current emphasis on teamwork has made emotional intelligence very important in the workplace. The more adept you are at working comfortably and productively with others (i.e., the more emotionally intelligent you are and the more you use this intelligence), the more likely you are to succeed.

Stay current

The working world is always in flux, responding to technological developments, global competition, and other changes. Reading newspapers and

Skills employers seek.

SKILLS	WHY?
Communication	Both good listening and effective communicating are keys to workplace success, as is being able to adjust to different communication styles.
Critical thinking	An employee who can assess workplace choices and challenges critically and recommend appropriate actions stands out.
Teamwork	All workers interact with others on the job. Working well with others is essential for achieving work goals.
Goal setting	Teams fail if goals are unclear or unreasonable. Benefit is gained from setting realistic, specific goals and achieving them reliably.
Acceptance	The workplace is becoming increasingly diverse. A valuable employee is able to work with and respect all kinds of people.
Leadership	The ability to influence others in a positive way earns you respect and helps advance your career.
Creativity	The ability to come up with new concepts, plans, and products is valuable in the workplace.
Positive attitude	If you show that you have a high level of commitment to all tasks, you may earn the right to tackle more challenging projects.
Integrity	Acting with integrity at work—communicating promptly, being truthful and honest, following rules, giving proper notice, respecting others—enhances your value.
Flexibility	The most valuable employees understand the constancy of change and have developed the skills to adapt to its challenge.
Continual learning	The most valuable employees stay current on changes and trends by reading up-to-the-minute media and taking workshops and seminars.

magazines, scanning business sites on the Internet, and watching television news all help you keep abreast of what you face as you make career decisions. Spend your time staying on top of two issues: growing and declining career areas, and workplace trends.

Growing and declining career areas

Try to stay on top of what careers are growing most rapidly. Rapid workplace change means that a growth area today may be declining tomorrow—witness the sudden drop in Internet company jobs and fortunes in 2001. Human Resources Development Canada keeps up-to-date labour market information available on their Web site. Check in periodically to keep up on current trends. Their Web site is located at **www.jobfutures.ca.**

Workplace trends. What's happening now? To save money, corporations are hiring more temporary employees (temps) and fewer full-time employees. When considering whether to take a permanent job or a temporary job,

get analytical!

CONNECT VALUES TO CAREER

Use your values as a career exploration guide.

First, look at the following list of "value words." Put a checkmark by those qualities that are most important to you as a working person. Circle your top five.

- Accepting
- Adventurous
- Ambitious
- Calm
- Caring
- Conscientious
- Co-operative
- Creative

- Decisive
- Demonstrating leadership
- Efficient
- Enthusiastic
- Focused on learning
- Honest/fair
- Independent
- Kind

- Loyal
- Organized
- Powerful
- Prompt
- Serious
- Trustworthy
- Wealthy

Keeping your top values in mind, answer the following questions:

The kind of work I enjoy most is _____

I can't see myself working as a _____

Self-fulfillment at work consists of _____

Being in charge of others makes me feel _____

Being responsible makes me feel _____

Working independently makes me feel _____

Working in a team makes me feel _____

Imagining that I'm being promoted after two years on a job, I think my employer would say it is because of these exemplary characteristics:

_____

_____

Source: Adapted from Gary Izumo et al., *Keys to Career Success.* Upper Saddle River, NJ: Prentice Hall, 2002, pp. 67–69.

---

consider the effects of each. Permanent jobs offer benefits (employer contribution to pension plan, paid vacations, and health insurance) and stability, but less flexibility. Temporary jobs offer flexibility, few obligations, and often more take-home pay, but have limited benefits.

Expect change

As you learned in Chapter 1, rapid change in the workplace means that workers are changing jobs and careers often. Today's workers have to be prepared to go back to the drawing board should jobs not work out. When you experience the stress of job and career shifts, look for the positive in the change. Even difficult changes can open doors that you never even imagined were there. For example, Canadian country singer Shania Twain's parents were both killed in a car accident when she was just 21 years old. She was left to take care of her two teenage brothers. Despite this, she did not give up her dream of becoming a singer/songwriter. She took whatever singing jobs she could to help pay for rent and food. Twain looks back on these days as "the best education I ever had."

If you think creatively about your marketable skills and job possibilities, you will be able to find new ways to achieve. What you know about your learning style should play an important role in your thinking.

What does your *learning style* mean for your career?

If you don't know exactly what you want to do, you are not alone. Many students who have not been in the workplace—and even some who have—aren't sure what career to pursue. Start with what you know about yourself. In your initial exploration, you might ask yourself questions like the following:

- What do I know best, do best, and enjoy best?
- Out of the jobs I have had, what did I like and not like to do?
- What kinds of careers could make the most of everything I am?

You may not realize it, but with what you know about your learning style from your work in Chapter 3, you already have a head start on the self-knowledge that will help you find the right career. You can use each half of your learning style profile in a different way. Because the Multiple Intelligences assessment gives you information about your innate learning strengths and weaknesses, your results can help point you toward areas that take advantage of your abilities and involve your interests.

Your Personality Spectrum assessment results are perhaps even more significant to career success because they provide insight on how you work best with others. Nearly every aspect of the search process—looking for, interviewing for, and winning a job—involves dealing with people. Succeeding in your chosen job depends, in large part, on your ability to communicate and function in a team.

Key 11.3 focuses the four dimensions of the Personality Spectrum on career ideas and strategies. Look for your strengths and decide what you may want to keep in mind as you search. Look also at your weaknesses because even the most ideal job involves some tasks that may not be in your area of comfort. Identifying ways to boost your abilities in those areas will help you succeed.

Keep in mind a few important points as you consider the information in this table.

Use information as a guide, not a label. You may not necessarily have all the strengths and challenges that your dominant areas indicate. Chances are, though, that thinking through them will help you narrow your focus and clarify your abilities and interests.

Avoid thinking that challenges are weaknesses. Work challenges describe qualities that may cause issues in particular work situations. They aren't necessarily weaknesses in and of themselves. For example, not many

Personality Spectrum in the working world.

DIMENSION	STRENGTHS ON THE JOB	CHALLENGES ON THE JOB	LOOK FOR JOBS/CAREERS THAT FEATURE...
Thinker	• Problem solving • Development of ideas • Keen analysis of situations • Fairness to others • Efficiency in working through tasks • Innovation of plans and systems • Ability to look strategically at the future	• A need for private time to think and work • A need, at times, to move away from established rules • A dislike of sameness—systems that don't change, repetitive tasks • Not always open to expressing thoughts and feelings to others	• Some level of solo work/ think time • Problem solving • Opportunity for innovation • Freedom to think creatively and to bend the rules • Technical work • Big-picture strategic planning
Organizer	• High level of responsibility • Enthusiastic support of social structures • Order and reliability • Loyal • Able to follow through on tasks according to requirements • Detailed planning skills with competent follow-through • Neatness and efficiency	• A need for tasks to be clearly, concretely defined • A need for structure and stability • A preference for less rapid change • A need for frequent feedback • A need for tangible appreciation • Low tolerance for people who don't conform to rules and regulations	• Clear, well-laid-out tasks and plans • Stable environment with consistent, repeated tasks • Organized supervisors • Clear structure of how employees interact and report to one another • Value of and reward for loyalty
Giver	• Honesty and integrity • Commitment to putting energy toward close relationships with others • Finding ways to bring out the best in self and others • Peacemaker and mediator • Able to listen well, respect opinions, and prioritize the needs of co-workers	• Difficulty in handling conflict, either personal or between others in the work environment • Strong need for appreciation and praise • Low tolerance for perceived dishonesty or deception • Avoidance of people perceived as hostile, cold, or indifferent	• Emphasis on teamwork and relationship building • Indications of strong and open lines of communication among workers • Encouragement of personal expression in the workplace (arrangement of personal space, tolerance of personal celebrations, and so on)
Adventurer	• Skilfulness in many different areas • Willingness to try new things • Ability to take action • Hands-on problem-solving skills • Initiative and energy • Ability to negotiate • Spontaneity and creativity	• Intolerance of being kept waiting • Lack of focus on detail • Impulsiveness • Dislike of sameness and authority • Need for freedom, constant change, and constant action • Tendency not to consider consequences of actions	• A spontaneous atmosphere • Less structure, more freedom • Adventuresome tasks • Situations involving change • Encouragement of hands-on problem solving • Travel and physical activity • Support of creative ideas and endeavours

people would say that a need for structure and stability (a challenge of the Giver) is a weakness. However, it can be a challenge in a workplace that operates in an unstructured manner. Look at items that may be challenges for you. Then, looking at the careers or jobs you are considering, see if you think you will encounter situations that will bring your challenges into play.

Know that you are capable of change. What you know about how you learn now will help you develop the ability to make positive changes in school and in your career. Use ideas about strengths and challenges as a starting point and make some decisions about how you would like to progress as a working person.

Now that you've done your homework, it's time to get to the search. What you know, along with the strategies that follow, will help you along the path to a career that works for you.

How can you find a career that's *right for you*?

Many different routes can lead to satisfying jobs and careers. In the career areas that interest you, explore what's possible and evaluate potential positive and negative effects so that you can make an educated decision about what suits you best. Maximize your opportunities by using the resources available to you, making a strategic search plan, and knowing some basics about résumés and interviews.

Use available resources

Use your school's career planning and placement office, your **networking** skills, classified ads, on-line services, and employment agencies to help you explore possibilities both for jobs you need right away and for post-graduation career opportunities.

Your school's career planning and placement office. Generally, the career planning and placement office deals with post-graduation job placements, whereas the student employment office, along with the financial aid office, has more information about working while in school. At either location you might find general workplace information, listings of job opportunities, sign-up sheets for interviews, and contact information for companies.

The career office may hold frequent informational sessions on different topics. Your school may also sponsor job or career fairs that give you a chance to explore job opportunities. Start exploring your school's career office early in your college life. The people and resources there can help you at every stage of your career and job exploration process.

Networking. Networking is one of the most important job-hunting strategies. With each person you get to know, you build your network and tap into someone else's. With whom can you network? You can network

NETWORKING

The exchange of information or services among individuals, groups, or institutions.

with friends and family members, instructors, administrators, alumni, employers, co-workers and others.

Classified ads. Some of the best job listings are in newspapers. Individual ads describe the kind of position available and give a telephone number or post office box for you to contact. Some ads include additional information such as job requirements, a contact person, and the salary or wages offered. You can run your own classified ads if you have a skill to advertise.

On-line services. The Internet has exploded into one of the most fruitful sources of job listings. There are many different ways to hunt for a job on the Web:

- Look up career-focused and Canadian job listing Web sites such as **www.monster.ca, www.canjobs.com, www.actualjobs.com,** or Canada's job bank at Human Resources Development Canada, **http://jb-ge.hrdc-drhc.gc.ca.** In addition to listing and describing different jobs, sites like these offer resources on career areas, résumés, on-line job searching, and more.

- Check the Web pages of individual associations and companies, which may post job listings and descriptions.

- If nothing happens right away, keep at it. New job postings appear; new people sign on to look at your résumé. Plus, sites change all the time. Do a general search using the keywords "hot job sites" or "job search sites" to stay current on what sites are up and running.

Make a strategic job search plan

After you've gathered enough information to narrow your career goals, plan strategically to achieve them by mapping out your long-term timeline and keeping track of specific actions.

Make a big-picture timeline. Make a career timeline that illustrates the steps toward your goal, as shown in Key 11.4. Mark years and half-year points (and months for the first year), and write in the steps when you think they should happen. If your plan is five years long, indicate what you plan to do by the fourth, third, and second years, and then the first year, including a six-month goal and a one-month goal for that first year.

Using what you know about strategic planning, fill in the details about what you will do throughout your plan. Set goals that establish who you will talk to, what courses you will take, what skills you will work on, what jobs or internships you will investigate, and any other research you need to do. Your path may change, of course; use your timeline as a guide rather than as an inflexible plan.

The road to a truly satisfying career can be long. Seek support as you work toward goals. Confide in supportive people, talk positively to yourself, and read books about career planning such as those listed at the end of this chapter.

Keep track of details. After you establish your time frame, make a plan for pursuing the jobs or careers that have piqued your interest. Organize your approach according to what you need to do and how much time

Career timeline.

1 month	Enter university on part-time schedule
3 months	Meet with advisor to discuss desired major and required courses
6 months	Declare major in Child Studies
1 year	Switch to full-time class schedule
2 years	Pick up courses during spring and summer
3 years	Graduate with B.A.
4 years	Transfer to teacher's college
5 years	Work part-time as classroom aide as part of teacher's college training
	Graduate with teaching certificate
6 years	Have a job teaching high school

you have to do it. Do you plan to make three phone calls per day? Will you fill out three job applications a week for a month? Keep a record—on index cards, in a computer file, or in a notebook—of the following:

- People you contact
- Companies to which you apply
- Jobs you rule out (e.g., jobs that become unavailable or that you find don't suit your needs)
- Responses to your communications (phone calls to you, interviews, written communications), information about the person who contacted you (name, title), and the time and the dates of contact

Keeping accurate records enables you to both chart your progress and maintain a clear picture of the process. You never know when information might come in handy again. If you don't get a job now, another one could open up at the same company in a couple of months. In that case, well-kept records enable you to contact key personnel quickly and efficiently. Key 11.5 illustrates a sample file card.

Job/company:	Child-care worker at Morningside Daycare
Contact:	Kim McKay, Morningside Daycare, 136 Rockwood Avenue, St. Catharines ON L2P 3R8
Phone/fax/email:	(905) 555-3353 phone, (905) 555-3354 fax, no email
Communication:	Saw ad in paper, sent résumé and cover letter on October 1
Response:	Call from Kim to set up interview — Interview on Oct. 15 at 2 p.m., seemed to get a positive response, said she would contact me again by the end of the week
Follow-up:	Sent thank-you note on Oct. 16

Your résumé, cover letter, and interview

Information on résumés, targeted resumes, cover letters, and interviews fills entire books. You'll find specific sources listed at the end of the chapter. To get you started, here are a few basic tips on giving yourself the best possible chance at a job.

Résumé and cover letter. Your résumé should always be typed or printed on high-quality paper. Design your résumé neatly, using an acceptable format (books or your career office can show you some standard formats).

Proofread it for errors and have someone else proofread it as well. Type or print it on a heavier bond paper than is used for ordinary copies. Include a cover letter along with your résumé that tells the employer what job you are interested in and why he or she should hire you.

Prospective employers often use a computer to scan résumés. The computer program will select résumés if they contain enough *keywords*—words relating to the job opening or industry. Résumés without enough keywords probably won't even make it to the human resources desk. When you construct your résumé, make sure to include as many keywords as you can. For example, if you are seeking a computer-related job, list computer programs you use and other specific technical proficiencies. To figure out what keywords you need, check out job descriptions, job postings, and other current résumés.[2]

Interview. Be clean, neat, and appropriately dressed. Choose a nice pair of shoes—people notice. Bring an extra copy of your résumé and any other materials that you want to show the interviewer, even if you have already sent a copy ahead of time. Avoid chewing gum or smoking. Offer a confident handshake. Make eye contact. Show your integrity by speaking

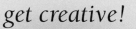

honestly about yourself. After the interview, no matter what the outcome, follow up right away with a formal but pleasant thank-you note.

Being on time to your interview makes a positive impression—and being late will almost certainly be held against you. If you are from a culture that does not consider being late a sign of disrespect, remember that your interviewer may not agree.

Having a job may not only be a thought for the future; it may be something you are concerned about right now. Many students need to work and take classes at the same time to fund their education. Although you may not necessarily work in an area that interests you, you can hold a job that helps you pay the bills and still allows you to make the most of your school time.

What will help you *juggle* work and school?

What you are studying today can prepare you to find a job when you graduate. In the meantime, though, you can make work a part of your student life to make money, explore a career, and increase your future employability through contacts or résumé building.

As the cost of education continues to rise, more and more students are working and taking classes at the same time. Being an employed student isn't for everyone. Adding a job to the list of demands on your time and energy may create problems if it sharply reduces study time or family time. However, many people want to work and many need to work to pay for school. Weigh the potential positive and negative effects of working so that you can make the most beneficial choice.

Effects of working while in school

Working while in school has many different positive and negative effects, depending on the situation. Evaluate any job opportunity by looking at these effects. Potential positive effects include:

- Money earned
- General and career-specific experience
- Being able to keep the job you currently hold
- Enhanced school and work performance (working up to 15 hours a week may encourage students to manage time more effectively and build confidence)

Potential negative effects include:

- Demanding time commitment
- Reduced opportunity for social and extracurricular activities
- Having to shift gears mentally from work to classroom

If you consider the effects and decide that working will help you, consider what you need from a job.

Establishing your needs

Think about what you need from a job before you begin your job hunt. Key 11.6 shows questions you may want to consider. Evaluate any potential job in terms of your needs.

In addition, be sure to consider how any special needs you have might be accommodated. If you have a hearing or vision impairment, reduced mobility, children for whom you need daycare, or any other particular need, you may want to find an employer who can and will accommodate it.

Your experiences in exploring careers and working are closely tied to your experiences with money. An important part of becoming a working person is earning the money you need to live. For that reason, investigating your financial needs and your particular strategies of dealing with money is important as you move toward the career for you. With what you learn about your finances, you are able to find the job and career that fit your needs.

No matter where your money comes from—financial aid or paycheques from one or more jobs—you can take steps to help it stretch as far as it can go. Using budgeting skills and strategic planning, you can more efficiently cover your expenses and still have some left over for savings and fun.

How can you *create a budget* that works?

For the vast majority of students, college is not a time to be "rolling in money." Even if you are a fully independent adult who has returned to school after years of working, money is probably tight, perhaps making it necessary to skimp in order to meet expenses. Similarly, if you depend on money from relatives or financial aid, not having enough to meet your monthly expenses can add stress to your daily life.

Evaluate what you need from a job you take when in school.

NEED	EVALUATION QUESTIONS
Salary or wage level	How much do I need to make for the year? How much during the months when I am paying tuition? What amount of money justifies the time my job takes?
Time of day	When is best for me? If I take classes at night, can I handle a day job? If I take day classes, would I prefer night or weekend work?
Hours per week (part-time vs. full-time)	If I take classes part time, can I handle a full-time job? If I am a full-time student, is part-time work best?
Duties performed	Do I want hands-on experience in my chosen field? Is the paycheque the priority over choosing what I do? What do I like and dislike doing?
Location	Does location matter? Will a job near school save me a great deal of time? What does my commute involve?
Flexibility	Do I need a job that offers flexibility, allowing me to shift my working time when I have an academic or family responsibility?
Affiliation with school or financial aid program	Does my financial aid package require me to take work at the school or a federal organization?

Every time you have to figure out whether the money in your pocket will pay for what you want at a store, you are **budgeting** your money. Budgeting is a process that considers your resources (money flowing in) and expenditures (money flowing out) and adjusts the flow so that you come out even or perhaps even ahead. Being able to budget effectively relieves money-related stress and helps you feel more in control.

Your biggest expense right now is probably the cost of your education, including tuition and room and board. However, that expense may not hit you fully until after you graduate and begin to pay back your student loans. For now, include in your budget only the part of the cost of your education you are paying while you are in school.

BUDGETING

Making a plan for the coordination of resources and expenditures; setting goals regarding money.

The art of budgeting

Budgeting involves a few basic steps: Determining spendable income (how much money you have after taxes), determining how much money you spend, subtracting what you spend from your after-tax income, evaluating the result, and deciding how to adjust your spending or earning based on that result. Budgeting regularly, using a specified time frame, is easiest. Most people budget on a month-by-month basis.

Determine your spendable income

Add up all of the money you receive during the year—the actual after-tax money you have to pay your bills. You may earn some of this money every month—from a part-time, after-school job, for example—while other income may come from summer and holiday employment that you have saved and then pro-rated for your monthly expenses. Common sources of income include:

- Your take-home pay from a regular full-time or part-time job during the school year
- Your take-home pay from summer and holiday employment
- Money you earn as part of a work-study program
- Money you receive from your parents or other relatives for your school expenses
- Scholarships or grants that provide spending money

If you have savings specifically earmarked for your education, decide how much you will withdraw every month for your school-related expenses.

Figure out how much you spend

If you have never paid much attention to how you spend, examine your patterns. Start by recording every cheque you write for fixed expenses like rent and telephone. Then, over the next month, record personal expenditures in a small notebook. Indicate any expenditure over $5, making sure to count smaller expenditures if they are frequent (e.g., a bus pass for a month, soft drinks, or newspaper purchases per week).

Money can't buy you happiness. It just helps you look for it in more places.

MILTON BERLE

Some expenses, like insurance, are billed only a few times a year. In these cases, convert the cost to a monthly expense by dividing the yearly cost by 12. Be sure to count only *current* expenses, not expenses that you will pay after you graduate. Current expenses might include:

- Rent or mortgage
- Tuition that you are paying right now (the portion remaining after all forms of financial aid, including loans, scholarships and grants, are taken into account)
- Books, lab fees, and other educational expenses
- Regular bills for utilities (electricity, gas, oil, phone, water)
- Food, clothing, toiletries, and household supplies
- Child care
- Transportation and car expenses (gas, maintenance)
- Credit cards and other payments on credit (car payments)
- Insurance (health, car, homeowner's or renter's, life)
- Entertainment and related items (cable television, movies, restaurants, books and magazines)
- Computer-related expenses, including the cost of your on-line service
- Miscellaneous unplanned expenses

Use the total of all your monthly expenses as a baseline for other months, realizing that your expenditures will vary depending on what is happening in your life.

Evaluate the result

Focusing again on your current situation, subtract your monthly expenses from your monthly income. Ideally, you have money left over—to save or to spend. However, if you are spending more than you take in, your first job is to analyze the problem by looking carefully at your budget, your spending patterns, and priorities. Use your critical-thinking skills to ask some focused questions.

Question your budget. Did you forget to budget for recurring expenses such as the cost for semi-annual dental visits? Or was your budget derailed by an emergency expense that you did not foresee, such as the cost of a new transmission for your car? Is your budget realistic? Is your income sufficient for your needs?

Question your spending patterns and priorities. Did you spend money wisely during the month? Did you go to too many restaurants or movies? Can you afford the luxury of your own car? Are you putting too many purchases on your credit card and being hit by high interest payments? When you are spending more than you are taking in during a "typical month," you may need to adjust your budget over the long term.

Make decisions about how to adjust spending or earning

Look carefully at what may cause you to overspend and brainstorm possible solutions that address those causes. Solutions can involve either increasing resources or decreasing spending. To deal with spending, prioritize your expenditures and trim the ones you really don't need to make. Cut out unaffordable or wasteful extras. For example, you can save a lot of money each month by renting movies at your local video rental store instead of going to the theatre. You can save even more if you borrow movies, which are often free, from your local library.

As for resources, investigate ways to take in more money. Start your summer job search early so you have the choice of the highest-paying positions. Taking a part-time job, hunting down scholarships or grants, or increasing hours at a current job may also help. You may also want to look for a job that pays more than you are currently making.

A sample budget

Key 11.7 shows a sample budget of an unmarried student living with two other students in off-campus housing with no meal plan. Included are all regular and out-of-pocket expenses with the exception of tuition expenses, which the student will pay back after graduation in student loan payments. In this case, the student is $190 over budget. How would you make up the shortfall?

Not everyone likes the work involved in keeping a budget. For example, whereas logical–mathematical learners may take to it easily, visual learners may resist the structure and detail of the budgeting process (see Chapter 3).

MULTIPLE INTELLIGENCE STRATEGIES FOR

Budgeting ←

Looking into the strategies associated with your strongest intelligences helps you identify effective ways to manage your money.

INTELLIGENCE	WHAT WORKS FOR YOU? SUGGESTED STRATEGIES	WRITE NEW IDEAS HERE
Verbal–Linguistic	• Talk over your budget with someone you trust. • Write out a detailed budget outline. If you can, keep it on a computer where you can change and update it regularly.	
Logical–Mathematical	• Focus on the numbers; using a calculator and amounts as exact as possible, determine your income and spending. • Calculate how much money you'll have in 10 years if you start now to put $500 in an RRSP account each year.	
Bodily–Kinesthetic	• Consider putting money, or a slip with a dollar amount, each month in different envelopes for various budget items—rent, dining out, etc. When the envelope is empty or the number is reduced to zero, your spending stops.	
Visual–Spatial	• Set up a budgeting system that includes colour-coded folders and coloured charts. • Create colour-coded folders for papers related to financial and retirement goals—investments, accounts, etc.	
Interpersonal	• Whenever budgeting problems come up, discuss them right away. • Brainstorm a solid five-year financial plan with one of your friends.	
Intrapersonal	• Schedule quiet time and think about how you want to develop, follow, and update your budget. Consider financial-management software. • Think through the most balanced allocation of your assets—where you think your money should go.	
Musical	• Include a category of music-related purchases in your budget—going to concerts, buying CDs—but keep an eye on it to make sure you don't go overboard.	
Naturalistic	• Remember to include time and money in your budget to enjoy nature. • Sit in a spot you like. Brainstorm how you will achieve your short- and long-term financial goals.	

A student's sample budget.

A STUDENT'S SAMPLE MONTHLY BUDGET

- Wages: $10 an hour (after taxes) × 20 hours a week = $200 a week × 4 1/3 weeks (one month) = $866.
- Withdrawals from savings (from summer earnings) = $200
- Total income per month: $1,066

MONTHLY EXPENDITURES

School-related expenses (not covered by student loans, grants, scholarships—including books and supplies)	$ 150
Public transportation	$ 90
Phone	$ 40
Food	$ 450
Credit card payments	$ 100
Rent (including utilities)	$ 200
Entertainment	$ 100
Miscellaneous expenses, including clothes and toiletries	$ 100
Total monthly spending	**$1,230**

$1,066 (income) − $1,230 (spending) = $−164 ($164 over budget)

Visual learners may want to create a budget chart such as the one in the example or use strategies that make budgeting more tangible, such as dumping receipts into a big jar and tallying them at the end of the month. Even if you have to force yourself to use a budget, you will discover that the process can reduce stress and help you take control of your finances and your life.

Savings strategies

Your challenge is to figure out ways to save money and still enjoy life. This involves being honest with yourself about your *needs* versus your *wants*. If your current running shoes are falling apart, you certainly *need* a new pair. However, your decision to buy an especially expensive pair is a *want* because other equally serviceable brands may cost far less.

Here are some savings suggestions for cutting corners. Small amounts can eventually add up to big savings and may keep you out of debt.

- Share living space with one or more roommates.
- Eat at home more often than at restaurants.
- Use your local library for books, CDs and videos. They're free to borrow.

- Use coupons, take advantage of sales, buy store brands, and buy in bulk.
- Find discounted play and concert tickets (students often receive discounts).
- Walk or use public transportation.
- Bring your lunch from home.
- Shop in second-hand stores.
- Use email or write letters.
- Ask a relative to help you with child care.

Add your own suggestions here:

_____

_____

_____

Making successfully intelligent financial decisions

Every budgetary decision you make has particular effects, often involving a trade-off among options. When you spend $120 for that new pair of running shoes, for example, you may not have enough for movie tickets and dinner with friends that weekend. That is, there is an *opportunity cost* in addition to money. In this case, the new running shoes deprive you of the chance to attend the movie and go to dinner. Although buying the running shoes may be the right decision for you, look at the whole picture before you spend your money.

Being strategic with your money primarily means taking that big-picture look before making any financial decision, large or small. Use what you know about decision making to make the decisions that work best for you.

1. *Establish your needs.* Be honest about what you truly need and what you just want. Do you really need a new bike? Or can the old one serve while you pay off some credit card debt?
2. *Brainstorm available options.* Think about what you can do with your money and evaluate the positive and negative effects of each option.
3. *Choose an option and carry it out.* Spend it—save it—invest it—whatever you decide.
4. *Evaluate the result.* This crucial step builds knowledge that you can use in the future. What were the positive and negative effects of what you chose? Would you make that choice again?

Often, making some short-term sacrifices in order to save money can help you a great deal in the long run. However, this doesn't mean you should never spend money on things that bring you immediate satisfaction. The goal is to make choices that provide both short-term satisfaction and long-term money growth.

MAP OUT YOUR BUDGET

get practical!

Arrive at a basic estimate of whether you are operating at a gain or a loss.

Step 1: Estimate your current expenses in dollars per month, using the following table. This may require tracking expenses for a month, if you don't already keep a record of your spending. The grand total is your total monthly expenses.

Expense	Amount Spent
Rent/mortgage or room and board payment	$
Utilities (electric, heat, gas, water)	$
Food (shopping, eating out, meal plan)	$
Telephone (land line and mobile phone)	$
Books, lab fees, other educational expenses	$
Loan payments (educational or bank loans)	$
Car (repairs, insurance, payments, gas)	$
Public transportation	$
Clothing/personal items	$
Entertainment	$
Child care (caregivers, clothing/supplies, etc.)	$
Medical care/insurance	$
Other	$
TOTAL	**$**

Step 2: Calculate your average monthly income. If it's easiest to come up with a yearly figure, divide by 12 to derive the monthly figure. For example, if you have a $6,000 scholarship for the year, your monthly income would be $500 ($6,000 divided by 12).

Income Source	Amount Received
Regular work salary/wages (full-time or part-time)	$
Grants or work-study programs	$
Scholarships	$
Assistance from family members	$
Other	$
TOTAL	**$**

Step 3: Subtract the grand total of your monthly expenses from the grand total of your monthly income:

Income per month	$
Expenses per month	– $
CASH FLOW	**$**

Step 4: If you have a negative cash flow, you can increase your income, decrease your spending, or both. Think about what's possible for you to accomplish. List here your two most workable ideas about how you can get your cash flow back in the black.

1. _____

2. _____

It is thrifty to prepare today for the wants of tomorrow.

AESOP

Following are two final pointers for being strategic with your hard-earned money:

- **Live beneath your means.** Spend less than you make. This strategy helps you create savings. Any amount of savings gives you a buffer zone that can help with emergencies or bigger expenditures.
- **Pay yourself.** After you pay your monthly bills, put whatever you can save in an account. Paying yourself helps you store money in your savings where it can grow. Make your payment to yourself a high priority so that you honour it as you do your other bills.

One final part of keeping an accurate, useful budget is being a strategic consumer of banking services.

Use bank accounts wisely

Paying your bills and saving require that you form your own relationship with a financial institution such as a bank. Choose a bank with convenient locations, hours that fit your schedule, account fees that aren't too high, and a convenient network of automatic teller machines (ATMs).

Most banks issue debit cards that look like credit cards but take money directly out of your chequing account immediately (unlike cheques, which clear after one or more days). Many banks now have phone or on-line payment services that help you bank from your home, as well as services that allow you to set up the automatic payment of bills directly from your account each month.

The two specific services you need when you use a bank are chequing and savings accounts.

Chequing accounts. Most banks offer more than one chequing plan. Some accounts include cheque-writing fees, a small charge on every cheque you write or on any cheques above a certain number per month. Some accounts have free chequing, meaning unlimited cheque writing without extra fees—but you often have to maintain a minimum balance in your account to qualify.

Some accounts charge a monthly fee that is standard or varies according to your balance. Interest chequing pays you a low rate of interest, although you may have to keep a certain balance or have a savings account at the same bank.

Savings accounts. The most basic savings account, the interest savings account, pays a rate of interest to you determined by the bank. Many interest savings accounts do not have a required balance, but the interest rate they pay is very low.

STRESSBUSTER

SONYA BEEL   Sprott-Shaw Community College, Duncan, British Columbia

How do you manage the conflicting demands of work and school? How do you find positive ways to manage this stress?

I decided to go back to school after my third son was born. I have three children, all under ten years of age, which meant that I waited eight years to get my career training started. I was a little nervous about taking out a student loan, especially since I had to get one from outside of the province, but that was the only way I could get the money for my education.

I have a part-time job on weekends. My spouse, Tony, works full-time at a door factory. With him working full time, and me working part time, things were very comfortable financially. Unfortunately, he was laid off in September and was out of work for six weeks. I have never been so scared. What would I do? How could I feed three small boys, pay the rent, and cover all the expenses on a part-time salary? Every day, I kept telling myself that it would get easier and less stressful. For a little peace of mind, I talked to my family and friends about it. The staff at the school was very helpful, and would let me know what resources were available to me.

The biggest stressbusters I have are my children, even though they do cause a lot of financial worry. I try to play with them every night after their bath. It really seems to help me forget, for a few hours, all the stress I feel about having a young family, a job, and school. If you have similar stress and children, I recommend that you take a few hours every day, get out the toys, and play with your kids.

How can you manage your *credit cards?*

It is common for students to receive dozens of credit card offers from different financial institutions issuing VISA and MasterCard. These offers—and the cards that go along with them—are a double-edged sword: They have the power to help you manage your money, but they also can plunge you into a hole of debt that may take you years to dig out of.

When used properly, credit cards are a handy alternative to cash. They give you the peace of mind of knowing that you always have money for emergencies and that you have a record of all your purchases. In addition, if you pay your bills on time, you will be building a strong credit history that will affect your ability to take out future loans, including car loans and mortgages.

However, it takes self-control to avoid overspending, especially because it is so easy to hand over your credit card when you see something you like. To avoid excessive debt, ask yourself these questions before charging anything: Would I buy it if I had to pay cash? Can I pay

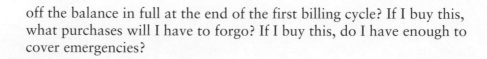

off the balance in full at the end of the first billing cycle? If I buy this, what purchases will I have to forgo? If I buy this, do I have enough to cover emergencies?

How credit cards work

When you make purchases on credit—everything from your textbooks to holiday presents for friends and family—the merchant accepts immediate payment from the credit card issuer and you accept the responsibility to pay the money back. *Every time you charge, you are creating a debt that must be repaid.* The credit card issuer earns money by charging interest on your unpaid balance. With rates that are often higher than 20 percent, you may soon find yourself wishing that you had paid cash.

Here's an example of how quickly credit card debt can mount. Say you have a $3000 unpaid balance on your credit card at an annual interest rate of 18 per cent. If you make the $60 minimum monthly payment every month, it will take you eight long years to pay off your debt, assuming that you make no other purchases. The math—and the effect on your wallet—is staggering:

- Original debt—$3000
- Cost to repay credit card loan at an annual interest rate of 18 per cent for eight years—$5760
- Cost of credit—$2760

By the time you finish, you will repay nearly twice your original debt.

To avoid unmanageable debt that can lead to a personal financial crisis, learn as much as you can about credit cards, starting with the important concepts in Key 11.8

Learn to use credit wisely while you are still in school. The habits you learn today can make a difference to your financial future.

Managing debt

The majority of Canadians have some level of debt, and many people go through periods when they have a hard time keeping up with their bills. Falling behind on payments, however, could result in a poor credit rating that makes it difficult for you to make large purchases or take out loans. If you are having trouble keeping up with your payments, seek out the advice of a credit counsellor. Their services are often free.

David Thompson, a credit counsellor in Ottawa, says students need to be careful when using credit cards. Abusing credit cards can damage your credit rating, which can affect you when applying for jobs in the future. Two companies in Canada track and collect credit information: Equifax Canada and TransUnion Canada. They document your credit history, including your payment history and any missed payments.[3]

The most basic way to stay in control is to pay bills regularly and on time. On credit card bills, pay at least the minimum amount due. If you get into trouble, deal with it in three steps. First, admit that you made a mistake, even though you may be embarrassed. Then, address

Learn to be a smart credit consumer.

WHAT TO KNOW ABOUT . . .	. . . AND HOW TO USE WHAT YOU KNOW
Account balance—a dollar amount that includes any unpaid balance, new purchases and cash advances, finance charges, and fees. Updated monthly on your card statement.	Charge only what you can afford to pay at the end of the month. Keep track of your balance. Hold on to receipts and call customer service if you have questions about recent purchases.
Annual fee—the yearly cost some companies charge for owning a card.	Look for cards without an annual fee or, if you've paid your bills on time, ask your current company to waive the fee.
Annual percentage rate (APR)—the amount of interest charged on your unpaid balance, meaning the cost of credit if you carry a balance in any given month. The higher the APR, the more you pay in finance charges.	Credit card companies compete by charging different APRs. Shop around, especially on the Web. Two sites with competitive APR information are **www.studentcredit.com** and **www.bankrate.com**. Also, watch out for low, but temporary, introductory rates that skyrocket to over 20 percent after a few months. Look for *fixed* rates (guaranteed not to change).
Available credit—the unused portion of your credit line. Determine available credit by deducting your current card balance from your credit limit.	It is important to have credit available for emergencies, so avoid charging to the limit.
Billing cycle—the number of days between the last statement date and the current statement date.	Knowledge of your billing cycle can help you juggle funds. For example, if your cycle ends on the 3rd of the month, holding off on a large purchase until the 4th gives you an extra month to pay without incurring finance charges.
Cash advance—an immediate loan, in the form of cash, from the credit card company. You are charged interest immediately and may also pay a separate transaction fee.	Use a cash advance only in emergencies because the finance charges start as soon as you complete the transaction. It is a very expensive way to borrow money.
Credit limit—the debt ceiling the card company places on your account (e.g., $1,500). The total owed, including purchases, cash advances, finance charges, and fees, cannot exceed this limit.	Credit card companies generally set low credit limits for college students. Many students get around this limit by owning more than one card, which increases the credit available but most likely increases problems as well.
Credit line—a revolving amount of credit that can be used, paid back, then used again for future purchases or cash advances.	Work with the credit line of one card, paying the money you borrow back at the end of each month so you can borrow again.
Delinquent account—an account that is not paid on time or for which the minimum payment has not been met.	Avoid having a delinquent account at all costs. Not only will you be charged substantial late fees, but you also risk losing your good credit rating, affecting your ability to borrow in the future. Delinquent accounts remain part of your credit record for many years.
Due date—the date your payment must be received and after which you will be charged a late fee.	Avoid late fees and finance charges by mailing your payment a week in advance.

Continued.

WHAT TO KNOW ABOUT . . .	. . . AND HOW TO USE WHAT YOU KNOW
Finance charges—the total cost of credit, including interest and service and transaction fees.	Your goal is to incur no finance charges. The only way to do that is to pay your balance in full by the due date on your monthly statement.
Grace period—the interest-free time period between the date of purchase and the date your payment for that purchase is due once it appears on your statement. For example, a purchase on November 4 may first appear on your November 28 statement with payment due 25 days later.	It is important to know that interest-free grace periods only apply if you have no outstanding balance. If you carry a balance from month to month, all new purchases are immediately subject to interest charges.
Minimum payment—the smallest amount you can pay by the statement due date. The amount is set by the credit card company.	Making only the minimum payment each month can result in disaster if you continue to charge more than you can realistically afford. When you make a purchase, think in terms of total cost, not monthly payments.
Outstanding balance—the total amount you owe on your card.	If you carry a balance over several months, additional purchases are immediately hit with finance charges. Pay cash instead.
Past due—your account is considered "past due" when you fail to pay the minimum required payment on schedule.	Three credit bureaus note past due accounts on your credit history: Experian, Trans Union, and Equifax. You can contact each bureau for a copy of your credit report to make sure there are no errors.

CREDITOR

A person or company to whom a debt is owed, usually money.

the problem immediately to minimize damages. Call the **creditor** and see if you can pay your debt gradually using a payment plan. Finally, examine what got you into trouble and avoid it in the future if you can. Cut up a credit card or two if you have too many. If you clean up your act, your credit history will gradually clean up as well.

Sacrifici

In Italy, parents often use the term *sacrifici,* meaning "sacrifices," to refer to tough choices that they make to improve the lives of their children and family members. They may sacrifice a larger home so that they can afford to pay for their children's sports and after-school activities. They may sacrifice a higher-paying job so that they can live close to where they work. They give up something in exchange for something else that they have decided is more important to them.

Think of the concept of *sacrifici* as you analyze the sacrifices you can make to get out of debt, reach your savings goals, and prepare for a career that you find satisfying. Many of the short-term sacrifices you are making today will help you do and have what you want in the future.

Developing Successful Intelligence

PUTTING IT ALL TOGETHER

Personal qualities and career success. Much of what brings success in any career area is being able to match who you are to the personal qualities that are valued for a given profession. Use your successful intelligence to investigate where you fit.

Step 1. Think it through: *Analyze who succeeds and why.* Pick one career area to focus on. What are the characteristics of people who are successful in this career? Think about success-promoting qualities that aren't obvious. Investigate, using information from the Internet, conversations with successful working people, and reading.

Career area that interests you: _____

Qualities and characteristics of people who succeed in this career: _____

_____

What you have in common with these people: _____

_____

Do you see yourself and your talents reflected in the people you learned about? _____

_____

Step 2. Think out of the box: *Generate ideas about what inspires you.* What topics, tasks, and interests make you feel creative, capable, and joyful?

create your future

What motivates you to do more? Brainstorm a few ideas, keeping in mind that career success often comes from pursuing what you love to do.

_____

_____

Step 3. *Make it happen: Look for practical ways to test what you've learned.* From the people you talked to and where they work, make a list of three summer or winter internship possibilities.

1. _____

2. _____

3. _____

On a separate piece of paper, map out a three-month plan for contacting these people, determining the possibility of interning, and applying formally for internships.

Team Building

COLLABORATIVE SOLUTIONS

Building interview skills. Divide into pairs—each student will have a turn interviewing the other about themselves and their career aspirations. Follow these steps.

1. Independently, take three minutes to brainstorm questions you'll ask the other person. Focus on learning style, interests, and initial career ideas. You might ask questions like these:
   - If you could have any job in the world, what would it be?
   - What do you think would be the toughest part of achieving success in that profession?
   - Who are you as a learner and worker—what is your learning style?
   - What sacrifices are you willing to make to realize your dreams?
   - What is your greatest failure, and what have you learned from it?
   - Who is a role model to you in terms of career success?
2. Person A interviews Person B for five to ten minutes and takes notes.
3. Switch roles: Person B interviews Person A and takes notes. Remember that each person uses their own questions that they developed in Step 1.
4. Share with each other what interesting ideas stand out to you from the interviews. If you have any, offer constructive criticism to your interviewee about his or her interview skills.
5. Finally, submit your notes to your instructor for feedback.

This exercise will build your ability to glean information from others and to answer questions during an interview. You will use this skill throughout your professional life. Probe deeply when interviewing others so that you develop the ability to draw out the best in someone. Be as interested—and interesting—as you can.

Writing

Record your thoughts on a separate piece of paper or in a journal.

Money and you. Describe your relationship with money. What do you buy? How much do you spend? Are you careful? Reckless? Inattentive? Focused on every detail? How much do you use credit cards—and do you pay credit card bills in full each month or run a balance? If you could change how you handle money, what would you do?

Career Portfolio

PLAN FOR SUCCESS

Complete the following in your electronic portfolio or on separate sheets of paper.

Being specific about your job needs. As you consider specific job directions and opportunities, you will have to begin thinking about a variety of job-related factors that different employers offer and that may affect your job experience and personal life. Among these factors are the following:

- Benefits (including health insurance, vacation)
- Integrity of company (What is its reputation?)
- Integrity of organization in its dealings with employees
- Promotion prospects/your chances for advancement
- Job stability
- Training and educational opportunities (Does the company offer in-house training? Will it pay for job-related courses or degrees?)
- Starting salary
- Quality of employees
- Quality of management
- Nature of the work you will be doing (Will you be required to travel extensively? Will you be expected to work long hours? Will you be working in an office or in the field?)
- Your official relationship with the company (Will you be a full-time or part-time employee or an independent contractor?)
- Job title
- Location of your primary workplace
- Company size
- Company's financial performance over time

Think about how important each factor is in your job choice. Then rate each on a scale of one to ten, with one being the least important and ten being the most important. As you consider each factor, keep in mind that even if you consider something very important, you may not get it right away if you are just beginning your career.

Finally, consider the results of a recent survey of college students conducted by the National Association of Colleges and Employers. When asked their top two reasons for choosing an employer, students named *integrity of organization in its dealings with employees* as number one and *job stability* as number two. How do these top choices compare to your own?[4]

SUGGESTED READINGS

Adams, Robert Lang, et al. *The Complete Résumé and Job Search Book for College Students*. Holbrook, MA: Adams Publishing, 1999.

Beatty, Richard H. *The Resume Kit*, 5th ed. New York: John Wiley & Sons, 2003.

Boldt, Laurence G. *Zen and the Art of Making a Living: A Practical Guide to Creative Career Design*. New York: Arkana, 1999.

Bolles, Richard Nelson. *What Color Is Your Parachute? 2003: A Practical Manual for Job Hunters and Career Changers*. Berkeley, CA: Ten Speed Press, 2003.

Detweiler, Gerri. *The Ultimate Credit Handbook*, 3rd ed. New York: Plume, 2003.

Goleman, Daniel. *Emotional Intelligence*. New York: Bantam Books, 1997.

Goleman, Daniel. *Working with Emotional Intelligence*. New York: Bantam Books, 2000.

Kennedy, Joyce Lain. *Job Interviews for Dummies*. Foster City, CA: IDG Books Worldwide, 2000.

Tyson, Eric. *Personal Finance for Dummies*. Foster City, CA: IDG Books Worldwide, 2000.

INTERNET RESOURCES

For information on on-line job searches and targeting your resume, check out Monster.ca: **www.monster.ca**

The University of Saskatchewan offers students tips on money management: www.usask.ca/sas/elo/ budgeting_sociallife.html

Advice on how to write a resume can be found at The Resume Edge: **www.resumeedge.com**

What's the latest on what Canadian employers want? Find out from the Conference Board of Canada: **www.conferenceboard.ca**

If you're looking for varied and current labour market information, as well as what skills you have to offer potential employers, check out Canada Prospects: **www.careerccc.org**

Prentice Hall Student Success Supersite—Money Matters: **www.prenhall.com/success/MoneyMat/ index.html**

1. Daniel Goleman, *Working with Emotional Intelligence*. New York: Bantam Books, 1998, pp. 26–27.

2. ResumeEdge.com, "Resume Keyword Search," 2004 [on-line]. Available at: www.enetsc.com/ResumeTips23.htm (May 2004).

3. Colin Campbell, "The Danger of Debt" [on-line]. Available at: http://www.carleton.ca/ottawainsight/2002/pfinance/s4.html. Downloaded October 30, 2002.

4. Eduardo Porter and Greg Winter, "'04 Graduates Learned Lesson in Practicality," *New York Times*, May 30, 2004, pp. A1 and A24.

G R O W

12

IN THIS CHAPTER

In this chapter you will explore answers to the following questions: • How will what you've learned bring success? • How can you make a difference in your community? • How can you continue to activate your successful intelligence? • How can you create and live your personal mission?

354

Creating your life

AS YOU COME to the end of your work in this course, you have built up a wealth of knowledge. You will soon be analyzing how you fared in your first college semester. You are facing important decisions about what direction you want to go in school—and starting to think about where the choices you make now will ultimately lead you.

This chapter will help you connect college to the rest of your life. You will see how the skills and attitudes you acquire in school fuel your future success. You will learn to think of yourself as a member of broader communities and to take on the challenge of being an active participant. You will gather 20 important tools that will help you transfer the power of successful intelligence into your post-college life. Finally, you will create your personal mission, exploring how to use it to guide your dreams.

building a successful future

How will what you've learned *bring success?*

You leave this course with far more than a final grade, a notebook full of work, and a credit hour or three on your transcript. You have gathered important attitudes and skills, developed flexibility, and opened the door to lifelong learning.

New attitudes and skills prepare you to succeed

The attitudes and skills you gained this semester are your keys to success now and in the future (see Key 12.1). As you move through your college years, keep motivation high by reminding yourself that you are creating tools that will benefit you in everything you do.

Flexibility helps you adapt to change

As a citizen of the twenty-first century, you are likely to move in and out of school, jobs, and careers in the years ahead. You are also likely to experience important personal changes. How you react to the changes you experience, especially if they are unexpected and difficult, is almost as important as the changes themselves in determining your future success. The ability to "make lemonade from lemons" is the hallmark of people who always land on their feet.

Successfully intelligent thinking will help you adapt to and benefit from both planned and unexpected changes. Your goal is flexibility as you analyze each change, generate and consider options, make decisions, and take practical actions. With flexibility and resourcefulness, you can adapt to the loss of a job or to getting an exciting job offer, a personal health crisis or a happy change in family status, failing a course or winning an academic scholarship.

Although sudden changes may throw you off balance, the unpredictability of life can open new horizons. Margaret J. Wheatley and Myron Kellner-Rogers, leadership and community experts and founders of the Berkana Institute, explain: People "often look at this unpredictability with resentment, but... unpredictability gives us the freedom to experiment. It is this unpredictability that welcomes our creativity."[1] Here are some strategies they recommend for making the most of unpredictable changes:

- Look for what happens when you meet someone or something new. Be aware of new feelings or insights that arise. Observe where they lead you.

- Be willing to be surprised. Great creative energies can come from the force of a surprise. Instead of turning back to familiar patterns, explore new possibilities.

The word "impossible" is not in my dictionary.

NAPOLEON

Student success skills are career and life success skills.

ACQUIRED SKILL	IN SCHOOL, YOU'LL USE IT TO...	IN YOUR CAREER, YOU'LL USE IT TO...
Investigating resources	... find who and what can help you have the post-secondary experience you want	... get acclimated at a new job—find the people, resources, and services that can help you succeed
Knowing and using your learning style	... select study strategies that make the most of your learning style	... select jobs and career areas that suit what you do best
Setting goals	... complete assignments and achieve educational goals	... accomplish work tasks and reach career goals
Managing time	... get to classes on time, juggle school and work, turn in assignments when they are due	... finish tasks on or before your supervisor says they are due, balance different on-the-job duties
Critical thinking	... think through writing assignments, solve math problems, see similarities and differences among ideas in literature, history, sociology, etc.	... find ways to improve product design, increase market share, present ideas to customers and employees, and so on.
Reading	... read course texts and readings	... read operating manuals, work guidebooks, media materials in your field, and continuing education materials
Note taking	... take notes in class and in study groups	... take notes in work meetings and during important phone calls
Test taking	... take quizzes, tests, and final exams	... take tests for certification in particular work skills
Writing	... write essays and reports	... write memos, letters, reports, or media material
Building successful relationships	... get along with instructors, students, student groups	... get along with supervisors, co-workers, and team members
Staying healthy	... manage stress and stay healthy so that you can make the most of school	... manage stress and stay healthy so that you can operate at your best at work
Managing money	... stay on top of school costs and make decisions that earn you the money you need	... budget the money you are earning so that you can pay your bills and save for the future
Establishing and maintaining a personal mission	... develop a big-picture idea of what you want from your education	... develop a big-picture idea of what you want to accomplish in your life and make choices that guide you toward those goals

- Use your planning as a guide rather than a rule. If you allow yourself to follow new paths when changes occur, you are able to grow from what life gives you.

- Focus on what is rather than what is supposed to be. Planning for the future works best as a guide when combined with an awareness of the realities of your situation.

Lifelong learning

As a student, your main focus is on learning—on acquiring knowledge and skills in the courses you take. Though you will graduate knowing much more than you did when you started college, you are not finished learning. On the contrary, with knowledge in many fields doubling every two to three years and with your personal interests and needs changing every day, what you learn in college is just the beginning of lifelong learning. With the *habit* of learning you will be able to achieve your career and personal goals—those that you set out for yourself today and those that you cannot anticipate but that will be part of your future.

You can make learning a habit through asking questions and being open to exploring new ideas and possibilities. Here are some ways to make that happen:

Seeking experiences that broaden your horizons is part of lifelong learning. These students are learning both academic and life lessons during their travel in China.

Investigate new interests. When information and events catch your attention, take your interest one step further and find out more. Instead of dreaming about it, just do it.

Read, read, read. Reading expert Jim Trelease says that people who don't read "base their future decisions on what they used to know. If you don't read much, you really don't know much. You're dangerous."[2] Decrease the danger to yourself and others by opening a world of knowledge and perspectives through reading. Ask friends which books have changed their lives. Keep up with local, national, and world news through newspapers and magazines.

Pursue improvement in your studies and career. After graduation, continue your education both in your field and in the realm of general knowledge. Stay on top of ideas, developments, and new technology in your field by seeking out **continuing education** courses. Sign up for career-related seminars. Take single courses at a local college or community learning centre. Some companies offer additional on-the-job training or pay for their employees to take courses that will improve their knowledge and skills.

Spend time with interesting people. When you meet someone new who inspires you and makes you think, keep in touch. Form a study group, a film club, or a walking club. Host a potluck dinner party and invite

CONTINUING
EDUCATION
Courses that students
can take without
having to be part of a
degree program.

people from different corners of your life—family, school, work, or neighbourhood. Learn something new from everyone you meet.

Talk to people from different generations. Younger people can learn from the experienced, broad perspective of those belonging to older generations; older people can learn from the fresh and often radical perspective of those younger than themselves. Communication builds mutual respect.

Delve into other cultures. Talk with a friend who has grown up in a culture different from your own. Invite him or her to dinner. Eat food from a country you've never visited. Initiate conversations with people of different races, religions, values, and ethnic backgrounds. This is not difficult in a multicultural country like Canada. Travel internationally and locally. Take a course that deals with some aspect of cultural diversity. Try a semester or year abroad.

Nurture a spiritual life. You don't have to attend a house of worship to be spiritual, although that may be part of your spiritual life. Wherever you find spirituality and soul—in music, organized religion, friendship, nature, cooking, sports, or anything else will help you find balance and meaning.

Experience the arts. Art is "an adventure of the mind" (Eugène Ionesco, playwright); "a means of knowing the world" (Angela Carter, author); something that "does not reproduce the visible; rather, it makes visible" (Paul Klee, painter); "a lie that makes us realize truth" (Pablo Picasso,

get creative!

THINK 50 POSITIVE THOUGHTS

Appreciate yourself, and plan to expand your horizons.

On a piece of paper, list 25 things you like about yourself. You can name anything—things you can do, things you think, things you've accomplished, things you like about your physical self, and so on.

Next, list 25 things you would like to do in your life. These can be anything from trying Vietnamese food to travelling to Ellesmere Island in Canada's Arctic. They can be things you'd like to do tomorrow or things that you plan to do in 20 years. At least five items on each list should involve your current and future education.

Finally, come up with five things you can plan for the next year that combine what you like about yourself and what you want to do. If you like your strength as a mountain biker and you want to explore a province you've never seen, plan a mountain biking trip. If you like your writing and you want to be a published author, write an essay to submit to a magazine. Be creative. Let everything be possible.

1. _____
2. _____
3. _____
4. _____
5. _____

painter); a revealer of "our most secret self" (Jean-Luc Godard, filmmaker). Through art forms you can discover new ideas and shed light on old ones. Seek out whatever moves you—music, visual arts, theatre, photography, dance, domestic arts, performance art, film and television, poetry, prose, and more.

Make your own creations. Take a class in drawing, writing, or quilting. Learn to play an instrument. Write poems for your favourite people or stories to read to your children. Concoct a new recipe. Design and build a set of shelves for your home. Create a memoir of your life. Express yourself, and learn more about yourself, through art.

Lifelong learning is the master key that unlocks every door you encounter on your journey. If you keep it firmly in your hand, you will discover worlds of knowledge—and a place for yourself within them.

You are part of a world community of people who depend on one another. Giving what you can of your time, energy, and resources to those who need help makes you a valued community member.

How can you *make a difference* in your community?

Everyday life is demanding. You can become so caught up in your own issues that you neglect to pay attention to anything else. However, you can make a difference in your **community**—by helping others; being an active, involved citizen; and doing your share for the environment.

COMMUNITY

(1) A group of people living in the same locality.

(2) A group of people having common interests.

(3) A group of people forming a distinct segment of society.

You can help others

What you do for others has enormous impact. Giving others hope, comfort, or help can improve their ability to cope. Reaching out to others can also enhance your career. Being involved in causes and the community shows caring and community spirit, qualities companies look for in people they hire.

You can help others by volunteering, participating in service learning, and setting an example in how you live your life.

Volunteering. Look for a volunteering activity that you can fit into your schedule. Key 12.2 lists organizations that provide volunteer opportunities; you might also look into more local efforts or private clearinghouses that set up smaller projects.

Never doubt that a small group of committed citizens can change the world; indeed, it's the only thing that ever has.

MARGARET MEAD

- Amnesty International
- Women's shelters
- Big Brothers and Big Sisters
- Canadian Blood Services
- Canadian AIDS Society
- Churches, synagogues, temples, and affiliated organizations such as the YM/YWCA

- Educational support organizations
- Environmental awareness/support organizations such as Greenpeace
- Food banks
- Hospitals
- Hotlines
- Kiwanis/Knights of Columbus/Lions Club/Rotary

- Libraries
- Meals on Wheels
- Nursing homes
- Planned Parenthood
- Scouting organizations
- Share Our Strength/other food donation organizations
- Shelters and organizations supporting the homeless

Service learning. In the past few years, looking for a way to help students become involved citizens as well as successful learners, many colleges have instituted *service learning* programs. These are sometimes referred to as citizenship courses or volunteer hours. The basic concept of service learning is to provide the community with service and the students with knowledge, creating positive change for both and including specific opportunities for students to reflect on and analyze their experiences.[3] Service learning builds a sense of civic responsibility, helps students learn useful skills through doing, and promotes values exploration and personal change. Service learning is a "win–win" situation—everyone has something to gain.

You can get involved locally and nationally

Being an active citizen is another form of involvement. On a local level, you might take part in your community's debate over saving open space from developers. On a provincial level, you might contact legislators about building sound barriers along a highway that runs through your town. On a national level, you might write letters to your MP to urge support of an environmental, energy, or health bill. Work for political candidates who adopt the views you support, and consider running for office yourself—in your city, provincially, or nationally.

Most important, vote in every election. Your votes and your actions can make a difference—and getting involved will bring you the power and satisfaction of being a responsible Canadian citizen. Having the right to vote places you in a privileged minority among people around the world who have no voice in how they live.

You can help to preserve your environment

Your environment is your home. When you help to maintain a clean, safe, and healthy place to live, your actions have an impact not only on your

get analytical! **EVALUATE YOUR INVOLVEMENT IN COMMUNITIES**[4]

Look closely at your ties to communities that are important to you.

Thinking about the definition of "community" that you read in the margin on page XXX, come up with a list of communities to which you belong—professional, family, spiritual, academic, athletic, political, and so on. Write them here.

_____

_____

_____

Choose two of these communities that are especially important to you. On a separate sheet of paper, answer the following questions for each community. These questions will help you analyze your involvement and how you and your communities benefit.

- How do I help others in this community?
- How do others in this community help me?
- Do I get more than I give, or give more than I get, from this community?
- What about this community concerns me?
- What have I done, or can I do, to address my concerns?
- What is the extent of my commitment to this community and to its success?

immediate surroundings but also on others around you and on the future of the planet. Every environmentally aware person, saved bottle, and reused bag is a step in the right direction. Take responsibility for what you can control—your own habits—and develop sound practices that contribute to the health of the environment.

Recycle anything that you can. Many communities have some kind of recycling program. If you live on campus, your college may have its own recycling program set up. What you can recycle—plastics, aluminum, glass, newspapers, magazines, other scrap paper—depends on how extensive the program is. Products that use recycled materials are often more expensive, but if they are within your price range, try to reward the company's dedication by purchasing them.

Respect the outdoors. Use products that reduce chemical waste. Pick up after yourself. Through volunteering, voicing your opinion, or making monetary donations, support the maintenance of parks and the preservation of natural, undeveloped land. Be creative: One young woman planned a cleanup of a local lakeside area as the main group activity for the guests at her birthday party (she joined them, of course). Everyone benefits when each person takes responsibility for maintaining the fragile earth.

Remember that valuing yourself is the base for valuing all other things. Improving the earth is possible when you value yourself and think you deserve the best living environment possible. Part of valuing yourself is doing whatever you can to create the life you want to live. Activating your successful intelligence and developing your personal mission are two ways to guide yourself to that life.

How can you continue to activate your *successful intelligence?*

hroughout this text you have connected analytical, creative, and practical thinking to academic and life skills. You have put them together in order to solve problems and make decisions. You have seen how these skills, balanced and used consistently, can help you succeed.

As you complete your work in the course, know that you are only just beginning your career as a successfully intelligent learner. You will continue to discover the best ways to use your analytical, creative, and practical thinking skills to achieve goals that are meaningful to you.

Robert Sternberg has found that successfully intelligent people, despite differences in thinking and in personal goals, have several particular characteristics in common. He calls them "self-activators"—things that get you moving and keep you going. According to Sternberg, successfully intelligent people:[5]

1. *Motivate themselves.* They make things happen, spurred on by a desire to succeed and a love of what they are doing.

2. *Learn to control their impulses.* Instead of going with their first quick response, they sit with a question or problem. They allow time for thinking and let ideas surface before making a decision.

3. *Know when to persevere.* When it makes sense, they push past frustration and stay on course, confident that success is in their sights. They also are able to see when they've hit a dead end—and, in those cases, to stop pushing.

4. *Know how to make the most of their abilities.* They understand what they do well and capitalize on it in school and in work.

5. *Translate thought into action.* Not only do they have good ideas, they are also able to turn those ideas into practical actions that bring ideas to fruition.

6. *Have a product orientation.* They want results; they focus on what they are aiming for rather than on how they are getting there.

7. *Complete tasks and follow through.* With determination, they finish what they start. They also follow through to make sure all the loose ends are tied and the goal has been achieved.

8. *Are initiators.* They commit to people, projects, and ideas. They make things happen rather than sitting back and waiting for things to happen to them.

9. *Are not afraid to risk failure.* Because they take risks and sometimes fail, they often enjoy greater success and build their intellectual capacity. Like everyone, they make mistakes—but tend not to make the same mistake twice.

10. *Don't procrastinate.* They are aware of and avoid the negative effects of putting things off. They create schedules that allow them to accomplish what's important on time.

11. *Accept fair blame.* They strike a balance between never accepting blame and taking the blame for everything. If something is their fault, they accept the responsibility and don't make excuses.

12. *Reject self-pity.* When something goes wrong, they find a way to solve the problem. They don't get caught in the energy drain of feeling sorry for themselves.

13. *Are independent.* They can work on their own and think for themselves. They take responsibility for their own schedule and tasks.

14. *Seek to surmount personal difficulties.* They keep things in perspective, looking for ways to remedy personal problems and separate them from their professional lives.

15. *Focus and concentrate to achieve their goals.* They create an environment in which they can best avoid distraction and they focus steadily on their work.

16. *Spread themselves neither too thin nor too thick.* They strike a balance between doing too many things, which results in little progress on any of them, and too few things, which can reduce the level of accomplishment.

17. *Have the ability to delay gratification.* While they enjoy the smaller rewards that require less energy, they focus the bulk of their work on the goals that take more time but promise the most gratification.

18. *Have the ability to see the forest and the trees.* They are able to see the big picture and to avoid getting bogged down in tiny details.

19. *Have a reasonable level of self-confidence and a belief in their ability to accomplish their goals.* They believe in themselves enough to get through the tough times, while avoiding the kind of overconfidence that stalls learning and growth.

20. *Balance analytical, creative, and practical thinking.* They sense what to use and when to use it. When problems arise, they combine all three skills to arrive at solutions.

Make these characteristics your personal motivational tools. Return to them when you need reactivation. Use them to make sure that you move ahead toward the goals that mean most to you.

How can you *create and live* your personal mission?

If the trees are your goals, then the forest is the big picture of what you are aiming for in life—your personal mission. To define your mission, craft a *personal mission statement.*

Dr. Stephen Covey, author of *The Seven Habits of Highly Effective People*, defines a mission statement as a philosophy outlining what you

JENNIFER ARMOUR   University of Guelph, Guelph, Ontario

Do thoughts of your future path after school cause you stress? What steps are you taking now to prepare yourself for life after graduation?

Of course thoughts about my future frustrate me and cause me stress all the time! I don't think a day goes by that I don't worry about what I'm going to do after I graduate or someone asks, "So what exactly are you going to do with this degree?" Unfortunately, our society never thinks positively about the workforce, which creates a tremendous amount of pressure on students. One is more inclined to hear, "It's so hard to find a job nowadays," "The unemployment rate rose again," and "All that money for an education when there aren't any job opportunities in your field." Honestly, I really don't know what kinds of jobs are going to be available after graduation since the world is constantly changing. My plan, though, is to remain positive and ambitious, and not be afraid to take risks.

To prepare myself for the real world, I'm focusing on the areas I'm interested in and looking for connections that may open doors in the future. I'm also looking into some entry-level positions to familiarize myself with certain aspects of my field, so I'll be better prepared when it comes time to find a job. I ask questions and study hard because I believe the knowledge I've acquired will make me an asset to the workforce. If I could give one piece of advice to anyone about the future, it would be to have the courage to pursue your dreams even when they seem unattainable. So just remember that you are not alone in your worries about the future. Make the most out of each day and reach for your goals because they will lead to greater things.

want to be (character), what you want to do (contributions and achievements), and the principles by which you live (your values). He describes the statement as "a personal constitution, the basis for making major, life-directing decisions."[6]

Here is a mission statement written by Carol Carter, one of the authors of *Keys to Success*.

> My mission is to use my talents and abilities to help people of all ages, stages, backgrounds, and economic levels achieve their human potential through fully developing their minds and their talents. I aim to create opportunities for others through work, service, and family. I also aim to balance work with people in my life, understanding that my family and friends are a priority above all else.

How can you start formulating a mission statement? Try using Covey's three aspects of personal mission as a guide. Think through the following:

- **Character.** What aspects of character do you think are most valuable? When you consider the people you admire most, which of their qualities stand out?

get practical!

EXPLORE YOUR PERSONAL MISSION

Work toward a concrete description of your most important life goals.

As a way of exploring what you most want out of life, consider one or more of the following questions, which ask you to look back at the life you imagined you would have. Freewrite some answers on a separate piece of paper.

1. You are at your retirement dinner. You have had an esteemed career in whatever you ended up doing in your life. Your best friend stands up and talks about the five aspects of your character that have taken you to the top. What do you think they are?

2. You are preparing for a late-in-life job change. Updating your résumé, you need to list your contributions and achievements. What would you like them to be?

3. You have been told that you have one year to live. Talking with your family, you reminisce about the values that have been central to you in your life. Based on that discussion, how do you decide you want to spend your time in this last year? How will your choices reflect what is most important to you?

Thinking about your answers, draft a personal mission statement here, up to a few sentences long, that reflects what you want to achieve in life. Focus on the practical—on what you want to do and the effects you want to have on the world.

_____

_____

_____

_____

_____

_____

- **Contributions and achievements.** What do you want to accomplish in your life? Where do you want to make a difference?
- **Values.** How do the values you established in your work in Chapter 2 inform your life goals? What in your mission could help you live according to what you value most highly? For example, if you value community involvement, your mission may reflect a life goal of holding elected office, which may translate into an interim goal of running for class office at college.

Because what you want out of life changes as you move from one phase to the next—from single person to spouse, from student to working citizen—your personal mission should remain flexible and open to revision. If you frame your mission statement carefully so that it truly reflects your goals, it can be your guide in everything you do, helping you to live with integrity and to work to achieve your personal best.

Live with integrity

Having integrity puts your **ethics** into day-to-day action. When you act with integrity, you earn trust and respect from others. If people can trust

ETHICS

A system of moral values; a sense of what is right to do.

PERSONAL TRIUMPH

SHANIA TWAIN   country/pop recording artist

"I'm always trying to explore new things." That's Shania Twain's philosophy on life and learning. It's a remarkable comment from the Canadian Grammy award winner who has sold more than 50 million records worldwide to both country and pop music fans. Her fourth album Up *was released in late 2002. But like most people, Twain's life has had its share of "ups" and "downs."*

In 1965, Eileen Regina Edwards was born in Windsor, Ontario, to Sharon and Clarence Edwards. When she was two, her parents divorced and Eileen moved to Timmins with her mom and her two sisters. In 1971, her mom married Jerry Twain, who was an Ojibwa Indian.

Her stepdad was often between jobs and there were times when the family had troubles making ends meet. Frequently, there wasn't enough money or food to send her to school with a lunch. Twain remembers walking home from school and wishing her family had a "roast beef house." That refers to being able to smell what other people in the neighbourhood were having for supper. Unfortunately, her family didn't experience that often. She also remembers a time a friend from school had spent the night and was pouring herself a glass of milk in the morning. Twain remembers, "It was such an indulgence in my eyes. So I grabbed the glass and said, 'You can't have that. We have to share.'"

However, Twain didn't let these obstacles get in the way of her dream. Besides going to school, Twain was already working hard at refining her singing talents. By the time she was just 8, she was singing in the bars and taverns of Northern Ontario. Her mom used to wake her up around 11:30 p.m. and take her to the bars after midnight, when bars used to stop selling liquor and it was legal for minors to be there. By the time she

was in high school, she was in a cover band called, ironically enough, "Longshot," and she had sung on the CBC to a national audience on the Tommy Hunter Show.

When she was 21, life dealt her a crushing blow. Her mother and stepfather were both killed in a car crash. Twain was left to raise her two younger brothers, Mark and Darryl. According to Twain, "I felt totally lost, I was on automatic pilot, doing what I had to do. It was a stressful time. What I learned through all of it was how strong I was capable of being." It was during this period that she would eventually embrace the Ojibwa name "Shania," out of respect for her stepfather and his native culture.

Through all these difficult times, Twain continued singing at clubs, resorts and bars around Ontario. In 1991, she caught the ear of a Nashville producer and in 1993, her debut album, simply called *Shania Twain*, was released. It wasn't a big seller, but it led to a meeting with producer and future husband Robert "Mutt" Lange. The two soul mates married in December of 1993, only nine months after meeting each other.

Since that time, Twain has worked hard to achieve and maintain her success. Her albums *Come on Over, The Woman in Me,* and *Up!* have sold millions of copies and have won Grammy and Juno awards. She's not only in control of her professional life, but her personal one. She took a break from the spotlight touring and recording and started a family of her own. She and Robert had a son, Eja, in 2001. Shortly after Eja's arrival, Shania and Robert went to work on her fourth album, *Up.*

As Twain has shown over the years, anything is possible if you have the desire and passion to live your mission. Incidentally, in Ojibwa, Shania means, "I'm on my way." Are you now on your way?

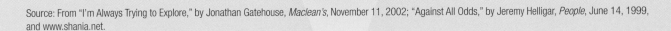

Source: From "I'm Always Trying to Explore," by Jonathan Gatehouse, *Maclean's*, November 11, 2002; "Against All Odds," by Jeremy Helligar, *People*, June 14, 1999, and www.shania.net.

you to be honest, to be sincere in what you say and do, and to consider the needs of others, they will be more likely to encourage you, support your goals, and reward your work.

Living with integrity helps you believe in yourself and in your ability to make good choices. A person of integrity isn't a perfect person, but is one who makes the effort to live according to values and principles, continually striving to learn from mistakes and to improve. Take responsibility for making the right moves, and you will follow your mission with strength and conviction.

And life is what we make it, always has been, always will be.

GRANDMA MOSES

Aim for your personal best in everything you do. As a lifelong learner, you will always have a new direction in which to grow and a new challenge to face. Seek constant improvement in your personal, educational, and professional life. Dream big, knowing that incredible things are possible for you if you think positively and act with successful intelligence. Enjoy the richness of life by living each day to the fullest, developing your talents and potential into the achievement of your most valued goals.

Dave E. Redekopp, Barrie Day, and Marnie Robb of Edmonton's Life-Role Development Group sum up the main points of this chapter with their "High Five" checklist:[7]

- **Change is constant.** Remember to be flexible. It will help you adapt to the changes that will occur in your personal or professional life.
- **Follow your heart.** Create and live out your personal mission.
- **Focus on the journey.** While goal setting is important, it's also important to enjoy what life offers you.
- **Stay learning.** Remember that learning is a lifelong process. It helps us grow as people.
- **Be an ally.** Spend time with friends and family and remember to get involved in your local community.

改善

Kaizen is the Japanese word for "continual improvement." Striving for excellence, finding ways to improve on what already exists, and believing that you can effect change are at the heart of the industrious Japanese spirit. The drive to improve who you are and what you do provides the foundation of a successful future.

Think of this concept as you reflect on yourself, your goals, your life-long education, your career, and your personal pursuits. Create excellence and quality by continually asking yourself, "How can I improve?" Living by *kaizen* helps you to be a respected friend and family member, a productive and valued employee, and a truly contributing member of society. You can change the world.

Developing Successful Intelligence

PUTTING IT ALL TOGETHER

Learn from the experiences of others. Look back to Shania Twain's Personal Triumph on page 367. After you've read her story, relate her experience to your own life by completing the following:

Step 1. Think it through: *Analyze your experience and compare it to Shania's.* How does she try to explore new things? How could that philosophy be applied to your life? How can this help you activate your successful intelligence?

Step 2. Think out of the box: *Imagine ways to contribute.* Think about the ways in which you could serve. How might your talents and skills give something to others? Brainstorm ideas about how you could use what you do well to help others in your community. How can you take your skills and talents to try new things that might make a difference in your community?

Step 3. Make it happen: *Make a practical plan to get involved.* Decide on a specific way to help others, then form a plan to pursue this goal. As you think about your decision, consider how you will "try to explore new things": Write down what you intend to do and the specific steps you will take to do it and live your personal mission.

create your future

Team Building

Giving back. In your group, research volunteering opportunities in your community. Each group member should choose one possibility to research. Answer questions such as the following: What is the situation or organization? What are its needs? Do any volunteer positions require an application, letters of reference, or background checks? What is the time commitment? Is any special training involved? Are there any problematic or difficult elements to this experience?

When you have the information, meet together so that each group member can describe each volunteering opportunity to the other members. Choose one that you feel you will have the time and ability to try next semester. Name your choice and tell why you selected it.

Writing

Record your thoughts on a separate piece of paper or in a journal.

Your learning for life. Review the strategies for lifelong learning on pages xx-xy. Which three do you feel you already do well? Which three do you think you need to develop further? For the three you want to develop, brainstorm ideas for how you will grow in those areas. Include your prediction for how this effort will benefit you.

Career Portfolio

Complete the following in your electronic portfolio or on separate sheets of paper. When you have finished, read through your entire career portfolio. You have gathered information to turn to again and again on your path to a fulfilling, successful career.

A Wheel for Life. In Key 12.3 you see a blank Wheel of Life. Without looking at the first wheel from the beginning of the semester, evaluate yourself as you are right now, after completing this course: Where would you rank yourself in the eight categories? After you have finished, compare this wheel with your previous wheel. Look at the changes: Where have you grown? How has your self-perception changed? Let what you learn from this new wheel inform you about what you have accomplished and what you plan for the future.

Continue to update your Wheel of Life so that it reflects your growth and development, helping to guide you through the changes that await you in the future. Add or change the categories as your college, career, and life priorities evolve.

Use this wheel to evaluate your progress.

Rate yourself in each area of the wheel on a scale of 1 to 10, 1 being least developed (near the centre of the wheel) and 10 being most developed (the outer edge of the wheel). In each area, at the level of the number you choose, draw a curved line and fill in the wedge below that line. Be honest—this is for your benefit only. Finally, look at what your wheel says about the balance in your life. If this were a real wheel, how well would it roll?

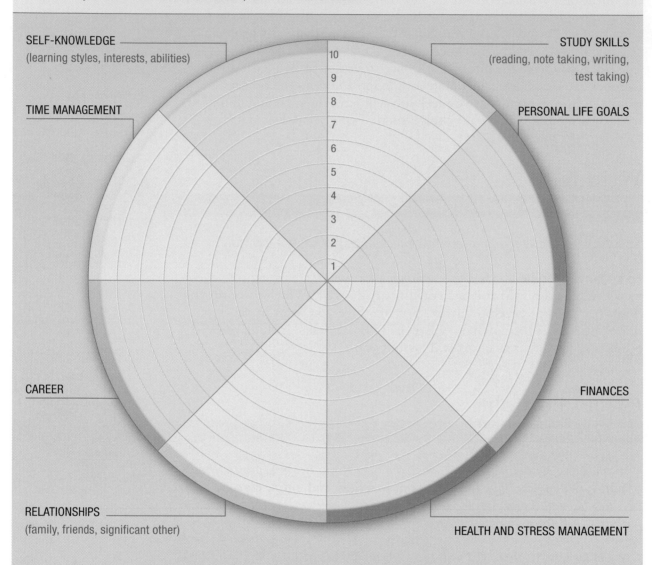

SELF-KNOWLEDGE
(learning styles, interests, abilities)

TIME MANAGEMENT

CAREER

RELATIONSHIPS
(family, friends, significant other)

STUDY SKILLS
(reading, note taking, writing, test taking)

PERSONAL LIFE GOALS

FINANCES

HEALTH AND STRESS MANAGEMENT

Source: Based on "The Wheel of Life" model developed by the Coaches Training Institute, © Co-Active Space 2000.

SUGGESTED READINGS

Blaustein, Arthur I. *Make a Difference: America's Guide to Volunteering and Community Service.* San Francisco: Jossey-Bass, 2003.

Delany, Sarah, and Elizabeth Delany, with Amy Hill Hearth. *Book of Everyday Wisdom.* New York: Kodansha America, 1996.

Jones, Laurie Beth. *The Path: Creating Your Mission Statement for Work and for Life.* New York: Hyperion, 1998.

Moore, Thomas. *Care of the Soul: How to Add Depth and Meaning to Your Everyday Life.* New York: HarperCollins, 1998.

Wheatley, Margaret J., and Myron Kellner-Rogers. *A Simpler Way.* San Francisco: Berrett-Koehler Publishers, 1998.

INTERNET RESOURCES

Volunteer Canada is dedicated to volunteerism in Canada: **www.volunteer.ca**

Helping out in your community can be easy as donating blood: **www.bloodservices.ca**

Help out someone in need of guidance and support. Big Brothers and Big Sisters can always us an extra person: **www.bbbsc.ca**

Need help with career development? Check out Edmonton's Life Role Development Group: **www.life-role.com**

ENDNOTES

1. Margaret J. Wheatley and Myron Kellner-Rogers, "A Simpler Way," *Weight Watchers Magazine* 30.3 (1997), pp. 42–44.

2. Linton Weeks, "The No-Book Report: Skim It and Weep," *Washington Post*, May 14, 2001 p. C8.

3. National Service Learning Clearinghouse, "Service Learning Is..." 2004 [on-line]. Available at: **www.servicelearning.org/article/archive/35/** (May 2004).

4. Adapted from Katherine Woodward Thomas, *Calling In the One.* New York: Three Rivers Press, 2004, pp. 298–299.

5. List and descriptions based on Robert J. Sternberg, *Successful Intelligence.* New York: Plume, 1997, pp. 251–269.

6. Stephen Covey, *The Seven Habits of Highly Effective People.* New York: Simon & Schuster, 1989, pp. 70–144, 309–318.

7. Adapted from Dave E. Redekopp, Barrie Day, and Marnie Robb' s *The High Five of Career Development*, available at: **http://www.life-role.com/documents/High%20Five.pdf**

SUCCESSFUL INTELLIGENCE

Demonstrate What You Know in an Oral Exam

In an oral exam, your instructor asks you to verbally present your responses to exam questions or to discuss a pre-assigned topic. Exam questions may be similar to essay questions on written exams. They may be broad and general, or they may focus on a narrow topic that you are expected to explore in depth.

The material in this Study Break is designed to help you master the skills you need in order to perform well during an oral exam. These skills have lifelong benefits. The more comfortable you are speaking in front of instructors, the more prepared you will be for any kind of public speaking situation—in school, in the community, and at work.

Keep in mind that if you have a documented learning disability that limits your ability to express yourself effectively in writing, you may need to take all your exams orally. Speak with your advisor and instructors to set up an oral exam schedule.

Preparation strategies

Because oral exams require that you speak logically and to the point, your instructors will often give you the exam topic in advance and may even allow you to bring your notes to the exam room. Other instructors ask you to study a specified topic and they then ask questions about the topic during the exam.

Speaking in front of others—even an audience of one, your instructor—involves developing a presentation strategy before you enter the exam room:

Learn your topic. Study for the exam until you have mastered the material. Nothing can replace subject mastery as a confidence booster.

Plan your presentation. Dive into the details. Brainstorm your topic if it is pre-assigned, narrow it with the prewriting strategies you learned in Chapter 7, determine your central idea or argument, and write an outline that will be the basis of your talk. If the exam uses a question-and-answer format, make a list of the most likely questions, and formulate the key points of your response.

Do, or do not. There is no "try."

YODA (*THE EMPIRE STRIKES BACK*)

Use clear thinking. Make sure your logic is solid and that your evidence supports your thesis. Work on an effective beginning and ending that focus on the exam topic.

Draft your thoughts. To get your thoughts organized for the exam, make a draft, using "trigger" words or phrases that will remind you of what you want to say.

Practise your presentation

The element of performance distinguishes speaking from writing. As in any performance, practice is essential. Use the following strategies to guide your efforts:

Know the parameters. How long do you have to present your topic? Where will you be speaking? Will you have access to a podium, table, chair, or white board?

Use index cards or notes. If your instructor doesn't object, bring note cards to the presentation. Keep them out of your face, however; it's tempting to hide behind them.

Pay attention to the physical. Your body positioning, voice, eye contact, and what you wear contribute to the impression you make; therefore, try to look good and sound good.

Time your practice sessions to determine whether you should add or cut material. If you are given your topic in advance, make sure you can state your points in the allotted time. During the exam, make sure you don't speak too quickly.

Try to be natural. Use words you are comfortable with to express concepts you know. Be yourself as you show your knowledge and enthusiasm for the topic.

Be prepared for questions

After your formal presentation, your instructor may ask you topic-related questions. Your responses and the way you handle the questions will affect your grade. Here are some strategies for answering questions effectively:

Take the questions seriously. The exam is not over until the question-and-answer period ends.

Jot down keywords from the questions. This is especially important if the question has several parts, and you intend to address one part at a time.

Ask for clarification. Ask the instructor to rephrase a question you don't understand.

Think before you speak. Take a moment to organize your thoughts and to write down keywords for the points you want to cover.

Answer only part of a question if that's all you can do. Emphasize what you know best and impress the instructor with your depth of knowledge. If you draw a blank, simply tell the instructor that you don't know the answer.

Handling your nerves during an exam

If you are nervous, there are things you can do to help yourself:

Keep your mind on your presentation, not yourself. Focus on what you want to say and how you want to say it.

Take deep breaths right before you begin, and carry a bottle of water. Deep breathing will calm you, and the water will ease a dry mouth.

Visualize your own success. Create a powerful mental picture of yourself acing the exam. Then visualize yourself speaking with knowledge, confidence, and poise.

Establish eye contact with your instructor and realize that he or she wants you to succeed. You'll relax when you feel that your instructor is on your side.

Decide how well these techniques work for you

Practice makes perfect, especially when it comes to public speaking. Gauge your ability to speak effectively during an oral exam with the following team exercise:

- Team up with another student to prepare for a written essay, then quiz each other as if you were taking an actual oral exam. How did your partner evaluate your presentation? What were your strengths? Your weaknesses?
- Do you think that your answers demonstrated all you know about the subject or that you could have done better in writing? If you answered the latter, what obstacles prevented you from doing your best in your oral presentation?
- Describe three actions you will take to improve your next presentation.

1. _____

2. _____

3. _____

SELF STUDY QUIZ

MULTIPLE CHOICE

Circle or highlight the answer that seems to fit best.

1. Students who experience stereotype vulnerability may
   A. call attention to themselves as members of a minority group.
   B. be self-conscious because they see themselves as underachievers.
   C. feel superior to others because of their minority status.
   D. distance themselves from the qualities they think others associate with their group and avoid asking for help because they fear perpetuating a group stereotype.

2. The goal of stress management is to
   A. eliminate all stress from your life.
   B. focus only on school-related stress.
   C. learn to blame all stressful situations on others.
   D. develop strategies for handling the stresses that are an inevitable part of life.

3. Emotional intelligence is defined by Daniel Goleman, as a combination of
   A. empathy and social skills.
   B. self-regulation and motivation.
   C. Thinker qualities and Giver qualities.
   D. personal competence and social competence.

4. *Networking* can be defined as
   A. visiting your instructor during office hours.
   B. the exchange of information or services among individuals, groups, or institutions.
   C. discovering your ideal career.
   D. making a strategic plan.

5. Being flexible in the face of change involves
   A. changing your direction when you encounter obstacles in your life and work.
   B. acknowledging the change and assessing what new needs it brings.
   C. reacting in a way that you have seen work for others.
   D. focusing on an aspect of your life not affected by the change.

6. To be open to unpredictability,
   A. put your energy into building existing relationships.
   B. make a plan and stick with it even in the face of change.
   C. focus on what is rather than on what is supposed to be.
   D. don't let surprises throw you off.

FILL-IN-THE-BLANK

Complete the following sentences with the appropriate word(s) or phrase(s) that best reflect what you have learned. Choose from the items that follow each sentence.

1. _____ factors play an important role in how _____ are interpreted. (Personal/body movements, Biological/verbal cues, Cultural/non-verbal cues)

2. _____ criticism involves goodwill suggestions for improvement. (Non-constructive, Direct, Constructive)

3. The three most common eating disorders are _____, _____, and _____. (anorexia nervosa/food allergies/binge drinking, anorexia nervosa/bulimia/binge eating, constant dieting/eating too much fat/bulimia)

4. Two effective ways to build career knowledge and experience are _____ and _____. (job hunting/networking, internships/volunteering, learning style/critical thinking)

5. The debt ceiling a credit card company places on your account is called a _____. (cash advance, account balance, credit limit)

ESSAY QUESTIONS

The following essay questions will help you organize and communicate your ideas in writing, just as you must do on an essay test. Before you begin answering a question, spend a few minutes planning (brainstorm possible approaches, write a thesis statement, jot down main thoughts in outline or think link form). To prepare yourself for actual test conditions, limit writing time to no more than 30 minutes per question.

1. Discuss the mind–body connection—specifically, the impact of diet, exercise, sleep, and medical care on the development and management of stress. Describe the changes you hope to make in your stress-management plan as a result of the information you have read in this textbook.

2. Choose three important skills you have developed during this course. Explain how they will contribute to your success for the remainder of your post-secondary experience and beyond.

Answer Key

For Self Study Quizzes

Page 128

MULTIPLE CHOICE	FILL-IN-THE-BLANK
1. D	1. commitment
2. A	2. initiative
3. D	3. learning preferences/personality traits
4. A	4. interests/abilities
5. C	5. mission
6. A	6. flexible

Page 261

MULTIPLE CHOICE	FILL-IN-THE-BLANK
1. D	1. taking in information/asking questions about information/using information
2. B	2. creativity
3. A	3. context
4. D	4. cue column
5. B	5. mnemonic device
6. C	6. Freewriting/uncensored/planning

Page 377

MULTIPLE CHOICE	FILL-IN-THE-BLANK
1. D	1. Cultural/non-verbal cues
2. D	2. Constructive
3. D	3. anorexia nervosa/bulimia/binge eating
4. B	4. internships/volunteering
5. B	5. credit limit
6. C	

Index

A

AA. *See* Alcoholics Anonymous (AA)
Abstracts, 200
Academic integrity. *See* Integrity, academic
Acceptance, 327
Achievements, personal, 366
Acquired immune deficiency syndrome (AIDS), 200, 316
  see also Human immunodeficiency virus (HIV)
Acronyms, 187–188, 189
ADD. *See* Attention deficit disorder
Addiction Research Foundation, 308
Addiction, 308
  identifying and overcoming, 312–313
Aesop, 344
AIDS. *See* Acquired immune deficiency syndrome (AIDS)
Alcohol, 306–308, 310
Alcoholics Anonymous (AA), 312–313
Algonquin College, Ottawa, ON, 182
Allen, Woody, 8
Alta Vista, 202
Altschuler, Glenn C., 50
American Psychiatric Association, 309
American Psychological Association (APA), 215
Amnesty International, 361
Analogy, 104
Analytical thinking, 8, 9
Anger management, 283, 284
Anorexia nervosa, 305–306
Anxiety. *See* Test anxiety
AOL Canada, 202
APA. *See* American Psychological Association (APA)
Apprenticeship of Duddy Kravitz, The, 200
Armour, Jennifer, 365
Assertiveness, 282, 283
Assessments, 65, 66
  personality, 66, 67–68
  scoring, 68
  see also Test questions
Assumptions, 99–100
  personal, 100–101
Astronomy Today, 258

ATDs. *See* Automatic teller machines (ATDs)
Attention deficit disorder (ADD), 166
Atwood, Margaret, 33
Audience, 205, 206
Australia, 36
Automatic teller machines (ATDs), 344

B

Bachman, Randy, 97
Back matter, 143
Bank accounts, 344, 345
Bard College, New York, 203
Bates, Marilyn, 68
BC. *See* British Columbia
Beel, Sonya, 345
Behaviour, 35, 278
Benson, Dr. Herbert, 302
Berkana Institute, The, Washington, 356
Berle, Milton, 338
Bias(ed), 100
BiblioCentre, 200
Bibliography, 143
Big Brothers, 361
Big Sisters, 361
Binge eating, 306
Birth control, 314, 315
Bishop, Dr. Joyce, 68, 69, 72, 86, 88
Blackberry, (handheld device), 104
Block, Judy R., 36, 153, 281
Body language, 279, 280, 282
Books in Print, 199
Boolean operators, 204
Boom, Bust and Echo 2000: Profiting from the Demographic Shift in the New Millennium, 20
Boone, Louis E., 36, 153, 281
Botstein, Leon, 203
Boyd, Monica, 266
Brainstorming, 104, 105, 173, 206–209, 217, 222, 225, 248, 283, 297, 304, 324, 340, 342, 375
Brazil, 36
Brett, Alicia, 219
Briggs, Katharine, 68
British Columbia (BC), 192
Buddha, 301

Budgeting, 337–338, 339, 340, 339–341—343–357
  successful, 342–344
Buffalo Springfield, 98
Bulimia, 306
Burka, Jane B., 48
Burnout, 304
Burns, Daniel, 20
Bush, George W., 147

C

Calgary, 289
Campbell, Colin, 346
Canada Yearbook, 199
Canada, 36, 133
  alcohol use in, 308, 310
  culture in, 35
  debt in, 346
  diversity in, 265, 266, 267
  food guide for, 299
  foreign policy of, 96
  hate crimes in, 270–271
  immigration to, 266
  internet use in, 201
  job listing web sites in, 332
  multiculturalism in, 35, 274, 359
  nutrition in, 298
  obesity in, 298
  prime ministers of, 201
  rock music in, 97, 98
  sexual assault in, 287
  stress in, 51
  violent crime in, 286
Canadian AIDS Society, 361
Canadian Almanac Directory, 199
Canadian Blood Services, 361
Canadian Broadcasting Corporation (CBC), 367
Canadian Centre for Addiction and Mental Health, 308
Canadian Centre on Substance Abuse, 308
Canadian Charter of Rights and Freedoms, 265, 270
Canadian Criminal Code, 270
Canadian Encyclopaedia Plus, 199
Canadian Federation of Students, 286–287
Canadian Global Almanac, 199
Canadian Journal of Communication, 196

Canadian National Mental Health Association, 51
Canadian Newsdisk, 199
Canadian Oxford Dictionary, 199
Canadian Parliamentary Guide, 199
Canadian Periodical Index, 200
Canadian Social Trends, 199
Canadian Who's Who, 199
Career, 322–356
  areas, 327
  centre, 325, 331
  changes in, 328–329
  exploration strategies, 83, 325
  goals, 28, 60
  learning style and, 329–331
  matching curriculum to, 193
  paths, 324–325, 326
  satisfaction, 331, 332
  skills, 326, 327, 358–357
  success, 5
  timeline, 332
  values, 328
Carlyle, Thomas, 149
Carnegie, Andrew, 183
Carter, Angela, 360
Carter, Carol, 37, 365
Cave, Charles, 103
CBC. *See* Canadian Broadcasting Corporation (CBC)
CD-ROM, 199, 200
Census of Population, 2001, (Canada), 23–25
Center for Academic Integrity, The, Kenan Institute for Ethics, Duke University, North Carolina, 33
Center for Critical Thinking and Moral Critique, 95
Center for Media Literacy, The, 152
Chaisson, Eric, 247
Champlain St. Lambert CEGEP, St. Lambert, QC, 312
Character, 366
China, 36
Chinese, 25
Chisholm, Patricia, 51
Chrétien, Jean, 96, 147–148
Christianity, 197
Churchill, Sir Winston, 127
Citizenship, 7
  involvement, 361, 362
Classroom benefits, 75–77
College, 4, 5, 16, 25–26, 63, 93, 264, 287, 290–297, 323, 355
  budgeting at, 337–338, 339
  career, 133, 236
  diversity at, 266–267
  library, 195, 196, 197, 199–200—201, 205, 232, 314
  minority students at, 273

reading in, 130–131
  support groups on, 312–313
Come on Over, 367
Commitment, 14
Common sense. *See* Thinking, practical
Communication,
  across cultures, 280, 281–282
  effective, 275
  non-verbal, 280
  problems, 275
  skills, 277
  styles, 275, 276, 277
Communicators,
  adventurer-dominant, 276
  giver-dominant, 275, 276
  organizer-dominant, 275, 276
  thinker-dominant, 275, 276
Community, 360
  involvement, 7, 360, 362
Competence,
  personal, 326
  social, 326
Condition of Education, The, 1996, 160
Conference Board of Canada, 5, 6, 31, 63, 77, 93, 160, 163, 195, 231, 265, 297, 324
Conflict management, 282, 283
Conflict resolution, 283
Contemporary Business Communication, 281
Context, 132
Contributions, personal, 366
Coon, Dennis, 104
Copeland, Lennie, 280
Cornell note-taking system, 145, 155, 169, 174–176, 179
  see also Note taking, systems
Cornell University, New York, 175
Counselling, 312
Covey, Dr. Stephen, 365, 366
Cramming, 236, 238, 255
  see also Last-minute studying
Creative thinking. *See* Thinking, creative
Creativity, 103–104
  setting stage for, 106
Credit card management, 345–346, 348
Creditor, 348
Criteria for Substance Dependence and Criteria for Substance Abuse in the Diagnostic and Statistical Manual of Mental Disorders, 309
Critical thinking. *See* Thinking, analytical (critical)
Criticism, 275, 278
  constructive, 278-, 279

non-constructive, 278
receiving, 279
Crosby, Stills, Nash and Young, 98
Cross-training, 301
Cultural competence, 35–36, 268
Culture, 35
  high-context, 36, 280, 281
  low-context, 36, 280, 281
Curriculum, 193

D

Daily, The, 266
Date rape, 286–288
Day, Barrie, 368
de Bono, Edward, 105
Dead Sea Scrolls, 197–198
Debt management, 346–348
Decision making, 114, 116–118, 120–121
DeGeneres, Ellen, 8
Dell, Michael, 107
Depression, 266, 303–305–306
Detox. *See* Detoxification (detox) centres
Detoxification (detox) centres, 312
Dewar, Sir James, 267
Dewey Decimal system, 200
Dictionary, 140–142
Discipline, 19
Discrimination, 267, 270, 271, 272
Diversity, cultural, 35, 36, 265, 266, 268, 269, 270, 359
  adapting to, 271–272
  on campus, 266–267
Dodson, John E., 51
Douglas, Claire, 150
Dowdall, G. W., 308
Down time, 46
Drafting, 211–213, 223, 248
  checklist, 216, 217

E

Eating disorders, 305–306
Ebbinghaus, Herman, 181
Ebsco Host, 200
Economy, global, 23
Ecstasy. *See* Methylenedioxymethamphetamine (MDMA) (Ecstasy)
Editing, 222–221, 222, 249
Educating Yourself about Alcohol and Drugs: A People's Primer, 311
Education, 4, 5, 7, 20, 32–33
  continuing, 358
  costs of, 337, 338
  goals, 4
  income and, 5
  post-graduate, 4
  post-secondary, 7, 13, 21, 163, 243

research as, 195
styles of, 63
values and, 33
writing as, 195
Educational Resources Information
    Center (ERIC), 200
Edwards, Clarence, 367
Edwards, Eileen Regina, (Shania
    Twain), 328, 367, 370
Edwards, Sharon, 367
Edwards, Tryon, 184
Einstein, Albert, 260
Ellesmere Island, NWT, 359
Emerson, Ralph Waldo, 18
Emotional intelligence quotient
    (EQ), 110
Emotional intelligence, 110, 326
Empathy, 326
Empire Strikes Back, The, 375
Employability Skills 2000+ profile.
    5, 6, 31, 63, 77, 93, 265
England, 36
English as a Second Language
    (ESL), 289
English, 133, 253, 289
Enron, 183
Environment preservation, 362–363
EQ. *See* Emotional intelligence
    quotient (EQ)
Equifax Canada, 348
ERIC. *See* Educational Resources
    Information Center (ERIC)
Erindale College, University of
    Toronto, Mississauga, ON,
    201
ESL. *See* English as a Second
    Language (ESL)
Essay questions, 247, 249, 250,
    252–251, 263
Ethics of the Fathers, 155
Ethics, 35, 366–368
Evaluating finances, 339
Exam overview, 240
Excellence, academic, 4
Excite, 202

F
Fact, 99, 100
Failures, learning from, 22–22
Fairness, 33
Farrell, Elizabeth F., 103
Fears, facing your, 17
Financial Post Corporate Reports,
    200
Flexibility, 49, 80, 327, 328, 337,
    356
    change and, 356–358
Foot, David K., 20
Formula, 137
Forseth, Kevin, 42

*Frames of Mind: The Theory of
    Multiple Intelligences,* 69
France, 36
Frank, Steven, 241
Freewriting, 209, 212, 225, 279
French, 317
Freud, Sigmund, 284
Front matter, 143
Fry, Arthur, 103
Fry, Ron, 235

G
Gage Canadian Dictionary, 199
Gandhi, Indira, 280
Gardner, Howard, 66, 69
Gatehouse, Jonathan, 367
Gates, Bill, 8
Generalizations, 269
Georgia, 274
Gerber, Linda, 157, 190
Germany, 36
Ghana, 289
Gibran, Khalil, 233
Glass, Colby, 101
Gledhill-Hoyt, J., 308
Globalization. *See* Economy, global
Glossary, 140
Goals, 30–32–33, 36, 41, 43, 93,
    110–112, 222, 290
    achieving, 39–40
    career, 60, 332
    fulfillment, 80
    life-success, 5–7
    long-term, 37, 44–78, 154
    multiple paths to, 56
    personal, 363, 364
    prioritize, 38, 39
    reading, 134
    reasonable, 48
    see also Education, goals
    setting career, 28, 357
    setting personal, 40, 52
    setting, 31, 327
    short-term, 37, 44, 78, 154
    teamwork, 153
    thinking skills and, 94
Godard, Jean-Luc, 360
Goldberg, Natalie, 221
Goleman, Daniel, 110, 326
Gomery inquiry, 147, 183
Gonzalez, Alejandra, 23
Google, 202, 203
Grammy award, 367
Greek, 119, 140, 156
Greenpeace, 361
Griffin, Anna, 182
Griggs, Lewis, 280
Grigorenko, Elena L., 110
Grisham, John, 137

H
Habits, 14, 15
Hall, Edward, 36
Hancock, Ophelia H., 147
Harris, Philip R., 280
Harris, Robert, 201
Harris, Sherwood, 134
Harvard University,
    Massachusetts, 66
Hate crimes, 270–271, 272
Hawkins, Rita Lenken, 18
Hayes, J. R., 105
Health and Welfare Canada, 298
Health Canada, 299
Health, mental, 303–304, 306
Health, personal, 7, 297–298
    improving, 318–319
    see also Wellness
Healthy eating. *See* Nutrition
    (healthy eating)
Hebrew, 54
Helligar, Jeremy, 367
Henson, Jim, 105
Hesse, Douglas, 148
Hierarchy, 179
High school, 4
Highlighting, 145, 147–146,
    145–147
Hindu, 190
HIV. *See* Human immunodeficiency
    virus (HIV)
Hochman, David, 203
Holliday, Billie, 310
Holmes, T. H., 51
Homer, 202
Honesty, 33–34
Hopper, Grace Murray, 103
Hot Bot, 202
Human immunodeficiency virus
    (HIV), 316
    see also Acquired immune
    deficiency syndrome (AIDS)
Human Resources Development
    Canada, 327, 332
Humanities Index, 200
Hunt, Diana Scharf, 39
Hunter, Dr. William, 95, 108
Hymowitz, Carol, 50

I
Igali, Baraladei Daniel, 190, 191,
    192
Illegal drugs, 310–312
Immigration, 266
Index Medicus, 200
India, 190
Inert intelligence, 8
Information, 137
    analysis, 97–98, 195
    creativity and, 103–104

evaluation of, 101–103
gathering, 97
search strategy, 197–198
Initiative, 16
Integrity, academic, 33, 35, 243, 327
positive consequences of, 35
Integrity, personal, 368
Intellectual property, 214
Intelligence quotient (IQ), 7–8, 119, 326
Intelligence strategies,
multiple for reading, 138
Intelligence, 7–8, 9, 66, 277
see also Thinking, analytical (critical); Thinking, creative; Thinking, practical
successful, 8, 9, 10–11, 93, 94, 95, 97, 119, 195, 363–364
Intelligent guessing, 241–242
Internet Service Providers (ISPs), 202
Internet, 15, 23, 37, 46, 83, 86, 152, 195, 196, 199, 215, 226, 314, 327
evaluation of information, 204–205
job postings on, 332
research, 201–202, 203–204
Internships, 4, 123, 325
Interviews. *See* Jobs, interviews for
Ionesco, Eugène, 360
Ipsos Reid poll, 298
IQ. *See* Intelligence quotient (IQ)
Iran, 289
Iran-Iraq war, 289
Irving, Washington, 33
ISPs. *See* Internet Service Providers (ISPs)
Israel, 106
Italy, 36, 340
Ivory Coast, 289
Izumo, Gary, 328

J
Jack, Stephanie, 248
Jacobs, Gregg D., 302
Japan, 36, 280
Japanese, 156, 370
Jobs, 325–326, 328
interview cover letter, 229–228
interviews for, 335, 350–351
listings, 332
needs, 336–337, 351–352
opportunities, 331
setting boundaries for, 319–320
strategic search plan for, 332, 333
testing for, 256–257
John Hopkins University, Maryland, 309
Johnson, Floyd H., 204
Journal of the American Medical Association, 200

Judaism, 197
Judgement, 36, 268
Juno award, 367

K
Kanungo, Soumik, 312
Keirsey Sorter assessment, 68
Keirsey, David, 68
Keller, Helen, 135
Kellner-Rogers, Myron, 356
Keys to Career Success, 328
Keyword search, 198
King, Dr. Martin Luther, Jr., 271, 274
King, Mark A., 268
Kiwanis clubs, 361
Klee, Paul, 360
Knights of Columbus, 361
Knowledge, 22, 86, 109, 132, 163, 233, 238, 247, 252, 269, 324, 325, 326, 355, 358, 360
acquired, 35
cultural, 271
shared, 155
solidified, 155
Kurtz, David L., 36, 153, 281
Kwantlen University College, Surrey, BC, 248

L
Lange, Robert (Mutt), 367
Lao Tzu, 13
Last-minute studying, 236–238
Latin, 140, 253
Laurence, Margaret, 133
Lazear, David, 72
LD Online (Learning Disabilities Information and Resources), 84, 86
Leadership, 327
Learning Disabilities Association of Canada, The, 86
Learning disabilities, 84, 86, 166
managing, 86
Learning,
from others' experiences, 88, 290–291
lifelong, 358, 360, 368–370
preferences, 64
see also Education
service, 361
styles, 64, 65, 66, 75, 77, 78, 83, 329–331
Lee, H., 308
Leibovich, Lori, 204
Levine, Dr. Mel, 218
Liberal Party of Canada, 147, 191
Library of Congress system, 200
Library. *See* College, library; University, library
Life skills, 4

Life success goals, 5–7
Life-Role Development Group, (Edmonton, AB), 368
Link, Henry C., 240
Listening, 163, 164
challenges of, 165, 166
effective, 166–167
note taking and, 169, 170
personal habits, 168
stages of, 164, 165
Los Angeles riots (1992), 272
Lowery, Lawrence F., 96
Lycos, 202

M
Machine-scored tests, 242–243
Macionis, John J., 157, 158
Maclean's, 196, 200, 367
Maenner, G., 308
Magazines for Libraries, 200
Mahler's Symphony No. 2 *(Resurrection Symphony)*, 106–107
Mahler, Gustav, 106
Major (subject), 61, 77–78, 79, 80, 83, 109, 116
Malekzadeh, Ali, 36
Mars Exploration Rover, 99
MasterCard, 345
Math test anxiety. *See* Test anxiety, math
MBTI. *See* Myers-Briggs Type Inventory (MBTI)
McCarthy, Sheryl, 272
McGill University, Montreal, QC, 50
McKenzie, Diane, 308
McMillan, Steve, 247
MDMA. *See* Methylenedioxy-methamphetamine (MDMA) (Ecstasy)
Mead, Margaret, 361
Meals on Wheels, 361
Media, 152
Memory, 181–183–184
techniques, 137, 163, 181, 184, 185, 186–190, 232
Mental health. *See* Health, mental
Methylenedioxymethamphetamine (MDMA) (Ecstasy), 311
Mexico, 201
Microfiche, 197
Microfilm, 197
Middle East, 106
Minnesota Mining and Manufacturing Company. *See* 3M (Minnesota Mining and Manufacturing Company)
Mitchell, Joni, 97
MLA. *See* Modern Language Association (MLA)
Mnemonic devices, 186–188

Modern Language Association (MLA), 215
Moidel, Steve, 139
Montreal, 266
Morgan, J. P., 183
Morris, Charles G., 74, 245
Moscovich, Ivan, 96
Moses, Grandma, 368
Motivation, 13, 15, 17, 27, 31, 37, 38, 49, 66, 110, 155, 283, 304, 326, 356, 363
Mount Everest, 152
MSN Search, 202
Mulroney, Brian, 201
Multiple Intelligences theory, 14, 66, 67, 68, 69–72, 78, 81
Multiple Pathways to Learning, 66, 71–74
Multiple-choice tests, 242, 261–262
Myers, Isabel Briggs, 68
Myers-Briggs Type Inventory (MBTI), 66, 68
Mynah Birds, The, 98
Myth of Laziness, The, 218

N
NA. *See* Narcotics Anonymous (NA)
Nahavandi, Afsaneh, 36
Napoleon Bonaparte, 358
Narcotics Anonymous (NA), 313
National Center for Cultural Competence, 268
National Center for Learning Disabilities, The, (NCLD), 84, 85, 86
National Service Learning Clearinghouse, 361
NCLD. *See* National Center for Learning Disabilities, The, (NCLD)
Networking, 331, 332
New England Journal of Medicine, 196
Newton, Sir Isaac, 13
Nicholl, Malcolm J., 20
Nichols, Ralph, G., 164
Niebuhr, Reinhold, 306
Nigeria, 190, 191
Noran, Robert T., 280
Note taking, 168–169, 171–173, 179–181, 357
    creating a team for, 192
    reviewing, 173, 234, 236
    revising, 173
    summarizing, 174
    systems, 175–176, 175–176, 178–179
Nutrition (healthy eating), 298

O
Obesity, 298, 300
Ojibwa, 367
Opinion, 99, 100
Oral,
    examination, 374–375, 376, 377
    presentation, 222, 224–225
Osher, David, 268
Ottawa, 346
Overeaters Anonymous, 313

P
Palestine, 106
Palm Pilot, (handheld device), 104
Palmer, Jay, 23
Pauk, Walter, 175
Paul, Dr. Richard, 95
PDA. *See* Personal digital assistant (PDA)
Pelvic inflammatory disease (PID), 316
People, 367
Perception puzzles, 106
Perfectionism, 48
Personal digital assistant (PDA), 42
Personal growth, 4, 7
Personal health. *See* Health, personal
Personal mission, 360, 366–368
Personality spectrum, 66, 67–68, 70–71, 74–73, 74, 78, 275, 276, 329, 330
Personality traits, 64, 66
Personality types, 89–90
Perspective, 99–100
    personal, 100–101
    shifting, 105
Physical exercise, 301, 302
    improving, 303
    types of, 301
Picasso, Pablo, 187
PID. *See* Pelvic inflammatory disease (PID)
Piggrem, Gary W., 245
Pitino, Rick, 18
Plagiarism, 214–216, 215–216
Planned Parenthood, 361
Porter, Eduardo, 352
Positive attitude, 238–239, 327, 359
Positive self-talk, 18
Positive thinking, 18–19
Practical thinking, 8, 9
Prefixes, 140–141
Prejudices, 265, 267, 268, 269, 270, 272
Preparation, 238
Pretest, 236
Prewriting strategies, 206, 209, 210, 211
Primary sources (of texts), 134
Prioritizing, 38, 45

Problem solving, 113–116
    close to home, 291
    group, 121–123
Procrastination, 47–49, 112, 364
Procrastination: Why You Do It and What to Do About It, 48
Progressive Conservative Party of Canada, 201
Prologue, 140
Proofreading, 222
ProQuest, 200
Psychological Abstracts, 200

Q
Questioning, 95, 144, 151, 166–167, 225, 234

R
Rahe, R. H., 51
Rape, 286–288
Reader's Guide to Periodical Literature, 200
Reading comprehension, 132, 147
    choosing setting for, 134–135
    strategies for, 133, 134
Reading, 144–145, 147, 148
    challenges, 137–139
    critically, 150–151, 152
    practically, 137
    purposes, 135, 137
    skills, 160–161
    speed, 139
Reciting, 148–149
Red River College, Winnipeg, MB, 114
Redekopp, Dave E., 368
Relationships, personal, 284, 285, 288
Research, 195
    internet, 201–202, 204–204
    prewriting strategies as, 210
    search strategy for, 198–199
    team, 226
Respect, 33–34
    mutual, 35
Responsibility, 15–16, 33–34, 110
Résumé, compiling, 77, 292, 334
Resurrection Symphony. See Mahler's Symphony No. 2 *(Resurrection Symphony)*
Reviewing, 149–150, 234, 252
Revising, 216–218, 219, 220–221, 222–221, 222, 249
Richler, Mordecai, 200
Rise, Colin, 20
Risk taking, 107–108
Robb, Marnie, 368
Robinson, Francis P., 142
Rohypnol (Roofies), 286
Romeo and Juliet, 188
Roots (of words), 140

Rotary clubs, 361
Ruggiero, Vincent, 95
Russian, 156

S
Safe, staying, 302–303
Sanskrit, 190
Sapolsky, Robert M., 50
Saudi Arabia, 36
SAVE. *See* Suicide Awareness Voices of Education (SAVE)
Savings strategies, 341–342
Scandinavia, 36
Scanning, 142
Scheduling, 41–42, 43, 45
   techniques, 45–47
Schroedter, Gabriel, 114
Schuckit, Marc Alan, 311
Search directories, 202
Search engines, 202
Seeds of Peace, 106
Self-activators, 363
Self-awareness, 77, 326
Self-esteem, 14, 18, 20, 35, 304
Self-knowledge, 40, 271
   wheel of life and, 54–55
Self-management, 31
Self-portrait, 91–91
Self-regulation, 326
Selye, Hans, 50–51
Seneca College, Toronto, ON, 23
Sesame Street, 105
Seven Habits of Highly Effective People, The, 365
Seven Pathways of Learning, 72
Sexual harassment, 285–286
Sexual relationships, 313
   critical thinking and, 313–314
Sexually transmitted diseases (STDs), 313, 314, 315, 316
Shahriari, Tooka, 289, 290–291
Shakespeare, William, 18, 188
Shania Twain, 367
Shanks, Hershel, 197
Share our Strength, 361
Shaw, Nancy E., 287
Sheehy, Gail, 252
Shorthand, 179, 180
Shoshone Indian, 225
Silver, Spencer, 103
Silverman, Rachel Emma, 50
Simon and Schuster Handbook for Writers, 148, 215
Sims, Anthony, 268
Single, Eric, 308
Skidmore College, New York, 52
Skills, 304
   employability, 5
   fundamental, 5
   life-success, 357

personal management, 5
   teamwork, 5
Skimming, 142
Slaboch, Kate, 50
Sleeping, 302, 303, 304
Smith, Thomas M., 160
Social competence, 110, 326
Social Readjustment scale (Holmes-Rahe scale), 51
Sociology, 157, 158
Soloway, Eliot, 204
Source note, 210
Spanish, 86
Spendable income, 338
Sports Illustrated, 137
Sprott-Shaw Community College, Duncan, BC, 42, 345
SQ3R. *See* Survey, question, read, recite, and review (SQ3R) reading technique
St. Francis Xavier University, Antigonish, NS, 219
St. Jerome, 166
St. Lawrence College, Kingston, ON, 287
Standard Periodical Directory, 200
Stanford-Binet IQ test, 66
Starkman, Randy, 191
Statistics Canada, 5, 23, 201, 266, 271
Staying current, 327
STDs *See* Sexually transmitted diseases (STDs)
Stereotyping, 267, 268, 269, 270
Sternberg, Robert J., 8, 9, 94, 101, 103, 106, 107, 110, 119, 363
Stevenson, Robert Louis, 66
Stoffman, Daniel, 20
Stone Angel, The, 133
Stress, 30–31, 41, 42, 45, 49, 50–64, 114, 219, 238, 297, 304, 328
   dealing with, 319
   levels of, 51
   management, 52–54, 238, 297, 301, 307, 312, 345, 365
   relieving, 52
   see also Test anxiety
Strunk, William Jr., 214
Stuart, Eileen M., 302
Student,
   activities, 313
   employment, 335–345
   post-secondary, 4
   returning, 239
Study benefits, 75
Study group, 153
   leaders of, 154
   note taking in, 174
   organizing, 159

participation in, 153–154
   see also Teamwork
   strategies for success of, 154
   tests for, 255–256
Study plan, 233–234
Study Skills Library, California Polytechnic State University, San Luis Obispo, California, 47
Study techniques, 157–159
Subject Guide to Books in Print, 199
Substance abuse, 306–312, 313
Success is Choice, 18
Success, celebrating, 20–21, 22
Successful Intelligence: How Practical and Creative Intelligence Determine Success in Life, 8
Suffixes, 140–141
Suicide Awareness Voices of Education (SAVE), 305
Suicide, 304, 305
Summary, 149, 234
Supreme Court of Canada, 287
Survey, question, read, recite, and review (SQ3R) reading technique, 130, 132, 138, 142, 144, 145, 148, 157, 159, 190, 232, 234, 255
Surveying (reading strategy), 143
Sydnor, William E., 48
Sympatico, 202

T
Tai Chi, 114
Tardif, T. Z., 106
Taugher, Meghan E., 103
Teaching styles, 75
Teamwork, 77, 152–155, 326, 327
   benefits of, 155, 156, 157
   see also Study group
Technology, 23
TechnoTrends: 24 Technologies That Will Revolutionize Our Lives, 20
Test anxiety, 238, 239, 248
   math, 258–261
   returning student and, 239
Test questions, 243
   fill-in-the-blank, 246–247, 255–263
   matching, 246
   multiple-choice, 243–244, 245
   objective, 243
   see also Multiple-choice tests
   subjective, 243
   true-or-false, 245
Test taking, 231, 357
   learning from mistakes, 252, 253
   on-the-job, 256–257

preparation for, 232, 233, 234, 236, 237, 238, 254–255
strategies for, 240, 241, 242, 243
Test type, 232–233
Thesis statement, 210
Thinking, 95, 113–116–115, 116, 118–117, 118–119
  5.6
  analytical (critical), 94, 97, 101–103, 132, 151, 164, 173–205, 234–236, 242, 324, 325, 327, 357
  creative, 8, 9, 94, 103–104, 327
  flexible, 94
  intelligent, 356
    4.16–4.22, 4.25–4.27, 4.31–4.35, 4.39–4.40, 4.43–4.45
  positively, 132
  practical, 94, 108–109, 110, 111, 110–112
Thomas, Katherine Woodward, 362
Thomas, Matt, 94
Thompson, David, 346
Thomson, Roy, 98
Thoreau, Henry David, 133
3M (Minnesota Mining and Manufacturing Company), 103
Three Women, The, 187
Time management, 31, 40, 41, 42, 45, 59–60, 112, 233, 239, 357
Timm, Paul, 41
Timmins, ON, 367
Timoshenko, Gary, 308
Tobacco, 308–310
Togo, 289
Tommy Hunter Show, 367
Toronto Sun, 191
Toronto, 266
TransUnion Canada, 348
Trelease, Jim, 358
Troyka, Lynn Quitman, 148, 203, 207, 215
Trust, mutual, 33, 34
Turkey, 289
Turnbull, Helen, 36
Twain, Jerry, 367
Twain, Shania. *See* Edwards, Eileen Regina, (Shania Twain)
Tyco, 183

U
U.S. National Institute of Health, 304
U.S. National Research Bureau, 23
Ulrich's International Periodicals Directory, 200
Understanding Psychology, 74, 258

Understanding the Dead Sea Scrolls, 197
United States of America, 36, 201, 280
Universal Resource Locator (URL), 202, 205
University of British Columbia, Vancouver, BC, 289
University of Guelph, Guelph, ON, 365
University of Michigan, Michigan, 204
University of Virginia, Virginia, 216
University, 4, 5, 16, 25, 63, 289–290
  budgeting at, 337–338, 339
  career, 133, 236
  diversity at, 266–267
  library, 195, 196, 197, 199–200—201, 205, 232, 314
  minority students at, 273
  support groups on, 312–313
Up!, 367
URL. *See* Universal Resource Locator (URL)
Uto-Aztecna language, 225

V
Values, 32, 37, 366
  career, 328
  cultural diversity and, 35
  education and, 33
  exploring, 34
  identifying and evaluating, 32
  moral, 33
Van Truong, Minh, 308
Vancouver, 266, 289
Verbal signposts, 167
Vickers, Michael, 266
Violent relationships, 286
Virgil, 77
VISA, 345
Visualization, 176–178
Vocabulary, 132
  expand, 139
Vocalization, 139
Voltaire, 116
Volunteering, 326, 360–361
von Goethe, Johann Wolfgang, 324
von Oech, Roger, 104, 105

W
Wall Street Journal, 95
Washington, Irving, 78
Webster's Biographical Dictionary, 199
Wechsler, H., 308
Weeks, Linton, 358
Wellness, 297–298
  see also Health, personal

Wheatley, Margaret J., 356
Wheel of life, 54–56
Wilgoren, Jodi, 50
Windsor, ON, 367
Winter, Greg, 352
Wisdom, 86
Woman in Me, The, 367
Wong, Rita, 206
Working with Emotional Intelligence, 326
Workplace, 326, 331
  benefits, 77
  boundaries, 319–320
  success, 324
  trends, 327–329
World War I, 266
World War II, 188
World Wide Web, 202, 332
Writing, 195
  analytically, 218–219
  conclusion, 213
  editing, 222–221, 222
  elements of effective, 205, 206
  informative, 205
  introduction, 213
  persuasive, 206
  planning stages of, 225
  process, 206–207, 209, 210
  revising, 216–218, 219, 220–221, 222–221, 222

Y
Yahoo!, 202
Yale University, Connecticut, 8
Yerkes, Dr. Robert M., 51
YMCA. *See* Young Men's Christian Association (YMCA)
Yoda, 375
York University, Toronto, ON, 150
Yoshigahara, Nob, 96
Young Men's Christian Association (YMCA), 301, 361
Young Women's Christian Association (YWCA), 361
Young, Neil, 97, 98
Yuen, Lenora M., 48
YWCA. *See* Young Women's Christian Association (YWCA)

Z
Zull, James, 181

Photo Credits

Unless otherwise specified, all photo objects throughout this text are courtesy of Herema Technology © 2001.

Page 2, Dynamic Graphics; p. 30, Michael Stravato/NY Times; p. 36, Wonderfuke/Masterfile; p. 38, Joyce Dopkeen/NY Times; p. 42, Kevin Forseth; p. 52, James Estrin/NY Times; p. 62, Edward Keating/NY Times; p. 86, CP Photo/Fred Chartrand; p. 92, Dynamic Graphics; p. 99, Jonathan Wiggs/Boston Globe; p. 103, Michael Quan/NY Times; p. 130, Wonderfile/Masterfile; p. 150, Claire Douglas; p. 162, © Images 100 Ltd.; p. 184, Suzanne Kreiter/Boston Globe; p. 190, Igali.com; p. 194, Jamume Gaul/Firstlight.ca; p. 196, Michelle V. Agins/NY Times; p. 219, Alicia Brett; p. 230, Stephanie Klein-Davis/NY Times; p. 241, Ozier Muhammad/NY Times; p. 264, Keith Meyers/NY Times; p. 272, Michelle V. Agins/NY Times; p. 287, Nancy E. Shaw; p. 296, PhotoDisc, Inc.; p. 312, Soumik Kanungo; p. 322, Ruby Washington, NY Times; p. 354, Digital Vision, p. 358, NY Times; p. 361, Anne-Marie Beaton/The Canadian Press; p. 365, Jennifer Armour; p. 367, Anne-Marie Beaton/The Canadian Press.